HELIOS UNBOUND:

PAGAN THEURGY TO CONNECT TO YOUR HIGHER GENIUS

I0211820

Helios Unbound: Pagan Theurgy to Connect to Your Higher
Genius by Nick Farrell
© 2020 First edition

All rights reserved, including the right to reproduce this book, or
portions thereof, in any form.

The rights of Nick Farrell to be identified as the author of this
work have been asserted by him in accordance with the Copyright,
Designs and Patents Act, 1988.

Layout: Nick Farrell
Cover Design: Nick Farrell

ISBN: 978-1-912241-15-6
MB0207

Set in Book Antiqua

A Megalithica Books Publication
An imprint of Immanion Press
info@immanion-press.com
www.immanion-press.com

HELIOS UNBOUND:

PAGAN THEURGY TO CONNECT TO YOUR HIGHER GENIUS

NICK FARRELL

Megalithica Books

STAFFORD ENGLAND

To Paola

AND

Θὼθ τρισμέγιστος

ACKNOWLEDGMENTS

This book is drawn from many different sources and influences in my life. This book has developed from the magical and academic work of: Aaron Leitch, Jake Stratton-Kent, Jeffrey Kupperman, Samuel Mathers, Florence Farr, Alistair Crowley, Sam Block, Eleni Pachoumi, Hans Deiter Betz, Kieren Barry, Chic and Tabatha Cicero, Chris Brennan, David Goddard, Josephine McCarthy, Pat Zalewski, Christine Zalewski, João Pedro Feliciano, Frater Acher, Sorita D'Este, Tony Mierzwicki, Brian Copenhaver, Gareth Knight, Stephen Skinner, Joseph Peterson, John Greer, Jane Gibson, Mike Magee and Christopher Warnock. I was assisted in developing a more credible approach to the Greek language by Dr Alfonso Ricca and Eirini Tsotsou. Angelo Albano and Carina Rina were a great help with the proofing and thanks to the Magical Order of the Aurora Aurea members, and the Facebook *Helios Unbound* Group who acted as guinea pigs and proofers.

CONTENTS

There is only Chaos which seeks to know itself. This act of knowing required a mirror of condensed ordered patterns where the story of the One Thing played out. The mound of Order arose from the ocean of Chaos and became the stage for the drama of Understanding. We are creatures of Chaos, understanding ourselves through an ordered existence.

A∴A∴T∴

INTRODUCTION

In 2003, I attempted the six-month "Abramelin process" to meet my *Holy Guardian Angel*. I was living in Bulgaria. The system I used was based on Alistair Crowley's *Liber Resh* invocations to the Sun, the Order of the Golden Dawn Watchtowers ritual and the long prayers required by the *Sacred Book of Abramelin the Mage*. I had a temple set up in the basement of my house in Sofia, and it started well. There was a small amount of weirdness at the beginning (for example, several red squirrels began paying too much attention to the house. They were always staring in the windows and had a habit of tapping on them when I was working). However, this settled down.

The biggest problem was with praying. I had been a Christian before beginning my magical path and had no problems with Christianity, but my real impulse was towards the Ancient gods. At that point, I had not developed my philosophy of the gods and had a general agnostic view of a Supreme God. It was a state where I could accept anything from elementals to angels but lacked a framework. The more I heard myself talking to this abstract Christian god, the less I liked it. The prayers contained Christian elements which I had rejected for lacking logical sense and felt hollow and like I was going through the motions to obtain the desired end.

In the second month, I was praying that this god would help me have knowledge and conversation with my *Holy Guardian Angel*, and I started to wonder what that meant and what were the implications. Modern occultists considered that the *Holy Guardian Angel* was what the Ancients call *Higher Genius* and I realised that was this being that I needed to meet. But, I started to feel that the *Holy Guardian Angel* was something else, and while knowledge and conversation with it was laudable, it was not going to resolve the central issue which had been teased out during the concentration of effort so far during the work. I didn't know what I believed, and it was only by meeting my *Higher Genius* that I would get there.

While I noted these thoughts in my diary, I persisted with the Abramelin because I felt that I was getting something from it, and it was possible that this thought was a move by my *Lower Self* to get me to give up. The following month's work was dry, and then my house was burgled, and my tools were stolen. I took it as a sign and abandoned the practice.

What I had learnt was that the concentrated effort of regular focused work over a proscribed period did work. What I needed to do was focus on what I wanted to achieve from the process rather than sticking religiously to the Abramelin format. Abramelin worked like an initiation process with an alchemic formula to awaken to the *Higher Genius*. Over a weekend, I designed a draft for a new programme focused on Pagan gods and a more ceremonial approach. Rather than prayers, it involved ritual purification and consecration and similar techniques but forced the person to follow an intense, disciplined approach. It ended up being seven months of going upwards through the Moon, planets, stars and finally meeting with your *Higher Genius*.

A week after I had finished this outline, my tools were returned with the burglar begging me to remove the bad luck that he felt had been placed on him since he stole them.

I started on this newer process and obtained the result I needed. However, some of the methods were too tied up with what I knew at the time and needed considerable polishing before letting someone else try. The idea that you dedicate seven months to this goal based around a set of exercises appeared to pay off. The seven-month outline sat in a file with the revealing title oldlinuxbackup2003 which somehow managed to get transferred across many different computers over the years.

The years that followed marked a change in my magical approach. While I still held onto my Golden Dawn training, it became increasingly adapted by Ancient magic and the religion which had formed its roots. I was not the only one. Many people from my generation started working on the same sort of ideas. These ideas were threaded through medieval grimoires, Arabic Hermetic books, and Ancient Greek papyri. My Neoplatonic Hermetic approach had built into a working system which used old texts and systems which was being continuously updated. My focus appeared to be set in the Roman period Alexandra and what had been agnosticism, had been converted into a Pagan syncretism.

I started writing this system as a Pagan grimoire, but it swiftly got out of hand and just kept growing without being released outside my own *Magical Order of the Aurora Aurea*.

In 2017, I was asked by Jenny Alexander if it were possible to create a "boot camp" approach to my Pagan magic system. I initially thought it wasn't because it would require dedication and focus which many magical students lack. However, then I thought – isn't that really what the aim of the Abramelin six-month system? Remembering that I had written something like that years earlier, I did a computer search and found the file.

What surprised me was that it tightly fitted my current thinking. I could see my Hermetic rituals, alongside actual historical techniques, slotting in neatly into a structure to unite with the *Higher Genius*.

Writing this book took more time than I thought. There was more magical work and testing to repurpose the different systems to the goal. This process started to affect me and bring out new information and, in many ways, a new me. I parcelled out bits of the work for people to try, and they seemed to get the required results. This was important because the seven-month process builds a structure where a symbol of unification is repeatedly beaten into the candidate's *Sphere of Sensation* while a purification and consecration process take place. This builds up pressure in your sphere of sensation, which could draw out any psychological issues you might have and force you to deal with them.

When not working in their temple, the operator finds real-life acting as a teacher and helps development.

For me, the process became about issues of destiny and what you were meant to be and do. The result became clearer on the second day of the retreat when I experienced Mithras-Aion and understood what it was all about -- at least for me. The third day then became about building and working that experience into life.

Afterwards, it took another rewrite to make sure that those experiences were duplicated for those who try them.

HELIOS UNBOUND PROCESS OUTLINE

The *Helios Unbound* process works by providing consistent and powerful symbols which remind the person that their *Higher Genius* is within them. This process creates "an acceptable illusion" that the magician is ascending towards their *Higher Genius* as it simultaneously advances towards them. The reality is that over an intense period, you are hammering your *Lower Self* until it accepts the truth of the divine spark within and integrates that knowledge. During that time, the magician learns the outline of a Pagan magician system which acts as a trellis upon which a spiritual rose can grow. They invoke their *Higher Genius* three times a day for seven months alongside a practice called *Prima Materia* which is a sequence of exercises where the person rehearses what it is like if they had already obtained their spiritual goals and united with their *Higher Genius*.

Helios Unbound's first chapter looks at the terms, some of the philosophy and the rituals that you will need to conduct the working.

The First Month: involves confession, purification, consecration, and the framing of a vow to carry on the work. The idea is to break down what is wrong with a person and their life and return misused power towards the will of their *Higher Genius*.

The Second Month: invokes the balancing of the elements within the sphere of sensation to bring the person into a balance between the various aspects of themselves. This balancing mirrors some of the work which would typically be done in a magical order.

The Third Month: shows how the Ancients used the sacred Greek language and texts to connect to the more abstract aspects of the divine self. It uses an adapted continental German Rosicrucian technique to begin the process of drawing the *Higher Genius* to the Lower.

The Fourth Month: opens the person up to their astrological destiny and the seven planetary powers. Using their chart, the magician works with the spirits behind the planets to understand how they work, starting with the most abstract expression of the planetary forces and moving down to their "earthing." Rather than sitting back and being a victim to these spirits, the magician opens a line of communication with those forces and understands how to co-operate with them.

The Fifth Month: works with the Moon, which was a crucial spiritual force in the ancient world. Nature and everything within it are under the Moon's direct control. The magician discovers the spirits which rule a person as the Moon goes through her mansions in the sky throughout the year and invokes their Moon spirit.

The Sixth Month: expands the astrological work to the spirits of the twelve zodiacal signs and the spirits of the decans and the underused Hellenistic Lot astrology. The Ancient Egyptians saw the Decan spirits as vital forces over a person's destiny and these spirits show the instincts of a person and their life direction.

The Seventh Month: This is the last month of the seven-month programme which ends with a weekend retreat where the magician is cut off from the rest of the world to await the arrival of their *Higher Genius*. The first three weeks are equally crucial at building up the magical pressure to attain this goal. Ritual work increases as the magician encounters more abstract Pagan Angels and invokes the forces of Divine Love, which help them unite to their *Higher Genius*.

The Retreat: The Retreat is three-day working through an intense ritual programme. With the world silenced, you focus entirely on the goal of meeting your *Higher Genius.*

Day One: The theme of the first day is death and destruction. It is a central part of any initiation system to involve the candidate's spiritual death so that they might awaken to their new spiritual life

The first sequence includes the initial invocation and the lighting of the sacred candle, which begins the final process. The candle acts as a beacon (or Pharos) throughout the entire retreat and is a physical symbol of your *Higher Genius.* This creates an immediate reaction where the candidate is forced to confront themselves as the God Serapis and dying. The second sequence focuses on the death process and the return to the Chaos from which you were born. The Third sequence is a journey into the Egyptian underworld and meeting the spirits there while seeing your own *Higher Genius* awakening.

Day Two: Today's theme is of ascension and immortalisation. The first sequence involves invoking the higher Pagan angelic forces to provide you with a ladder to ascend to more rarefied spiritual states which only become accessible after "death." The second sequence attempts to meet the spiritual forces behind all gods and angels – the seven rays on Helios' crown. The third sequence is an ascension through the levels to have a vision of a form of your *Higher Genius* and the Fates. This ritual seeks to grant a vision of your immortal aspects and see the Hero within.

Day three: The last day of the process is Know Yourself which involves a ritual which is designed to cause the barriers between the magician and their *Higher Genius* to break down and for you to begin direct communication. The first sequence is a ritual invocation to your *Higher Genius* this then merges into a second sequence in which you chant until you have a *Higher Genius* experience.

I should warn people who are trying this that such an intense approach to magic requires more dedication and focus than many will have in them. If they complete it, they will be better magicians than I ever was when I started. The process is heavy on the practical but is based around a core of ancient theoretical esoteric teaching, which I hope to develop in later books so that the full system can be seen.

My advice is to read through the entire book to see the whole system from start to finish so that there are no surprises. In your spare time read anything you can find from the reading list. I also recommend that you take a course in Hellenistic astrology or work through Chris Brennan's recently published book *Hellenistic Astrology: The Study of Fate and Fortune*.

Gather all the equipment in advance and make a few dry runs at following the schedule. Once you start you must be stubborn – fighting with yourself, your family, work and hobbies to stick to the plan for seven months

Good luck and may you find your destiny.

Nick Farrell

Rome 2019

CHAPTER ONE

INFORMATION YOU WILL NEED

This book is based on the Pagan magical systems predominant in Ancient Alexandria between the first and fifth century. It does include some later Christian and Islamic developments which owe much to their Pagan sources. These include the *Goetia*, the *Key of Solomon* and some (heavily edited) ritual systems found within the *Order of the Golden Dawn*. In the magical field, magicians like Jake Stratton-Kent* and Aaron Leitch† have conclusively proven the dependence of Christian and Islamic magic on Pagan ‡myths and systems.

Ancient Alexandria is not just a historical period or place but a philosophical approach to magic called eclectic syncretism. The Greeks founded Alexandria on Egypt's black Earth. Under the Greek Ptolemies, it became a centre of learning and philosophy and a melting pot for different religious and magical thought including Egyptian, Greek, Hebrew, Gnostic, Hermetic, Christian, Persian, African and Syrian. It is from Alexandria we can see Jewish mystics adopting the Greek letter numbering systems and Platonic philosophies and creating the early forms of Kabbalah. It is possible to see the rudiments of magical systems which would be given a Christian gloss and repurposed for the later High Christian ceremonial magic.

There was no such thing as cultural appropriation in the ancient world. Pagans respected other gods and used them alongside their own, sometimes mixing them into approaches and philosophies in a way which would be considered alien today.

It is from this period we have the *Greek Magical Papyri*§ [PGM] which were magical spells from the Greco-Roman Egypt which

---

* Stratton-Kent, J. (2010). *Geosophia*. [Dover]: Scarlet Imprint/Bibliothèque Rouge.

† Leitch, A. (2003). *Secrets of the Magickal Grimoires*. St. Paul, Minn.: Llewellyn.

‡ Throughout this book I have reluctantly used the world "pagan" to describe any European or Middle Eastern non-Judaeo-Christian religion. I am aware that is a Christian term of abuse, but it is a handy single word term which is recognisable by everyone.

§ Betz, H. (n.d.). *Greek Magical Papyri in translation, including the demonic spells.*

have been collected since the 19th century. These show the eclectic syncretism of the period and are stripped of later magicians' fantasies about magic. Thanks to Theosophy, the 20th century saw a rise in magic, where the Christianity of the time was projected onto a fantasy Ancient past. In this imaginary history, the Ancient Egyptians were heirs to an ancient Atlantean heritage which aspired to the highest moral code and magic. However, the *Greek Magical Papyri* were magical manuals which were an anathema to this view. In its spells we see magicians strangling cats and drowning birds to obtain divine assistants, cursing people, and providing love spells. The way that the modern magicians coped with this approach was to either ignore them or sniff that the *Greek Magical Papyri* were degenerate "sorcery" after the fall of the great Egyptian temples.

The *Greek Magical Papyri* agree with what we know about the magic and religion of the period. They fit into an ancient society and culture where magicians were outsiders and "amoral" but not necessarily bad. They had a role and there were logical reasons for most of their actions. Sacrificing an animal was not considered evil, although it was falling from fashion as a method to attract a god's attention. However the magician's sacrifices were more symbolic and once it is understood how symbols work, the literal nature of the more drastic PGM spells becomes unimportant and the spells can be safely adapted to modern life – to the great relief of the local feline population.

Similar programmes to *Helios Unbound* are part of the magical corpus – not only are they found in the *Greek Magical Papyri*, they also appear in later magical documents. The most famous of these is the *Sacred Magic of Abramelin the Mage** which was a 16th-century book designed to contact an entity called the *Holy Guardian Angel*.

Such programmes are deliberately tricky and are a remedy to the modern world's assumption that you can do anything by pressing a button or downloading an App. They are based on a principle of purification and consecration of the *Lower Self* to enable awareness of the spiritual aspects of self and eventually, a union with the *Higher Genius*.

The discipline required in this book forces the *Lower Self* to give up its control of a person's life and surrender to the needs of the *Higher Genius*. The process is psychologically difficult and is opposed at all stages by the *Lower Self*, which considers its "learnt by experience" way safer. Its rebellion will involve opposition to

---

* Mathers, S. (2012). *The Book of the Sacred Magic of Abramelin the Mage*. Newburyport: Dover Publications.

the imposed discipline to all-out psychological revolt through fear and even hallucinations. When you believe you have quietened it, you will see even darker sides of yourself emerging waiting to be balanced, purified, and consecrated. Once these shadows are integrated, your *Higher Genius* will emerge to start enacting its magical destiny for you.

The spiritual forces behind this book hope that its use will help 21st-century people push past the barriers which are confining their spirituality. Rather than making the process easier, which has so far has not produced enough adepts, it condenses it makes it harder. A 21st-century person must push themselves to overcome the weaknesses of their generation so that they can either start their magical career or empower their existing spiritual progress.

The book's power depends on repeating a series of daily exercises three times a day without fail. There are three sessions connected to various times of the day. Waking, sleeping, and Mid-day. One of these can be the "main session" and is likely to be the night-time session. The two supporting sessions are half an hour each. The initial session is an extra hour long, meaning that you will be dedicating two and a half hours a day to the process. The last few days of the seven-month process will need you to be isolated from other people to begin the work of integrating your *Higher Genius.*

You might experience your *Higher Genius* at any time in the process. However, you should continue for the remaining seven months. It is quite possible that an earlier appearance is a *Lower Self* trick, an external testing spirit, or a move from your Higher to encourage you. It is unlikely that anyone's *Higher Genius* would want them to stop the process under any circumstances.

RELIGION

Understand that this is a "religious" process. You are meeting with your divine spark, and the way to do that is mystical. It would be best if you believed in a divine force which created the universe. Which god you follow is irrelevant, but there is little hope for an atheist in this system. Each day you will be required to make three prayers to the highest aspect of the One Thing (which is primarily abstract and unknowable without the aid of your *Higher Genius*), but this act will help you attune to those aspects of your *Higher Genius* which aspire to that unity. The system uses a Neoplatonic view of the universe, but there is no reason why it should not translate into any other belief pattern, provided that the person is sympathetic to Pagan symbolism.

EXPERIENCE

This system is "advanced" in that it uses techniques which are hard for beginners. However, it has been written assuming that the person following the process knows nothing. Even if your practice is not perfect, the momentum will build over time and overcome any experience issues. Because these exercises are repeated intensively, they will have more impact than many of the initiations in esoteric orders.

Experienced people will have simple techniques explained and a new way of working alongside the more challenging material.

SPACE

You will need to set aside some space for a small table which you can move around for most of your workings*. It is helpful to see the night's sky, the Sun and the Moon in some cases. Most times, you can disassemble your sacred space, but in the last few days, you will need your altar set up all the time. Ideally, this should be in the same place at the same time every day. Some of this work can be done in your imagination during a morning commute, but this is less desirable.

EQUIPMENT

I have listed the material you will need to make for each month's work in Appendix One at the back of this book. While the list is extensive, it boils down mostly to different types of candle and incense.

THE HIGHER GENIUS

Helios Unbound is a purification and consecration process which leads you to contact an entity called the *Higher Genius*. The *Higher Genus* is the divine spirit of a human which has the powers of a *Numen*. According to the Roman senator, Cicero, the *Numen* was part of the Divine Mind" (*divina mens*), a god "whose *Numen* everything obeys" and a "divine power" (*vim divinam*) "which pervades the lives of men." It was the power of the spiritual aspect of a human making itself known.

The *Higher Genius* is your spiritual aspect which rides in the lower part of the personality and the body to see the universe and

---

* You could use a traditional double cube altar.

experience the drama of your life. It is the "I" which experiences your life, above your emotions and thoughts, and has become so lost in the movie of existence it has forgotten its true identity. For this reason, it needs to "wake up" but any process of waking up appears like an divine encounter for the personality on earth. The earth-bound *Higher Genius* cannot remember its own face and when it sees itself again, it sees God and cannot believe this is its own reflection,

It is a paradox that the *Higher Self* is both in and outside the personality. Part of it still looks to the divine which created it and is aware of its destiny; most of it becomes trapped in the dream. In an ordinary person's life that is not an issue – the *Higher Genius* reintegrates with itself at death, but a magician wants to work with their *Genius* while they are still living.

HIGHER GENUIS

SPHERE OF SENSATION

When we invoke our *Higher Self*, and concentrate on that part of ourselves, our localised *Higher Self* remembers its *True Nature*, and the bigger *Higher Self* appears. Once experienced, it is life changing and enables a magician to take on a form closer to their true destiny. Often part of the *Lower Self*, with its associations and reactions, breaks. For example, if a family interfered with your development and their behaviour patterns are still doing so, a *Higher Self* event could cause these associations to snap. Sometimes the appearance of the *Higher Genius* can force a personality change.

While this *Genius* has been part of the Western Mystery Tradition for millennia, during the late-Christian period, it became identified with a mere *Guardian Angel* which was supposed to oversee a person's life. It was only with the rise of psychology that this significant spiritual force was re-discovered and bought back into the occult stream.

Dr Carl Jung described the *Higher Self* * as a royal archetype

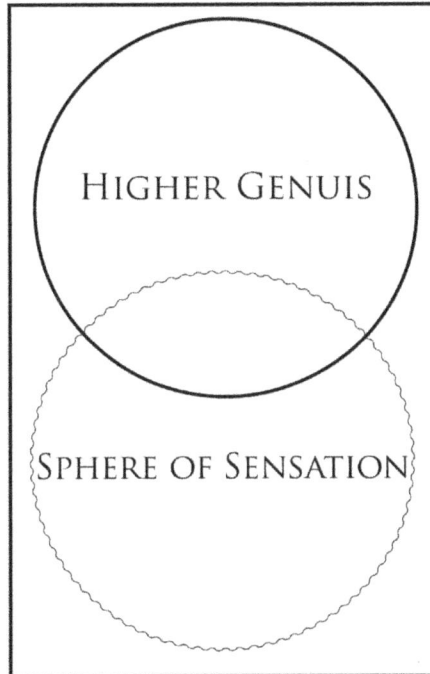

---

* Journalpsyche.org. (2019). *The Jungian Model of the Psyche | Journal Psyche.* [online] Available at: http://journalpsyche.org/jungian-model-psyche/

of the whole person and said the Self is the totality and purpose of the psyche; the Self is the *Imago Dei* (image of God), the "God in us." He saw the discovery of this Self, the highest authority of our personality, as fundamental to the wholeness and balance of our selfhood. It oversees our organic, biological, mental, emotional, and spiritual centres, in addition to controlling our concept of life and the world. It's the totality of our conscious and unconscious psyche.

Jung believed most of the problems in our life were rooted in an "undeveloped *Higher Self*." When the ego behaves excessively or destructively, the *Higher Self* becomes the healing self, responsible for re-establishing balance and inner harmony. Its work is to remove hidden obstacles and harmonise all dimensions of the person.

Where Jung differed with magical thinking was seeing this *Higher Genius* as the highest aspect of mind rather than the real self effectively driving a vehicle within a *Sphere of Sensation*. The difference is crucial. If the *Higher Self* were the best part of a personality, as Jung thought, then it is much smaller than the indwelling spiritual force seen in magic. Its powers are limited to "human powers" – great though they might be. It is a situation where a magician and an analyst can explain the same human actions without agreeing. Both agree that contacting the *Higher Self* or *Genius* is vital for a person's well-being. But a magician does not believe that a *Higher Genius* can be "undeveloped," instead they would think that the rest of a personality and life patterns shut it down to the point it has little influence.

The human who gets up, goes to work, goes home, watches TV and goes to bed does not need an active *Higher Genius*. A *Higher Genius* will have few lessons to learn and will have a minor observation role.

A person living their life to the full develops a closer relationship with their *Higher Self*, which benefits from the many experiences they have. Such a life is typically seen as hard because it breaks the rules. More magicians end up dying broke and alone despite having lives that would be the envy of many muggles. It does not always happen; it depends on the destiny or story of the individual for their survival. Money magicians, like Bill Gates, have been known to change their story and go from evil software villain to saint without needing to give up their wealth. Magicians who are working with their *Higher Genius* tend to find that change is part of their life.

Working with the *Higher Genius* gives the magician knowledge of their destiny and the instinct to the true story of their life. Their

[Accessed 16 May 2019].

Higher Genius has access to the powers of a god, so making contact is vital to a magician even if there is only brief contact.

According to Iamblichus,[*] the *Higher Genius* is created by the *Master of Dæmons* or the King of the Underworld, and it is essential when trying to contact your Genius to contact this King. Unfortunately, there was no god identified as being the Master of *Dæmons,* and many think Iamblichus was referring to Hades or Serapis.

The iconography of the *Higher Genius* is essential not because your spirit has a form, but because human minds need something to latch onto – particularly in the first stages of the operation. It is a cliché that a picture can tell a thousand words, but it is an idea built on truth. Symbolic forms provide us with a way to meet something infinite. When we see an image covered with symbols, they tell us about the subject. If it is the form of a man wearing a belt shaped like a serpent eating its tail, we know it is a symbol of infinity, and the being is immortal.

Because humans love forms, it is possible to begin building a connection with spiritual beings using an image. *Higher Genius* forms help us move from the symbolic to the truth. No real *Higher Genius* is going to look like anything you have seen before, even "light" is a bit too literal. A symbol helps us understand its nature. A symbol is like a phone number which connects to a host of other ideas.

One candidate for a *Higher Genius* form could be the Egyptian god Tutu *(pictured)* who related (among other things) to the *Higher Genius* of the Pharaoh. Tutu was a popular and accessible God to whom people could turn for help in their everyday existence.

Tutu appeared in the form of a striding royal sphinx composed of a lion's body and a human head, with usually a snake for a tail. In later periods, he was depicted in a more pantheistic mode with a crocodile or lion head attached to His body. He was shown in a side view often but with his

---

[*] See Iamblichus' commentary on Plato's *Sophist*, the first fragment, as well as the translator's notes on that fragment. In *Platonis DiaLogos Commentariorum Fragmenta*. Translated by Dillon, John M. Wiltshire, UK: Prometheus Trust, 2009. (thanks Jeffrey S. Kupperman)

head turned to be viewed frontally, emphasising this approachability.

Many of Iamblichus' ideas came from the Hermetic current in Egypt where Tutu was still accessible, Tutu follows my theme of a *Higher Genius* being a chaotic spirit searching for experience in a world of Order. Tutu is the "son of Neith" and "Atum's God." Neith is the goddess of the dark and limitless sky and a fitting symbol for the underworld of Chaos from which all order sprang. The Egyptians said that Neith "bought forth the first land from the Chaotic Primaeval waters of Nun."

Being her son, Tutu is the primal force which wants to know itself and it being a human *Higher Genius* makes sense.

There was no consistent standard in the depiction of *Higher Genius*. The Etruscans and the Romans depicted it as a divine man or a woman with angelic wings. One of the symbols of the *Higher Genius* was the cicada because they were supposed to sing in spiritual ecstasy. They also had other powerful symbolic characteristics. The Romans believed that the cicada was "born from the Earth," and was capable of resurrection and a symbol of immortality. This was because it shed its skin and sprouted wings on a new white body and must always be in a state of perpetual youth. The Romans used to make stylised brooches to represent cicadas.

The Tithonus myth tells the story of a young man, who fell in love with the Dawn Goddess. She granted him the gift of immortality. As in all such stories, this divine gift was not a blessing. Tithonus got older and smaller until there was nothing left of him but his shrill voice and he turned into a cicada. While on the surface this is a terrible story about the problems of immortality, it encodes a hidden story of a magician who looks for awakening (loves the dawn). He realises his immortality, and while his body ages, he becomes more like his *Higher Genius* until finally becoming its symbol.

The *Higher Genius* was also associated with snakes. Like the cicada, serpents were symbols of regeneration. There are legends which associate serpents with primal chaotic forces, which again ties them to the earth (like the cicada). They have strong protective associations which are proper for any power which aims to ensure the fulfilment of destiny.

The *Higher Genius* is shown as a human with a lion's head. Lions were associated with the Sun and there were many different gods who had a lion's head. Chnubis, for example, was a snake with the head of a lion.

One of the more essential *Higher Genius* symbols is the god Aion, who was a feature of the Roman version of the Mithras mysteries.

Aion had a lion's head and four wings. On his breast was an eye and he had lion heads on his stomach and knees. He sometimes had four arms and one held a sceptre. Aion is seen by many as a variation of the Time God Chronos, but his name can mean eternity and his symbolism suggests infinity in a state of limitation. The fact that his symbol did not just mean time or was limited to Mithras can be found in the *Greek Magical Papyri* Pnouthios spell* where a lion-headed magical "assistant" who is a "mighty angel has the same symbolism."

The Pnouthios process uses a magical image of a lion-headed god, holding a whip, surrounded by a serpent to be carved on a stone (which is an earth symbol). All these things are similarities to Aion that suggest it might be a representative of the divine nature of humanity, which was bound by time and trapped within the rock of matter.

> "When you go abroad, he will go abroad with you; when you are destitute, he will give you money. He will tell you what things will happen both when and what time of the night or day. If anyone asks you "What do I have in mind?" or "What has happened to me?" or even "What is going to happen?" question the Angel, and he will tell you in silence. When you are dead, he will wrap up your body as befits a god, but he will take your spirit and carry it into the air with him. For no aerial spirit which is joined with a mighty assistant will go into Hades, for to him all things are subject. Whenever you wish to do something, speak his name alone into the air and say, "Come!" and you will see him standing near you. Say to him, "Perform this task," and he does it at once, and after doing it, he will tell you, "What else do you want? I am eager for Heaven." If you do not have immediate orders, tell him, "Go, Lord," and he will depart. In this fashion, then, you will see the

*Papyri graecae magicae I.54

god alone, nor will anyone ever hear his speaking, just you alone. He will tell you about the illness of a man, whether he will live or die, even on what day and at what hour of the night. He will also give you wild herbs and the power to cure, and you will be worshipped as a god since you have a god as a friend. These things, the mighty assistant will perform competently."

The "assistant" appears more of a familiar, but his attributes show he is more than that. The magical process used to get him is a spiritual revelation with strange visions similar to what you will experience during the *Helios Unbound* process. The powers attributed to him are the same as the *Higher Genius.* Had not the writer written that it would obey your commands and treated it a servant, the *Higher Genius* attribution would be clear. But this dumbing down could be a cover for a mystery which either the writer did not know or was deliberately obscuring (something we see in the Egyptian scrolls which might have been based on a Mystery School or Egyptian temple practice but simplified for the magical market). It could also be possible Pnouthios is creating a "messenger" for his *Higher Genius,* which functions comparably but is simpler to attain and comprehend.

> *"He will serve you suitably for whatever you have in mind, Oh, blessed initiate of the sacred magic (hieras mageias, ιερᾶς μαγείας), and will accomplish it for you, this most powerful assistant. I share this mystery (mystirion) with no-one else, but conceal it, by Helios, since you have been deemed worthy by the Lord god."*

(125 - 133).

The concluding lines show that the magician is a *mystes* (μύστης) or initiate of the Mysteries who uses sacred magic. The magician is conscious of being the principal actor in a procedure that is magical and sacred. Such a practice must be kept hidden because of the exceptional powers that it assures.

Other symbols of the *Higher Genius* come in the form of the Egyptian God Harpocrates (Heru-pa-Khered) the son of Osiris and Isis and destined to become Horus. An example of this form of the *Higher Self* can be found in Athanasius Kircher's copy of a *Stele of Horus (pictured)* which showed a polymorphic *Dæmon* which he called the mind of the Supreme *Numen* (Power of the *Higher Genius*) as it descends into the breadth of nature (*Oedipus Egyptus* Volume III).

Kirche was a little imaginative when describing what he saw in the Stele and did not know Egyptology other than from Greek and Latin sources. He saw things in the stele, which were more artistic style rather than anything else. For example, he thought his "*Numan (sic)*" was crowned with symbols of the Sun and had a lion's head when it is human. He sees female breasts when there are none*. He says that the horns stand for the Moon and energy and fertility by having a plait twisted into the shape of a horn. (The latter was a standard symbol of a child's plat in Ancient Egypt and had no symbolic attributions connected to fertility). The fact Heru-pa-Khered holds snakes and scorpions show its domination over life and death is plausible, but Kircher sees a lion and the dog when an Egyptian would see an ass and a hippopotamus which were

Set's creatures. He says that the crocodiles were symbols of Typhon (Set) which is correct. Egyptian temple courtyards often had steles depicting Heru-pa-Khered standing on the back of a crocodile and holding snakes in his outstretched hands. These steles were immersed or lustrated in water for blessing and healing. The divine name Heru-pa-Khered was a protective and healing word of power.

For all his faulty attributions, Kircher correctly intuited that Heru-pa-Khered was a good symbol for the *Higher Self*; this was picked up by the *Order of the Golden Dawn* who saw "Harpocrates as sitting upon a lotus flower in the Nile" in its Neophyte ritual and marked it as a form of the Candidate's *Higher Genius.*

This book uses the Mithraic Aion as a symbol to use as a representative of the *Higher Genius.* It has connections to lots of gods including Aion, Chronos, Serapis, Horus and Eternias and Phanes. I found an association between my *Higher Self* and a lion-headed Aion I saw in a Roman museum, and it has shown up in that form ever since. However, there is no reason why you could not use the Stele of Heru-pa-Khered instead.

---

* He was a celibate Jesuit, so probably saw women's breasts when there were none.

The images of the lion (or Helios headed) god have four wings, one for each of the elements. He usually is surrounded by the zodiac and entwined by the serpent of nature. He has a lion on his heart centre and a staff of rulership in his hand. He holds typically a key which allows him to enter or exit matter at will. He either stands on a globe or emerges from a rock. The symbolism shows a divine being indwelling in nature and exposed to the planetary and zodiacal forces.

THE DÆMON IN ASTROLOGY

Something as crucial as the *Dæmon*, or *Higher Genius* could not escape making an appearance in astrology. While modern astrologers might have mostly lost its presence, the Ancient Greeks considered the position vital. Fortunately, the teaching was passed to the Arabs who described the *Dæmon* as one of their Arabic Parts of Fortune. Recently there have been moves to restore ancient astrology*, and this is proving a gold mine for Pagan magicians who prefer their astrology authentic and stripped of 20th-century psycho-babble.

The *Dæmon's* placement on an astrological chart shows the influence of the part of the *Sphere of Sensation* (or aura), which is connected intricately to our *Higher Genius*. It does not show our Cosmic *Higher Self*, but that part of the *Genius* which decided to incarnate in this personality. There is a slight difference between the two. The *Higher Genius* outside of the body is less restricted in its vision and less influenced by the life it has chosen. The *Dæmon*

---

* Brennan, C. (n.d.). *Hellenistic Astrology*.

shown in astrology is the one which is more personalised through our life experience. The *Dæmon's* position can show us what our spiritual purpose is, the connections of the world inside us. It can supply clues as to how our *Higher Genius* will appear to us, and there are several esoteric traditions which can give us a word of power to help contact it.

Hellenistic astrologers were interested in what they called the Lot of the *Dæmon* and the Lot of Tyche (Fortune), which was its opposite on the astrological chart.

In his *Anthology*, * the second century Alexandrian astrologer Vettius Valens called the Lot of Tyche "archetypal" and the *Dæmon* the 'second.' The Lot of Tyche helps during a chart interpretation. The importance of the two was religious – in Ancient Alexandria *Agathe Tyche* and *Agathos Dæmon* were worshipped. Tyche and *Agathos Dæmon* had assimilated native Egyptian deities like Shai (Fate God) and Renenet (a protective snake goddess). Cults of *Agathe Tyche* and *Agathos Dæmon* had appeared to propitiate these deities, and they were flourishing at the same time as Hellenistic astrology's development.

While the idea of personal *Higher Genius* had been around at least before Plato, the Platonist Plutarch (CE 46 – CE 120), popularised the concept of each person having a personal *Dæmon* and Tyche. In his *Parallel Lives*, Plutarch† said that each person was aided or not by fortune and a correspondingly good or bad, strong, or weak, higher *Dæmon*. When a *Dæmon* was "weak" in the chart it meant that the life it had chosen would be one where spiritual concerns were insignificant or where the person had to try to communicate with the *Dæmon* continually or lose contact.

In the second century book *Tabula Cebetis*,‡ the unknown author interprets an allegorical picture (said to have been dedicated by someone in the temple of Cronus at Athens) showing the whole of human life with its dangers and temptations. The *Dæmon* guides the entry into being, which contains a Tyche who gives and takes away a fortune for those entering.

The astrological house assigned to the Good *Dæmon* was the 11th which symbolises goals, friendships, and group membership. It

---

* A full translation of the text by Mark Riley can be found here https://www.csus.edu/indiv/r/rileymt/Vettius%20Valens%20entire.pdf

† Plutarch., Dryden, J. and Clough, A. (1952). *The lives of the noble Grecians and Romans*. Chicago: Encyclopdia Britannica.

‡ Cebes Thebanus and Parsons, R. (1892). *Cebes' Tablet*. Boston: Ginn.

was associated with the king's (or ruler's) favourites, councillors, servants, their associates or allies, parliament, and government supporters. It is a house of optimism and confidence, personal strength, motivation, and increase. Helios, the Sun god, ruled it.

However, a house placement for the *Higher Genius* was not enough. It had so much power, which came from several aspects of the Chart, that further calculations were required. These were the Sun and the Moon. The Moon is associated with the body, and the Sun with the mind, the soul and spirit.

The Moon is the traditional planet associated with Fortune because she was a symbol of the cycles of waxing and waning. The Sun was part of the *Dæmon,* in that it is metaphorically associated with mind and spirit.

There was a difference between being born in the day or the night. For Lots of Fortune, you take the arc from Sun to Moon in a daytime chart and the arc from Moon to Sun in at night and project this arc from the ascendant to find the position of the lot.

You take the degrees of the Asc + Moon - Sun (D) or Asc + Sun - Moon (N)

For the Lot of *Dæmon,* the formula reverses: Asc + Sun - Moon (day) or Asc + Moon - Sun (night)

Fortunately for people like me to whom maths is a mystery, calculating the Lot of Fortune (Tyche) or the Lot of the Spirit (*Dæmon*) can be done on a computer using a programme like Janus* in seconds.

Having obtained the position of your Lot of Tyche and Dæmon, you can start to understand how your *Higher Genius* works in your life.

Say that a magician has their *Dæmon* in the fourth house at 9.42 degrees Scorpio and their Tyche 10.58 Taurus in the tenth house.

Cancer and the Moon rule the fourth house which gets on with the Watery Scorpio. The *Dæmon* is strong, although its more Martian aspects are blunted. The *Dæmon* is highly spiritual and intense (Scorpio). However, Scorpio brings the Moon to its fall so there might be some problems for the magician to overcome, such as strong ties to an unhealthy or an emotionally unsupportive family or environment (fourth house). The *Dæmon* will be seeking to build a spiritual or can help other people find meaning, direction, and purpose to life. To do that, a magician finds these things for themselves first before giving anything to anyone else. The *Higher Genius* directs them to have an "interesting life" which means they will experience great

---

* Janus software can be found here https://www.janus5.com/getjanus5. htm

heights and great depths within their lives. They will seek a spiritual family of some sort, although that might not work through the traditional means but might be an esoteric group. The *Higher Genius* provides deep, authentic internal emotional roots and contact with that family to help open the magician. They will find their *Dæmon* through intense mystical experiences. This person's *Higher Genius* is more connected to the element of water.

Another magician has their *Dæmon* at 10.26 Aries in the Ninth house of philosophy and their Tyche 18.04 in the fourth house of Sagittarius. The *Higher Genius* supplies practical harmony and wisdom. It brings Taurian responsibility to the value of higher knowledge, philosophy, psychology, religion, higher education, and sharing this with others. The creative talents of Taurus involved in mental pursuits bring an ability to expand knowledge, to bring innovative ideas and concepts to what is already known. Their *Higher Genius* is not happy with what is known but prefers to expand and grow within the framework of what is accepted. This innovation is expressed through Aries, although there might be a tendency to be too fixed and dogmatic. Sagittarius rules the Ninth House so the person's spirituality might be a little self-centred, but it could also bring spiritual leadership. Those with a *Genius* in this house are spontaneous people and have enthusiasm for ideas and plans which interest them and a unique ability to impart that enthusiasm to others. There is a strong ability to communicate spiritual ideas to others and initiate action. This person's *Higher Genius* responds to fire.

THE LOWER DÆMON

The Ancients had the concept of a *Lower Dæmon* who brought terrible luck and harm. It was the shadow of the Higher *Dæmon* and was in the 12th house in the same way that the Higher *Dæmon* was in the 11th. The *Lower Dæmon* is in the next anti-clockwise house. So, if the *Higher Genius* is in the ninth, it will cast its shadow into the tenth. If it is in the fourth, the evil demon is in the fifth.

Just as the *Higher Genius* turns planets positive, the Shadow is harmful and will often blight the house and the planets within it. It might make those positive aspects appear detrimental to a person's life. Success in one area might come at the expense of the *Higher Genius*.

These will be your life's challenges and the issues you must overcome. The closer you draw to your *Higher Self*, the more these problems will appear and demand resolution. These things are often your fated story. When the *Lower Genius* is quietened, then the powers which it has locked up will suddenly be available or more positive.

Our first example has his shadow falling in the fifth house of sex and pleasure. What this will mean is the closer the relationship with the *Higher Genius* gets, the more he will experience an inability to express joy and happiness. There is a danger that the magician will become too shut off and mystical for his good. The *Lower Dæmon* will be undermining his happiness until the lesson that spirituality and sensuality both need to be expressed appropriately. The fifth house is Sagittarius, so the *Dæmon* is effectively stopping the magician having fun and happiness. It might be that it causes them to move around too much to earth their philosophy.

The fifth house contains the magician's south node which means it is a life lesson he needs to learn, and the shadow will make it elusive (as he might not even be aware of the issue). It might be that he isolates himself from contact or gets grumpy with others as he gets more intimate with his higher.

In our second example, the *Lower Dæmon* is undermining the tenth house – the house of work and status. So, the closer the magician gets to his *Higher Genius*, the more problems will erupt to distract him. The deeper he gets into his magical world with his higher, the more he will be pulled back to deal with matters related to work and career and sorting out other people. The person has Jupiter, Mercury, Venus, and Sun under the shadow of the *Higher Genius*, which means that they have much to work out to find a balance.

Third example: The magician has Leonine *Higher Genius* and connected to fire, and it focuses on the seventh house. It might appear fixed, and as if it knows all the answers and will drive the magician to take some leadership role (even if they don't want it). It has a strong focus on initiating and starting spiritual relationships (which practically means you will be better at this sort of magic than other things). Its approach is a little more unusual than most, and the *Genius* can appear less rational and fiercer than the native feels. The house of the *Higher Genius* throws light on Saturn, and the Sun in Cancer and these will be enhanced aspects of their spiritual self. The life story will depend on making relationships and partnerships which will be unusual but stable and long-term (Saturn). What the *Higher Genius* needs them to do requires a degree of patience and stability. It might often be at odds with what they feel is right (Sun in Cancer is introverted in comparison with Leo) and encourage them into the spotlight much more than they want.

The shadow of the *Higher Genius* is the eighth house, and these are the things which the *Higher Genius* has incarnated to resolve (by bringing the focus onto seventh house relationships). The shadow *Dæmon* is Leo in the eighth house and hits Mars. The eighth house is to do with death, and other people's resources and the position of Mars gives a drive for significance. Mars in Leo builds a strong need to *create* in some way. They want their lives to have a significant meaning. If the *Higher Genius* focuses on spiritual relationships, the shadow wipes all that out with bursts of ego and over-idealism, self-righteous behaviour, and quarrels. The *Shadow Dæmon* might prevent necessary spiritual "near death" transformations and initiations as it seeks to maintain the spiritual status quo.

THE HIGHER GENIUS IS SOLAR

From the classical age to modern magic, the solar nature of the *Higher Genius* is always assumed. The most commonly used current method for contacting the *Higher Genius* is *Aleister Crowley's Helios prayers* in *Liber Resh vel Helios* where three prayers are provided for the morning, noon and night. Few have questioned this logic because the Sun is a perfect symbol of the *Higher Genius*. The Sun is not the One Thing but has a crucial role in the physical creation of the world and humanity. All life on Earth is dependent on the Sun, making it the physical representation of the One Thing in the solar system. The Solar System can be seen as the Sun's sphere of sensation or aura.

The Sun symbolically follows human life. The Egyptians said that it was a child in the morning when the Sun rises, an adult at noon, and an older man in the evening. Like the Sun, the *Higher Genius* disappears into the chaotic underworld of dreams at night only to be reborn the next day. Following the Sun is copying the progress of your *Higher Genius* through your life story. Our bodies are made from mostly solar material which goes with us throughout our life story and withdraws when it is over.

Like the Moon, the Sun is a setter of time. In Pagan cosmology, Time is the first thing that the Divine Triad created from the dark waters of Chaos to provide a frame in which its story of self-discovery began. The Sun numbers our days on earth and follows us throughout our destined life span and beyond.

What this tells us is that by aligning ourselves to the Sun by ritual, we build an associative form where the Sun is our *Higher Genius*, and through that form, it can communicate with us.

In the fourth century, the Roman philosopher Emperor Flavius Claudius Julianus wrote:

> *"I earnestly entreat the Sun, the king of the universe, that he will be propitious to me for my affection to his divinity; that he will impart to me a good life; more perfect wisdom; a divine intellect; and a gentle departure from the present state of my earth life."*

PARTS OF THE SOUL

In *Phaedrus*,† Plato implies that the reason that the *Higher Genius* gets trapped in matter is due to factors within the soul that are part of being in matter. When the *Higher Genius* takes on its human space suit to enter matter, it finds itself in a three-fold world dominated by information gathered from the senses, animal desires, genetic programming and social needs.

Plato believed that the soul (which is what is called the lunar body or *Lower Genius* in this system) was made up of three parts. The first was Reason or the *logistikon (λογιστικόν)*, which is the thinking part of the soul. The next part of the lunar body is *thymoeides (θυμοειδές)* or *thumos (θύμος)*, which was our emotional self. The last part was the *epithymetikon (πιθυμητικόν)* (sometimes called *Eros (ἔρως)*, or desire) which was is the animal part of the soul through which we experience the sex-drive, hunger, thirst, and cravings.

The *logistikon* is the closest to the *Higher Genius* because it seeks to work out what is real, judges what is right and what is false and wisely makes just decisions. It is the soul's ruler. However, while the *logistikon* is like the *Higher Genius*, it is a bit like a computer in that it relies on the data it is given from the other bodies, if it gets wrong information from the animal instincts or the senses, it will react badly. However, it is through the *logistikon* that people contact their *Higher Genius*. It feels like whispering to the mind when you think about a problem, and you produce a solution which never would have occurred to you.

In Homer's poems, *thumos* meant emotions, desire, or inner urges. A human's thinking and feeling were part of it. *Thymos* comes from the verb *thyo* or *thyno (θύω or θύνω)* which means "I rush", or I "run," mainly in battle. Derivatives include the following words:

---

* Julian and Taylor, T. (1932). *Two orations of the Emperor Julian, one to the Sovereign Sun and the other to the Mother of the gods.* Chicago: Hermetic Publishing.

†Yunis, H. and Plato. (2011). *Phaedrus.* Cambridge: Cambridge University Press.

a) *thymos* (anger), b) *thyra* (door) because air passes through a door and c) *thymiama* (incense) because the offerings to the gods were accompanied by incense, and from that word it received the concept of "sacrifice." Homeric heroes externalise their *thumos* and converse with or scold it when one of them dies their *thumos* leaves the body. Plato saw *thumos* as "passion" or the emotional element. He saw it as a 'high spirit', and in the ideal personality, it represents a flowering of the ancestral spirit. Ideally, it should ally with the *logistikon* and provide the power for highly intellectual ideas. It is similar to the Polynesian concept of *mana,* which was a person's spiritual power, prestige and authority. It contains aspects of the soul which come from the ancestors and the higher learning and influences which have built up over time.

In an unjust soul, the *thumos* ignores the *logistikon* and aligns with the animal desires and demands pleasures of the body.

Plato used the image of the Charioteer to explain how these three bodies worked in the soul. This image is the same as the Tarot card *The Chariot,* one of those things which get missed by many Tarot experts.

The *logistikon* was the rider, and he controlled two horses. One of the horses being noble and immortal (*thumos*) and the other being rougher and mortal (*epithymetikon*).

The mortal horse (*epithymetikon*) is deformed and obstinate, a "crooked lumbering animal, put together anyhow...dark, with grey eyes and red complexion". Plato said that it was the "mate of insolence and pride, shag-eared and deaf, hardly yielding to whip and spur."

The immortal horse (*thumos*), on the other hand, is noble, "upright and cleanly made...his colour is white, and his eyes dark; he is a lover of honour and modesty and temperance, and the follower of true glory; he needs no touch of the whip, but word and admonition are its guide."

The Charioteer (*logistikon*) must rein in these disparate steeds, guiding and harnessing them to propel the vehicle with strength and efficiency.

The white horse wishes to rise to Heaven, but the dark horse pulls the chariot back towards the earth. The Charioteer tries to get the horses back into sync, and his chariot goes above the sky and drops down again. The rider catches the occasional glimpses of Heaven before sinking once more.

Lower Genius thinking has problems. It can unlock much of the secrets of the universe. Plato said that if the Charioteer can get the horses working correctly, he can see the world and his place within it. However, it is far too hard for most mortals.

A good Charioteer understands how each of the three forces of his soul work together, and he guides them without usurping their function. He achieves harmony among the elements. Thus, instead of dissipating his energies in opposite and detrimental directions, he channels those energies towards his goals.

In his *Republic*, Plato said this is a precursor to tackling any other endeavour of life:

> *"First, having attained self-mastery and beautiful order and harmonised these three principles... made himself one man instead of many, self-controlled and in harmony, he can turn to issues like obtaining wealth, focusing on the body, taking part in politics or business. In all such doings, he will follow the just and honourable action which preserves and helps to produce this condition of the soul."*

Fortunately, the *Higher Genius* is part of the *Lower Genius* and has a perfect view of the universe and can supply guidance.

Π   **THE CHARIOT**   ♋

Golden Dawn Temple Deck: The Chariot
(c) Wendrich artHouse

When inhabiting the body, the *Higher Genius* in its purest state is known as the *Nous* (Νοῦς). Homer used the term *Nous* to signify mental activities of mortals and immortals, but it later came to mean an almost divine Higher mind. In *Philebus*† Plato wrote that "*Nous* is king of Heaven and earth and sees reality in the same eternal way of gods and *Dæmons*.

In the *Enneads*,‡ the Neoplatonic philosopher Plotinus said that the *Nous* was the image of God and used more descriptions which make it the indwelling *Higher Genius*

---

*Plato., Emlyn-Jones, C. and Preddy, W. (2013). *Republic*. Cambridge, Mass.: Harvard University Press. Line 443d

† Plato. and Frede, D. (1993). *Philebus*. Indianapolis: Hackett Pub. Co.

‡ Plotinus. (1989). *Enneads*. Cambridge, Mass.: Harvard University.

within a human. He thought that *Nous* thinks its thoughts in terms of Platonic ideas. Thinking like this is the highest activity of life as it actualises forms. This Intellect is the first principle or foundation of existence. Intellect is called an emanation of the One. The One is the possibility of this foundation of reality. The Solar body or the *Higher Self*, or *Nous*, has access to a rational mind (*logistikon*) which it whispers driving suggestions but often it is the other two aspects which shout it down. In time this three-fold *Lower Self* takes on a life of its own, becoming a self-serving *Dæmon* of limitation.

For the *Higher Genius* to manifest, it must reduce the influence of this *Lower Genius* by working on the *logistikon* and encouraging the *epithymetikon* to follow it, instead of the animal desires.

The traditional way to do this was to repress the animal self and, to a lesser extent, the *epithymetikon*. Modern psychology has shown the danger of doing this as it amounts to damming within the psyche, which eventually causes an explosion. It is easier to try to get the animal self onside by making sure that it is happy and that it has not learnt any harmful defence mechanisms. The real key to bringing the animal self under control is through discipline.

The *Lower Genius* can be tamed by careful reward or punishment, like any animal. The key to any occult training programme is to do regular exercises over a long period. After a while, the lessons that these exercises bring will cause the *epithymetikon* to act in a trained way to experience. Since it no longer is distracted by the *epithymetikon*, the *thumos* will look more to the *logistikon*, and the chariot will run smoother. Since the Charioteer no longer worries about his ill-matched horses, he can listen more closely for the voice of the *Nous*.

Any discipline, such as this book, is an ideal way to bring *epithymetikon* under control (even if in the initial stages it causes problems).

PROMETHEUS AS A HIGHER GENIUS ALLEGORY

According to Hesiod's *Theogony**, Prometheus (Προμηθεύς, forethought) and his brother Epimetheus (Ἐπιμηθεύς afterthought) are trickster gods of the Greek pantheon and a thorn in the side of Zeus. The Ancients might have seen them as the "spirits of humanity." In one tradition, Prometheus shaped humanity out of mud, and Athena breathed life into it. Prometheus allowed his brother, Epimetheus, to dispense various qualities to the animals

---

*Hesiod. and Lattimore, R. (1991). *Hesiod*. [Michigan]: Ann Arbor Paperbacks.

and man. Epimetheus gave animals the best traits such as swiftness, courage, cunning, stealth, and he had nothing to give to man. Prometheus took over and gave humanity an upright posture like the gods. This gift enabled humans to survive. Prometheus later assumed the role of humanity's protector, although it is unclear if this is part of his game of one-upmanship with Zeus. As a Titan, he was said to have provided humanity with fire, and all the means to survive. Had Zeus got his way, humanity would have been dead a long time ago.

Epimetheus is unfairly depicted as Prometheus' stupid brother, but there are some things about his nature, which provide humanity with its specific power. We might be quicker thinkers, thanks to Prometheus, but Afterthought brought humanity other abilities; dependency on one another sharing, caring, meeting and loving. It is for this reason that he allows humanity to fall in love with Pandora. Prometheus saw humanity needed a companion.

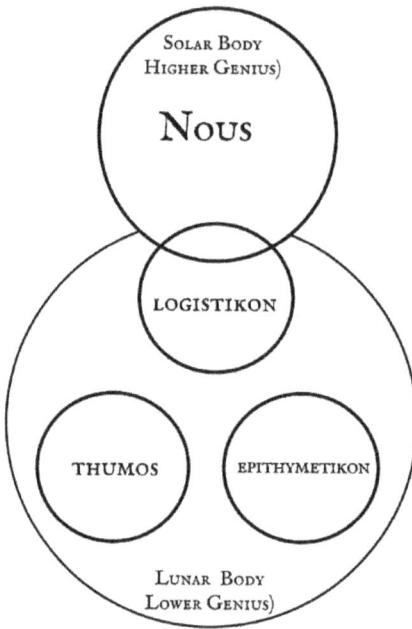

Solar Body (Higher Genius)

Nous

Logistikon

Thumos   Epithymetikon

Lunar Body (Lower Genius)

Their two brothers, Atlas (Ατλας) and Menoetius (Μενοίτης) shared humanity's quirks. Menoetius is humanity's inherent conservatism, which forces them to be on the wrong side of change. Atlas could separate the astral from the physical and create the divided world in which humanity lives. Menoetius is human hubris which makes the race believe that they are the centre of the universe and blundering on through mistakes ranging from wars to global warming. Atlas and Menoetius were on the wrong side of the Titan's revolt (which means that they are aspects of humanity which are antagonistic to the gods). If we follow Atlas and Menoetius, we will either end up separating our spirituality from the material or, get walloped by a lightning bolt from a highly miffed principal deity. Prometheus is the ability to think quickly, intuitively before things happen, and Epimetheus is the ability to learn from mistakes. In the weird way that the myths tell us things, Hesiod implies that these four Titans are bound up with the way we are. During the Greco-Roman period, the Egyptian alchemist Zosimos of

Panopolis (2nd-3rd Century CE) developed the idea. He saw Prometheus as a human's *Higher Genius* while Epimetheus was the physical body. The story where Prometheus warns his brother against accepting the gifts of Zeus is a Pagan description of the fall of man. Epimetheus says that the only thing that he wants from life is a "shapely woman" and wealth. Effectively re-enforcing the occult teaching that the *Higher Self* looked towards matter and found it beautiful and "fell into it." Once incarnate, the gods provided him with Pandora who arrived with her jar and forced him to conform to "fate" which was all the pains of living in matter.

> *"Zeus set yet another fetter upon him - Pandora, whom the Hebrews call Eve. For Prometheus and Epimetheus are, by the allegorical method, a single man, that is, soul and body; and so Prometheus sometimes takes the form of soul, sometimes that of mind, and sometimes that of flesh because of Epimetheus' disregard when he disregarded the advice of Prometheus, his foresight. For our Mind says: "The Son of God, being capable of everything and becoming everything, when he wills, as he wills, appears to each."* *

The legend told by 5th-century BCE Greek tragedian Aeschylus† *Prometheus Bound* said that Prometheus gave humanity fire. This "fire" was the divine spark in man. Prometheus effectively was the being who brought divine consciousness to the animal-human body (represented by this brother). Prometheus taught humanity civilisation, writing, mathematics, agriculture, medicine, and science. These are the tools of the *Higher Genius* and enabled humanity to thrive when Zeus tried to wipe us out.

As punishment for giving humanity these tools, Zeus sentenced Prometheus to eternal torment for his transgression. The immortal was bound to a rock, where each day an eagle, the emblem of Zeus, was sent to feed on his liver. The liver would grow back overnight to be eaten the next day again. (The Ancient Greeks believed the liver to be the seat of human emotions). Prometheus' punishment is the perfect description of the *Higher Genius* being trapped in nature (the rock) and tortured because it is an astral creature being made to feel things.

Hercules, a human, frees Prometheus which means that the work of becoming a perfected hero liberates the *Higher Genius*. Hercules drives away Zeus's Eagle with arrows. To the Greeks, arrows were symbols of perception and knowledge.

---

* Jackson, H. and Zoximos (1979). *Zosimos of Panopolis on the Letter Omega.* Claremont, Calif.: Claremont Graduate School.

† Aeschylus., Podlecki, A., Aeschylus. and Aeschylus. (2005). *Prometheus bound.* Oxford: Aris & Phillips.

The implication is that you do not literally rise "upwards" towards the *Higher Genius* to liberate it. By being a hero in your life and using your powers of perception, you can find your *Higher Genius* within yourself and liberate it.

THE SPHERE OF SENSATION

Throughout this book, I use the old term *Sphere of Sensation*. These days it is called the aura, but the Western concept of *Sphere of Sensation* contains associations which are unconnected to the aura. I have gone into detail about the *Sphere of Sensation* in my book, *Magical Imagination** which I have summarised in this book.

The *Sphere of Sensation* is the energy field through which we interact with the physical world. This energy not only colours your world but draws to you the experiences you need and acts as an unconscious memory for everything we experience. Golden Dawn Adept John Brodie Innes wrote that the *Sphere of Sensation* was an egg-shaped aura around the body. Each time we learn something new, a little part of our *Sphere of Sensation* changes to adapt to the latest information. From then on, we will see the world through that information. If a dog bites you when you are small, your *Sphere of Sensation* will activate all the warning systems when a dog comes into sight. It will tell your brain to start all the physical reactions to avoid the terrible experience you had before.

While that can be useful, there are times when it no longer becomes right or is wrong – such as when information comes to us second-hand from our parents, friends or teachers. A racist father who, because of his own experience or lousy programming, tells you that Jews were involved in human sacrifice, will get into your *Sphere of Sensation* and dominate your worldview.

Getting rid of that information is extremely difficult, which is why people who learned unhealthy behaviour patterns from their families repeat them. If your family upbringing has programmed you to see life as unfair, and that you never get any breaks, then your *Sphere of Sensation* will build you a universe based on those beliefs. Historically there are cases of such people who have won the lottery and lost it all in a few years because generations of such thinking had so corrupted their *Sphere of Sensation*.

To make matters worse, your *Sphere of Sensation* builds association trees which connected the information it has gathered.

---

* Farrell, N. (2013). *Magical Imagination: The Keys to Magic*. 2nd ed. London: SKYLIGHT.

So if we believe that the *Bible* is the word of God then everything it contains must be historically true. We start to believe that there really was a Moses who crossed the Red Sea and get terribly confused when scholars point out that the Red Sea was a mistranslation of the "Sea of Reeds" which was more of a swamp to the North of Egypt.

These associations built a web, which is our impression of reality – a unique image of the universe from their perspective. This universe is created from many experiences since birth. These are the lessons that we have taught ourselves or accepted as gospel from our parents, teachers, friends, and society. Over the years, our universe becomes more defined, meaning that we can handle more of what our life throws at us.

The New Age movement teaches a half-truth that our mental picture of the universe is such a powerful force for stability that it eventually creates the circumstances that support it. In other words, how we see our world becomes a self-fulfilling prophecy. The person who is rich either in material or spiritual terms is unlikely to be poor, while the poor will be forever locked in their misery. Occultism teaches that since the imagination builds such a universe under many, it can be changed – and indeed in most cases, it must.

I said it was a half-truth as is not always accurate or a universal law. There are some things in life which are cornerstones of your life which must happen for your story to take place. For example no amount of visualising can change your family and your genetics and they have a huge influence on your story and *Sphere of Sensation*. Some life changing events appear in a manner which could even have been imagined by the participants.

Over the millennia, many different techniques enabled people to master their universe using their imagination and change the wiring of their minds to let in things like success, happiness, and well-being.

The most common of these tools is pathworking or guided meditation, which we will look at in a moment. This technique which had long been part of the western magical tradition was tested in the 1970s by scientists who were shocked to discover that it was a powerful way to change ways of thinking.

For example, a friend of mine used a pathworking to visit a destructive first relationship to see how it made her feel now. She imagined undoing that event so that the plot of her life was no longer based on the false lessons that relationship taught her. It unlocked a tremendous amount of energy which was locked up in her sphere of sensation, and her life path changed.

It is essential to look at the Neo-Platonist idea of mind and symbols to understand the concept of how the Sphere works and communicates. Firstly, the Neo-Platonists believed that all things are the products of divine consciousness, and the way that an object is created by using physical material. The One Thing can do neither because it is infinite and cannot take any outside source and can only make its universe within its own mind. Once you realise the universe works *like* a mind*, you can use the information to bring about change.

The Universal Mind does not communicate in words – it uses symbols. A word is a symbol, but it only generally means one or more ideas. A real symbol is understood on many various levels.

Likewise, the *Sphere of Sensation* works on symbols, which it uses a bit like a computer language to programme the environment. It takes Macrocosmic symbols and converts them into personal ones. These reflect the Nephesh and the physical body. Our spiritual side communicates with us through the *Sphere of Sensation* using symbols.

We are born facing the wrong way. Our loyal servant, our *Sphere of Sensation,* shows us a distorted vision of the Universe. It builds our lives on incorrect beliefs founded on clouded understandings of the symbols. We see symbols but 'in a glass, darkly.' Soon optimism gives way to depression, the trivial becomes important, and our view becomes narrow and clouded. People form links with others through shared magnetism and corrupted symbols. Their Spheres of Sensation become linked, and spiritual energy become depleted. As people age, they become more fixed. They either keep symbols of their universe or live their lives as they always have done. In such circumstances, the higher aspects of the personality lose their ability to influence the *Sphere of Sensation,* it gives up and the person finally dies.

BASIC RITUALS

This book uses adapted rituals from *Order of the Golden Dawn.* It does so because they do the job and are publicly available. I see no reason not to use something which works and when adapted, brings in the same sort of energy. While some of the details of this might sail over the head of non-initiates and open me to the accusation that this book is a "Golden Dawn" system, anyone who is in that order will tell you that this book is nothing like the Golden Dawn. Since this

---

* This is not saying that the Universe *is* a Mind, just that it has similarities to one. The difference is like saying my computer is a Stoic philosopher because it uses a similar logic in its software.

system is "Ancient Alexandrian," the eclectic mix of Golden Dawn, Greek, Hebrew, and Egyptian systems is perfectly acceptable.

GREEK CROSS

All actions during *Helios Unbound* start with an adaption of the Kabbalistic cross which is an excellent method of balancing the *Sphere of Sensation* before and after any working to limit any unbalancing that the work causes. I have replaced the Hebrew of the Golden Dawn with Greek. Note that the visualisations of the cross are NOT a crucifix, but the equal-armed rose cross.

Reach up and tap between your eyebrows and visualise the crown centre above your head (see this as diamond light) realise that this is your spiritual centre in your body.

Say **SU EI [SY EE]** (ΣΥ ΕΙ) (This means literally "you are" when you touch and visualise this sphere you think of your *Lower Self*, placing itself in the hands of the higher. It is acknowledging that the divine is indwelling in your body)

When you have this visualised this take your hand down to your belly button while drawing this white diamond light down with it. Turn your hand to point to the floor and see this light continue down to your feet. See a sphere of dark violet form beneath your feet.

Say **E ARCHE ['E AR-CH'E]** (Η ΑΡΧΗ) which means Kingdom. Realise that your physical world connects the spiritual world. Everything you see around you is Divine. Now keeping on visualising that line of light, tap your right shoulder and see a sphere form of scarlet.

Say **KAI E DUNAMIS [KE 'E DY-NA-MEES]** (ΚΑΙ Η ΔΥΝΑΜΙΣ) which means "and the Power." Think of how you act, how you move and every activity you are doing. How you bring order to your universe. Draw a line across your body to your left shoulder. See a sphere of bright blue form.

Say **KAI E DOXA [KE 'E THO-XA]** (ΚΑΙ Η ΔΟΞΑ) which means "and the Glory." Think about what you are passively doing in your life and how you forgive. Interlock your fingers and touch your thumbs together so that they are in an upward pointing triangle level to your heart.

You are balancing Heaven, Earth, mercy, and severity, Order and Chaos in your *Sphere of Sensation*. When you have done this rotate your wrist so that your thumbs are pointing downwards. See a rose-pink ball of light in your heart centre [turning the wrist opens the heart centre]. All feelings to come to the surface (opening the heart centre always brings feelings. Note what they are.

Say **AEI [EYE-EE]** [Forever] (A-EE) and see yourself as a rose cross of white light with a rose centre broadcasting balanced golden light.

LESSER RITUAL OF THE PENTAGRAM·

Memorise this essential mini-ritual as it is used before any session in its invoking form and banishing form as part of the clearing out work done on the *Sphere of Sensation*.

Trace any image or figure in the air with the finger, dagger or another magical instrument. What is critical is the visualisation of everything at the right moment is vital.

Facing East perform a Greek Cross. Draw, in the air facing EAST an invoking pentagram about three feet across. ✶ bringing the point of the dagger to the centre of the Pentagram, vibrate the Name **AIΩ** (pronounced *AH, EE, AW*)

Imagine that your voice carries forward to the LIMITS of the UNIVERSE.

Without moving the dagger trace a semicircle before you as you turn towards the SOUTH. Again, trace the pentagram ✶, bring the dagger to the centre of it, and vibrate the name **ΩIA**, (pronounced *AW, EE, AH*)

Again, trace the semicircle with the dagger to the WEST, trace the Pentagram, ✶ bringing the blade to the centre, and vibrate the name **ΩAI**, (pronounced *AW, AH, EE*) Then, turn towards the NORTH, while tracing the circle, trace the pentagram ✶, bring the point of the dagger to the centre and vibrate the name **AΩI**, (pronounced either *AH, AW, EE*)

Return to the EAST, completing tracing the circle of brilliant white light, bringing the dagger point to the centre of the EAST pentagram.

---

* This ritual borrows from the Golden Dawn. However, the divine names used in this ritual have been changed to those more likely to have been used Greco-Roman Egypt. Thus the medieval cabbalistic names have been replaced with the variants of IAΩ. This was a divine name of Jupiter and the Jewish god YHVH. Pagan magicians used Archangels' names, so I have kept them but replaced the cabbalistic names of YHVH with variations of the name IAΩ. My personal theory is that the Jewish Kabbalah appeared in Greco-Roman Egypt based on an earlier Greek technique. The proof of this can be found in the first notable cabbalistic book Sefer Yetzirah in which the universe is created with Hebrew letters. The letters used are not YHVH but YHV which is a Hebrew variation of IAΩ.

Say **BEFORE ME** (then vibrate) **RAPHAEL** (pronounced **RA-FA-EL**[*])

Imagine a scintillating brilliant golden Archangel in front of you and facing you. In his/her right hand is caduceus.

Then, say, **BEHIND ME** (then vibrate) **GABRIEL** (pronounced **WA-VREE-EL**)

Imagine a scintillating brilliant silver Archangel behind you and facing you, holding in their right hand a silver chalice.

Raise your right arm at right angles pointing towards the South

Then, say, **AT MY RIGHT HAND** (then vibrate) **MICHAEL** (pronounced **MEE-KA-EL**)

Imagine a scintillating brilliant flaming Archangel at your right, facing you, and holding a sword of flame.

Keeping your right hand raised, raise your left arm at right angles pointing towards the North so you are standing as a cross.

Then, say, **AT MY LEFT HAND** (then vibrate) **Souriel** (pronounced **SOO-REE-EL**)

Imagine an Archangel of blue lightning holding a thunderbolt.

Imagine yourself as a golden cross radiating yellow light to fill the room and say,

ABOUT ME FLAME THE PENTAGRAMS, AND BEHIND ME SHINES THE SIX-RAYED STAR.

Imagine that behind you is a golden hexagram. It is a symbol of your *Higher Self*. See it unite with you and that the room is flooded with golden light.

Vibrate the name **IAΩ** (**E, AH, AW**)

Repeat the Greek Cross.

LESSER RITUAL OF THE PENTAGRAM RITUAL NOTES

In this system, the *Lesser Ritual of the Pentagram* [LRP] is used in the same way as it was within the *Order of the Golden Dawn* as a complete, classic 'magical sign' that the operator drew in four directions.

The pentagram is associated with the planet Venus because when viewed from earth, successive conjunctions of the planet plot a perfect pentagram shape around the zodiac every eight years. Another attribution is with Mars as that planet is connected to the number five. The pentagram represents humanity's ability to control things and spirits because of its five-fold nature. Since elemental or purely spiritual beings populate most of the universe, and a human is a mixture of both, this gives them considerable protection and

* In the PGM the names of the Archangels were written in Greek not Hebrew. Therefore the pronunciation would follow Greek rules.

power. As far as occultists are concerned, the pentagram is a symbol of a perfected human being. It is a symbol of spirit ruling over the elemental nature.

The LRP has the operator/candidate standing in the centre of their universe, between two pillars of Order and Chaos, with his or her *Higher Genius* within the heart centre, flanked by four Archangels and on all sides a symbol of the dominion of spirit. All this imagery sends a powerful message to the unconscious mind that they are a channel for their *Higher Genius*.

The LRP changes to the *Sphere of Sensation* by placing powerful symbols within it and each repetition enforces them over time. In time the person gradually develops to live in harmony with them.

The insistence on the LRP before ritual implies that the LRP has a hygienic effect and can be used to create sacred space. It does this in two ways. The first is by elevating the consciousness of the operator. It creates physical change in the environment occupied by the *Sphere of Sensation*. The *Sphere of Sensation* is spiritualised and expanded to the four quarters. The spiritualised sphere produces a high range energy hum. This hum prevents lower astral beings which operate on a lower spiritual note (which cause most of the problems in ceremonial magic) from entering the space.

The *Sphere of Sensation* is projected outwards and stretched magically to include the entire temple space. Over the years, many people, inside and outside the Golden Dawn, have reported beneficial effects caused by the regular performance of the LRP.

Besides drawing other forces to you, the invoking pentagram directly affects the person performing it. Rather than just being 'guardians' and 'protectors,' the angels and divine names send their transformative energies into your *Sphere of Sensation* and alchemically transmute and orientate it.

You will note that throughout what I have described I have used the "invoking" ritual of the pentagram. In the last 30 years, Western Magic has been obsessively using the "banishing" version of the rite. This is the same ritual, but the banishing pentagram is drawn from bottom to top ☆.   While the Golden Dawn used banishing pentagrams, it was only if they were in space which felt wrong or was used for other things. It was *never* used in a fully consecrated temple. The banishing protects by "reversing the polarity"[*] of the *Sphere of Sensation* to push away lower astral nasties while connecting the person to their *Higher Self*. It can be used to remove those parts of

---

[*] Yes I am aware it is a Dr Who reference.

your personality, such as habits, that you do not want. The invoking ritual allows you to bring things into your life that you desire and brings about your connection with spiritual forces. Lesser banishing pentagrams prevent you drawing these forces to you.

Once you have performed your ritual, it will stay working until Sunrise or Sunset.

If you want to attract an angel or a god, you will use the invoking one before your working. If you were doing your general daily meditation, you would perform the invoking pentagram ritual because you would want to gain information. However, if you were meditating on your shortcomings, you would do a banishing because you would want to get rid of something inside you.

THE ELEMENTAL PENTAGRAM RITUAL

The purpose of this ritual is to assist in balancing the elements. The mechanics of this ritual will be explained later. It is based on the Golden Dawn's *Supreme Ritual of the Pentagram*, but it has been tweaked to fit into this system. It uses the divine names of the gods which ruled each element according to Empedocles and the secret names of the Elemental Kings from Coptic Egypt. The room is to be orientated towards the East. Those who know the *Order of the Golden Dawn's Ritual of Opening by Watchtowers* should notice a few key differences. The active and passive spirit pentagrams are called Order and Chaos to fit with Empedocles elemental theory.

1. Face East and perform the Greek Cross

2. Vibrate: **ANLALA LAI GAIA APA DIACHANNA CHORYN (AN-LA-LA LAY GUY-AH AH-PAH DEE-ACH-AN-NA CH-OR-IN)**
Say, **Hear Me and make all spirits subject unto Me so that every Spirit of the Firmament and the Aether; upon the earth and under the Earth, on dry land or in the water, of whirling air or of rushing fire and every spell and scourge of God may be obedient unto Me. May the elemental gates open, and may I be free of anything that limits me.**

3. Visualise a landscape beyond the East with a tall tower in front of it. Draw the Order pentagram ☆ while vibrating **PHILOTÊS (FEEL-OT-ES)** (Φιλοτης) and draw a Spirit wheel ✹ in the centre while vibrating *Logos* (Λογος). Draw the Chaos pentagram ☆ vibrating **NEIKOS (NEE-KOS)** (Νεικος) and draw a Spirit wheel ✹ in the centre while vibrating **KHAOS** (Χαος).

4. Visualise the pentagrams hanging in the air and creating a vortex of power (like a spiralling galaxy). See Zeus (man-headed) stand before it.

5. Draw the Air pentagram ✩ vibrating **AKRAMATHA**. In the centre draw the sign of Aquarius ♒ and vibrate **ZEUS** (Ζευς). Say, **Spirits of Air adore your creator.**

6. Face South. Visualise a landscape beyond the South with a tall tower in front of it.

7. Draw the Order pentagram ✩ while vibrating **PHILOTÊS (FEE-LO-T'ES)** and draw a Spirit wheel ✺ in the centre while vibrating *Logos*. Draw the Chaos pentagram ✩ vibrating **NEIKOS (NEE-KOS)** and a Spirit wheel ✺ in the centre while vibrating **KHAOS**.

8. Visualise the pentagrams hanging in the air and creating a vortex of power (like a spiralling galaxy). See Hades (lion-headed) stand before it.

9. Draw the Fire Pentagram ✩ vibrating the divine names **ZOROTHION**. In the centre draw the sign of Leo ♌ and vibrate and **HADES** (Αδης). Say, **Spirits of Fire, adore your creator.**

10. Face West. Visualise a landscape beyond the West with a tall tower in front of it. Draw the Order pentagram ✩ while vibrating **PHILOTÊS (FEE-LO-T'ES)** and draw a Spirit wheel ✺ in the centre while vibrating *Logos*. Draw the Chaos pentagram ✩ vibrating **NEIKOS (NEE-KOS)** and a Spirit wheel ✺ in the centre while vibrating **KHAOS**.

11. Visualise the pentagrams hanging in the air and creating a vortex of power (like a spiralling galaxy). See Persephone (eagle-headed) stand before it.

12. Draw the water Pentagram ✩ vibrating the divine name **PERITON**. In the centre draw the sign of Scorpio ♏ and vibrate **PERSEPHONE** (Περσεφονη). Say, **Spirits of Water, adore your creator.**

13. Face North. Visualise a landscape beyond the West with a tall tower in front of it. Draw the Order pentagram ✩ while vibrating **PHILOTÊS (FEE-LO-T'ES)** and draw a Spirit wheel ✺ in the centre while vibrating *Logos*. Draw the Chaos pentagram ✩ vibrating **NEIKOS (NEE-KOS)** and draw a Spirit wheel ✺ in the centre while vibrating **KHAOS**.

14. Visualise the pentagrams hanging in the air and creating a vortex of power (like a spiralling galaxy). See Hera (bull-headed) stand before it.

15. Draw the Earth Pentagram ⛤ vibrating the divine name **PARAMAH**. In the centre draw the sign of Taurus ♉ and vibrate and **HERA** (Ἥρᾱ). Say, **Spirits of Earth, adore your creator**.

16. Go to the altar and face east. Say, **I invoke the forces of the Spirit of Life**. Draw the Order pentagram ⛤ while vibrating **PHILOTÊS (FEE-LO-T'ES)** and draw a Spirit wheel ⊛ in the centre while vibrating *Logos*. Draw the Chaos pentagram ⛤ vibrating **NEIKOS (NEE-KOS)** and draw a Spirit wheel ⊛ in the centre while vibrating **KHAOS**.

17. Say, **I invoke the Dæmons of the Celestial spheres, whose dwelling is in the invisible. You are the guardians of the gates of the Universe, become the guardians of this mystic space. Keep far removed any unbalanced forces. Strengthen and inspire me so that I may preserve unsullied this abode of the mysteries of the eternal gods. Let my sphere be pure and holy so that I may enter in and become a partaker of the secrets of the divine light.**

18. Stand in the form of a cross and say, **I am a creature of Chaos searching for meaning in Order. I stand between the Sun and the Moon, the gods and matter, and the Light and the Dark. I am balanced and the perfected vehicle for my Higher Genius.**

19. See a line of light coming from each of the quarters and the beings there meeting in the centre and forming into a rose. You are at the Centre of a Rose Cross. The rose opens with you in the centre from its heart emerges is the vision of the Higher Self. Commune with it. This is the beginning of Knowledge and Conversation with the Higher Self.

THE ZODIACAL PENTAGRAM

The Golden Dawn had a simple and highly effective way of using the pentagrams to open zodiacal portals. The method involved drawing the elemental pentagram for the zodiac sign and putting the astrological symbol in the middle while vibrating the name from the spheres on the Tree of Life.

Fire (Aries, Leo, Sagittarius) ⛤
Earth (Taurus, Virgo, Capricorn) ⛤
Air (Gemini, Libra, Aquarius) ⛤
Water (Cancer, Scorpio, Pisces) ⛤

ZALAMOIRLALITH

If you wanted to open a portal to Aries, you would face where Aries was at the time and draw an invoking pentagram of fire. You would place the symbol of Aries and vibrate the Hebrew name **Elohim Gibor** (God is Mighty).

In our case, though it is better to draw the invoking pentagram and then draw magic sigils of the planets and vibrate the mystical name of the sign. Thus, for Leo you would do an invoking Fire Pentagram and vibrate **ZALAMOIRLALITH**. We will be giving a list of these mystical names of the signs later.

LVX FORMULA

The LVX formula was a crucial part of the Golden Dawn system of magic. It "calls down the light" into a ritual and animates thought-forms, symbols, and geometric shapes. Over the years it has been proven to work, but there are intellectual holes in the process which make some things redundant and others clumsy or wrong. It is possible to do it the way the GD did it (which was hardwired into their 5=6 initiation or using a more "Pagan" approach).

THE GOLDEN DAWN APPROACH

INRI
Yod, Nun, Resh, Yod
The sign of Osiris slain
L – the Sign of Mourning Isis
V – the sign of Typhon and Apophis
X- the sign of Osiris Risen
L.V.X Lux, the light of the cross!

Virgo, Isis, Mighty Mother
Scorpio, Apophis Destroyer
Sol Osiris slain and Risen
Isis, Apophis, Osiris
(The spirit Enochian names are invoked to equilibrate the
force*)
Let the Divine White Brilliance Descend
I.A.O.

The LVX formula is a shorthand version of the Golden Dawn's
adept ritual which starts with three officers representing the divine
name IAO cause the light to descend on the candidate. INRI refers to
the candidate bound on the cross of suffering and becoming Osiris
slain. The door of Light (LVX) is shown to the candidate, who is
exposed to the forces which resurrect Osiris, causing the Divine
White Brilliance to descend from the Crown of God to re-animate
and bring things to life.

INRI was the form placed above the Cross of Jesus of Nazareth.
It is short for "IESUS NAZARENUS REX IUDAEORUM" meaning
in English "Jesus of Nazareth, King of Jews." John 19:20 states that
this was written in three languages — Hebrew, Latin, and Greek.
If you translate INRI into Greek, you would get the initials INBI,
standing for Ἰησοῦς ὁ Ναζωραῖος ὁ Βασιλεὺς τῶν Ἰουδαίων (ee-'e-
soos na-zo-re-os o va-si-lefs ton ee-oo-de-awn). The "traditional"
translation into Hebrew is מידוהיה דלמי ירצנה עושי this would give the
acronym Yod, Heh, Vau, Heh but before anyone gets excited this is
because the words Jesus of Nazareth, King of Jews are not correctly
translated. Our YHVH translation is Hebrew for "Jesus the Nazarite
and King of the Jews" and the correct rendering would be תרצנמ עושי,
מידוהיה דלמ Yod, Mem, Mem, Heh. Either way, the Hebrew keyword
is a mess and does not reach the place that *Order of the Golden Dawn*
intended. The idea that Yod, Nun, Resh, Yod could be a cypher for
INRI was found by Israel Regardie in an esoteric masonry paper and
has been lovingly copied ever since, perhaps because INRI matches
the rest of the GD's Christian aspects.

Regardie quotes the Golden Dawn document *777* as the source
that Apophis represents "death," and equates to Set-Typhon in the
Egyptian myths. However, Apophis was not part of the Isis and Osiris
myth. His role in Egyptian magic was not that of the destroyer, which

---

*This appears to have been a modern edition to the ritual added by Israel
Regardie

was appropriate for Set-Typhon, but a grand opposer of all order. He was not so much death as "total oblivion" and "raw Chaos." The temple of Karnak dedicated itself to doing hourly workings to ensure the weakening of Apophis so the Sun god Ra could defeat him. The Egyptians saw death as a good thing, but Apophis had no redeeming qualities. Apophis was despised and never worshipped by the Egyptians. His main rival was not Isis or Osiris, but Ra. Apophis's goal is to snuff out everything and were it not for the actions of Ra, creation would cease to be. Mention of his name in the LVX formula has always bothered me. It was too powerful and unbalances it – Isis and Osiris do not limit Apophis energy.

Set/Typhon does fit all the attributions given in the formula. He was worshipped and was never quite the devil of the Christian pantheon. Restoring Set-Typhon makes the issue go away completely. My thought was Apophis was bought in as a replacement for Set-Typhon, because his Greek name started with the letter A and Set-Typhon did not. We will look at this unnecessary red herring later.

THE LIGHT OF THE CROSS

This phrase, which is usually accompanied by the magician standing in the sign of the cross or visualising a golden cross does not come from the *Bible*. While it was a common saying in late-Christian terminology, in the Christian tradition the cross does not cast any light. It is a symbol of darkness and polarises against the resurrection, which is the source of Light.

What is being referred to here is how the Latin letters of LVX can be extended and made into three crosses. Magically this is because light moves through three phases. The three gods Isis, Typhon and Osiris represent these crosses.

The writer of the LVX ritual uses Isis, Apophis and Osiris because the letters of their names equal the word of power I.A.O. I.A.O was an important word. Not only was it a replacement for יהוה in the Greek translation of the *Bible*, it was a Divine Name of Jupiter, the King of the Gods. In the so-called *Mithras Liturgy*, IAO is associated with "fire" and "light." It is the perfect name for "calling down the Divine White Brilliance" (think of Zeus with his lightning bolt)

But the writer of the GD LVX formula either did not know or ignored the fact that IAO was written I.A.Ω. Omega is a different vowel from Omicron. *Bible* based material written around this divine name is always associated with Ω – the last letter of the alphabet. "I am the Alpha and the Omega, the First and the Last, the Beginning and the End." — Revelation 22:13. . "I" was associated with Christ and the Sun and Alpha was the first letter and Omega was the last. Osiris's name in Greek was spelt with the letter O (omicron) not Ω.

The *Order of the Golden Dawn* pronounced IAO as Ee, Ah, Oh. Yet Omega is pronounced like the AW in "law"; while omicron which was like the shorter O in "pot"* Ancient Greek vowels in their long form (which is best for vibration) gives us the Ee (e as in bean) Ah (a as in father) Aw (as in law). This means that the godforms *cannot* be defined by the first letter of their name. If Osiris is not spelt Ωsiris then A does not need to be the problematic Apophis and could be the more logical Set-Typhon.

THE HELIOS UNBOUND VERSION

Osophoophe (OS-OR-NOO-F'E) (Οσορνουφη) **The sign of Osiris slain** [At shoulder level, hold arms straight out at the sides to form an equal-armed cross.]

L – the Sign of Mourning Isis [Right arm is bent at 90°, upper arm parallel with the ground, forearm pointing upwards, fingers extended. Left arm is the same, but with the forearm arm pointing downwards. Head faces to the left and down. Right foot rests on its ball, with the knee bent.]

V – the sign of Set-Typhon the destroyer [Raise arms above the head at an angle of 60° to each other, and throw the head back, as if looking upwards.]

X- the sign of Osiris risen [Standing upright, cross the arms over the chest, right over left, so that the open hands rest on the shoulders.]

L.V.X [repeat the signs for each letter] **Lux, the light of the cross** [Stand in the sign of Osiris slain, visualise yourself as a golden cross sending out light]

Virgo, Isis, Mighty Mother [raise arms slightly]

Scorpio, Typhon Destroyer [raise arms slightly]

Sol Osiris slain [sign of Osiris slain] **and Risen** [sign of Osiris risen]

Isis, Typhon, Osiris [lift arms up again]

In the name of [Thoth-Hermes, Hekate Jupiter, Zeus, YHVH†]

---

* In Greek the word "mega" means "big" so we have "o-mega" which literally means "o-big" while the greek word "micron" means "small" so we have "o-mikron" which means "o-small" and for both the "big" and "small" refers to the duration.

† Use which ever god or goddess you are using as your Light Bringer.

Let the Divine White Brilliance Descend [Draw your arms down quickly]

I.A. Ω. (Ee-Ah-Aw)

[Vibrate **IAΩ** three times while visualising light descending from the above to below]

LESSER RITUAL OF THE HEXAGRAM

Another ritual which I am lifting from the Golden Dawn corpus, is a mini-rite called the *Lesser Banishing Ritual of the Hexagram*. It is performed after a LRP by adepts and assorted reasons have been provided for its existence mostly centred on an apparent need to neutralise any planetary energy before beginning a working.

Based on the drawing of two different triangles in distinct positions in the quarters it is the most used of a collection of "lesser" invoking and banishing hexagrams. However, the root of the lesser hexagrams might provide us with some clues as to its use and why it is an important daily practice for the modern magician.

One of the founders of the Golden Dawn took the triangle diagrams from a drawing of the *Key of Solomon* magic Circle where it is placed in the outside circle along with the highest magical names of power. The triangles are not explained, but it seems likely to me that that they are Geomantic symbols. Two of them (in the South and West) are variations on the Geomantic symbols for Carcer, the East is Fortuna Minor and the last, in the North is Conjunctio. Within the circle of Key Solomon, these Geomantic symbols make a great deal of sense. In this case, their role is creating a ring of protection around the magician.

Geomantic figures are a recipe which is fused to create a strong effect. In this case, we have a strong Saturnian flavour which separates the inside of the circle from the outside world. Carcer means Prison and is attributed to Saturn. The northern hexagram is the Geomantic opposite to Carcer. Conjunctio is attributed to the mutable Mercury and draws things together rather than separate them. However, Conjunctio tends to follow the influence of the other hexagrams so that that it is a "good symbol with good" and "bad with bad." Mercury was also a god of boundaries, so it would appear the role of this hex is to unite the other hexagrams to mark off and seal the protective circle.

Fortuna Minor in the East is a unique addition to the magic circle. It stands for the setting Sun – the Sun as an old man. It is a symbol of the beginning of the night, the light shining in the dark. It is the beginning (Genesis counted the day beginning at Sunset) and the end, which makes it a good symbol for the start of a magic circle. The image of the old man works with the concept of this magic circle being Saturnian and marking the passage of time. The Sun, in any format, is always going to have some protective aspect against darkness, but in this case, it is the herald of night. The East is where the Sun rises, so this Geomantic symbol reverses that idea. It is Time as the protector of order (Aion the Roman god of time was lion faced) and the continuation of everything that was.

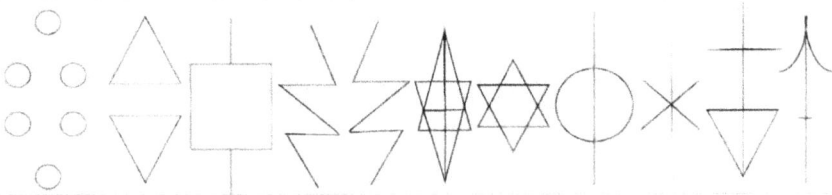

Drawing Geomantic symbols is a creative art. Traditionally they could be drawn by joining up the dots of a Geomantic figure differently. Geomantic figures do not have to be constructed using lines, they could use shapes and curls. Lines containing the dots could be drawn closer or further apart to make more geometrically balanced shapes. Golden Dawn members were shown a list of some of these Geomantic shapes, but this was only a starter kit so that the students were aware of the possibilities.

Geomantic symbols are important because they represent planetary force manifesting in the earth. They bring down power to a level where the magican can directly use it.

The Golden Dawn added to the symbols of this by placing the points of each triangle onto the Tree of Life. One of the missing parts of Golden Dawn teaching about the Lesser hexagram was the placement of the solar symbol in the centre. So far, I have only seen this solar symbol in the NISI documents which I published in *Mather's Last Secret**. It might have been unique to the AO, but I doubt it, as NISI is early in AO history and did not deviate much from early Golden Dawn teaching.

By doing this, Mathers provided an additional overlay of teaching which connected the triangles to the Tree of Life and showed how the planetary forces moved around Tiphareth. This enabled another

---

* Farrell, N. (2011). *Mathers' Last Secret revised - the rituals and teachings of the Alpha et Omega*: Rosicrucian *Order of the Golden Dawn*.

EAST

NORTH

SOUTH

WEST

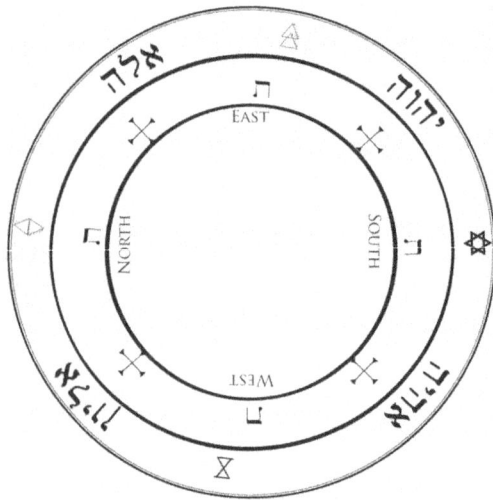

Mathers' innovation – the idea of creating a banishing and invoking aspect to the hexagram. If you wanted to remove a force, you drew the triangles anti-clockwise from the planetary point and if you wanted to invoke you drew the towards the planetary symbol from the one before it. The second triangle is the mirror opposite of the first. This does not apply to the fourth hexagram where the triangles were flipped.

In the *Lesser Banishing Ritual of the Hexagram*, the use of banishing versions of the Geomantic symbols makes for an impressive symbolic system. Rather than providing a magical circle, which the invoking ritual would still do, the banishing breaks down existing restrictions and structures. Rather than allowing the constrictive, separate prisons of the double Carcer symbols, it removes barriers to change. Rather than setting boundaries or uniting forces in the circle with the Conjunctio symbol it is breaking them down or destroying all connections. The banishing of the Sun at midnight is the removal of the element of time and the divine order. It makes the immediate environment chaotic.

When you perform a magical act, you are creating a change in the status quo and challenging the natural Saturnian forces. These energies will act to prevent the ritual's intention from happening. Some of these limitations will exist in the magician, others from society and the natural flow of the universe. By making the space antagonistic to Saturnian inertia, you are giving your magic a chance. Do not forget that with this ritual you are creating Chaos which allows the universe to be reassembled in a new image. This means that for some types of magic a *Lesser Banishing Hexagram*

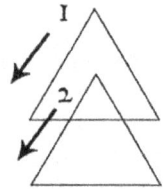

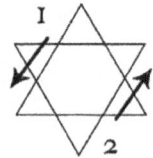

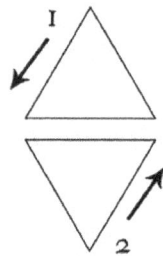

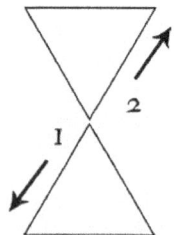

beforehand would not make sense. If you are trying to use magic to take control of an already chaotic situation, it would be unwise to banish Saturn because it will make matters worse.

There is an added point which applies more when you have made magic your life. That is that continual attempts to change the universe or do anything significant creates a backlash from Saturnian forces which try to maintain the status quo. The myth of Saturn and Jupiter and the war of the Titans applies here. At a certain point in your magical career, you will be a symbol for change and like Jupiter be a target for forces of inertia that insist that things stay the same.

What is worrying is often you are unaware of it or might mistake the process for a spiritual test. First, you notice is that your magic does not work in the same way as it did, you might find it harder to meet your spiritual contacts or find yourself too tired to do magical work. It is similar to the inertia that someone has when starting magical work. However, unlike that stage of your personal development, forcing yourself to be more disciplined does not resolve the matter.

While performing a daily *Lesser Banishing Ritual of the Hexagram* would help prevent this backlash before it becomes too crippling, you will always face this issue (it is part of the natural way the universe works), but at least it will not harm you as much.

The *Lesser Banishing Ritual of the Hexagram* has less to do with its planetary attributions and more to do with the forces of Order and Chaos and creating the right circumstances for your magic to work. It deserves to be performed in most workings (after the first LRP) when the ritual requires some change to an existing order. It should be done regularly to counteract those forces of normality which restrict evolution.

THE GREATER RITUAL OF THE HEXAGRAM

The last Golden Dawn feature used in *Helios Unbound* is the *Greater Ritual of the Hexagram* which brings in focused planetary force into a ritual. The Golden Dawn made this ritual a little too elaborate and I have simplified it. In *Helios Unbound*, they are not needed that often and it is best to only draw one.

The hexagram is based on the arrangement of the spheres on the Kabbalistic Tree of Life with each of the points representing one of the spheres. A hexagram is made up of two triangles. The triangle (point up) is made up of Saturn (Daath), Venus (Netzach) and Mercury (Hod). The Triangle pointing downwards is Moon (Yesod), and Mars (Geburah) and Jupiter (Chesed). The Sun (Tiphereth) is in

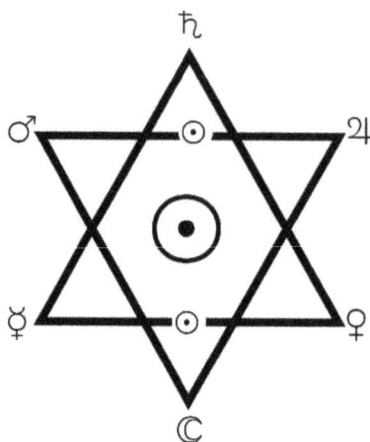

the centre. However, that association with the Tree of Life is less critical than the fact that there are six planets with the Sun in the centre.

You invoke the force by starting on the sphere immediately before the one you intend to invoke and draw your line clockwise towards it. If you wanted to involve Jupiter, you would start at Mars and move to Jupiter and continue to complete the triangle. Once you have finished the triangle where the planet you wish to invoke is found you then do the mirror opposite in the other triangle. In the above example, you would start your second triangle from Venus and go to Mercury.

The issue is how you draw the solar hexagram. The GD produced the inelegant solution of making the person draw all six planetary hexagrams. Symbolically this is a mess as the six planetary energies do not add up to the Sun. The Sun is a unique energy and not the sum of the other planets. Instead, it is better to take the starting point from the mid-points of the top of the lower triangle (before the point of the Abyss on the horizontal path of Gimel) and continue to Jupiter and complete the triangle. The second point should be started in the middle part of the path of Peh (before the veil of Paroketh on the path of Sahmek). You can see this in the above diagram.

Once the hexagram has been drawn a solar symbol should be placed in its centre and the divine name of the god of the planet vibrated. Once this is completed the IAΩ formula is conducted to call light onto the hexagram to charge it.

HEADLESS ONE

Those who follow Aleister Crowley will be familiar with his use of the Bornless One as part of his programme to contact his *Holy Guardian Angel*. It has long been assumed that Crowley adapted it from his reading of Charles Goodwin's 1852 *A Fragment of a Graeco-Egyptian work upon Magic*. Golden Dawn researcher Tony Fuller has confirmed that Crowley received it from Golden Dawn member Allan Bennett and then adapted it for his Thelemic cult. Bennett received it as a Golden Dawn adept where it had been adapted for that order by Samuel Mathers. It was recommended that the adept perform it daily. The Golden Dawn and Felkin's *Stella Matutina* extensively used it. The Golden Dawn version was different from the original and Crowley's and depended on the image of the ankh cross to provide an elemental and ritual basis.

The original ritual can be found in the *Greek Magical Papyri* and superficially appears to be a rite to invoke a being called Akephalos(Ακέφαλος) to exorcise and drive out an evil spirit which is possessing a victim. Towards the end of the ritual the magician switches from simply invoking Akephalos to channelling the god. The Golden Dawn saw this as a form of self-exorcism, to allow the divine presence of Akephalos.

What Mathers saw, which was unrecognised at the time, is that the rite was not just about exorcism and covers banishing, empowerment, and an invocation to the *Higher Genius*. The grade in which Mathers gave his version of the ritual out was one where the candidate was expected to meet and work with their *Higher Genius* after perfecting their personality (at least as much as possible). Mathers interpreted Akephalos as "Bornless" because the Hebrew word for "head" can also mean "start" or "beginning." Something which has no head has no beginning or birth and is in a sense "bornless" and eternal. It is a nice theory, but denies Occam's razor – the word was Greek and cannot be flipped into Hebrew to sound better. Jake Stratton-Kent points out that the ritual was correctly titled *The Headless One*.

Fuller said in a private conversation that the title *Headless One* was used by some Golden Dawn members and was mentioned in an annotation of the rituals by Dr. Carnegie Dickson. Dickson uses Kabbalistic terms to say that the "Headless One" is a T-shaped cross. This represents Malkuth or everything below Tiphareth. By performing the ritual and using other higher-Grade material one enables the Headless One to recover its "Head," or the *Higher Genius* which is separated by Daath.

Once this "Head" is restored to the T Cross we have, of course, the Ankh, symbol of the 7=4 and of the completed Adept of the Third Order.

Elsewhere Dickson suggests that the "Head" (Vesica, Egg) is Aima, the Great Mother of the Headless, or Bornless One. The first "step" towards the restoration of Headless Son (Sun) and mother is entering Tiphareth via the Door of Venus.

The original identity of Akephalos is uncertain. The name is connected to ἀκέφαλοι (akepfaloi, a-ke-fa-lee) who were spirits of the Dead who died a violent death, through accident or beheading (hence also called βίαιοι (vee-e-ee), βιαιοθάνατοι (vee-e-o-tha-na-tee)).

This might suggest that Akephalos was a god of violent death. The fact that the ritual contains a word of power associated with Set or Typhon has led many modern magicians and academics to conclude that he was an aspect of the Egyptian God Set.

However, David Frankfurter from Boston University* has pointed out that Akephalos was a cypher for the god Osiris in his solar form which "clearly invokes a form of Osiris — as a spirit, not as the august temple god we imagine Osiris to have been in places like Abydos."

"The epithet "headless [Akephalos]" seems to have been an esoteric priestly epithet for acclaiming a god's solar nature at a time when identification with the Sun was a form of ultimate glorification for gods all around the Roman Empire."

Frankfurter points out though that in the *Greek Magical Papyri* Akephalos was an epithet that circulated among other gods and may even have spawned its own distinct innovation – the Akephalos Theos (Ακέφαλος Θεός).

"Reivet Atheleverseth" which means "awesome and invisible god" is usually a term for Typhon but other scholars have suggested that this description could also be used for other deities.

The title cited as belonging to Set in the original spell could easily apply to any other god. The spell specifically says that the God

---

* Fairies, Demons, and Nature Spirits: 'Small Gods' at the Margins of Christendom *The Threat of the Headless Being: Constructing the Demonic in Christian Egypt.* Palgrave Macmillan; 2017.

was OSORONNŌPHRIS which is a corruption of Osiris-Onophris which means "he who is good, he who is happy."

THE HEADLESS OSIRIS

Osiris married Isis, and they ruled Egypt together. but Set, Osiris's and Isis's brother, wanted to rule Egypt instead. He tricked Osiris to get into a coffin which he sealed and cast into the Nile drowning him. Set took the throne while Isis went looking for the body of her husband.

When she found it, she returned home. Set found the body and hacked it into 14 pieces and scattered it down the Nile. The Ancient Egyptians considered that dismemberment of the body was the worst thing you could do to someone. A dismembered body suffered a second death which prevented the person living in the afterlife. Death by beheading symbolically killed a human twice, which was why Set did it to Osiris.

Isis, Nephthys and Anubis looked for the body parts, and Isis magically rebuilt Osiris' body. Once the body had been rebuilt, Osiris existed as the King of the Underworld. The ancient Greeks and Romans loved this legend, and it became an essential feature of the Isis cult in Rome. Some elements of the faith appear to have found their way into Christianity.

The idea of a headless god was a symbol of something which was impossibly alive, something which existed purely by the magic of Isis. By identifying with Osiris, a person could be magically restored into their divine self no matter how much a mess they had made of their life. Identifying Akephalos as Osiris links him much closer to the *Higher Genius*. Like the *Higher Genius* Osiris had lived on Earth, died, and was resurrected after passing through the underworld. Osiris stood for the chance of humanity to recognise its divine self and rise with the Sun god Re.

New Kingdom magical texts such as the *Amduat* and the *Book of Gates* say Ra is within a dead soul. In them, he travels through the Duat and unites with Osiris to be reborn at dawn. Osiris enabled rebirth for the dead while renewing the Sun. With some meditation, the connection to Osiris, Re and the *Higher Genius* and the *Lower Self* becomes apparent.

THE RITUAL

This version of ritual is based on the original *Greek Magical Papyri* PGM V. 96-172 known as the *Stele of Jeu the Hieroglyphist*. An original

English literal text of this stele reads:

Write the names to a new paper and extend (it) from the one side of your temple to the other side of your temple (side of the forehead). Face north saying the six names.

Subject to me all the Demons, to be obedient to me every heavenly and ethereal and earthly and underground and of dry land and aquatic demon and every enchantment and scourge of the god.

Grant me the god's powers of enchantment, or punishment. Compel all Dæmons to obey me, whether they are in the heavens, in the aether, on the Earth, or the underworld, or on dry land or in the swirling waters or the flashing fires.

And the *Dæmons* are always obedient to you.

This is the beneficial sign:

I call you, the Headless,
The creator of Earth and Heaven,
The creator of night and day,
You, the creator of light and darkness,
You are Osoronofris, whom nobody has ever seen.
You are Iavas! You are Iapos!
You distinguished the just and the unjust.
You created the female and the male.
You showed the seed and the fruits.
You created the men to love each other and to hate each other.
I am Moses, your prophet who transmitted your mysteries which are accomplished in Israel.
You showed the liquid and the dry and every food.
Hear me!
I am the messenger of Pharo Osoronofris.
This is your true name which was given to the prophets of Israel.

Hear me.

ΑΡΒΑΘΙΑΩ ΡΕΙΒΕΤ ΑΘΕΛΕΒΕΡΣΗΘ ΑΡΑ ΒΛΑΘΑ ΑΛΒΕΥ ΕΒΕΝΦΧΙ ΧΙΤΑΣΓΟΗ ΙΒ ΑΩΘ ΙΑΩ

(AR-VA-THEE-A-AW REE-VET A-THE-LE-VER-S'ETH A-RA VLA-THA AL-VE-Y E-VEN-CHEE CHEE-TAS-GO-'E EEV A-AWTH EE-A-AW)

ARVATHIAO REIVET ATHELEVERSITH ARA VLATHA ALVETH EVENFCHI CHITASWOI IVAOTH IAO

Hear me and turn away this Dæmon.
I call you with the empty spirit terrible and unseen god.

ΑΡΟΓΟΓΟΡΟΒΡΑΩ ΣΟΧΟΥ ΜΟΔΟΡΙΩ ΦΑΛΑΡΧΑΩ ΟΟΟ

(A-RO-GO-GO-RO-VRA-AW SO-CHOO MO-DO-REE-AW FA-LAR-CHA-AW O-O-O)

AROWOWOROVRAO SOCHOU MODORIO FALARCHAO OOO

Holy Headless! Set him free from the Dæmon that keeps him.

ΡΟΥΒΡΙΑΩ ΜΑΡΙ ΩΔΑΜ ΒΑΑΒΝΑΒΑΩΘ ΑΣΣ ΑΔΩΝΑΙ ΑΦΝΙΑΩ ΙΘΩΛΗΘ ΑΒΡΑΣΑΞ ΑΗΟΩΥ

(ROO-VREE-A-AW MA-REE AW-THAM VA-AV-NA-VA-AWTH ASS A-THAW-NA-EE AF-NEE-A-AW EE-THAW-L'ETH A-VRA-SAKS A-'E-O-AW-Y)

ROUVRIAO MARI ODAM VAAVNAVAOTH ASS ADONAI AFNIAO ITHOLITH AVRASACH AIOOI

Powerful Headless! Set him free from the Dæmon that keeps him.

ΜΑΒΑΡΡΑΙΩ ΙΟΗΛ ΚΟΘΑ ΑΘΟΡΗΒΑΛΩ ΑΒΡΑΩΘ

(MA-VAR-RE-AW EE-O-E'L KO-THA A-THO-R'E-VA-LAW AV-RA-AWTH)

MAVARRAIO IOIL KOTHA ATHORIVALO AVRAOTH

Set him free/Release him.

ΑΩΘ ΑΒΡΑΩΘ ΒΑΣΥΜ ΙΣΑΚ ΣΑΒΑΩΘ ΙΑΩ

(A-AWTH AV-RA-AWTH VA-SYM EE-SAK SA-VA-AWTH EE-A-AW)

AOTH AVRAOTH VASIM ISAK SAVAOTH IAO

This is the Lord of the gods.

This is the Lord of the world.
This is who the winds are afraid of.
This is who created with the command of his voice everything himself.
Lord! King! Master! Helper!
Save my soul!

ΙΕΟΥ ΠΥΡ ΙΟΥ ΠΥΡ ΙΑΩΤ ΙΑΗΩ ΙΟΟΥ ΑΒΡΑΣΑΞ ΣΑΒΡΙΑΜ ΟΟ ΥΥ ΕΥ ΟΟ ΥΥ ΑΔΩΝΑΙΕ

(EE-E-OO PYR EE-OO PYR EE-A-AWT EE-O-OO A-VRA-SAKS SAV-REE-AM O-O E-Y O-O Y-Y A-THAW-NE-E)

IEOY PIR IOU PIR IAOT IAIO IOOI AVRASACH SAVRIAM OO II EI OO II ADONAIE

Now, now, good messenger of the god.

ΑΝΛΑΛΑ ΛΑΙ ΓΑΙΑ ΑΠΑ ΔΙΑΧΑΝΝΑ ΧΟΡΥΝ

(AN-LA-LA LA-EE GE-A A-PA DEE-A-CHAN-NA CHO-RYN)

ANLALA LAI GAIA APA DIACHANNA CHORIN

I am the Headless Dæmon, having the sight in the feet.
I am the Powerful that has the immortal fire.
I am the Truth that hates the unfair acts done in the world.
I am the lighting and thunder.
I am he who is the sweat storm of rain falling upon the Earth to fertilise.
I am he whose mouth is altogether burned.
I am the begetter and the destroyer.
I am the grace of the eternity.
My name is heart girt with serpent.
Come forth and follow.

HELIOS UNBOUND VERSION

There is nothing wrong with using the literal PGM version, but the *Helios Unbound* version fuses most of the original but arranged into the Golden Dawn structure which fits into this book by supplying links to the elements. I have also downplayed the words of power used for an exorcism and made the text a little less literal. The ritual is based on the ankh cross. The base of the ankh is attributed to the element of Air, the left arm is the element of Fire and the right arm is the element of Water. The element of Earth is at the intersection of the three elements. This forms the headless body of Osiris.

The elements appear to be in an odd position, if you consider the normal direction of the elements. The way it was explained to me was that the Air element was the foundation of Yesod and the middle pillar of the Tree of Life. Because "back into the cross" your right hand was the sphere of Geburah and the pillar of Fire, while on the left hand to Chesed and the pillar of Water. This leaves the Earth quarter which has no function at all (some Golden Dawn manuscripts ignore it or just place it in the centre of the cross uniting the other three elements).

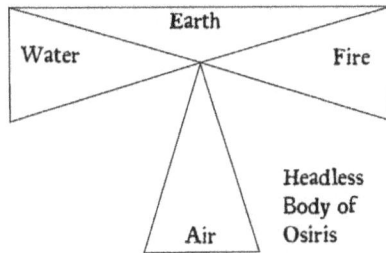

HELIOS UNBOUND HEADLESS ONE

The *Greek Magical Papyrus* requires a person to make a paper crown which is worn on the head during the ritual. On it you write

ΑΩΘ ΑΒΡΑΩΘ ΒΑΣΥΜ ΙΣΑΚ ΣΑΒΑΩΘ ΙΑΩ
And this symbol underneath.

It is not clear what the symbol means, but it might refer to the eyes of the Headless One. It is placed on the forehead. Stand and face north. Place the crown on your head and vibrate,

ΑΩΘ ΑΒΡΑΩΘ ΒΑΣΥΜ ΙΣΑΚ ΣΑΒΑΩΘ ΙΑΩ

(A-AWTH A-VRA-AWTH VA-SYM EE-SAK SA-VA-AWTH EE-A-AW)*

---

* This is a corruption of "SABAÔTH, SABAÔTH, in the name of ISAAC's SABAÔTH-IAÔ" and according to T. F. Raaion it is a scribal error which was repeated throughout the spell. Through some careful research Raaion reached the conclusion that it was supposed to start with a vowel string ΑΙÊ ΑΙÔΙ ÊÔΙΑÊ ΑÊ ΙÔ ÔÊ ΑΙÊΟΥΕΥÔΑΙ ΕΑΙ ΥΟ ΙΑÔ ΙÔÊ ΟΑΥ ΑΕÊ ΥÔΥÔ and then the six word name of power CHABRACH PHNESCHÊR PHICHRO PHNYRÔ PHÔCHÔ BÔCH see Raaion, T. (2019). *The Six Names*. [online] Sublunar.space. Available at: https://sublunar.space/2017-08-the-six-names.html [Accessed 31 Jul. 2019]. It is a case of experimentation and

Then say,

Grant me the god's powers of enchantment, or punishment. Compel all *Dæmons* to obey me, whether they are in the heavens, in the aether, on the Earth, or the underworld, or on dry land or in the swirling waters or the flashing fire.

Go to the East draw the Order pentagram ☆ while vibrating **PHILOTÊS** (FEEL-OT-'ES) (Φιλοτης) and draw a Spirit wheel ✹ in the centre while vibrating *Logos* (Λογος). Draw the Chaos pentagram ☆ vibrating **NEIKOS** (NEE-KOS) (Νεικος) and draw a Spirit wheel A in the centre while vibrating **KHAOS** (Χαος). Draw the Earth Pentagram ☆ vibrating the divine name **PARAMAH**. In the centre draw the sign of **Taurus** ♉ and vibrate and **HERA**. Say,

ΑΡΒΑΘΙΑΩ ΡΕΙΒΕΤ ΑΘΕΛΕΒΕΡΣΗΘ ΑΡΑ ΒΛΑΘΑ ΑΛΒΕΥ ΕΒΕΝΦΧΙ ΧΙΤΑΣΓΟΗ ΙΒ ΑΩΘ ΙΑΩ ΙΒ ΑΩΘ ΙΑΩ

(AR-VA-THEE-A-AW REE-VET A-THE-LE-VER-S'ETH A-RA VLA-THA AL-VE-Y E-VEN-PH-CHEE CHEE-TA-SGO-'E EEV A-AWTH EE-A-AW)

I invoke, Akephalos – the Headless.
The creator of Earth and Heaven.
The creator of night and day.
You created darkness and light.
You are Osiris-Onophris who no man has ever yet seen.
You are **IAVAS** and **IAPŌS**.
You separate the fair and the unfair.
You created men and women.
You revealed the secrets of seeds and fruit.
You created humanity to love and to hate each other.
I speak your will on Earth and channel your mysteries.
You reveal the moist and the dry,
the hot, the cold and provide all nourishment.
Hear me,
I am the Angel of Pharaoh Onophris.
And know your true names which you delight to hear.

Hear me and grant me the god's powers of enchantment, or punishment. Compel all *Dæmons* to obey me, whether they are in the heavens, in the aether, on the Earth, or the underworld, or on dry land or in the swirling waters or the flashing fires.

---

sticking to one which works for you.

Go to the South draw the Order pentagram ✮ while vibrating **PHILOTÊS** (FEEL-OT-'ES) (Φιλοτης) and draw a Spirit wheel ✪ in the centre while vibrating *Logos* (Λογος). Draw the Chaos pentagram ✮ vibrating **NEIKOS** (NEE-KOS) (Νεικος) and draw a Spirit wheel ✪ in the centre while vibrating **KHAOS** (Χαος). Draw the Fire Pentagram ✮ vibrating the divine name **Zorothion**. In the centre draw the sign of **Leo** ♌ and vibrate and **Hades** and say,

ΑΡΟΓΟΓΟΡΟΒΡΑΩ ΣΟΧΟΥ ΜΟΔΟΡΙΩ ΦΑΛΑΡΧΑΩ ΟΟΟ

(A-RO-GO-GO-RO-VRA-AW SO-CHOO MO-DO-REE-AW FA-LAR-CHA-AW O-O-O)

Hear me and turn away harmful *Dæmons*. This is your true name. Hear me and grant me the god's powers of enchantment, or punishment. Compel all *Dæmons* to obey me, whether they are in the heavens, in the aether, on the Earth, or the underworld, or on dry land or in the swirling waters or the flashing fires.

Go to the West draw the Order pentagram ✮ while vibrating **PHILOTÊS** (FEEL-OT-'ES) (Φιλοτης) and draw a Spirit wheel ✪ in the centre while vibrating *Logos* (Λογος). Draw the Chaos pentagram ✮ vibrating **NEIKOS** (NEE-KOS) (Νεικος) and draw a Spirit wheel ✪ in the centre while vibrating **KHAOS** (Χαος). Draw the Air pentagram ✮ vibrating the divine name **Akramatha**. In the centre draw the sign of **Aquarius** ♒ and vibrate and **Zeus** and say,

ΡΟΥΒΡΙΑΩ ΜΑΡΙ ΩΔΑΜ ΒΑΑΒΝΑΒΑΩΘ ΑΣΣ ΑΔΩΝΑΙ ΑΦΝΙΑΩ ΙΘΩΛΗΘ ΑΒΡΑΣΑΞ ΑΗΟΩΥ
(ROO-VREE-A-AW MA-REE AW-THAM VA-AV-NA-VA-AWTH ASS A-THO-NA-EE AF-NEE-A-AW EE-THAW-L'ETH A-VRA-SAKS A-'E-O-AW-Y)

Hear me and turn away harmful *Dæmons*. Holy Headless One, hear me and grant me the god's powers of enchantment, or punishment. Compel all *Dæmons* to obey me, whether they are in the heavens, in the aether, on the Earth, or the underworld, or on dry land or in the swirling waters or the flashing fires.

Go to the North draw the Order pentagram ✮ while vibrating **PHILOTÊS** (FEEL-OT-'ES) (Φιλοτης) and draw a Spirit wheel ✪ in the centre while vibrating *Logos* (Λογος). Draw the Chaos pentagram ✮ vibrating **NEIKOS** (NEE-KOS) (Νεικος) and draw a Spirit wheel ✪ in the centre while vibrating **KHAOS** (Χαος). Draw the Water Pentagram ✮ vibrating the divine name **PERITON**. In the centre draw the sign of **Scorpio** ♏ and vibrate and **Persephone**. Say,

ΜΑΒΑΡΡΑΙΩ ΙΟΗΛ ΚΟΘΑ ΑΘΟΡΗΒΑΛΩ ΑΒΡΑΩΘ
(MA-VAR-RE-AW EE-O-E'L KO-THA A-THO-R'E-VA-LAW
AV-RA-AWTH)

I call you with the empty spirit, for you are the terrible and unseen god.

ΑΡΟΓΟΓΟΡΟΒΡΑΩ ΣΟΧΟΥ ΜΟΔΟΡΙΩ ΦΑΛΑΡΧΑΩ ΟΟΟ
(A-RO-GO-GO-RO-VRA-AW SO-CHOO MO-DO-REE-AW
FA-LAR-CHA-AW O-O-O)

Holy Akephalos Set me free from *Dæmons* that restrain me.

ΡΟΥΒΡΙΑΩ ΜΑΡΙ ΩΔΑΜ ΒΑΑΒΝΑΒΑΩΘ ΑΣΣ ΑΔΩΝΑΙ
ΑΦΝΙΑΩ ΙΘΩΛΗΘ ΑΒΡΑΣΑΞ ΑΗΟΩΥ
   (ROO-VREE-A-AW MA-REE AW-THAM VA-AV-NA-VA-
AWTH ASS A-THAW-NA-EE AF-NEE-A-AW EE-THAW-L'ETH
A-VRA-SAKS A-'E-O-AW-Y)

Powerful Akephalos! Set me free from the *Dæmons* that restrain me.

ΜΑΒΑΡΡΑΙΩ ΙΟΗΛ ΚΟΘΑ ΑΘΟΡΗΒΑΛΩ ΑΒΡΑΩΘ
(MA-VAR-RE-AW EE-O-E'L KO-THA A-THO-R'E-VA-LAW
AV-RA-AWTH)

Set me free. Hear me and grant me the god's powers of enchantment, or punishment. Compel all *Dæmons* to obey me, whether they are in the heavens, in the aether, on the Earth, or the underworld, or on dry land or in the swirling waters or the flashing fires.

Go to the altar. Draw the Order pentagram ☆ while vibrating **PHILOTÊS** (FEEL-OT-'ES) (Φιλοτης) and draw a Spirit wheel ⊕ in the centre while vibrating *Logos* (Λογος). Draw the Chaos pentagram ⛤ vibrating **NEIKOS** (NEE-KOS) (Νεικος) and draw a Spirit wheel ⊕ in the centre while vibrating **KHAOS** (Χαος). Then say, :

ΙΕΟΥ ΠΥΡ ΙΟΥ ΠΥΡ ΙΑΩΤ ΙΑΗΩ ΙΟΟΥ ΑΒΡΑΣΑΞ ΣΑΒΡΙΑΜ
ΟΟ ΥΥ ΕΥ ΟΟ ΥΥ ΑΔΩΝΑΙΕ
(EE-E-OO PYR EE-OO PYR EE-A-AWT EE-A-'E-AW I-O-OO
AV-RA-SAKS SAV-REE-AM O-O Y-Y E-Y O-O Y-Y A-THAW-NE-E)

Powerful Akephalos. Set me free and send away any Dæmons that limit me.

ΜΑΒΑΡΡΑΙΩ ΙΟΗΛ ΚΟΘΑ ΑΘΟΡΗΒΑΛΩ ΑΒΡΑΩΘ
(MA-VAR-RE-AW EE-O-E'L KO-THA A-THO-R'E-VA-LAW
AV-RA-AWTH)

Set me free and release me

Go to the west and face East:

ΑΩΘ ΑΒΡΑΩΘ ΒΑΣΥΜ ΙΣΑΚ ΣΑΒΑΩΘ ΙΑΩ
(A-AWTH A-VRA-AWTH VA-SYM EE-SAK SA-VA-AWTH
EE-A-AW)

Lord of the Gods,
Lord of the Universe,
You whom the winds fear.
You made everything by the power of your words.
Lord, King, Ruler, help empower and save my soul.

ΙΕΟΥ ΠΥΡ ΙΟΥ ΠΥΡ ΙΑΩΤ ΙΑΗΩ ΙΟΟΥ ΑΒΡΑΣΑΞ ΣΑΒΡΙΑΜ
ΟΟ ΥΥ ΕΥ ΟΟ ΥΥ ΑΔΩΝΑΙΕ
(EE-E-OO PYR EE-OO PYR EE-A-AWT EE-A-'E-AW I-O-OO
AV-RA-SAKS SAV-REE-AM O-O Y-Y E-Y O-O Y-Y A-THAW-
NE-E)

Now, now, good messenger of the god. Hear me and grant
me the god's powers of enchantment, or punishment. Compel
all Dæmons to obey me, whether they are in the heavens, in the
aether, on the Earth, or the underworld, or on dry land or in the
swirling waters or the flashing fires.

Stand in the form of a cross with your head bowed

ΑΝΛΑΛΑ ΛΑΙ ΓΑΙΑ ΑΠΑ ΔΙΑΧΑΝΝΑ ΧΟΡΥΝ
(AN-LA-LA LA-EE GE-A A-PA DEE-A-CHAN-NA CHO-RYN)

*Pause. Visualise yourself in space and slowly build yourself a body out
of the galaxies. Remember not to give yourself a head. Then speaking as this
god of the darkness of space say,*

I am the Dæmon Akephalos with sight in his feet.
I am power who holds the immortal fire.
I am Truth that hates the world's unfairness.
I am lighting and thunder.
I am he whose sweat is the rainstorm fertilising the Earth.
I am he whose mouth is eternal fire.
I create and destroy existence.
I am the World's Beauty.

Visualise the egg of creation surrounded by a snake. This is
your own universe and creation. It is your heart. Now say,

My name is "HEART ENTWINED WITH A SERPENT"
καρδία περιεζωσμένη ὄφιν
(KAR-DEE-A PE-REE-E-ZOS-ME-N'E O-FIN)

Come forth and follow. For I have the powers of enchantment, or punishment. I compel all *Dæmons* to obey me, whether they are in the heavens, in the aether, on the Earth, or the underworld, or on dry land or in the swirling waters or the flashing fires.
Vibrate **IAŌ SABAŌTH** [seven times]
ΙΑΩ ΣΑΒΑΩΘ
(EE-A-AW SA-VA-AWTH)

GODFORMS

A magician sees gods differently from religion. The magician knows that gods are masks for divine forces. Magicians know them to be big and powerful, and activated by worship, but don't often worship them as such.

In his book, *Witches Abroad*, the fantasy writer Terry Pratchett put it well when he said:

> *"Most witches don't believe in gods. They know that the gods exist, of course. They even deal with them occasionally. But they don't believe in them. They know them too well. It would be like believing in the postman."**

A magician respects the gods and will often admire them, but the role of the relationship is different. The magician *works* with the gods.

This can be seen in the difference between a magical invocation and a prayer. On the surface, they are similar. Both tend to start by saying how big and powerful the god is. For the follower, such statements are devotion. To quote Monty Python in their film *The Meaning of Life*:

> *"Oh Lord, oooh you are so big. So absolutely huge. Gosh, we're all really impressed down here, I can tell you. Forgive us, O Lord, for this dreadful toadying and barefaced flattery. But you are so strong and, well, just so super. Fantastic. Amen."*

But for a magician, those devotional statements are simply aligning themselves to the mask which they are hoping to use in the ritual. They are taking those divine titles and weaving them into the form of a god about themselves.

A Priest in the Roman Catholic Eucharist rite will take the wafer

---

* Pratchett, T. (2013). *Witches Abroad*. London: Corgi.

and wine and ask god to make them into the body and blood of Jesus. Compare that with the Golden Dawn *Magical Eucharist* where the "priest" takes on the godform of Osiris and does it himself.

> *"I am Osiris Onnophris who is found perfect before the gods. I hath said: These are the elements of my body perfected through suffering, glorified through trial. The scent of this dying rose is as the repressed sigh of my Suffering. This flame-red Fire as the energy of mine undaunted Will. The Cup of Wine is the pouring out of the blood of my heart, sacrificed unto regeneration, unto the newer life. This bread and salt are as the foundations of my body, which I destroy so that they may be renewed."*

In a magic ritual, the magician takes on the form of a god to do the work. Here is one technique

GODFORM ASSUMPTION

Shut your eyes and relax and concentrate on your breathing.

Visualise a small statue of a god or saint or angel which you are familiar with. See it as about 30 cm.

In your mind's eye draw it to your groin centre or chakra.

Now imagine your personal divine light (which is a white sphere over your head). This is your slice of god which you carry around with you.

Imagine a line of light from that divine source send a line of white gold light down you your back and connect to the statue. Silently say the name of the god you have visualised.

See the statue breathe and come alive.

With each in breath see energy come down that line of light into the statue and for it to get bigger

… and bigger

Until it has grown to just below your eyes. The statue's eyes are shut.

With your mind reach out to the god form inside you connecting with that ancient divine force.

Now allow your consciousness to enter the statue, so you become the god.

Open your eyes and see the world as the god sees it.

You are the god looking through the eyes of a human.

Now shut your eyes again. Thank the god for taking part and withdraw from the statue

See the white light withdraw from the statue and see it begin to shrink.

And shrink.

Until it becomes a tiny dot.

Now open your eyes as a human again.

The practical use of this experiment is to take on the god's powers in a ritual. So that when the magician wants something it is not them who is asking, but the god itself.

After all a human is too small in the scale of the universe to make anything happen outside their sphere of control. As a god, the magician has the power to negotiate with other gods, or beings.

Throughout the *Greek Magical Papyri* we find this technique used. The magician says things like: "It is not me who does this but the god who does this." "It is not Nick Farrell who orders you to change the orbit of the Sun, but it is Helios the god of the Sun who orders this."

Something you will have realised from your little experiment is that while you might have felt the power of the being you invoked into your aura, there was nothing in this technique which could be remotely called worship.

The priest of any religion would say that what you had just done was heresy. You are not supposed to USE the god, you are supposed to reverently worship it at a distance and, if you are lucky, that god might not smite you, or may give you a blessing. But the truth of the matter is that by using that technique, the magician can stand in sacred space as the god and re-negotiate creation.

Sometimes a magician might use one god to order another about. You have a paradox – the magician acknowledges the gods and their power and yet at the same time is directing them in the same way that someone might turn a stage light onto an actor.

When a magician uses these divine forces, he or she does not care which is the right religion. Instead of taking a Richard Dawkins' approach saying all religions are wrong, and god does not exist, the magician says all religions are in some measure true and all gods exist*.

PLOTINUS' THEURGIC GODFORM VISUALISATION TECHNIQUE

What follows is an ancient theurgic visualisation method devised by the Neoplatonic philosopher Plotinus. I have modernised it and added a few things to make it more practical. It shows a link between

---

* I should point out that there is less proof of the existence of Richard Dawkins than there is for many Gods.

our techniques and those of antiquity.

Place a statue or picture of the god on the altar with a tealight before it. Perform a lesser invoking pentagram ritual. Purify and consecrate (see later). Light a candle and invoke the god using the normal method.

Visualise yourself as being in a crystal ball with the night's sky reflected in it.

Then visualise yourself as being within that universe. You should see planets, stars and know that this is your universe. You are a soul at the centre of the shining universe.

Vibrate the word **IAO** which calls down the light into your universe. As you vibrate it, allow the universe to fade and melt into the light. The mass of the universe dissolves.

Now invite the god into your universe. Not as something small but as something which fills the whole sphere. Chant its name or proper barbarous name of power until it can be seen and felt within your sphere.

Then you can communicate with the being. When you have finished, open your eyes focusing on the statue or picture and be aware that the god is with you in your *Sphere of Sensation*.

Close with the Greek Cross.

PATHWORKING

Pathworking is a visualisation exercise where the person listens to a story, either on tape or read to them. During the process, they notice what symbols or events they see presented symbols and listen to what entities say to them. These must be done in a relaxed state so that the person can obtain the most significant impact. At its most basic, pathworking is a journey through the magician's *Sphere of Sensation* and is training for more in-depth methods of so-called astral projection.

Pathworking is the magical use of imagination and has been a magical tool since the shamanic period of human history. Some of the written descriptions of magical events are literal descriptions of pathworkings.

Mythological journeys to the underworld are pathworkings. The Greek poet Homer wrote a vivid description of a magical underworld rite where Odysseus journeys to a magical spot, does a ritual and then pathworks a meeting with the dead.

Pathworking can be a mixed bag. Some of pathworkings are

barely controlled daydreams, but others speak truths about us which are more powerful and direct than any oracle or dream. Others allow us to interact with divine powers. Unfortunately, magic has an issue about separating the sheep from the goats when it comes to pathworking. How was it possible to know if you were compensating for your poor relationship with your mother in a vision, or have met a spirit which wants you to be the new Messiah for its new religion?*

If an 18th-century magician dreamt of being attacked by a black dog while defending a girl, they would think the dog was the Dog-Star, and the girl must be Virgo. In the 20th century, a psychologist would ask "who is the dreamer, and what do they understand by those symbols?" While the symbolic approach would supply a thought-provoking and esoteric response, the psychological model would give a more practical answer.

As I wrote in my book, *Magical Imagination,* pathworking has become more flexible thanks partly to work carried out in the 1970s by psychological researchers. By partially applying the psychological model to pathworking, we can see that some of what we imagine is driven by the desires and wishes of the *Lower Self*. Sometimes this can be useful, particularly when we are trying to understand our unconscious desires, but magically they are less appealing.

The psychological model started to make an impact on magic in the 1930s. It had champions such as Dion Fortune, Paul Case, and Israel Regardie. To them, and modern magicians, it supplied an explanation of occult processes of the mind. It was especially good at pinpointing those processes which stood in the way of successful living and magical attainment.

When doing a ritual and something happens, it is vital to rule out any psychological quirks as influencing the working. Divine beings rarely say what we want to hear. If spirits tell you that you are the new Messiah or the prophet of a New Aeon, then it is more likely to be your ego doing the talking. You might have visions of a past life where you were a high Tibetan Lama or High Priest of Atlantis. But, if you are a sad alcoholic while failing to convince others of your superiority, your pathworkings are projecting a desire for success to an imaginary time.

---

* If any spirit tells you that you are Messiah, or wants you to form a new religion you must ignore and banish it. A surprising number of experienced magicians fall for what is a low level astral trick from an entity which wants to inflate their ego. Greek legends say that you can only become a god after you are dead and if you want to become a prophet you should seek a non-magical path.

As the 20th century magician W.E. Butler pointed out, a modern psychologist would see some of the experiences of Christian saints as neurotic complexes often based on sexual repression.

The psychological approach supplied an excellent explanation of the processes that a student suffers during the beginning of their training. Teachers with some understanding of what their students were dealing with could help them overcome psychological issues which might have been misidentified as magical visions. As psychologists started to enter in the magical arena and define or dismiss all magical experiences in psychological terms, they undid essential parts of magic. Magical spirits, contacts, gods suddenly became complexes. The complex, and problematic, work of mediation with divine entities was written off as a form of elaborate talking to yourself.

Writing off all occult experiences as subjective and, open to psychological interpretation is dangerous. A psychologically minded occultist can become a narcissistic basket case rather than having a tempered ego. If everything is "all in your head," esoteric experiences are just a nihilistic horror, perception is everything, and nothing exists outside your mind.

There is another issue to do with boundaries. Psychologists have recently started to comment on the Celestial, which is well above the astral, which is their area of expertise. It has crossed the line of being helpful and become something to be discouraged. If occultists do not believe spiritual experiences with spirits, angels and gods are real, they will not have any.

THE INNER TEMPLE

An extension of the pathworking technique is the inner temple. This is an inner landscape which is built by the magician and used as a halfway house to enable spirits to come down the levels. This book uses an inner temple design based on a rose cross and helps the realisation of the *Higher Genius*. It is a representative of your *Sphere of Sensation* and anything which happens within that temple is happening within you.

Once it is built, it is projected onto your physical space and rolled up again when you have finished. If you get good at this, you should feel that your physical space is much bigger.

This inner temple is not based on a real physical counterpart, although it could be Greco-Roman. It is four chapels united in the centre by your *Higher Genius*. When you start working on this level, you will use the following pathworking and description. It might be a good idea to place it on tape.

PATHWORKING

Sit comfortably and begin your four-fold breathing. After a few moments visualise a large door with the image of a lion's head, in gold in the centre. Touch the lion's head.

The door swings open and you enter to find yourself standing in a silvery mist. The mist slowly clears, and you find yourself looking at a large Roman temple like the Pantheon. The portico is made of seven pillars and on the front lintel is the phrase

ΤΟ ΧΑΟΣ ἘΠΙΔΙΩΚΕΙ ΤΟ ΓΝΩΘΙ ΣΑΥΤΟΝ.
To Chaos epidiokei to gnothi sauton.

[TO CHA-OS E-PEE-DEE-AW-KEE TO GNO-THEE SAF-TON]
Which means "Chaos seeks to know itself."

Before the steps, there is an altar of burning incense and on the left is a fountain of water. Consecrate yourself in the incense smoke and wash yourself in the fountain of purification.

Walk up the seven steps of the temple to enter in the lead doors which are in the north. The door swings shut behind you and, as your eyes adjust, you find yourself standing looking at a giant statue of Hera made from black obsidian. The statue is standing on a cubic altar. Ten golden lamps illuminate the room and the walls are lined with frescoes of birds, plants and animals and mountain scenes. The images are unusual because, rather than looking natural, they seem stylised with perfect proportions. It is as if the artist tried to perfect nature.

Straight ahead there is another door which you go to and enter.

You blink

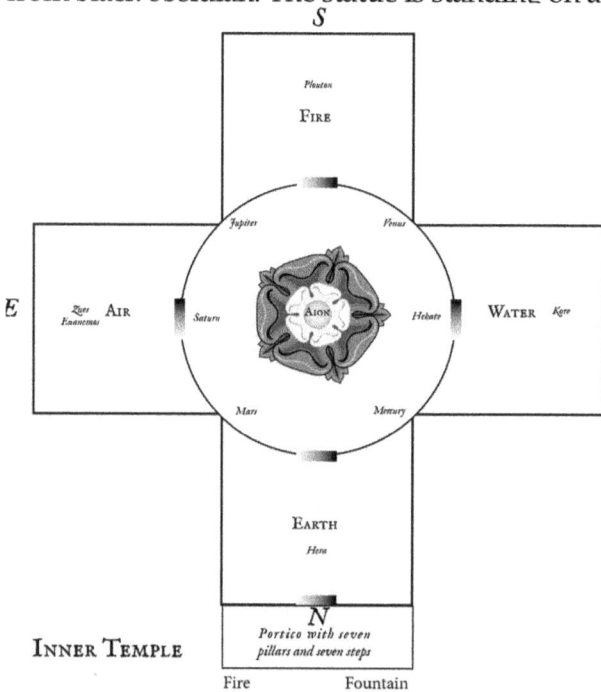

INNER TEMPLE

at the brightness. There is an oculus in the room's domed ceiling. Sunlight streams downward from the dome onto a golden statue of Aion. Beneath the dome, there are seven windows of violet, indigo, blue, green, yellow, orange, and red. And then there are 16 windows (four in each quarter) beneath them.

The massive statue of lion-headed Aion is standing on a double cubic altar and around him is carved a huge five petalled rose. It has been designed to look as if he has emerged from an unfolded rose. He is holding a key in his left hand and a staff in his right. A large serpent coils up his body.

A few feet back from the walls are statues of six planetary gods: Jupiter, Mars, Saturn, Venus, Hekate, and Mercury all carved to look as if they are worshipping the solar force within.

On your right side is a door. You open it and find yourself in the Water temple of Kore. In the centre is her statue. From a vase she is holding pours water into a pool. The walls are decorated with images of water creatures both from nature and myth. The room feels cool. It is lit from a line of blue stained-glass windows which surround the temple on three sides.

You leave and go to the right. This takes you to the South and the temple of Fire. The walls of this temple are carved as if they were made from lava and it is illuminated by large triangular windows of red stained-glass. In the centre is a statue of Pluto emerging from flames.

Go back to the centre of the temple and your right, behind the statue of Saturn, is a door leading to the East.

This temple is roofed with glass and the walls are painted with clouds and sky as if you were in the heavens. There are frescoes of the gods of Olympus sitting on the clouds.

In the centre is a statue of Zeus Euanemos (giver of gentle breezes) enthroned and holding a staff, and a lightning bolt.

Return to the centre and project this room onto your physical space so that anything that happens here happens there and as above so below.

THE SUN BREATH

The Sun breath is an Ancient Egyptian technique which found its way into the so-called Mithras initiation in the PGM. There is enough evidence to suggest the idea was commonplace, and it is not difficult to work out. The effects should be to energise yourself and awaken yourself with the same energy used by your *Higher Self*. Initially, you should try it out during a Sunny day where you can see the Sun. Later you can just visualise the Sun being above you.

Sit comfortably and regulate your breathing. Breathe in through your nostrils while counting to four, hold your breath for two and then breathe out through your mouth. When you have the pattern regular enough allow yourself to draw down the light of the Sun into your lungs following the same rhythm. When you are confident in doing this, use the 4,2 rhythm and draw the Sunlight to your feet. When you breathe out, allow the energy to come up your spine and out of your mouth. Do this for ten breaths and then repeat the process with your groin centre. Ten breaths and then your solar plexus centre. Ten breaths and then your heart centre. Ten breaths and your throat centre. Then ten breaths and your brow centre.

You should see all the centres linked by yellow solar light. Focus on your feet centre, breath in and draw the light up your spine to your crown centre vibrate IAO and see golden light shower through your *Sphere of Sensation*. Do these six times.

CHAPTER TWO
THE FIRST MONTH
THE MYSTERIES OF PURIFICATION
AND CONSECRATION

Each chapter will begin with an outline of the work to be conducted that month. It will then provide details of the rituals you follow, and the teaching involved with those processes.

RITUAL WORK FOR THIS MONTH

Each day you will perform the invocation to the Sun daily at the correct time. However, for one of the sessions, you will carry out much longer ritual work. You can select whatever session you wish to make your "main ritual working". The only thing you will change is the prayer to the Sun which you will use. If you are doing your main ritual in the morning, use the dawn invocation where the ceremony calls for the invocation to the Sun.

You will perform the *Prima Materia* whenever you get a spare moment and at least once a day.

Week One (first seven days)
Perform the *Lesser Ritual of the Pentagram.*
Perform the Sun breath for five minutes.
Journey to the Inner Temple.
Recite the invocation to the Sun.
Perform the confession.
Perform the Oath ritual and the descent into Hades ritual.
Perform the binding ritual.
Perform the spell to become a magician.
Meditate on your work and write it up.

Week Two
Wash your hands and face using the purification prayer (you can do this in your bathroom).
In your Temple, Perform the *Lesser Ritual of the Pentagram.*
Perform the Sun breath for five minutes.
Journey to the Inner Temple
Recite the appropriate invocation to the Sun.

Perform the confession.

Assume the godform of Nephthys and perform the purification ritual.

Having purified the space, go East and say,

I who am Nephthys purify the *Sphere of Sensation* of [your name] so that it is a fit vehicle for his/her *Higher Genius*. Let the unbalanced forces flee from my purity.

Meditate on your weaknesses leaving you.

Perform the spell to become a magician.

Week Three

Wash your hands and face using the purification prayer (you can do this in your bathroom).

In your Temple Perform the *Lesser Ritual of the Pentagram*.

Perform the Sun breath for five minutes.

Journey to the Inner Temple.

Recite the invocation to the Sun.

Perform the confession.

Assume the godform of Isis and perform the consecration ritual.

Having purified the space go East and say,

I who am Isis consecrate the *Sphere of Sensation* of [your name] so that it is a fit vehicle for his/her *Higher Genius*. I burn out the dross. Let the unbalanced forces flee from my purity.

Meditate on your weaknesses leaving you.

Perform the spell to become a magician.

Week four

Wash your hands and face using the purification prayer (you can do this in your bathroom).

In your Temple Perform the *Lesser Ritual of the Pentagram*.

Perform the Sun breath for five minutes.

Journey to the Inner Temple

Recite the appropriate invocation to the Sun.

Perform the confession.

Assume the godform of Nephthys and perform the purification ritual.

Having purified the space go East and say,

I who am Nephthys purify the *Sphere of Sensation* of [your name] so that it is a fit vehicle for his/her *Higher Genius*. Let the unbalanced forces flee from my purity.

Invoke and assume the godform of Isis and perform the consecration ritual.

Having consecrated the space go East and say,

I who am Isis consecrate the Sphere of Sensation of [your name] so that it is a fit vehicle for his/her *Higher Genius*. I burn out the dross. Let the unbalanced forces flee from my purity.

Meditate on your weaknesses leaving you.
Perform the spell to become a magician.

———————

There was a fundamental belief in the Ancient World that it was impossible to approach a god because they were too holy. There were legends such as that of Semele who made Zeus promise on the River Styx to grant her anything she wanted. She then demanded that Zeus reveal himself in all his glory as proof of his divinity. When he did, she was "consumed in lightning-ignited flame." Proclus explained it as being to do with holiness. A god could not get close to a human because of divine contamination, which was why the gods used a network of *Dæmons* to act as messengers. Purification techniques gave you the ability to ascend to heavenly realms the closer you were to a god-like state the less matter had a grip on you.

There is a slight problem with this concept. Firstly, while it is fair enough that gods should be huge power sources, it does not make sense that they cannot go near matter. The whole idea of a *Higher Genius* indwelling in your body suggests divine force can indwell matter. The *Higher Genius* is a god, and when you meet it in all its glory, it can be equally as blinding. The concept that the gods were in the heavens, while we were down here has been disproved. As the Soviets dryly pointed out, God is not in heaven because the cosmonauts went up there and did not see him. What has replaced the idea is the concept that gods and heavens are within a dimension which is parallel to this one and the universe is an outward expression of internal divine consciousness. All the holiness that melted Semele was within her, just on a slightly different frequency.

When looking at purity, it is vital to consider its opposite – impurity. Throughout human existence, impurity has been the obsession of organised religion. It mostly sought to define impurity in terms of breaking social codes or religious rules. Usually, religion makes matters worse by making humans feel guilty for sins that they do not commit. Religion can make a good person believe they are going to suffer divine punishment for wanting sex, loving another human, or desiring bacon. However, what is a sin in one religion can be a requirement in others; what one culture finds offensive is fine for another. It is impossible to define spiritual impurity in terms of religious or social norms.

Judaism, which is famous for its laws and requirements, has an excellent concept of real "spiritual impurity" in its idea of Tumah. Tumah is not a sin, but rather an 'absence of holiness.' Kabbalists consider holiness a form of life, vitality, or spirituality. The opposite of it is a dead body or someone not performing actions that are disconnected from the One Thing. Purification is the act of making an object holy rather than purging or punishing..

Purity is still essential. We still live in a dimension which is ordered and fixed and we must loosen our mindset to see these other dimensions. If you look at all the techniques connected to purification, they are symbolic of losing those shackles and creating a death-like experience. In death, the *Higher Genius*, no longer bound by its earthly existence, tunes out of the world of matter and retreats into the hidden dimensions. Death has purified it enough to move on. With the rare exception of the Ancient Egyptians*, this is the esoteric reason why societies do their best to quickly get the dead body back to its components to enable this final purification.

Purification is an emblematic attunement to the spiritual forces we wish to contact and a symbolic death to our ordered world. The traditional methods of confession, purification, consecration and attunement still are highly effective means of tuning out of the material world, even if the central philosophy behind them has changed.

OATHS

There is a proper place for the fear-inspiring and for fear to sit high in the soul as its overseer: it is beneficial to learn good sense under the pressure of distress.

What man that does not at all nourish his heart on fear - or what community of men, it makes no difference - will still revere Justice?

Aeschylus, *Eumenides* 517-25 2

---

* Egyptian magical technology was such that the body was simultaneously purified and acted as an anchor for a *Higher Genius* to return to earth if it wished to commune with family members. Rougher societies removed this nicety by burying the body or burning it.

In your first working of *Helios Unbound,* you are required to swear an oath and make a personal sacrifice to the process. When I use the word "oath", I am referring to the Roman word *Sacramentum* which is an oath or vow "given to the gods." *Sacramentum* was pledged as a sacred bond and could be lost upon the oath's violation. However, *Sacramentum* was an essential part of a Roman consecration.

One of the reasons why magic does not work is because a person has not understood what they must sacrifice. In different systems of magic, there is the concept of sacrifice – of giving something up to achieve a desire or receive something from the gods. Usually, this is symbolic; a person killed an animal or poured wine into a trench to give something up to achieve a goal.

The victim could be a universe that you are desperately grasping. Say you have a problematic relationship with a person, and you were always fighting. One day you both worked out this was self-destructive and ended it. You find yourself alone and do a ritual to find a new partner. Nothing happens. The answer might be that the old destructive relationship is still in your life. You cannot ask the gods to create you a new universe with a new partner until you have a space to put a new person inside it.

This idea of "having space" to roll out the new universe is vital. When the creator gods of magic unfold your new shiny universe, there must be holes cut inside the design for all the things you want to remain. After all, if you invoke for a new job, you do not want your relationship to pack in, or your dog to vanish overnight. The problem is that if something in your life is central and antagonistic to your goal remains, then the new universe will end up like the old one.

While the creation of a new universe is one idea, with its own set of gods, we must ask the important question "what happened to the old one?" and "what needs to be chopped out of my universe to make this work?"

This god of sacrifice is a variation of one of the many underworld death gods within religion. They are Satan, Set, Baron LaCross, Typhon, Pluto, Dis Pater and Saturn. Before any creation ritual, they must be unleashed onto your existing universe, removing those things which stand in the way of what you want.

Attempting to hold on to a large chunk of your universe while at the same time hanging onto your old one is impossible. One change should create other dramatic ones and when you do your invocation, you unconsciously know what you need to sacrifice.

The concept of taking an oath is a form of sacrifice where the "victim" is the person making it. They can be seen as dying so that they can become something more. Making the oath is narrowing their life and promising not to do something so that they can be more than human.

This idea of making a commitment and a sacrifice of yourself has been a feature of magic since the dawn of time. In ancient societies, without the aid of police forces, order depended on people keeping their word. If an individual's word were broken, then the order would collapse. The gods in charge of oaths were the scariest, because the penalty for breaking an oath was high. Some ancient societies considered a broken oath equal to waging war on the gods.

In taking an oath, one called down a conditional curse on oneself which takes effect if one lies or broke a promise.

According to Hesiod in his *Works and Days*:

"Whoever wilfully swears a false oath, telling a lie in his testimony, he himself is incurably hurt at the same time as he harms Justice, and in after times his family is left more obscure, whereas the family of the man who keeps his oath is better in after times."[*]

An oath is a way of binding chaos and making it ordered. It is creating a new universe and setting the rules by which the new universe is bound. Making an oath is building a reality where you agree to do a certain amount of work in return for a universe where your *Higher Genius* is part of your conscious existence. Breaking that oath will, therefore, send this universe back into the chaos from which was created, and you will have to start from scratch. The oath gods, such as Orcus and Stix were chaotic because if the oath were broken, the reality which had been created by that oath was automatically destroyed and it takes such a god to destroy it..

In masonic-style magic orders, such as the *Order of the Golden Dawn*, oaths were a dull thing if you read it out loud and included many clauses that are almost legalistic in their phraseology. Strangely, it is common for candidates to say in the post-mortems afterwards that it was at this point they felt the most. The oath is an act of the *Lower Self* submitting to the Higher. *Lower Self* which draws down the *Higher Self* to take part. An Oath is being made to your *Higher Self* and not the group which is facilitating and witnessing the spiritual event.

Oaths are the basis for the grimoire tradition of pacts. In that you have agreed with a being to create a new universe together. The understanding is that if either one of you backs down and breaks

* Hesiod. and Cooke, T. (1743). *The Works of Hesiod*. London: Printed for T. Longman

the oath, they will suffer in some way. It is unlikely that breaking an oath might make a demon suffer, but it is likely to obey the pact because it depends in part on an ordered universe held together by oaths to carry out its work.

The God of Oaths being used in this book is the Roman God Orcus. Orcus was Etruscan and depicted as a bearded giant, and sometimes confused with Hades. He was so powerful that the Church in Spain had to prohibit the use of his name in oaths as late as the eighth century.

The Greek *Dæmon* Horkos (Όρκος) was a similar being – he was the personification of the curse inflicted on any person who breaks their oath. Oaths with Orcus acting as a witness are made with the understanding that he will act as an enforcer if something goes wrong.

In this operation, fear is not the motivator for you to keep your oath. There are many stories about the horrors that await those who break oaths or fail in the Abramelin process, but Orcus is not going to make your life a misery because you did not complete the *Helios Unbound* system. He *might* cause your regular habits to collapse or the work to fail (if you continue it). You cannot talk your way out of breaking your oath, Orcus will decide if it was intentionally broken and act accordingly. If you were hospitalised or could not continue because you were unwell, Orcus is not going to be an arse about it. However, if you could not face your practice because you stayed up all night playing computer games and slept until 3 pm he might think that is against the oath.

The oath is made on the symbol of the supernal triangle which represents the highest that the magician can aspire. You place your right hand on the symbol when you make the oath and your left hand in a bowl of spring water which represents the river Styx (Στυξ). (All Gods were required to make their oaths on the waters of the river Styx).

The Oath

I invoke you who protects the boundaries between life and death, darkness and light.

I call you who keeps away the living and draws the dead into his enclosure. Mighty Orcus, king of the shades stand witness to this pact between my *Higher Genius* and me. For I stand between the light and darkness, by the banks of the River Styx so that my Genius shall stand before the Holy and Secret Triad of the One Thing.

(Place your left hand in the water and your right on the triad. Visualise Orcus standing before you)

In the name of the One Thing

I (your full name) spiritually commit myself to this magical process to contact my Higher Genius and open myself to the changes that it will require for me to be a perfect vessel for it to manifest through me.

I swear to do all the exercises involved in this process and to see it to its conclusion no matter what darkness is revealed to test me.

I will allow myself to dissolve into the Chaos of what was before my birth so that I might be reborn as a more useful vessel for my Higher Genius.

I will perform all practical work concealed and apart from the gaze of the outer and uninitiated world.

I will, from this day forward, apply myself to the Great Work, which is to purify and exalt my spiritual nature so that with the Divine aid I may at length attain to be more than human, and thus gradually raise and unite myself to my Higher and Divine Genius.

I will not abuse the great magical power entrusted to me but will always serve humanity. As my *Higher Genius* sees the unity of humanity, so I too shall see all as an expression of the One Thing and will not discriminate due to gender, sexual preference, colour, religion or nationality.

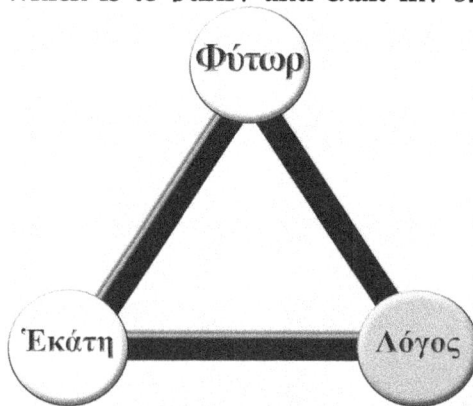

Divine triad of Father, Hekate and Logos (based on the Chaldean Oracles)

In return, my *Higher Genius* will work with me during this process, teach me magic, and how to serve the supernal triad better. It shall assist me in this trial and bring me the experiences I need.

And if I break this oath, I open myself to a wave of Chaotic force which will undo all I have done, end any pacts I have made and cause my *Higher Genius* to withdraw. Thus, I will have failed in this work and lost the magic I sought to obtain.

With this Oath, the sky quivers, the Earth quakes before me, for I am a magician, I possess magic.

THE DESCENT INTO CHAOS

This follows the oath and represents the descent into chaos, which starts the process. Like the concept of the harrowing of hell, it invokes Typhon to begin the process of breaking down old and outworn ideas in the candidate's sphere of sensation, which will be the main feature of the first month of work.

It uses the God Typhon *(pictured)*, who was a form of chaos which nearly overthrew Zeus. In Egypt, he was considered like Set, the Egyptian God of Sandstorms who murdered Osiris. In this process, they are used to remove blocks and complexes which prevent the *Higher Genius* awakening in the magician. It works because humanity is essentially a being of chaos which is living in an ordered universe. By helping to revert part of the sphere of sensation to its original chaotic state, Typhon opens the way for a stronger ordered universe. The ritual is based on a Greco-Egyptian Papyrus PGM IV. 154-285

Place some incense on the burner and say,

Mighty Typhon, sceptre-bearing almighty power and sovereign, god of gods; Lord ABEPAMEN ΘΩΟΥΛΕΡΘΕΞΑΝΑΞΕΘΡ ΕΛΥΟΩΘΝΕΜΑΡΕΒΑ

A V - E R - A - M E N - T H A W - O O - L E R - T H E - XA-NA-XETH-RE-LY-O- AWTH-NE MA-RE-VA

Disturber of the dark, bringer of thunder, sender of storms, lighting flasher of the night! You are the one who exhaled the cold and the heat. Stone-shaker, wall-breaker earth-quaker, boiler of the waters. You are the one who stirs the depths to motion,

ΙΩ ΕΡΒΗΤ ΑΥ ΤΑΥΙ ΜΗΝΙ
E-AW ER-V'ET AY TAY-EE M'E-NEE

I am he who searched the world to find the great Osiris, whom I brought you bound. I am he who together with you allied with the gods (others say against the gods); I am he who shut heaven's double door and put to sleep the unseen serpent, who at the edge of you kingdom, stopped the sea, the streams, and the flowing rivers. But, as your soldier, I was defeated by the gods and was cast face down on account of empty wrath. Awaken me, I beseech you, I implore you, friend; do not leave me here cast upon the earth, Oh lord of gods:

ΑΕΜΙΝΑΕΒΑΡΩΘΕΡΡΕΘΩΡΑΒΕΑΝΙΜΕΑ
AE-MEE-NA-E-VAR-AWTH-ER-RETH-AW-RA-VE-AN-EEM-EA

Return me into your world of chaos, break down that which stands in the way of unity with my Higher Genius. Fill me with power, I beg you, grant me this grace, that whenever I call upon any one of the gods, they come to me swiftly and appear visibly before me.

Sit down and set your timer for 20 minutes. Visualise before you a door opening into the chaotic underworld. Do not think of traditional associations here but see it as a universe of pure chaos, with the occasional form popping into existence. Step through the door and slowly allow yourself to merge with the chaos. The goal the moment is to allow your self to feel what chaos is like. Each time you have a thought let it pass through you. Do not hold onto any thought or concept of yourself. Breathing slowly, just let any stress pass into the chaotic field allowing you to relax further. You are aiming to reach a point where the *Sphere of Sensation* stops generating material and slows. After a while you will start to feel chaos field starting to tug at the ordered structures on the outer part of your *Sphere of Sensation*. As this happens, thoughts connected to some of your more active complexes will start to arise. These are the complexes which will be being tugged at by Typhon for destruction or at least looking at. Note them.

When the timer sounds, will yourself to step back into the door. Return to your body and say,

I am a being of chaos, operating in a world of order.
I am clothed in the elements.
I am crowned with Spirit.
The heat in my body is a fire.
I have air in my lungs.
I have water in my mouth and blood.
The weight of my bones is the earth.

The sky quivers, the Earth quakes before me, for I am a magician, I possess magic.

In the universe we have created for ourselves, we usually fail in some way. It is not, as some religions would have us believe, because we are sinful and lured from the path because of some devil or another. It is because we have lost sight of who we are in the cosmic scheme of things. Magic offers a philosophy that we can find our true destiny and work towards it. To do that, we have to recognise the mistakes of the past and rededicate ourselves to our destiny.

This process is called 'purification and dedication' and is represented by the elements of water and fire. Purification is the removal of everything that stands in the way of us becoming who we are meant to be, while consecration is the dedication of ourselves to our correct goal. In magic, objects are also purified and consecrated but for now the focus is the magician.

CONFESSION

The concept of "confessing sins" is not a Christian process, but like many things was borrowed from the Pagan mystery cults. The practice can be seen in Ancient Babylon, and in Greece, where everyone was required to make secret confessions to the priest, if they wanted to be admitted, or initiated, into the "mysteries" of their religion. The mysteries were so high, heavenly and holy, that no man with guilt lying on his conscience, and sin unpurged, could be initiated to them. The Gods themselves would be furious if a person who had guilt on their shoulders were given the secrets of the mysteries. We can see the negative confession of sin in the Ancient Egyptian *Book of the Dead*, where the soul tells the *Dæmons* in the Judgement Hall of Maat that he has not committed one of 42 sins.

The difference between the Christian and Pagan idea of a "sin to be confessed" is marked. A Pagan sin was a transgression against the gods or performing acts which makes one feels guilty. There is no concept of "all have sinned and fall short of the Glory of God" and no original sin which needed to be forgiven or you will face an eternity of hell.

Redemption was a Pagan concept with several Pagan gods having Sotara (savour) in their titles. From the first century before Christ onwards the idea of divine help to "save" a person became increasingly important. Pauline Christianity was one of many redemptive cults which sprang up at the time with the basic idea that we were trapped by an earthy nature and needed to be liberated from it.

Admitting sin, or acts which held you to the earth, allowed a spiritual force to liberate you. Stating your sin out loud, generally to another person, bought it out into the open so that it could be purified or forgiven by a god.

In the *Helios Unbound* process, confession is almost used psychologically to identify and remove those weaknesses which prevent the *Higher Genius* manifesting. Sin is defined as a self-destructive personality flaw which is contrary to the life direction intended for the *Higher Self*. For example, someone who is unable to form a proper relationship with another human but instinctively pushes them away, a person who shirks responsibly, a racist or sexist is unlikely to be a good vehicle for a *Higher Genius*. The first stage of any process is realising that you are doing it and confession is a technique which brings it into focus so that it can be transmuted into something more useful.

When a confession takes place in a ritual space, something curious happens. Psychically, a small dark force emerges from the magician's *Sphere of Sensation* and is pushed out of the sacred space. The purification and consecration of that space keeps the darkness dislodged enough for the magician to get a handle on it and understand it better.

Aleister Crowley wrote a good, if very Christian, confession ritual for his self-initiation system* which went:

> *Yea! but I am a Fool, a Flutterer!*
> *I am under the Shadow of the Wings!*
> *I am a Liar and a Sorcerer.*
> *I am under the Shadow of the Wings!*

---

* *LIBER DCLXXI vel PYRAMIDOS A Ritual of Self Initiation based upon the Formula of the Neophyte* By Aleister Crowley

I am so fickle that I scorn the Bridle.
I am under the Shadow of the Wings!
I am unchaste, voluptuous and idle.
I am under the Shadow of the Wings!
I am a Bully and a Tyrant crass,
I am under the Shadow of the Wings!
I am as dull and as stubborn as an Ass,
I am under the Shadow of the Wings!
I am untrusty, cruel and insane,
I am under the Shadow of the Wings!
I am a Fool and frivolous and vain.
I am under the Shadow of the Wings!
I am a Weakling and a Coward; I cringe,
I am under the Shadow of the Wings!
I am a Catamite and Cunnilinge.
I am under the Shadow of the Wings!
I am a Glutton, a besotted Wight;
I am under the Shadow of the Wings!
I am a Satyr and a Sodomite.
I am under the Shadow of the Wings!
I am as changeful and selfish as the Sea.
I am under the Shadow of the Wings!
I am a Thing of vice and vanity.
I am under the Shadow of the Wings!
I am most violent, and I vacillate,
I am under the Shadow of the Wings!
I am a blind Man and emasculate.
I am under the Shadow of the Wings!
I am a raging Fire of Wrath no wiser!
I am under the Shadow of the Wings!
I am a Blackguard, Spendthrift and a Miser.
I am under the Shadow of the Wings!
I am obscure and devious and null.
I am under the Shadow of the Wings!
I am ungenerous and base and dull.
I am under the Shadow of the Wings!
I am not marked with the white Flame of Breath.
I am under the Shadow of the Wings!
I am a traitor! Die the traitor's death!

Notice that there is a statement where the *Lower Self* announces that they hold a sin and then they place them under the Shadow of the Wings of Divinity. This is a call for divine protection. The only weakness in the prayer is that it calls upon you to confess to sins you did not commit or are only sins in Crowley's repressed Christian world (sorry Crowley, cunnilingus is not a sin).

It is far better for a person to sit down and work out their list of sins and what they feel guilty about. By doing so, they not only understand their weaknesses but will start to work out why they act this way. Setting aside time to find a list of the things you recognise are self-defeating practices and then using them in a regular ritual becomes a powerful tool of purification.

Make a list of 20 weak points in your personality. If you can't think of more than 10 then add "I am self-deluded" to the list.

Start the confession with a general invocation to the Sun:

Hail, O Lord, Great Power, Great Might, King, Greatest of gods, Helios, the Lord of heaven and earth, God of gods: mighty is your breath; mighty is your strength, oh Lord. Mighty Saviour who redeems your fragments cast into Earth. Absolve and dissolve my weaknesses.

Write them down and at the end of them say the line "I am under the shadow of the wings of Helios."

In other words:

I am unable to speak the truth; I am under the shadow of the wings of Helios.
I pick the wrong friends; I am under the shadow of the wings of Helios.
I need to be loved by others; I am under shadow of the wings of Helios.

You end the prayer with the following:

O Lord, while being born again, I am passing away; while growing and having grown. I am dying; while being born from a life-generating birth, I am passing on, released to death– as you have forgiven, as you have decreed, and have established the mystery. I am PHEROYRA MIOYRI. [FE-ROY-RA ME-OY-RI]

An additional visualisation which will help the process is to visualise a door to the chaos realm in front of you. Allow the door to swing open and see the chaotic space. As you say each line of your confession visualise yourself casting a shadow from your *Sphere of Sensation* through the door and into the chaotic space. Watch as it is dissolved into Chaos. After you have chanted PHEROYRA MIOYRI shut the door.

Purification and consecration of the circle must always follow

the confession.

The confession's goal is to change the weakness into something more useful. Christianity says that even if you believe you have been forgiven you are going to have to repent of your actions, or go the opposite way. Just confessing we are idiots rarely makes us Einstein. As we state our weaknesses before the gods, we attempt to discover why we do such self-destructive acts. During the meditation which follows a purification and consecration, we must pick one of our sins to examine. We look at when we first started acting this way and our motivations for doing so. A person who hates homosexuals might not have come to terms with their own sexuality. A person who beats their partner might have bottled in anger against their parents.

Just as the law or society does not accept such excuses for bad behaviour, your *Higher Genius* does not either.

There is no harm about talking about the issues that are dredged up during a confession process with a psychologist or counsellor.

PURIFICATION

In magic, we ritually clear out the *Sphere of Sensation*. The closest thing to this in organised religion is a baptism where a person is held under water and then born anew, usually struggling with water in their nose. The magician uses the symbol of water to do this, without the need to sneeze.

Take a large glass and fill it to about halfway. You will notice that the water stays where it is put. You will see that it cools the glass. If you knock the glass, after rippling a bit still returns to its glass shape. This is the clue to transforming some of those 'moths' in the *Sphere of Sensation*. In the glass, we are seeing what a perfect *Sphere of Sensation* looks like – it is a clear vessel for the One Thing. When it is troubled, it swiftly reverts to its calm still state.

This is neither possible nor desirable because there are symbols in our *Sphere of Sensation* that we want. If we purified ourselves too much, we would lose what makes us unique and human.

We use the symbol of water because it removes those things that we do not want and replaces them with the serene calm of the element. We settle those astral moths by becoming calm about them. We are not hard on ourselves about our 'sins' but we seek to transform them one by one until they are useful. We become tranquil. A purification is a form of self-exorcism.

Water is an important symbol which is associated with death and putrefaction. Water is primarily cool, which is the active quality that binds things together and allows formation and nourishment of composite entities. When water evaporates from a body, its absence causes decomposition. The ancients thought that the moistness of water permits the dissolution of structure and the loss of form. Water allows the growth and development of form.

Water was known as the Tears of Persephone and united the Earth and Air elements. Indeed, she is the daughter of Demeter (Earth) and Zeus (Air) and gets her power to unite (Cool) from Demeter and Her power to transform (Moist) from Zeus. So, she has the power to join that which is above with that which is below. In the Greco-Egyptian tradition, Persephone was associated with the Egyptian goddess Nephthys, who was sometimes called 'Black Isis.' Her name means 'throne,' and her symbol was a small cup on her head, based on the hieroglyph of her name. She was connected to the putrification of the body after death. She and her sister Isis were instrumental in the resurrection of Osiris and have a similar function in the work that we are doing.

MAKING "HOLY WATER"

Holy water is used for purifying people or spaces. It works by removing negative energy from the area or objects. It does this because it is a symbol of death, transition or the original chaotic waters.

Nephthys

Buy some still mineral water. Fill a bowl with the water and place it on the table top before you. Draw a *Lesser Banishing Pentagram* ✫ and say,

Creature of Water, I exorcise thee and cleanse thee for my purpose.

Draw a *Lesser Invoking Pentagram* ✫ over it and say,

Creature of Water, you are now the waters of the Primal Chaos. May you reflect the face of the One Thing, which moved upon the face of the waters of Chaos.

Visualise a golden hexagram in the centre of the water. Then, in your mind's eye, see it boil with white light. Chant the name

IAΩ (Ee-Ah-Aw)

Visualising the letters in the water until you feel that it is pure. If you need to purify yourself, see your *Sphere of Sensation* as being dark. Dip your finger in the water and draw a Greek Cross on yourself. See your *Sphere of Sensation* get more transparent and brighter, then draw an equal-armed cross on your forehead and say,

"I purify with water."

PURIFYING RITUAL SPACE

Whenever you carry out a purification, you should always adopt the godform of Persephone-Nephthys and hold it throughout the process. You do this by invoking her first.

She is visualised as a beautiful woman in a blue and orange robe with a blue cup. She has a headdress with a small cup on her head.

INVOCATION

I invoke thee, oh Stolistes of the sacred mysteries.
Come forth, Nephthys, and purify me so that I shall be cleansed.
Pour the waters of life through my sphere of sensation
that I may be pure and enter the holy of holies.
Make me like unto thee,
a manifestation of the highest.
Still the stormy waters of my soul
that I might be a perfect image
of the One Thing.
Let me drink from thy chalice
which are the living waters of eternal life.
Let the dark storm clouds that fill my soul
be washed away by thy power.

Assume the Godform of Persephone-Nephthys and go East

Dip your fingers in the water and draw an equal-armed cross in the air. Go to the south, west and north and do the same thing in each. Return to the east, hold the glass on high and say,

"I purify with water."

RITUAL ABLUTION

Before beginning any working, you must first wash your hands and face saying the following.

May you abolish my defilement,
Oh waters, may you wash my errant Dæmons.
Wash the face of Horus, Rub the face of Seth,
Wash the face of Neith.
Rub the face of her spinners.
Loosened my restrictions through Horus,
Opened are my limits through Seth.
My impurity is gone.
My purity is the purity of the divine triad.
I shall not fall on some evil obstacle.
I am pure.

CONSECRATION

Consecration is the term which is used to describe the setting aside of something to make it holy. It is an act by which a thing is separated from its mundane and profane use and dedicated to magical use. Usually, this is done by fire, which is a symbol of the consecration process. Fire burns away the dross and converts it into Spirit. Fire rises to the heavens, where it becomes the essence of the stars and lightning.

The ancients believed that before a soul can ascend through the spheres, Fire must purify it. Fire burns away the transient and imperfect, thereby freeing the soul and immortalising it. The Orphic tradition believes that if you entered the underworld you would be purified in the Earth's Fiery Womb in preparation for rebirth. The Zoroastrians believed that a Hero was the one who can make the perilous Hero's Journey and survive an ordeal by Fire and molten metal.

Fire has the power of discrimination but because of its dry nature it is inflexible. It is similar to a person's will power, which sees its purpose and cannot be swayed from it. Ancient elemental theory stated that Fire actively imposes a determinate form on things, and represents the creative impulse.

Fire was an integral part of the Promethean myth. To the Ancient Greeks Prometheus was a chaotic being which created us (and became later associated with Lucifer). Prometheus created humans by mixing Earth and Water to create the gross body; Athena breathed Air into it, imbuing it with a Spirit-Soul. Prometheus added the Higher Soul, which is the Fire that he took from the Wheel of the Sun and brought to humanity in a Narthêx (giant fennel) stalk. When we use fire in a ritual it is a symbol of our divine origins.

The Promethean myth shows us that consecration is a primary agent of transformation because it creates a self-determining form. It effectively breathes life into it. It takes the dead and chaotic form created by water and transmutes it to something more spiritual and alive.

For this reason, consecration followed purification. Once you had made something as holy as possible, you set it aside for the fire which was a representation of spirit. However, it was a process. Fire consecration, usually with incense on red hot coals, is seen as a replacement for animal, or even human, sacrifice. Burning creates a sacrifice. When incense is sacrificed, symbolicaly the flame and the smoke rise to heaven.

Consecration is a sacrifice, by dedicating ourselves or an object we are removing it from its mundane purpose, but this very act ensures that it becomes holy and pure. Consecration enables you to set aside space so that it becomes practically useful for magical ritual work. It "sets the space or object on fire." It raises its energy so that it becomes connected with the force you want to work with.

Thus, if a magician walks around a temple with incense, they have dedicated that space to the gods and the purpose of their ritual. By the nature of its sacrifice, lower astral creatures, ghosts and other similar beings cannot enter because, like the *Lesser Ritual of the Pentagram*, consecration lifts the vibration of the area which prevents lower astral beings from entering.

You must select the right incense. This is partly because the smell will assist in opening your senses to subtle influences and partly because each one has a specific planetary attribution which can intensify your work. Frankincense is one of the best general-purpose incenses. It is dedicated to the Sun and therefore works well in most rituals. Myrrh is dedicated to the Moon and is therefore good at working at the lower astral levels. It is also effective when mixed with frankincense for healing work

Isis

because it makes the *Sphere of Sensation* easier to manipulate.

The ancient Egyptians used an incense called kyphi, which was made ritually over a long period of time. It had some twenty ingredients in it which were magically supposed to do something. Alas, we don't know exactly what, but it makes for one of my favourite incenses and creates a thick ritual atmosphere.

This system uses specific incenses for the planets which are based on those mentioned in the *Greek Magical Papyri*.

Frankincense (Sun), Myrrh (Moon), Storax (Saturn), Indian Nard (Venus), Cinnamon (Mercury), Saussurea Costus (Mars) and Cinnamomum Tamala (Indian Bay Leaf) Jupiter. These may sound exotic but they can be found on Ebay or some herb shops.

On an hour of the planet draw a *banishing* pentagram over it ✮ and say,

Creature of Earth I banish thee of all impurity so that you will be a perfect sacrifice to [god].

Place your hand over the incense and draw an invoking pentagram ✮ and say,

ḤET NEBET NEFRIT WEB-IT-ET DED-IT PIT QE-MET TE ÌN-NET ḤOPI NE-ḤET NEṬER ÌM* **You are every good and pure thing that the Sky gives, the Earth creates, the inundation brings, on which the god lives.**

The thicker the incense smoke in a temple room, the better. This is because in a room full of thick smoke it is easier to 'see' things. One magical technique, called getting a spirit to physical manifestation, involves calling a spirit into a triangle of the art which has so many incense burners around it that it is possible to see the spirit in the smoke. Some theories are that the spirit can use the special planetary-tuned smoke to build its physical body. It is more likely that the heavy smoke and the intense ritual make it easier for the participants to project the image of the spirit upon it. In my experience, people seeing physical manifestations all see something different, which would not be possible if the creature had built a body out of smoke.

SELF-CONSECRATION

Light the charcoal and place the incense on it. When it is burning, draw a cross the same as a Greek Cross in your *Sphere of Sensation*. Then draw an upward-pointing triangle, which is a symbol of fire,

---

* This is Ancient Egyptian and is pronounced as it is written.

starting at the top which would be midway between your eyes, going towards your left hip, then your right hip, then returning to your forehead. Holding the incense on high, say,

I consecrate with fire.

CONSECRATION OF SPACE

If you wish to purify a space before your working, take the incense to the east. Draw the fire triangle with the burning incense, from the tip downwards as before, in the air. Go to the south, west and north and do the same thing in each. Return to the east, hold the incense on high and say,

I consecrate with fire.

GODFORM WORKING

Whenever you carry out a consecration, you should always adopt the godform of Isis and hold it throughout the process. She is visualised as a beautiful woman in a red robe with an incense burner and a vulture's headdress. Before talking on the godform you should look to the west and say the following Invocation.

INVOCATION

I invoke thee, oh Dadouchos of the sacred mysteries.
Come forth, Isis, and consecrate me with fire
so that the desire for Adonai shall eat me up
and that through my sacrifice I shall be made whole,
that my life shall be set aside from the mortal inclination,
and that I shall walk the path of magic.
Consecrate this sphere of sensation,
So that it may be a holy abode of the mysteries.
Make me like unto thee,
a manifestation of the highest.
A perfect image of the One Thing.
Let me burn with desire for the One
and be a spark of infinity.

PRAYERS TO THE SUN

These prayers to the Sun at different parts of the day form the backbone of the *Helios Unbound* process. They are taken from PGM where they were a single prayer* and expanded to provide some more meaning.

You should start each day by waking up and washing your hands and face (preferably saying the ablution prayer) and then face the Sun. Ideally, you should see the Sun when you make the invocation.

MORNING PRAYER TO THE SUN

I invoke You, the Greatest God, Eternal Lord, World Ruler, who are over the World and under the World, Mighty Ruler of the Sea, rising at Dawn, shining from the East for the Whole World. Come to me, You Who Rise from the Four Winds, benevolent and lucky *Agathos Dæmon,* for whom Heaven has become the Processional Way.

I call upon Your Holy and Great and Hidden Names which You rejoice to hear.

ΗΑΡΠΕΝΚΝΥΦΙ ['EAR-PEN-KNY-FEE]
ΒΡΙΝΤΑΝΤΕΝΟΦΡΙ [VRI-NTA-NTE-NO-FREE]
ΒΡΙΣΞΥΛΜΑΣ [VREES-KSYL-MAS]
ΑΡΟΥΡΖΟΡΒΟΡΟΒΑ [AR-OOR-ZORV-ORO-VA]
ΜΕΣΙΝΤΡΙΦΙ [MES-EEN-TREE-FEE]
ΝΙΠΤΟΥΜΙ [NIP-TOO-MEE]
ΞΜΟΥΜΜΑΟΦΙ [KS-MOOM-MAO-FEE]

The Earth flourished when You shone forth, and the Plants became fruitful when you laughed; the Animals begat their Young when You allowed.

Awaken to me *Higher Genius* so that I may be an awakened participant in my own life.

And be a specialised Channel for you and your Power.

Give Glory and Honour and Favour and Fortune and Power to me as I am purified and consecrated to your purpose.

I invoke You, Shining Helios, giving Light throughout the Whole World. You are the Great Serpent, Leader of all the Gods, who control the Beginning of the World and the End of the all that is: I awaken thee into my life with the secret names of power.

PSOI ΨΟΙ [PSEE]
PHNOUTHI ΦΝΟΥΘΙ [F-NOO-THEE]
ΝΙΝΘΕΡ [NIN-THER]

You are He who becomes Visible in my life.

---

* PGM IV.1600-1715

I invoke you in the First Hour where you have the form of a cat
ΦΑΡΑΚΟΥΝΗΘ [FA-RA-KOO-N'ETH] because you are reborn
each day. Teach me to be independent and to watch so that I act at
the right time

In the second Hour You have the Form of a Dog Your Name is
ΣΟΥΦΙ. [SOO-FEE] For you are my loyal protector. Teach me
strength and honour.

In the Third Hour You have the Form of a Serpent your name is
ΑΜΕΚΡΑΝΕΒΕΧΕΟ ΘΩΥΩ [AM-EK-RA-NEV-ECH-EO THAW-Y-
AW] For you are the creative life immortal life force. Teach me to
heal and continually renew my life.

In the Fourth Hour You have the Form of a Scarab, your name
is SENTHENIPS ΣΕΝΘΕΝΙΨ [SEN-THE-NEEPS], for you are a
symbol of the heavenly cycle. Teach me how to use these cycles to
transform bodies and souls.

In the fifth Hour You have the Form of a Donkey your name is
ΕΝΦΑΝ ΧΟΥΦ[EN-FAN CHOOF]. For you provide the power and
destruction of the world. Teach me how to weld the powers of the
sandstorm.

For the sky quivers, the Earth quakes before me,
for I am a magician, I possess magic.

NOON PRAYER TO THE SUN

*Wash your hands (preferably saying the ablution prayer) and then face the
Sun (if possible).*

You God of Life, you Lord of Love, All men live when you shine.
You are the crowned King of the Gods.
The goddess ISIS embraces you,
and enfolds you in all seasons.
You the King of Truth, the Lord of Eternity,
The Prince of Everlastingness,
You Sovereign of all Gods,
You God of Life, you Creator of Eternity,
You Maker of Heaven.
All the Gods rejoice at your rising.
Giver of all life,
The Earth rejoices when it sees your golden rays.
People who have been long dead
come forward with cries of joy
to behold your beauties every day.

You go forth each day over Heaven and Earth*.

In the sixth Hour You have the Form of a Lion; Your Name is ΒΑΙ ΣΟΛΒΑΙ [VAEE SOLVAEE], the Ruler of Time. Teach me the power of leadership and give me confidence to speak your will.

In the seventh Hour You have the Form of a Goat; Your Name is ΟΥΜΕΣΘΩΘ [OO-MES-THAWTH]. Teach me how to use my sexual power wisely.

In the eighth Hour You have the Form of a Bull; Your Name is ΔΙΑΤΙΦΗ (DEEA-TEE-F'E] because everyone can see you. Grant me passion, power and strength to fulfil my destiny.

In the Ninth Hour You have the Form of a Falcon; Your Name is ΦΗΟΥΣ ΦΩΟΥΘ [F'E-OOS FAW-OOTH], the Lotus Emerged from the Abyss. Teach me how to live as a being of chaos in a world of order.

In the tenth Hour You have the Form of a Baboon; Your Name is ΒΕΣΒΥΚΙ [VES VYKEE] because of your raw intelligence. Teach me to be as clever as Thoth

In the 11th Hour You have the Form of an Ibis; Your Name is ΜΟΥ ΡΩΦ [MOO RAWF] because you bring the word of the *Logos* to Earth.

In the 12th Hour You have the Form of a Crocodile; Your Name is ΑΕΡΘΟΗ [AER-THO- 'E] as you prepare to enter the underworld and chaos. Protect me as I enter the unknown.

For the sky quivers, the Earth quakes before me,
for I am a magician, I possess magic.

EVENING PRAYER TO THE SUN

Wash your hands (preferably saying the ablution prayer) and then go and face the Sun. This should be done either at Sunset or before you go to bed.

You who have set at Evening as an Old Man, who are over the World and under the World, Mighty Ruler of the Sea, hear my Voice in this Present Day, in this Night, in these Holy Hours. Hail to you setting Sun,
Self-made you fashioned your body,
Creator uncreated.
Descending into chaos and the unknown,
Sole one, unique one, who traverses eternity.
Remote one, with millions under his care;

---

* This prayer is taken from the wall of the 900 BCE tomb of *Shepenmut*: priestess of Thebes and then added to the last part of PGM IV.1600-1715

Your splendour is heaven's splendour,
Your colour brighter than its hues.
In a brief day you race
Hundreds of thousands, millions of miles.
A moment is each day to you,
It has passed when you go down.
You completed the hours of night,
You order it without pause in your labour.
Through you do all eyes see,
When you stir to rise at dawn,
Your brightness opens the eyes of the masses;
When you set in the western mountain,
They sleep as in the state of death."
Awaken to me.

ΚΜΗΦ ΛΟΥΘΕΟΥΘ [KM'EF LOO-THE-OOTH]
ΟΡΦΟΙΧΕ [OR-FOI-CHE]
ΟΡΤΙΛΙΒΕΧΟΥΧ [OR-TEE-LEE-VE-CHOOCH]
ΙΕΡΧΕ ΡΟΥΜ [EE-ER-CHE ROOM]
ΙΠΕΡΙΤΑΩ ΥΑΙ [EE-PER-EET-A-AW YAEE]

I conjure Earth and Heaven and Light and Darkness and the Great
God who created All, ΣΑΡΟΥΣΙΝ [SA-ROO-SEEN].
You, Agathon *Dæmon* the Helper awaken to me and transform my
life.
For the sky quivers, the Earth quakes before me,
for I am a magician and I have magic.

SPELL TO BECOME A MAGICIAN*

This is an ancient Egyptian spell which is designed to turn someone
into a magician. It was carved into the wall of the Great Pyramid.

I invoke you who are among the nobles of Atum.
I have come to you, so you respect me in proportion to what you
know.
I am he whom the One made
Before the sky and Earth came into being,
When he was alone in the darkness,
And spoke the words of creation and magic;
When his myriads of spirits protected his companions,
He spoke with Khepri the Sun,

---

* CT Spell 261. Middle Kingdom. After Faulkner.

Making him more powerful;
He took authoritative utterance upon his mouth.
I am the son of She who bore Atum,
I protect what the One created,
I am he who caused the Ennead to live,
My name is 'If-I-wish-I-do',
I am the father of the Gods. My standard is high.
The gods are endowed by the commands of the eldest,
Following the command of She who bore Atum,
I keep silence, I acknowledge the Higher.
I come into the presence of the Bulls of the Sky,
I sit among them.
My name is the 'Greatest of the *Dæmons*.'
I am the heir of Atum.
I have come to take possession of my throne
And that I may receive dignity and fulfil my destiny,
Which belonged to me before you had come into being,
You Gods; acknowledge me,
For [insert name] is a noble magician.

THE MAGIC OF THE PRIMA MATERIA – CONVERSING WITH YOUR GUARDIAN DÆMON

"You will discover for yourself the truth of what I say, if, without waiting to behold the outward and visible forms of the gods, you are content to behold their works; and with these before you, to worship and honour the Divine authors of them."

Socrates

It has been one of the most basic mistakes amongst the occultists to reject the material world in favour of a more spiritual approach. The assumption of spiritual ascent implies a rejection of the material world and yet we will be born into the material world, and it is our primary mission for at least the 70 or 80 years that we are put on Earth. If it was the duty of every magician to rush to the throne of God, then one has to question why you were born at all? The implication that the Earth is evil, and that humanity must escape its clutches implies a great heresy – that the One Thing makes mistakes.

The Golden Dawn made the spiritual experience of the Kingdom (Malkuth) that of knowledge and conversation with your *Holy Guardian Angel*. This experience was only attainable, according to the Abramelin system, through an arduous process like what you are undergoing in this book. It seemed strange to me that something indicative of real spiritual progress was so low on the kabbalistic tree of life. However, after working on this material, it started to make sense. There were two forces which Abramelin had fused the *"Guardian Angel or Dæmon"* and the *Higher Genius* into one. The *Higher Genius* was your Divine Self while *Guardian Angel* was a *Dæmon* of nature that had been sent to guide you through your material destiny.

The Greek philosopher Socrates pioneered this understanding of this being which he called his *Dæmonion* (a "divine something"). The difference of *Dæmon* in spelling is important – it is a neuter gender of the word. Obtaining knowledge and conversation with the *Dæmonion* was not indicative of spiritual attainment but something natural which he learned as a child. It appeared in fortuitous events; its function was to forewarn or to check in matters not so much of right and wrong as safety, expediency, or of good fortune. It was not the voice of conscience, which many have thought because it did not appear to have anything to do with moral choices. Some believed the *Dæmonion* was a quick exercise of judgment, based on knowledge and experience without consciousness of the process. However, that was hardly available to Socrates as a child. Others have thought that it was his divine self which in this book we call the Divine Genius. However, its action was too inflexible and limited. The consciousness of the Divine Genius is much more transcendental.

In Plato's *Apology* 31c, Socrates says: "I have a *Dæmonion* from the god. It began when I was a child. It is a voice, and it turns me away from something I am about to do whenever it speaks. It never turns me towards anything. It is what has prevented me from taking part in politics, and I think it was quite right to stop me. Be sure, gentlemen of the jury, I should have died long ago otherwise."

In the *Republic*, Socrates suggests that his *Dæmonion* enabled him to become a true philosopher. This statement puzzled many philosophy students because the *Dæmonion* does not offer any spiritual insight, but only tells Socrates not to do things and warns him.

In the *Euthydemus*, Socrates says: "I happened to be sitting alone in the place in the dressing room of the Lycaeum, and I thought I would leave. When I got up, the *Dæmonion*, came and I sat down.' Soon after Euthydemus and his companions arrived. "

In the *Theaetetus*, he says that the *Dæmonion* stops him talking to some people and not others.

In the *Phaedrus*, Socrates is quoted as saying: "When I was about to cross the river, the *Dæmonion* restrained me. I seemed to hear a certain voice, which did not allow me to proceed until I should have expiated myself, as having in some way offended against God."

The description of the relationship is precisely that of knowledge and conversation with his *Holy Guardian Angel*. The restrictive and limited nature of the discussion is what you expect from a guardian or protector whose role is to keep you following your life story or destiny with the potential to micro-manage the material world in such a way to get its message across.

In his *Memorabilia* iv 3 13 Socrates' student Xenophon uses one of Socrates dialogues, to give a clue of the nature of this Ruled by the *Dæmon:*

> *"You will discover for yourself the truth of what I say, if, without waiting to behold the outward and visible forms of the gods, you will be content to behold their works; and with these before you, to worship and honour the Divine authors of them."*

What that is saying is that Socrates' *Dæmonion* is talking to him through the material world and circumstance and since childhood, he had worked out a simple way to communicate with it so that the whole of nature was providing him with a continuous Oracle. When you perform traditional divination in an open and altered state of consciousness, you consciously look for some answers in the symbols you are using. This usually occurs when you are in some heightened emotional state, and your human failings doubt the intensity of the message that your *Higher Self* is trying to convey to you. If you have tarot cards, you will decide which symbols are correct for the reading. What happens if we apply the same rules to the universe that is around us? If reality is a result of the outpouring of the mind of 'God' what if we try to read it as if a *Dæmon* of God was speaking to us.

It would work like this if you are having a problem or want to try and see what lies ahead go for a walk and make the conscious decision to look at the universe unravelling around you as opposed to being just a passive subject and a reaction to it. Mentally invoke the *Dæmonion* for guidance.

Then say something like "by the time I get to the shops 10 minutes away; something will have occurred on my path that will provide me with some insight about whether or not to quit my job." Instead of worrying over the myriad of possibilities in any situation concerning one's livelihood, you are throwing it out to the Universe and in doing so, allowing yourself to become a more effective channel for your own divine Will.

Your eye might be drawn to some leaves dancing about in a gust of wind; something that under normal circumstances, you would have barely noticed. It could be inferred that the *Dæmonion* is telling you that it is time to reform, to change your job. By opening to the possibility of receiving divine answers in this way, you have enabled your *Dæmonion* to communicate to you more effectively in the same way that occurs when reading tarot cards or using any other divination process. However, rather than using someone else's symbolic system, you are using your own, and by choosing to interact with the world, you are closer to the mind of 'God' for it is more clearly reflected there, than anywhere else.

Another example of this principle in action can be seen in the case of two star-crossed lovers who life has decreed are unable to be together due to the fact they are married to other people. On an illicit drive one day, they decide to throw it out to fate and the Gods, to divine life to find out what would happen to them if they followed their overwhelming emotional impulses. They turn left into a road and find their way blocked by a rubbish truck collecting the recycling.

The truck has an eagle badge on the front which is an astrological symbol of Scorpio and intense emotions. The lovers had to pull over to the side of the road and wait patiently for the lorry to pass them by. As it did, they noticed the word 'together' on the side of the van. The symbols seemed to be saying that their relationship would be stopped dead in its tracks because they were recycling their emotional baggage.

Communicating with the *Dæmonion* in this way is tricky. It has to feel right, the first emotional response indicates a connection to the *Dæmonion*, and then the intellect explains the message. The intellect must be as honed as the mind of Socrates as there is a real danger that the person will hear only what their *Lower Self* wants them to hear. The star-crossed lovers mentioned above tried to read the message positively saying that eventually, the rubbish truck passed which meant everything would be ok. The *Dæmonion* was giving them a simple warning that the road was blocked, and they could go no further as a couple. Rationally the rubbish truck was always going to pass them; it was not part of the message. In hindsight, they would admit that their first thought when they saw the truck was that they were going to get stuck.

However, the *Dæmonion* works all the time, always trying to communicate its warnings through various circumstances. We must be looking at our material universe to enter into a dialogue with our

Holy Guardian Angel. This essential spiritual process is lost if we try to shut out matter and avoid existing successfully in the material world.

The *Guardian Dæmon* is the guide throughout your life and makes sure that you stay on mission throughout it. It appears to be formed from everything that influences you in your environment coupled with the forces of Destiny which manage your life story. It is also connected to the *Higher Genius* and is subordinate to it. What is clear from Socrates' description is that its actions could be good or bad depending on the person. It protects you so that you make the decisions that shape your fate. However, the fact that some people have terrible life stories creates questions:

Were such people fated by the gods to be miserable? Is this because they failed to listen to the voice of their *Guardian Dæmon*, which failed to protect them properly or is even punishing them? Certainly, at times the *Guardian Dæmon* has a dark side, keeping people in challenging situations for years so that they can learn a lesson. This is noticed when a person starts using magic and notices that sometimes it does not work (or does not work in the way it is intended). This is because the *Guardian Dæmon* is making sure it fails because, if it succeeds, the person's life story will go off mission. A person who uses love magic to get a partner without ever researching what is preventing it from happening is missing a valuable life lesson. This is one of the reasons that a spell to win the lottery is so unlikely to succeed. A person who has to work for their objectives is more use to the One Thing than the person who has it drop in their laps. Luck and good fortune are possible, but only if it is not going to get in the way of the real-life lesson.

It explains why those with intimate divine contacts find them silent at times of crucial life decisions when their advice is needed. If our stories are the sum of our choices, taking those decisions away from us by having our gods telling us what to do would be counterproductive.

In such cases, The *Guardian Dæmon* will merely block any magical or divine attempts at intervention until the person has made the important choice or learnt the necessary lesson. The *Guardian Dæmon* is also not above creating adverse events which will force the person to focus on their life goals.

It is important to remember that the *Guardian Dæmon* is making sure your life objectives are met, and you don't go too far off the plot. If your story is a miserable one, it is because you are at a point where you must escape it, kill a terrible monster, or make some changes. No one wants to read a story about someone who sits bemoaning their fate and stays the same. For a story to work it must be about someone overcoming their limits or finding a way to make those limits a garden rather than a prison.

ALCHEMY

The material world is our mission or story. If your *Higher Genius* didn't want us to live in matter you would not have incarnated. You are here to live whatever mission your *Higher Genius* has given you consciously. To do that you have to awaken your *Higher Genius* within matter so that it has its reigns on all aspects of your life. This mystery of nature had to be encrypted in mediaeval alchemy. Throughout most alchemical texts we see the term "first matter" used to represent the starting point for all transformations. The first matter is seen in two contradictory forms – it is holy and profane. Its uniqueness is so important that the alchemists say that finding the right stone which makes up the first matter is most of the work.

The Golden Dawn magician Arthur Waite claimed alchemical writers concealed the *Prima Materia*'s "true name" because it contains all the qualities and properties of elementary things, the names of all kinds of things were assigned to it. In the 17th century *Theatrum Chemicum** it was written:

> "Alchemists compare the "Prima Materia" to everything, male and female, a hermaphroditic monster, heaven and earth, body and spirit, chaos, microcosm, and the Hyle. Within itself, it contains all colours and metals. There is nothing more wonderful in the world. It begets, conceives, and gives birth to itself."

Many alchemists looking at this statement researched rocks that contain certain minerals which they thought likely to give the result they wanted. Sadly, there was only one thing that could genuinely fit a description like that. It had to be a creature that was made of both matter and spirit. The first matter was not a rock – it was the alchemist.

Rather than concentrating on escape, the magician then should be looking at themselves and nature to understand their spiritual mission. I believe that the first spiritual awakening happens when one focuses on seeing Nature and the body as a way of communicating with God and opens a dialogue with the *Dæmonion*. This can be found in the first exercises of the higher, more secret,

---

* Vaughan, R., Cross, T. and Ashmole, E. (1652). *Theatrum chemicum Britannicum ·*. London: printed by J. Grismond for Nath: Brooke, at the Angel in Cornhill.

levels of esoteric European masonry which are part of an alchemical process of transformation starting from the first matter which I have reworked as "catch" exercises in this book. The aims and results will be much different as the goal of this book is to help make a conscious connection with your *Higher Genus*, but I found these exercises useful in obtaining that goal.

PRIMA MATERIA

This exercise should be performed whenever you have a spare moment. At first, it will be challenging because it uses a very earthly mood of consciousness that you spend most of your life in and there are none of the shiny astral objects we associate with meditation or spiritual states. After a while, something happens and the scene changes. The divine seems to "wake up" deep inside you. It is hard to explain, which is why the esoteric lodge which gave me this exercise said it needed a master to transmit it. However, as the goals for this exercise are more limited its practice is straight forward.

STAGE ONE

Sit on a chair with your back straight and relax. There is no need to shut your eyes. You just have to be fully aware of your body and its presence in the physical space. Breath in slowly and as you do shift your awareness deeper into your body. Feel every cell, your blood moving around your system, your heart beating. Each breath centres you closer within your physical frame. You might note some odd things. For example, when I did it, I found my consciousness was not in my body or my brain at all but seemed to be focused close to my face. The exercise drew me into my physical body. Once you have reached a certain level of body awareness, allow yourself to "sense" your physical environment with your entire body. Don't move – feel and become more sensitive to the energies which surround you. Vibrate the word IAΩ three times (silently if you are in public).

STAGE TWO

This stage occurs after you have managed to attain the most definite form of body awareness and sensitivity and it might take a week, or longer before it happens. You start to notice gold flecks, or white light moving in your body; sometimes these extend to the environment. You might experience flashes of imagery (Sun rising is a common one) and feelings of warmth. Do not be too concerned about this, in fact, it is better at this stage to ignore it. But they are signs that the *Prima Materia* is starting to be transformed by your focus and awareness and the divine self is starting the long process of manifesting in matter.

The overall effect of this ritual is cumulative and will have effects the more it is done. We will build on this exercise over the coming months until its true nature is revealed along with the powers it unlocks. There is another stage of this process which we will look at in other months

CHAPTER THREE

MONTH TWO
THE MYSTERIES OF THE ELEMENTS

WORK FOR THIS MONTH

Perform your usual solar invocations and *Prima Materia* exercise at the correct time. Then on your main ritual time:

Week One

1.   Inscribe a black candle from top down with the sign of Taurus, Paramah, your name, Hera and an Earth triangle.

2.   Draw a banishing pentagram in front if and say, **Creature of Wax I exorcise you so that you will be a perfect sacrifice to the gods of the element of Earth so that I might better manifest the powers of this element in my life and be a more aware channel for my *Higher Genius*. As you are sacrificed so shall the elemental blocks and barriers which prevent this happening be removed.**

3.   Place the candle on the triangle on your altar and wash yourself as you did last month.

4.   Invoke the Sun for that time of day.

5.   Commence the solar breath for five minutes.

6.   Perform your confession.

7.   Go northeast and say,

The purpose of this ritual if it pleases the divine triad is to awaken in my sphere of sensation the powers of the element of Earth so that I might manifest these powers for my *Higher Genius* and that these will help me to awaken to my spiritual self.

8.   Open the quarters in the element of Earth (in all four quarters using the supreme pentagram ritual). *If the Earth element is over powered in your chart do not use the pentagrams but stand and vibrate the names.*

9.   Purify and consecrate (as last month).

10.   Invoke Hera* as the queen of the Earth.

Sister and spouse of mighty Zeus, I invoke you Earthly queen. You reside in your ancient shrine at Samos, which alone can pride itself on your birth and heard your infant cries, and receives your nurture.

You occupy in lofty Carthage, which worships you as the maiden who crosses the sky on a lion's back.

You guard the famed walls of the Argives, by the banks of the river-god Inachus, who now sings your praises as the bride of the Thunderer and as queen of all goddesses.

You, whom all the East reveres as the yoking goddess, and whom all the West addresses as Lucina, the goddess of childbirth.

Be for me in my most acute misfortunes Hera the Saviour, and free me from looming dangers in my weariness from exhausting toils.

Awaken your powers within me, raise your Earth spirits to help me manifest my Higher Genius' elemental power over Earth.

I offer you this sacrifice in the hope that you will assist me to awaken to my true self.

11.   Light candle and meditate.

Week Two

1.   Inscribe a blue candle from top down with the sign of Scorpio, Periton, your name, Persephone and a water triangle.

2.   Draw a banishing pentagram in front of it and say, **Creature of Wax, I exorcise you so that you will be a perfect sacrifice to the gods of the element of Water so that I might better manifest the powers of this element in my life and be a more aware channel for my Higher Genius. As you are sacrificed so shall the elemental blocks and barriers which prevent this happening be removed.**

3.   Place the candle on the triangle on your altar and wash yourself as you did last month.

4.   Invoke the Sun for that time of day.

5.   Commence the solar breath for five minutes.

---

* Apuleius, *The Golden Ass* 6. 3 ff

6.   Perform your confession.

7.   Go northeast and say,

The purpose of this ritual, if it pleases the divine triad, is to awaken in my sphere of sensation the powers of the element of Water so that I might manifest these powers for my Higher Genius and that these will help me to awaken to my spiritual self.

8.   Open the quarters in the element of Water (in all four quarters using the supreme pentagram ritual). *If the Water element is over powered in your chart do not use the pentagrams but stand and vibrate the names.*

9.   Purify and consecrate (as last month).

10.   Invoke Persephone* as the queen of the water.

Persephone, Daughter of Zeus, blessed and gracious Goddess,

Wife of Hades you are beloved and life-giving,

You hold the doors of Hades under the depths of the earth;

Transactor of Justice and the holder of the sacred olive branch of peace

Mother of the Eumenides, Queen of the Underworld, You, daughter from Zeus through secret begetting.

Mother of loud-shouting, many-shaped Bacchus.

Playmate of the moving seasons, light bringing, of beautiful form,

Ruler of all, maiden, showering fruits,

Radiant, horned, you alone are longed for by mortals.

You are Spring, delighting in fragrant meadows

Your body appears to us in growing fruits and branches.

You alone are life and death to distressed mortals.

Persephone, you are forever the nourisher and the death bringer.

Send up fruits from the Earth and the ever-nourishing waters from the underworld.

---

* Orphic Hymn *To Persephone*

Bring abundant life leading to richness of old age

Awaken your powers within me, raise your water spirits to help me manifest my Higher Genius' elemental power over water.

I offer you this sacrifice in the hope that you will assist me to awaken to my true self.

11. Light candle and meditate.

Week Three

1. Inscribe a yellow candle from top down with the sign of Aquarius, Akramatha, your name, Zeus and an air triangle.

2. Draw a banishing pentagram in front of it and say, **Creature of Wax, I exorcise you so that you will be a perfect sacrifice to the gods of the element of Air so that I might better manifest the powers of this element in my life and be a more aware channel for my Higher Genius. As you are sacrificed so shall the elemental blocks and barriers which prevent this happening be removed.**

3. Place the candle on the triangle on your altar and wash yourself as you did last month.

4. Invoke the Sun for that time of day.

5. Commence the solar breath for five minutes.

6. Perform your confession.

7. Go northeast and say,

The purpose of this ritual if it pleases the divine triad is to awaken in my sphere of sensation the powers of the element of Air so that I might manifest these powers for my Higher Genius and that these will help me to awaken to my spiritual self.

8. Open the quarters in the element of Air (in all four quarters using the supreme pentagram ritual). *If the Air element is over powered in your chart do not use the pentagrams but stand and vibrate the names.*

9. Purify and consecrate (as last month).

10. Invoke Zeus* as the King of the Air.

Nature's great consistent King,

---

* A much-hacked version of Cleanthes poem (c. 300 - 220 B.C.)

Omnipotent and just ruler who controls all,

King of the Air and mind, Father of Humanity,

We bear your image when we wander

And with songs of praise your power.

From your clouds you wield a two-edged sword

Pulsates through all that Nature brings to light;

Chaos by you becomes order.

Zeus, shrouded by darkness,

Whose lightning lightens the thunder-clouds;

You bring universal law for evermore.

Awaken your powers within me, raise your Air spirits to help me manifest my *Higher Genius'* elemental power over Air.

I offer you this sacrifice in the hope that you will assist me to awaken to my true self.

11.   Light candle and meditate.

Week Four

1.   Inscribe a red candle from top down with the sign of Leo, Zorothion, your name, Hades and a Fire triangle.

2.   Draw a banishing pentagram in front of it and say, **Creature of Wax, I exorcise you so that you will be a perfect sacrifice to the gods of the element of Fire so that I might better manifest the powers of this element in my life and be a more aware channel for my Higher Genius. As you are sacrificed so shall the elemental blocks and barriers which prevent this happening be removed.**

3.   Place the candle on the triangle on your altar and wash yourself as you did last month.

4.   Invoke the Sun for that time of day.

5.   Commence the solar breath for five minutes.

6.   Perform your confession.

7.   Go northeast and say,

"The purpose of this ritual if it pleases the divine triad is to awaken

in my sphere of sensation the powers of the element of Fire so that I might manifest these powers for my *Higher Genius* and that these will help me to awaken to my spiritual self.

8.   Open the quarters in the element of Fire (in all four quarters using the supreme pentagram ritual). *If the Fire element is over powered in your chart do not use the pentagrams but stand in each quarter and vibrate the names.*

9.   Purify and consecrate (as last month).

10.   Invoke Hades* as the King of the Fire.

Magnanimous Hades whose Kingdom is below the earth,

You are wrapped forever in the depths of night.

Zeus Khthonios with the keys to the Earth you unlock the Fires of Vulcan upon which all matter is tested.

You bring forth riches of the world and are the throne of creation.

Distant, unknown, surrounded by pale ghosts and the shrouds of the dead.

In Akheron's obscure depths you hold the flames hidden within everything.

The life animating, burning, and creating. Awaken your powers within me, raise your Fire spirits to help me manifest my *Higher Genius'* elemental power over Fire.

I offer you this sacrifice in the hope that you will assist me to awaken to my true self.

Light candle and meditate.

Week Five

1.   Make four elemental candles as you did in the previous weeks and place them at the East (Yellow), West (blue), North (black) and South (red). Take a white candle and write on it αἰθήρ (æther) your name and a spirit wheel. Draw a banishing pentagram in front of it and say,

2.   **Creature of Wax I exorcise you so that you will be a perfect sacrifice to the gods of the Aether so that I might better manifest**

---

* Adapted Orphic Hymn

my spiritual powers and balance the elements within. Help me be a more aware channel for my *Higher Genius*. As you are sacrificed so shall the elemental blocks and barriers which prevent this happening be removed."

2. Place the white candle upon the triangle and perform your ritual ablutions.

3. Invoke the Sun for that time of day.

4. Begin the solar breath for five minutes.

5. Perform your confession.

6. Go northeast and say,

The purpose of this ritual if it pleases the divine triad is to awaken in my sphere of sensation the powers of Spirit so that I might manifest these powers for my *Higher Genius* and that these will help me to awaken to my spiritual self.

1.   Open the quarters with Air in the East, Water in the West, Fire in the South, and Earth in the North. Do this even if your chart is unbalanced.

2.   Purify and consecrate (as last month).

3.   Invoke æther* as Quintessence.

Ever untamed æther who reigns high above Zeus' dominions of the sky; glorious Sun with dazzling brightness who gives the Sun, Moon and stars their light.
All taming power, ætherial shining æther, who blasts forth in the heat of life: Lord of the elements, light-bearing power, with starry radiance shining,
I invoke you spiritual life,
White flower on the crossroads of the elements.
By this sacrifice balance the elements within me
And awaken my spiritual self.
Awaken your powers within me, raise your spirits to help me manifest my *Higher Genius'* elemental power over Aether. I offer you this sacrifice in the hope that you will aid me to awaken to my true self.

4. Light candle and meditate.

---

* Adapted Orphic Hymn

For most of humanity's history, science consisted of the division of the universe into four elements – earth, air, fire, and water. Aristotle added a fifth – Aether which was the spirit that united them all. Modern magic has tripped over itself when adopting the elemental system by taking it far too literally and seeing the elements as their physical counterparts, rather than symbol metaphors. Seeing elemental Fire as something you put a log into and keep your house warm, or elemental Water as something you would swim in has given esoteric science an outdated feel.

Oddly, modern science and the elemental theory which would have been familiar to the Ancients are still in harmony. Instead of the word air a modern scientist would say "gas," Fire, radiant energy, water, liquid and earth a solid. Each element represents the state of matter in vibration. Fire is the highest vibration and Earth the slowest.

Where esoteric science and elemental theory part company is the association of those states with other associations and parts of the body. Water for example is associated with emotions and Air is connected to the mind. These associations found their way into astrology where they are said represent certain basic traits and give a certain "temperament".

Each of the four elements occurs in three states or qualities, respectively named the basic (cardinal), static (fixed) and moving (mutable). The difference can be seen most clearly in water. When water is frozen, it is fixed, when it is running it cardinal and when it his heated it becomes steam and mutable.

The ancestor of all elemental thinking was the Sicilian magician Empedocles who lived in the in the fifth century BCE. In *Tetrasomia*, or *Doctrine of the Four Elements*, Empedocles described the four elements as the roots of all existence which were controlled by two forces Love (Philotês) and Strife (Neikos). Love is the force that draws things towards Order while Strife causes them to break apart. In this system Philotês is the force which creates order while Neikos creates chaos. Empedocles said that Strife also divided the one immortal soul of Love into many individual souls, each making up both Love and Strife in some proportion and placed them into mortal bodies, which were compounded from different mixtures of four elements.

Like Albert Einstein, Empedocles did not believe that matter could be destroyed. In fact, he believed that the four elements were Gods:

Hear the fourfold Roots of all:
Life bringing Hera, Hades, Shining Zeus,
And Nestis (Persephone) who moistens the springs of humans
with tears.

In his *Ancient Philosophy, Mystery and Magic: Empedocles and Pythagorean Tradition**, Peter Kingsley worked out that Zeus is Air, Hera is Earth, Hades is Fire and Nestis (Persephone) is Water. The gods enable the elemental forces to be approached.

Empedocles' equation of the Roots with deities emphasises the fact that they were not literal material substances but spiritual essences manifesting differently in the material and spiritual worlds. They can be land, the sea, the sky and the Sun, and abstract concepts like the Underworld (which was said to be subterranean fire).

Plato (427 to 347 BC) named four "faculties of the soul" based on the elements: Imagination, Demonstration, Intelligence, and Opinion. A modern psychologist would say that the elements reflect components of the human psyche, but they could also represent the stages in various processes of growth and transformation or the Ascent of the Soul in the *Chaldean Oracles*. In the process outlined in this book an elemental progression from Earth, Water, Air and Fire is repeated (sometimes overtly and other times by implication).

The Elements are archetypes of psychology because they are structures in the collective unconscious, are universal beyond complete analysis; they can be "circumscribed but not described".

In the century that followed Empedocles, Aristotle developed the system further by looking at how the elements interacted with each other to create the world, Aristotle attributed double qualities on each of the elements: Warm versus Cool and Dry versus Moist. While these meanings could be used to understand nature, it was still important to see these elements as living spiritual qualities rather than just physicals things. One of the biggest mistakes that modern scientists make when commenting on Ancient Science is that they assume that Aristotle and those who followed him were using their elemental theory to describe physical reactions, when they were really talking about both a spiritual and a physical approach.

In each element, one Power is dominant. Earth is pre-dominantly Dry, Water pre-dominantly Cool, Air is pre-dominantly Moist, and Fire is predominantly Warm. Unlike the chemical elements, which

---

* Kingsley, P. (1995). *Ancient philosophy, mystery, and magic.* 1st ed. USA: Oxford University Press.

replaced this system, the spiritual elements could be transformed into each other. For example, Water is transformed into Air when the Water is acted on by a larger quantity of Air because the Water's Coolness is "overpowered" by the Air's Warmth. The Moist quality is retained through the transformation. This process can be reversed as Air can be transformed back into Water by acting upon it with sufficient Water. It was a belief that such transformations were possible, which allowed the Spiritual path of Alchemy to develop.

The *Greek Magical Papryi* also contained words of power which were specifically linked to the Elements. When these were vibrated they activated the part of the body connected to the element. The Magical Name of power which connected the magician to the Divine Mind was AEEIOYO. The name of Air was PPP SSS PHR (PPP SSS FREE], a popping, a hissing sound. It was common in spells of the period). Fire was MMM. EY EIA EE was Water. OOO AAA EEE was Earth and YE YOE was the complete Body.

In Ancient Rome and Greece elementals were seen as nature, spirits, which formed in significant places and were acknowledged as lesser gods or goddesses. The Romans called these the Genii Loci, while the Greeks called them *Dæmons*. They were seen as being guardian spirits connected with the land, but they were everywhere including buildings, corporations, the state, military units, and guilds of tradesmen.

Their elemental nature can be seen in various myths. For example, Cacus was a giant who was a son of Vulcan lived in a cave in the Aventine Hill in Italy, the future site of Rome. He ate humans and would nail the heads of victims to the doors of his cave. Hercules tried to kill him and Cacus attacked by spewing fire and smoke, while Hercules responded with tree branches and rocks the size of millstones. Hercules leapt into the cave, aiming for the area where the smoke was heaviest. Hercules grabbed Cacus and strangled him. Cacus fits what would be later described as a Fire elemental.

Another important Roman Goddess who may have been a Fire elemental was Vesta. Vesta is the virgin goddess of the hearth, home, and family in Roman religion. Vesta's presence is symbolized by the sacred fire that burned at her hearth and temples, but she was closely related to Cacus. Her sacred fire was kindled in every home in Rome and effectively made the whole city sacred. It was her elemental Fire which powered the Roman Legions in their conquests, and when it was extinguished in 394 CE by the Christian emperor Theodosius I in Rome, not only did he die within a year, but the empire swiftly collapsed.

The Romans did not consider any gods or goddesses elemental in anyway that would be understood by later occultists, but it does give us an idea as to how what we would now define as elemental might be divine and worshipped.

PARACELSUS

While the use of elements in Alchemy was important throughout the Middle Ages it was not until the splendidly named Swiss alchemist Philippus Aureolus Theophrastus Bombastus von Hohenheim (1493 – 1541) that the idea of elementals as creatures entered occult practice. Von Hohenheim who was better known as Paracelsus wrote a book called *Liber de Nymphis, Sylphis, Pygmaeis et Salamandris et de Caeteris Spiritibus**. In it, he made a link between the elements and all the creatures of myth and legend including the classical monsters, nymphs along with more Germanic creatures and mountain spirits. Around this, he built into them a philosophy to explain the existence of these beings.

Each element, Paracelsus claimed, had a type of being associated with it. The Water people were nymphs, who are also sometimes called undina. Air people are sylphs, and go by the name sylvestres. Mountain creatures are pygmies or gnomi. Fire races are salamanders, also called vulcani, whose monsters are will-o'-the-wisps.

Paracelsus told his readers saying that he was using the mythic names for these creatures so that people could understand what he is trying to describe. When you heard in Roman myth that a creature was a nymph it meant they were really talking about a water elemental. Not only did this give you an idea about what the being might be, it created a whole new philosophy which merged myth and the beginnings of science.

Paracelsus thought that elementals were like humans but lacked a soul and were half spirit. They could move through objects and traveling like spirits needed feeding and could get sick. In many ways, Paracelsus wrote, they were more like animals. However, they are to be treated well, and agreements made with them were binding. Elementals live completely in the sphere of their respective elements. Salamanders would live in all things which were manifestations of fire. Its word would be a mirror of this one, but with the other elements removed. While this means that they cannot enter another elemental realm, all of them can interact with this one.

---

* Paracelsus. and Blaser, R. (1960). *Liber de nymphis, sylphis, pygmaeis et salamandris et de caeteris spiritibus.*. Bern: Francke Verlag.

Paracelsus said that the world that the elementals live in is totally separate from that of humanity, but Earth and Fire elementals could serve people and Water and Air elementals could marry them (we will look that the marrying an elemental later).

Elementals were to act as guardians of the unfolding of nature's treasures. In his *Astronomia Magna** Paracelsus wrote that God did not want his secrets to be simply visible; he wanted them to become manifest and knowable through humanity. So contacting the elemental kingdoms was important to understand nature.

In *Liber de Nymphis* Paracelsus wrote that God has set guardians over nature, for all things, and he left nothing unguarded and it is the nature spirits, who make and protect what Paracelsus calls "tremendous treasures, in tremendous quantities".

"Everything must come out, creature, nature, spirit, evil and good, outside and inside, and all arts, and all doctrines, teachings and what has been created." In other words, these treasures are the power and knowledge present in the elements.

Paracelsus at once created problems as well as solutions in his elemental theory. As there is a tendency within modern occultism to be literal when it comes to elementals and a trend to see the elemental kingdoms as being populated by fantastic creatures which can be approached and talked to. The elementals in question are similar to Victorian fairies or garden gnomes, which dumbs them down to a point where they are nearly useless to a working magician. I remember one magician describing her experience with Air elementals as being "slow floating pieces of paper" and described how a gnome used to march up and down her hallway.

But the reality given by Paracelsus is a little less anthropomorphic. He said that there is as much difference between the bodies of men and the bodies of the Nature spirits as there is between matter and spirit.

Elementals were not spirits, because they had flesh, blood and bones; they live and propagate offspring; they can talk, act and sleep, &c., and consequently they cannot be properly called 'spirits.' They are beings occupying a place between men and spirits, resembling men and spirits, resembling men and women in their organization and form, and resembling spirits in the rapidity of their locomotion."

Being a Christian, Paracelsus thought that the Egyptians, Chaldeans, and Persians often mistook the salamanders for gods, because of their radiant splendour and great power. The Greeks,

---

* Daniel, D. (2006). Paracelsus' *Astronomia Magna* (1537/38). Ann Arbor, Mich: UMI.

following the example of earlier nations, deified the fire spirits and in their honour kept incense and altar fire, burning perpetually, he claimed.

ARTIFICIAL ELEMENTALS

Paracelsus also gave magic one of its most interesting concepts – that of the artificial elemental. He reasoned that since humanity had within them the "breath of God" they had the ability to create life. They could, with their imagination and emotion, forge an artificial elemental and give it life. This was the reality behind the myth of the magician's familiar. The magician would create a thought form which would act as a servant and carry out his or her bidding directly on the material.

The most physical of these can be seen in the legend of the Golem which was created by Judah Loew ben Bezalel in 16th-century Prague. In that case, an Earth elemental as animated clay robot which was controlled by a kabbalistic divine name. It was used to protect the Jews of Prague from anti-Semitic attacks. The concept also had echoes in Ancient Egypt where statues or shawabtis were placed in the tomb which would act as servants for the dead person in the afterlife. The statues were the form taken by the artificial elemental.

Another form of an artificial elemental is created by magical group to protect its members. These look like gods or angels and are sometimes "real" elemental beings who are ordered to serve by their Elemental King, who has to be approached by the group. More often, they are artificial constructs and are less intelligent.

But over the years I have seen that they have often acted against members who were causing trouble even before anyone was aware of what they were doing. In one group I was involved in a person secretly was planning to set up his own group. He had made up his mind that he was going to wait until he completed the next grade, which would have given him the authority to initiate people into that system. He could then take as many people who would follow him into the new group. At the next meeting, he complained that he could not "get into" the ritual because the temple guardian had forbidden him, even though he knew the password. Within a month, he had snapped and picked a fight with the group leader and resigned. In another case a person, who failed an initiation and projected his psychological anger onto others, found it difficult to get into the temple because the temple guardians did not let him in. Eventually they let him enter but his behaviour was closely watched until they refused to let him in at all. He left the group.

These artificial elementals are part of the selection process of candidates into the group. When a person applies to join, the group leader approaches the guardians and asks the new candidate to be tested to see if they should be admitted.

Another form of artificial elemental is the one which is created by a large crowd of people during a riot. Psychologists have noticed that people do funny things when they are amongst such a group of people. They suddenly become easily manipulated and can do things that they would not do normally. This is the psychology of a mob that suddenly forms and rampages through a city. Afterwards people who took part in a riot sometimes wonder how they managed to get so excited and do the sort of actions that they would not normally have done. In fact, my first experience with an artificial elemental was when I was a teen Christian and went to a *Youth for Christ* concert. These were organised by well-meaning fundamentalist Christian groups to lure kids away from their natural spiritual direction towards sex, drugs and shopping and get them back into the same churches as their parents. At the end of the concert, there was a long talk and kids were asked to come up and accept Jesus into their lives. People mobbed the stage, even I felt compelled to go to the stage. The speaker talked about a spirit of God moving among the people and said that he was "leading them by their heart" to come forward." Sure enough, I could see a swirling mass of cloud moving like a wave through the crowd urging them on. It did not feel like a religious experience, it felt like something else – a compulsion. A psychologist would tell you it was normal crowd behaviour, but what I was seeing was the artificial elemental which was doing it and it had been accidentally given form and a task by the speaker. As a conversion tool, the artificial elemental was counter-productive. People who went forward lacked the intellectual understanding of what they were doing and never really became Christians, if anything they were insulted and felt manipulated. The goal of the artificial elemental was not to lead them to God, but to get them to the front of the theatre and to give their lives to Jesus.

One thing that is a common belief about artificial elementals is that they can get out of control. They are like a computer or a machine in that if they are badly programmed they can carry out their tasks literally – much like the brooms in the story of the sorcerer's apprentice. In other cases, their elemental side can predominate, and they can act in ways that the user might not expect and cause general mischief. Earth elementals when out of control cause things to go missing or break. Now that we do not have many open fires, Fire elementals cannot cause wood or coal to fall onto the carpet and burn the house down, so they delight in electrical problems.

Rules

Paracelsus built the rules of elemental magic, which are still accepted by many modern occultists. For example, elementals did not have a soul and when they die their consciousness was not preserved. This was because there was no superior vehicle present to contain it. They lived to great age and those composed of Earth ether are the shortest lived; those composed of Air ether, the longest. The average life span of an elemental was between three hundred and a thousand years. Paracelsus maintained that they lived in conditions similar to our Earth environments and are somewhat subject to disease. Elementals are incapable of spiritual development, but most of them are of a high moral character.

The four fixed signs of the zodiac were assigned to the four kingdoms of elementals. The gnomes were Taurian. The undines were Scorpios. The salamanders were Leos and the sylphs Aquarian.

While Paracelsus was ahead of his time in many areas, the limitations he placed on the elementals were typical thinking for the 16th Century. He tended to see them as structured in terms of Kingdoms and said that they were capable of waging war upon one another. When nature spirits went to war you saw evidence on this level. For example, if lightning struck a rock and splintered it, the event could be a salamander attacking a gnome. Our world was the battleground because they could not attack one another on the plane of their own peculiar etheric essences because there was no vibratory correspondence between the four elements of which these kingdoms are composed. To make matters worse, the elementals were fond of Civil Wars.

Eliphas Levi

Since the 19th Century, occultists have said that Elementals were under the control of four Kings: Paralda (air), Nixa (water), Djinn (fire) and Gob (earth). The Kings' names were invented by the French occultist Eliphas Levi (1810 - 1875) whose real name was Alphonse Louis Constant.

Levi was a huge influence in the study of the elementals and his work influenced the *Order of the Golden Dawn* and groups that came from it. In a paper called the *Conjuration of the Four Elements*, Levi said that the elementary spirits were like young children and clearly he didn't like kids much because he said: "They torment those more who busy themselves with them, unless one has control of them by means of superior rationality and great severity."

Elementals prepare nasty dreams, move divining rods, and pretend to be dead people with raps on walls and furniture. They can never manifest any other thought than our own, and if we are not thinking, they talk to us with all the incoherence of dreams. They are without free will and consequently have no responsibility. They torment mystics with terrible visions such as the nightmares of Saint Antony, and Swedenborg, Levi wrote.

He warned that any magician who uses them assumes a terrible responsibility, all the evil which he makes them do. If you ask an elemental to kill someone, it would do it without feeling guilty and as far as the universe is concerned it is "not elementals that kill people, but people who kill people."

Fortunately, being able to control an elemental was not something a normal muggle could do. Levi said that you had to undergo the four trials of the ancient initiations. Since no one knew what these were, Levi suggested that you could expose yourself without fear to a raging fire, go across a chasm on using a plank bridge, or scaling a steep mountain during a storm, or getting away from a cascade, or from a dangerous whirlpool by swimming.

"The man who fears water will never reign over the undines; he who is afraid of fire cannot command the salamanders; as long as we are subject to dizziness we must leave the sylphs in peace, and not irritate the gnomes; for inferior spirits only obey a power that is proved to them by showing itself their master even in their own element," he wrote.

When the magician has "acquired by boldness and practice this incontestable power" he may impose upon the elements the mandate of his will, by special consecrations of Air, Fire, Water and Earth. This is the indispensable beginning of all magic operations.

Levi was partly right. While it is true that dealing with elementals you cannot be scared of them, facing your fears by performing daredevil acts will not cure anything other than a fear of heights, fires or drowning. The best way forward is to master the elements in your own personality before working with them.

This was the work of the *Outer Order of the Golden Dawn* but was part of the first degrees of most magical orders. Working on the personality was equal to working with the internal elementals.

Elemental Prayers of Levi

These prayers were keys to understanding the elements. Levi did not write the first one, which came from a book called *Comte de Cabalis*.

On first reading they appear Christian until you realise that they were designed to be invocations to the Elemental Kings. The Kings were the Divine Rulers of each element and lore said they were angelic. With a little tweaking they fit into a more overt Pagan approach nicely. The Prayer of the Salamanders, for example is directed at Hades and the Prayer of the Undines is for Persephone.

The Prayer of the Salamanders (Hades).

Immortal, eternal, ineffable and uncreated Father of all things who is borne upon the incessantly rolling chariot of ever-turning Worlds.

Ruler of the underworld immensity where the throne of your power is elevated; from whose height your dread-inspiring eyes discover all things, and your exquisite and sacred ears hear all.

Listen to your children whom you have loved from the beginning of the ages; for your golden, great, and eternal majesty is resplendent below the world and the sulphurous depths. You are the great supporter, Oh sparkling fire. There you illumine and support yourself by your own splendour; and there comes forth from thine essence overflowing streams of light which nourish your infinite spirit.

That infinite spirit nourishes all things and makes this inexhaustible treasure of substance ready for generation. It receives the forms with which you have impregnated it from the beginning.

Oh Chthonic Father, Hades the Father of blessed mortals and immortals. You have specially created powers who are marvellously like thine eternal thought and adorable essence.

PRAYER OF THE SYLPHS (ZEUS)

Spirit of light. Spirit of wisdom, whose breath gives and takes away again the forms of all things. Zeus, in whose presence the life of being is a shadow which changes, and a vapour which passes away. You who rises to the clouds and moves on the wings of the winds. When you breathe, infinite spaces are peopled. When you inhale, all that comes from you returns to you. Endless movement in eternal stability, be you eternally blessed. We praise thee and bless thee in the changing empire of created light, of shadows, of reflections and of images; and we long unceasingly for thine immutable and imperishable light.

Let the ray of your intelligence and the heat of your love penetrate us. Then what is movable will become fixed, the shadow will become a body, the spirit of the air will become a soul, the dream will become a thought. We shall no longer be borne away by the tempest but shall hold the bridle of the winged steeds of the morning and shall direct the course of the evening winds that we may fly into your presence.

Zeus mighty spirit of spirits. Zeus the eternal soul of souls. Zeus the imperishable breath of life. You are the creative inspiration. You breathe in and out the existence of all beings in the flux and reflux of your eternal Word, which is the divine ocean of movement and of truth.

PRAYER OF THE UNDINES (PERSEPHONE)

Terrible Queen of the sea. You hold the keys of the cataracts of heaven, and who encloses the subterranean waters in the hollow places of the Earth.

Persephone Queen of the deluge and of rains, of springtime. You open the sources of streams and fountains. You who commands the moisture (which is like the blood of the earth) to become the sap of plants. We adore and invoke thee.

Speak to us, you moving and changeable creatures. Speak to us in the great commotions of the sea, and we will tremble before thee. Speak to us also in the murmur of the limpid waters, and we will want your love.

Immensity in which all the rivers of being lose themselves, which ever spring up within us. Ocean of infinite perfections. Height which sees you in the depth. Depth which breathes you in the height. Bring us to the true life through intelligence and love. Lead us to immortality through sacrifice.

PRAYER OF THE GNOMES (HERA)

Invisible Queen who has taken the Earth as her support and has dug abysses in order to fill them with the omnipotence. You whose name makes the arches of the world tremble. You who make the seven metals circulate in the veins of stone; Monarch of seven luminaries. Rewarder of subterranean workers. bring us to the desirable air and to the kingdom of light.

We watch and work without respite. We seek and hope by the twelve Olympians of the Holy Mountain, for the talismans which are buried by the magnetic nail which passes through the centre of the Earth. Hera, Hera, Hera have pity upon those who suffer. Enlarge our hearts. Let us be free and raise up our heads. Exalt us.

Stability and movement. Day invested by night. Darkness veiled in light; you are the Master who never keeps the wages of his workmen. Silvery whiteness. Golden Splendour. Crown of Diamonds, living and melodious. You bear the sky upon your finger, like a ring of sapphire. You who hide under the earth, in the kingdom of gems, the wonderful seed of stars.

All hail. Reign; and be the Eternal Dispenser of riches, of which you have made us the guardians.

The divinity of the elements appeared in other cultures too – initially by implication. The four holy creatures are already mentioned in *Ezekiel*. This book was written during the Babylonian captivity around 600 – 560 BCE so pre-dated Empedocles and had little to do with the elements. At that point, the four holy creatures were symbols of the four directions.

The attribution of these forces to the elements meant that the concept of four beings in charge of the elements was universal. In syncretic Roman Egypt, these spirits were given names, which had been lost to the Western Mystery tradition until the discovery of an obscure Coptic manuscript they are Akramatha (Angel-Air), Zorothion (Lion-Fire), Periton (Eagle -Water) and Paramarah (Bull-Earth). These are not names you can really invoke as they are divine names of an Angelic collective and a hive mind of divine force. However, they can be used on angelic talismans as the highest name. Each of these four creatures has an archangelic force which enables a better interaction. These are the classical archangels of the elements Raphael (Air), Gabriel (Water), Michael (Fire) and Uriel (Earth). These Archangels were used by Ancient Pagans and it is fair to say that much of the lore associated with them comes from Pagan rather than Jewish or Christian sources.

By the time of the astrologer Ptolemy, 85-165 AD - each of the 12 zodiac signs is assigned the four elements.

Fire - Aries, Leo, Sagittarius
Earth - Taurus, Virgo, Capricorn
Air - Gemini, Libra, Aquarius
Water - Cancer, Scorpio, Pisces.

When mapped onto an astrological chart it is possible to see a person's elemental bias. A person who is lacking in water planets might not have much in the way of empathy, someone who has too many fire planets might be impulsive and aggressive.

Greek physician Galen (physician of the Emperor Marcus Aurelius and a contemporary of astrology's Ptolemy) gave credit to the fifth Century BC Greek physician Hippocrates when naming his four temperaments: Choleric, Melancholic, Sanguine, and Phlegmatic.

In Galen's *On the Elements** Hippocrates is quoted as being the first to determine "the qualities of the elements - qualities according to which one thing acts on others and is affected."

In the Renaissance, the 16th century AD physician, alchemist, and astrologer Paracelsus more created the concept of each element energy being a living creature. With the four elements being a race of nature spirits. These were Salamanders (fire), Gnomes (earth), Sylphs (air), and Nymphs (water).

FIRE

Fire is the senior element and the primal force of animation. Fire is the desire for life, the will to be and become. Fire signs embody leadership, initiative, and courage. People with a fiery emphasis tend to be impulsive, spontaneous, creative, and enthusiastic. Fire signs inspire others, stimulating creative action based on lofty ideals.

Fire can create an over-emphasis on self-expression without consideration for others' feelings, resulting in selfishness, egotism, or fanaticism. If someone is lacking in Fire, they may need to cultivate self-confidence, energy, bravery, and desire. Indeed, in alchemy Fire is considered the primary agent of change, and Empedocles said that Fire was the Agent of Action (*Kinêtikê*) among the Elements. He said fires burn beneath the Earth and that Volcanic Fire shoots to the Heavens and licks the stars. Fire is the highest and the lowest element. It would be a mistake to take this literally as there is some important teaching here. He is saying that fire exists in all matter, even when it is unseen and like a volcano it can erupt so that fire may connect with the heavenly fire. Empedocles was said to have died by throwing himself into a volcano which seems to imply that

---

* Galen. and Johnston, I. (2011). *Galen on diseases and symptoms*. Cambridge: Cambridge University Press.

he was using that internal fire to ascend to the stars. Diodorus of Sicily (8.75) wrote*,

> *"Thou, Empedocles, didst purify thy body with the Living Flame and Fire didst thou drink out from Immortal Craters... he leapt into the Craters of Fire and drank of Life."*

In Tantra, Fire is the kundalini sexual energy coiled like a sleeping serpent at the base of the spine or coiled around the feet.

Fire is separate from the rest of the elements because it corresponds to energy, while the other three Elements correspond to states of matter.

Hades, the brother of Zeus is the God of fire. His associations with death and the underworld make this attribution odd to modern minds. However the early Greeks did not have the same concept of universe that we have today. There was the Earth and the sky and that was it. Hades connection with volcanic fire and being Persephone's husband (a union of fire and water) make the attribution viable. A volcanic crater is filled with rivers of fire, which suggests a union of Fire and Water. Craters were a place of power and magic, for it is an entry to the Underworld. The "Fires of Hades" might have survived into Christianity with hell being a place of punishment. Empedocles thought that Hades' fire was the source of all life, order and creation (*Aidêlon*) and chaos, destruction (*Aidês*).

AIR

Air is the energy of the mind and communication. Air enables connections linking different people and with new ideas and information. Air energy is intellectual, objective, inquiring, social, supportive and communicative. Air enables detachment and perspective.

However sometimes it can be superficial and take impartiality to the extreme and become cold and distant. It tends to be all talk and not actually doing anything. The person who puts up a wall of words that mean nothing is channelling air (in more ways than one).

Air is important as a mediating element, which unites Fire and Water. Air also constitutes the cosmic breath, which unites the trapped aspects of the *Higher Genius* with its more aspects.

Zeus is a storm or sky god and associated with the turbulent air. There are invocations for him to bring fertilising rain which was Moisture from the Air. Like air, Zeus can shift into any shape and so air is a symbol of transformation.

---

* Diodorus (1985). *Bibliotheca historica*. Lipsiae: Teubner.

Air's power as a mediator means that Zeus has an essential role in uniting the *Higher Genius* with the body. Empedocles says the Breath-Soul or Spirit (Psukhê he associated with Air), unites the Body (Sôma) with the Principle of Motion (Kinêtikê). This is one of the reasons we use the name IAO which was a secret name of Zeus so much in this system.

WATER

Water is the realm of emotions and creates feeling and sensitivity in people. It creates empathy, psychism, intuition, compassion, creativity, and imagination.

However, fear is also an emotion and pain. Water often lacks direction and seeks extreme controls to avoid pain. It can over-react, cause paranoia and escapism. It is also connected to death and purification. This is because it can dissolve material because it's Cool (uniting) quality allows the Water to attach to solid matter of all sorts and its Moist (conforming) quality causes the result to have no fixed form. Dissolution is a passive loss of form and objects lose their rigid structure and identity. This is one of the reasons why Chaos was depicted as water in many Egyptian and Greek myths.

In the Greek tradition you find water sources being considered as important. They appear as central to the Eleusinian and Persephone Mysteries because springs were entrances to the Underworld. In the story of Persephone, Hades took her down the Kuanê spring. Persephone was the Queen of the Nymphs, the daughters of Ocean who are the spirits of springs and streams.

Persephone unites the Earth and Air. She is the daughter of the Earth Goddess Demeter and Zeus (who corresponds to Air and the Sky). Persephone obtains her power to unite (Cool) from Demeter and Her power to transform (Moist) from Zeus. In the Eleusinian Mysteries, Persephone joins the Underworld to life above the Earth and mediates between them.

EARTH

Earth is the lowest element and represents manifestation in the physical world. Earth is the spiritual principle of stable but inflexible synthesis, and the foundation of physical being. Earth is the energy of pragmatic building and physicality. It is the action of bringing dreams into reality. Earth focuses on the physical aspects of life and establishes structures and systems to increase security and comfort. Stamina, patience, practicality, determination, and sensuality are connected to the Earth-sign.

However, it can lead to materialism, greed, over-indulgence, stagnation and fear. In many ways losing our awareness of our *Higher Genius* is due to a fascination with the Earth element and a restriction to the five senses. However, without Earth it is much harder to bring ideas into form.

The Element is associated with Hera as protectress of the stable foundation of fertility. Empedocles called Hera *pheresbios* or "life-bringing" to emphasise the fact that the Earth element is just as holy and living as anything else. Earth is unchanging, and Hera is the protectress of the stable family and home, and social order. Hera is a more conservative fertility goddess since she provides the stable foundation of sex within an ordered family.

UNITING THE ELEMENTS

Occult theory says that when you balance the elements you create a fifth element of spirit (or Aether). This was called quintessence by medieval alchemists because it was beyond them and transcended the limitations imposed by the Four Elements.

Sir Isaac Newton wrote in his incomplete Index Chemicus that:

> *"Quintessence is a thing that is spiritual, penetrating, tingling and incorruptible, which emerges anew from the four elements when they are bound to each other... This perfect substance or balsam, thought to be beyond the realm of change and decay, was believed to be a panacea with miraculous healing properties and the power to transform the impure into the pure, the perishable into the imperishable."*

Quintessence was luminous but invisible to ordinary sight. Paracelsus believed the stars were made of Quintessence and that within every living thing there exists a hidden star that was that thing's Quintessence.

In Taoist alchemy, the Quintessence is known as chi, an unseen energy that flows through the body and can be accumulated and directed in moving meditations.

In all these traditions, both East and West Quintessence is the uniting divine aspect behind matter.

In our system the *Higher Genius* displays elements of Quintessence. The Quintessence of all the elemental aspects of your body and personality is your *Higher Genius.* The discovery of this element within your physical body or personality is therefore part of discovering your *Higher Genius.*

To find our personal Quintessence it is vital to find our elemental balance. The easiest way to do that is to look at your astrological chart. Note the position of each planet and its zodiacal position and give each one of the score based on the following.

ELEMENTS

FIRE	AIR	WATER	EARTH
Aries	Gemini	Cancer	Taurus
Leo	Libra	Scorpio	Virgo
Sagittarius	Aquarius	Pisces	Capricorn

Look at the element that the Sun and Moon is positioned and award it two points. So, if you have Sun in Leo (fire) and Moon in Scorpio (water) you have two points for fire and two for water.

Now give a point for the element of Rising Sign (the Ascendant), the mid-heaven, Mercury, Venus, Mars, Jupiter and Saturn sign

Now add an extra point for each for the element of the sign ruling Ascendant (use traditional ruling planets). If the Ascendant is in Leo, which is ruled by the Sun, which is fire.

Now add an extra point for the element ruling the zodiac where the Sun is found.

If a planet is within the 29th degree of any sign (on the cusp) split the point between that element and the element of the next sign, since it is so close to 0° of the next sign.

So if we have a person with Ascendant in Leo, Sun in Leo, Moon in Scorpio, Mercury in Leo, Venus in Virgo, Mars in Libra Jupiter in Gemini and Saturn in Pisces, MC in Aries it will add up like this

Fire: Asc (+1+1), Sun (2+1), Mercury (+1), MC (+1) = 7
Air: Mars (+1), Jupiter (+1) = 2
Water: Moon (+2) and Saturn (+1) = 3
Earth: Venus (+1) =1

An element is dominant if it gets five or more points. Having six or more points is unbalanced. In the above example the person is unbalanced towards fire and is weak in Earth.

It is important to realise that this is not bad. This person was clearly born to manifest the Fire element, but it is done at the expense of Earth. They will tend to be autocratic, arrogant and inclined to put their excessive amount of energy into what they do. They may have difficulty seeing other people with their own valid ideas, needs and desires. Weak Earth types are materially unstable, disorganised and not that good with money. What this person will find is that they have a lot of energy and can do things extremely quickly and creatively, but they will lack the focus and organisation to bring things to fruition. For a *Higher Genius* to function in such a person effectively they must strengthen the material aspects and slow down the some of the over-bearing fire.

Heraclitus of Ephesus, a pre-Socratic Greek philosopher, described the balancing process thus:

> *"Fire lives in the death of Earth, and Air lives the death of Fire;*
> *Water lives the death of Air, and Earth lives the death of Water."*

In our case study it means that the person should not just attempt to emphasise Earth qualities but sacrificing some of his fire to air and some of his water to Earth.

When this person effectively communicates, interacts or expresses themselves with others, the worse aspects of their fire will become mitigated. Sacrificing water to obtain more Earth means giving up some of their emotion-based ideas so that they can be more practical. It suggests that the reason why they fail to be balanced might be an emotional vulnerability, sensitivity or intensity which prevents them from being earthed. They might be emotionally dependant on another person to provide that Earth side of themselves as a sign that person cares about them.

All of these things are "issues" which prevent the sort of elemental balancing that the *Higher Genius* needs before it can use the personality as a vehicle. One might argue that the *Higher Genius* should have gotten its astrology right when it manifested in this body, but you will usually find that the imbalance was necessary for the person's life story to unfold. In the case of the above, the person might have had the sort of life where women did everything practical for him and he was happy to let them do that, perhaps because his mother had showed her affection by doing material things for him. The *Higher Genius* would want that sorted out as part of any balancing.

Magic offers a method of balancing using ritual. There are two ways it can do this. The slower way is the most common. It provides the unconscious with a symbol of a balanced elemental personality by opening four elemental gates in the sphere of sensation. This balanced approach enables the unconscious to see what the energies should look like and slowly move towards them. While this is effective it does take some time and regular practise to work properly.

The faster way, although potentially more dangerous and dramatic, is to concentrate only on the elements which are out of balance and not invoking those which are already reasonable. The person in our case study would invoke only the gates of Air, Water and Earth. Invoking Air would help kill of the overbalance of Fire while water and Earth would balance the weakness of Earth.

Before moving on we will use another example.

This person has Leo Asc, Sun and Venus in Gemini, Moon in Libra, Mercury, Jupiter and the MC in Taurus and Saturn and Mars in Leo.

Adding up the numbers we have:

Fire: Asc (+1+1), Saturn (+1) Mars (+1) =4
Air: Sun (+2+1), Venus (+1), Moon (+2) =6
Water: nothing
Earth: MC=(+1), Mercury (+1), Jupiter (+1) =3.

This person is balanced in Fire and Earth, overbalanced in Air without any Water.

Those without any Water have an emotional vacuum which they attempt to fill by turning to spiritual realms or universal truths. They have difficulty remaining in touch with and expressing their feelings may lead them to form relationships with overly emotional people or to become addicted to excitement and intensity. They try to prove their sensitivity by carrying out nurturing activities. With the heavy balance towards air this person lives in their head. They restlessly seek knowledge and sharing their thoughts with other people. Impersonal (emotionally detached), yet they thrive on communication and social interaction.

To fix this imbalance they would have to invoke Water, Fire and Earth. After a while the Air will slowly die down and bring in more Water.

A person who suffers from no over balances or lacks simply invokes all four gates to adjust any difficulties which might have developed over time.

Chapter Four

Month Three
Mysteries of the Sacred Language

The Work for the Month

Each day you will perform the invocations to the Sun each day at the correct time. However, for one of the sessions each day you will carry out much longer ritual work as outlined in the letters exercise later. You should also carry out your *Prima Matera* exercise when ever you get the chance.

I t is one of those occult myths that the Hebrew alphabet is the most magical and ancient. Certainly, it has had a significant role in the development of Western Magic, and it is the key to the mystical understanding of the Old Testament. Yet historically the Hebrew alphabet was not handed to Adam by God. We can see its roots as a development of Phoenician, which in turn borrowed ideas from the Ancient Egyptians. The Hebrew that we know of now is not the version of the Ancient Israelites but appears to have been tidied up into the neat square script during the Babylonian captivity. But we also know that a mystical belief in the letter's power did not exist until much later.

The Greeks took their alphabet from the Phoenician traders, which they adapted it to suit their speech, but they had vowels, and came to associate each letter with a number. The Hebrew letters did not become associated with numbers until after the Greeks invaded Israel and Egypt After the Maccabees threw out the Greek rulers their leaders had a problem. Greek was the most common language and the nation's entire financial system used its number system. The last thing you want, when you have spun the Greeks as oppressors is to continue using their number system so the Maccabees took Hebrew letters and gave it the Greek number system based on the similarity.

In Alexandria, where there was a huge Jewish population which mixed with the Greeks, Platonic ideas were added into the Hebrew mystical mix. It is from here that the first notably Kabbalistic work–

the *Sefer Yetzirah* was compiled. Not only did it use the Greco-Hebrew letter/number system it was also fused with the advanced Greek philosophy which was being developed in the City. It is those elements which evolved into modern kabbalah. It is worthwhile pointing out that the world Hebrew *gematria* comes from the Greek γεωμετρία, "geometry."

But Greeks and Romans used a gematria of their own in magical texts. We can see Greek letters being used magically and as means to encode ideas in the same way as Kabbalah. In the *Greek Magical Papyri*, the letters themselves have a power and a meaning similar to what is seen in Kabbalah and can be used the same way.

Greek gematria could be used to build magical phrases out of Greek classical texts and the titles of Gods – in the same way as the Kabbalah was used in by the Jews to explore their holy texts. That tradition ended with the fall of the Roman empire and the rise of Christianity. It is unclear where it would have ended if it could continue. Hebrew kabbalah went on to develop into a spectacular flowering of Judaic mysticism and magic. The question is what would have happened if Greek gematria had continued. Judaism was a religion which used its gematria to explain and experience mystical states. But Greek gematria was used to unlock the secrets of its philosophy and magic. It was used to work with the Egyptian texts and a Greek variant of Ancient Egyptian – Coptic was developed.

To resurrect this tradition then it is necessary to take the ancient tradition and incorporate what has been developed in the Jewish tradition since. This is not enormous difference, but once the door is unlocked then it is hoped that the new strain will enable Ancient Magic to be used more practically.

This is not to say that we replace the Jewish kabbalah or even create a Greek Kabbalah. I am one who believes that Kabbalah is inherently Jewish and exclusively tied to Judeo-Christian ideas.

HOW IT WORKS
The Greek Alphabet to function like gematria has to
1.   Add up.
2.   Work out astrologically.
3.   Have an Oracular power.
4.   Be useful magically.
5.   Each letter must mean something.

THE MEANING OF THE LETTERS
Phoenician script has 22 letters, the same 22 as modern Hebrew;

there's a one to one mapping between those two scripts. The Ionian Greek script, however, got rid of three of the letters (digamma/waw, qoppa, san/sampi), added four (phi, khi, psi, omega), and moved the position of the derived form of waw (which became upsilon) further back in the alphabet. Each of the Phoenician letters had their own name, many of which provided the names for their corresponding Greek letters. These names referred to, in many cases, earlier Egyptian hieroglyphs or related words that provided a basis for what the letter looked like. Many of these names were maintained in Greek, often in derived forms, such as Alpha from ʾĀlp, Bēta from Bet, Gamma from Gimel, and so forth.

Many of the meanings of the Greek letters for Hebrew are therefore going to be the same with a few additions.

Letter	Phoenician	Meaning
A	ʾĀlp	Ox
B	Bet	House
Γ	Gimel	Throwing stick
Δ	Dāleth	Door
E	He	Window
Z	Zayin	Weapon
H	Ḥeth	Wall, yard, thread
Θ	Ṭēth	Wheel, good
I	Yōdh	Hand, finger
K	Kaph	Hand, palm
Λ	Lāmedh	Goad
M	Mēm	Water
N	Nun	Fish, serpent, whale
Ξ	Simketh or Sāmekh	Fish, tent peg, prop support
O	ʿAyin	Eye
Π	Pē	Mouth
P	Rēš	Head
Σ	S (Simketh)	Tooth
T	Tāw	Mark, cross
Y	Wāw	Hook

Letter	Phoenician	Meaning
Φ	Qōph	Back of the head, sewing needle, eye of a needle, monkey
X		
Ψ		
Ω	From Omicron	

By the time the Ionian Greek script was adopted and spread throughout Greece, many of the letter forms were so far removed from their Phoenician counterparts (if any existed) that many of these meanings became meaningless or detached from the letters.

NUMBERS

Greek isopsephy (ἰσοψῆφία, literally "same pebble", is another system like Hebrew gematria when applied to the Greek alphabet. The Greek alphabet, having come from the same origin as the Hebrew alphabet, also used letters as numerals, and did so earlier than Hebrew. A big difference is the number of characters: Hebrew has 22 letters with five extra, adding to 27, while Greek has 24. To make up for the lost characters, Greek used three obsolete letters for the sole purpose of transcribing numbers: digamma (F) for 6, qopppa (Ϙ) for 90, and sampi (ϡ) for 900. Digamma was a "w" sound, qoppa a uvular "k" sound like Hebrew qoph, and sampi was probably a lengthened "s" or "ks" sound.

Value	Letter	Value	Letter	Value	Letter
1	A	10	I	100	P
2	B	20	K	200	Σ
3	Γ	30	Λ	300	T
4	Δ	40	M	400	Y
5	E	50	N	500	Φ
6	F	60	Ξ	600	X
7	Z	70	O	700	Ψ
8	H	80	Π	800	Ω
9	Θ	90	Ϙ	900	ϡ

The Greek alphabet comes into better use in astrology since, with 24 letters not counting the obsolete ones, it matches up well with divisors and multiples of 360.

It is possible to use the same Kabbalistic Nine Chamber method to reduce all Greek letters to their basic elements. This becomes vital for the construction of sigils, magic squares and other "kabbalistic" designs.

3,30,300 Γ, Λ, Τ	2,20,200 Β, Κ, Σ	1,10,100 Α, Ι, Ρ
6,60,600 F, Ξ,Χ	5,50,500 Ε,Ν, Φ	4,40,400 Δ,Μ, Υ
9,90,900 Θ, Ϙ, ϡ	8,80,800 Η, Π, Ω	7,70,700 Ζ, Ο, Ψ

Thus if we were to take the magic square of Saturn:

   4   9   2

   3   5   7

   8   1   6

Using the Nine Chambers you could convert it to Greek letters:

   Δ   Θ   Β

   Γ   Ε   Ζ

   Η   Α   F

Now say you wanted to create a sigil of the Goddess Hera to create a happy marital home. Saturn would be the physical building while Hera (Ηρᾱ), would be the Goddess of the Marriage and Home. Hera's name would be H= 8 P=100 A=1. Using the Nine Chambers we would have 8, 1, 1 and the following Sigil which could be placed on a talisman or drawn in the air as part of a magical ritual.

ASTROLOGY

The Greeks, Copts, and other Hermetic magicians are well-known for having attributed the seven vowels of the Greek alphabet to the seven visible planets and their spheres. The attribution of these letters can be seen throughout the Greek Magical Papryi and ancient Greek forms of gematria, especially in certain holy names and voces magicae. This is where the attributions change dramatically between the Hebrew. In this system, the attributions are:

- A, alpha, for the Moon
- E, epsilon, for Mercury
- H, eta, for Venus
- I, iota, for the Sun
- O, omicron, for Mars
- Y, upsilon, for Jupiter
- Ω, omega, for Saturn

The elements can be worked out as the following:

- Θ for Aether or the Quintessence
- Γ for Earth
- Δ for Water
- P for Air
- Π for Fire

There are 12 "simple" consonants:

- B for Aries
- Z for Taurus
- K for Gemini
- L for Cancer
- M for Leo
- N for Virgo
- Ξ, for Libra
- Σ for Scorpio
- T for Sagittarius
- Φ for Capricorn
- X, for Aquarius
- Ψ for Pisces

The following table describes the different attributions of all the letters of the Greek alphabet:

Letter Upper/ Lower Case	Planet/ Element/ Zodiac	God	Eng.	Time	N⁰·
A, α	Moon	Hekate	A	Monday	1
B, β	Aries	Athena	B	April	2
Γ, γ	Earth	Hera	G	Midnight	3
Δ, δ	Water	Persephone	D	Sunset	4
E, ε	Mercury	Hermes	E	Wednesday	5
F, ϝ		Prometheus	w*		6
Z, ζ	Taurus	Hesta	Z	May	7
H, η	Venus	Aphrodite	h	Friday	8
Θ, θ	Aether	Aether	Th		9
I, ι	Sun	Helios Apollo	I	Sunday	10
K, κ	Gemini	Apollo	K	June	20
Λ, λ	Cancer	Hermes	L	July	30
M, μ	Leo	Zeus	M	August	40
N, ν	Virgo	Demeter	N	September	50
Ξ, ξ	Libra	Themis	X	October	60
O, o	Mars	Aries	O	Tuesday	70
Π, π	Fire	Hades	P	Noon	80
Ϙ, ϙ		Dionysis	Q*		90
P, ρ	Air	Zeus	R	Dawn	100
Σ, σ	Scorpio	Hephaestus	S	November	200
T, τ	Sagittarius	Artemis	T	December	300
Y, υ	Jupiter	Zeus	U	Thursday	400
Φ, φ	Capricorn	Pan	Ph	January	500
X, χ	Aquarius	Ganymede	Ch	February	600
Ψ, ψ	Pisces	Poseidon	Ps	March	700
Ω, ω	Saturn	Cronos	o/aw	Saturday	800

* = was not pronounced by the Greeks. The letter had no sound in the Greek speech so was abandoned. It was kept for numeric reasons.

GEMATRIA OF GODS

If you look at the literary and magical works of the Greeks, you are struck by how much effort they go to giving their gods titles. These titles start to make sense when you apply Gematria to them.

So let's have a look at the name Zeus Ζεύς. He is made up of Zeta (Taurus), Epsilon (Mercury), Upsilon (Zeus) and Sigma (Artemis). His numbers add up to 7+400+300+200= 907 (reduces down to seven which is the letter Z, zeta which is Apollo). The number 907 is also the same as the word "Constant." From this we can see that Zeus's basic nature (because we have not included any of his "titles,") is practical, fixed and directed toward matter. Zeus is a constant power which expresses itself in Nature and through the Sun and through oracles. The fact that the upsilon is there, means that Zeus is present in his own name.

When Homer added a title to that name, the energy of Zeus changes to show a different side of his nature. Father Zeus is Πατερ (Pater) adds the Pi (Fire, Hades), alpha (Moon, Hekate), Tau (Sagittarius, Vesta), Epsilon, (Mercury, Hermes) Rho (air, Zeus). This version of Zeus fiery and closer to Earth. It communicates through the air. The number is 80+1+300+5+100=486 which reduces to 9 or Theta which is the Aether. When we invoke Father Zeus we want something powerful, fiery and closer to our material selves that unites the elements. 486 is also the same number as the word "Stone", "Honey" and "Gladness." By calling Zeus Father you are bringing happiness through sacrifice (honey was a popular sacrifice to the Greek Gods). The Stone has interesting masonic associations too.

This use of vowels and letters also explains some of those strange sounding names in the *Greek Magical Papyri* which are mostly made up of vowels. Each one is focusing the influence of a planet in the ritual. Thus, the famous IAO would be the Sun, the Moon and Saturn. This name, which appears in the Greek version of the Old Testament instead of the Hebrew YHVH does put an interesting spin on Tetragrammaton.

Vowel words like this shown in the *Greek Magical Papyri* would be vibrated or Sung using their musical notes to a certain number of counts. So you would vibrate the bottom line for a count of four, for example, the next line would be vibrated to a count of eight, divided by two letters with four beats each.

AEEIOUO

EEIOU

EIO

IO

O

I

The divine name used here is made up of the Moon, two Mercury, one Sun, two Mars and one Jupiter. It was used in a magical binding spell. The two Mars letters bind the beneficent Jupiter and the Mercury is emphasised. During the process of the chant, Jupiter is liberated from the powers of the Moon and Mars; Mercury and Mars then contain the Sun; then Mars expresses itself with the Sun and then finally all things have been dissolved into the Sun as the great god. You will have chanted an invocation to the Sun, Mercury and Mars five times and the Moon once.

CONDENSING POWER

It is possible to take a Homeric verse and convert it into a powerful vibratory chant. Write down all the vowels from the line in order. Thus:

Ω εἰὼ ἀοιο ἰήαε ὤυα ἴου [aw ee-aw a-ee-o e-e'e-a-e aw-y-a ee-oo]

This gives a magically condensed version of the verse which is particularly good at charging objects or moving magical/divine energy. If vibrating each vowel is a mini-invocation to the seven main gods we can see that the verse is made up of a formula of Saturn (3), Mercury (2), Sun (4), Moon (2), Mars (3) and Venus (1). Saturn would represent the obstacle, or the boundary Mars matches it. The Sun supplies most of the power for the chant while Venus less so. This would not be a good chant to overcome an obstacle in a relationship but would be good for overcoming depression.

You can use the musical notes for each vowel to make the chant even more interesting.

- A, alpha, for the Moon, musical note A

- E, epsilon, for Mercury musical note G

- H, eta, for Venus musical note F

- I, iota, for the Sun musical note E

- O, omicron, for Mars musical note D

- Y, upsilon, for Jupiter musical note C

- Ω, omega, for Saturn musical note B

Each letter should be Sung or vibrated on a single breath and in the order they are given. To be done properly the line of vowels should be vibrated once for every letter so in this case 18 times. While you vibrate or sing you should focus on the intention of your working.

I suspect that the use of vowels by themselves in the *Greek Magical Papyri* and other magical texts might represent this form of magical reduction to create a chant of power. They could represent divine names or phrases that have been boiled down to their vowel essence to create a more potent magical effect. If this is the case, it is a magical use of Greek which is impossible in Hebrew Kabbalah. The vowels are gods so care should be taking in using this method.

It does create some interesting theological questions if applied to divine names. The essence of Zeus are the letters E and Y which are Mercury and Jupiter. Zeus then combines the expansive Jupiter force with the communication, speed and "many turning" ways of Mercury. Hera combines the Venus, Mercury and the Moon and Hermes is made up of Venus and a double helping of Mercury. This would mean that the qualities of these gods are not "pure" powers. The process of humanising them has given them an interesting mixture of qualities. Zeus is Jupiter-like but has a mercurial streak. His wife is not at all Jupiter-like, but does have her husband's mercurial side. She also is a mother and magic goddess who has a sexual and creative side.

NOTE ON COLOURS

The vowels are also associated with colours, a fact which might be useful when drawing talismans or magical images of the gods.

- A, alpha, for the Moon, Colour Violet
- E, epsilon, for Mercury, Colour Orange
- H, eta, for Venus, Colour Green
- I, iota, for the Sun, Colour Yellow
- O, omicron, for Mars, Colour Red
- Y, upsilon, for Jupiter, Colour Blue
- Ω, omega, Colour Indigo.

Say we were drawing Zeus. His two essential vowels are εύ. You would therefore draw him from the colours Orange and Blue. The same would apply to a spell as is described above Ω εἰὼ ἁοιο ιήαε ὡυα ἵου.

If you were to visualise a *Dæmon* who would carry out your spell's work, you could visualise him in the colours of the vowels. This would mean six colours, but you would be more Yellow and a bit less Red and Indigo because there are more vowels with those colours and hardly any Green. On any talisman you could also colour each vowel in its appropriate colour.

MAGICAL TEXTS

One of the areas that the Judo-Christian-Islamic magical tradition had over more ancient methods of magic was that it was centred on written magical texts. There was a *Bible*, Mishnahs and a *Koran* which, being inspired by God and written in holy letters, was therefore magical already. But this underestimated how the Ancient Greeks and Romans saw certain texts. Homer's *Odyssey* and *Iliad* were not just treated as beautifully written poems but sacred texts which explained how the universe worked and just as spiritually important as the *Bible*.

The *Iliad* opened with this invocation to the Goddess:

> "Sing, goddess, the anger of Peleus' son Achilles and its
> devastation, which put pains thousand fold upon the Achaeans,
> hurled in their multitudes to the house of Hades strong souls of
> heroes, but gave their bodies to be the delicate feasting of dogs, of
> all birds, and the will of Zeus was accomplished since that time
> when first there stood in division of conflict Atreus' son the lord
> of men and brilliant Achilles."

The *Odyssey* opened with this invocation to the Muse:

> "Tell me, Muse, of the man of many ways, who was driven far
> journeys, after he had sacked Troy's sacred citadel. Many were
> they whose cities he saw, whose minds he learned of, many the
> pains he suffered in his spirit on the wide sea, struggling for his
> own life and the homecoming of his companions."

While this might seem like a poetic device it really was not. It was a sign that the words were channelled from the Muses themselves and were divine and true. The sentences were holy and could be taken out of context and used to make a point, in the same way that *Bible* verses were. Plato borrowed so many themes and phrases from Homer that the ancient Alexandrian writer Ammonious authored a book showing how much of a debt the philosophy owed to the poet.

This is ironic because philosophers of the time were running down Homer. Aristotle was fond of quoting Homer in his works too. He wrote an early work called *Homeric Questions* which looked at the problems with some of the words, phrases or stories with answers to them. This concept shows that the great minds of the age were seeing Homer as something to be dissected with the ideas depicted in them as something to be seriously looked at.

Homer was taught to the Greek and Roman upper classes. Partly for the purity of the Greek and partly for the moral lessons learnt. A child was expected to have memorised some, if not all of the Homeric verses, in much the same way that lettered children of the 18th century was expected to quote verbatim much of the *Bible*.

With the letters meaning something magical and coming directly from God the *Iliad* and the *Odyssey* have the potential to be powerful "spells" and mantras. These can be seen in the *Greek Magical Papyri*, and the principle used is not difficult. You look through either of these books for a sentence which reflects the need you have. Ideally the sentence should fit into context so that it is not isolated too much from its original meaning. If Homer is weaving words, you do not want to unpick his threads too much. Next it should be a complete line and written entirely in Greek. You can find literal texts of Homer with English and Greek above them. You can double check the meaning of the words with an Ancient Greek Dictionary. It might sound a lot of work and it is. But the payoff is worthwhile.

Here is a spell which was used to help a slave escape. The spell appears in PGM IV 2145 and it is taken from the *Iliad* book 10 line 564

"*Thus speaking he drove the single-hooved horses through the trench.*"

Ὡς εἰπὼν τάφροιο διήλασε μώνυχας ἵππους
[aws eepon tafreeo dee'elase mawnychas eepoos]
[Thus horses trench through single-hoof driven]

Within the *Iliad*, single-hoof horses are associated with speed. The trench referred to an obstacle placed around the Greek camp to stop enemy troops breaking into the Greek camp. When it was breached, it was a military disaster. In a spell to help a slave escape, boundaries are vital because if they got far enough away they would be safe. In this case the spell is designed to help a slave escape quickly.

In modern times, it could also be used to quickly overcome an obstacle and get us away from problems. When problems hit us, we often wish we can get through them quickly and move on. This spell could be used in that way.

It can be chanted as a mantra. Homer was written in Dactylic hexameter to create a poetic rhythm. Each line was carefully written so it could be divided into six feet; each foot would be a dactyl made up of a long and two short syllables. These could be substituted by a "spondee" of two long syllables instead. The fifth foot is often a dactyl. The sixth foot can be filled by either a trochee (a long then short syllable) or a spondee. When you learn, a phrase is easier to clap it in, one hard, two soft.

A dactylic line most normally looks as follows:

− !! | − !! | − !! | − !!| − u u | − X

So you have to chant your mantra according to these forms.
Ως (the first stress is on omega) εἰπὼν τάφροιο διήλασε μώνυχας ἵππους

Os eipon taphroio dielase monychas ippous (this is read ippus)
[Os Ei pon] [Ta phro-io] [die la-se] [mo-nychas] [ip pus]
(It sounds like òs eipòn tafròio dièlase mònychas îppus)

If you are feeling brave you can sing it in a 3/3 time using the notes I have given above playing only the lead vowels thus: [E,C, A], [D, G,A] [A,D,C] [G,F,D] [A,A]

Throughout the ancient world, we see these verses from the *Iliad* or Homer used for divination or the basis of spells. This use of Homeric verses pre-dates and suggests many of the same uses that modern magicians find for Psalms and *Bible* verses.

For example, a Roman lawyer put this phrase, in small print, in Greek on one of his writs in the hope of sending his opponent to sleep so that he made a mistake.

"The other gods, and the charioteer and indeed men did sleep all night. But sweet sleep did not bind Jupiter."

A lawyer friend of mine tried this as several experiments. For the first he wrote out the phrase on a piece of paper and then stuck it under the chair where his legal opponent would sit during a difficult negotiation. On that occasion the rival started off the meeting with a great deal of bluster assuming he was going to win. However, he quickly unravelled, started making mistakes in his arguments, and rapidly gave up. On another occasion, the lawyer used the same verse written in a Word document. He coloured the lettering white so that while it was there it could not be seen. This worked on several different legal letters to help the lawyer win the cases.

Homeric verses appear in the *Magical Papyri* as a prelude to the especially important *Mithras Liturgy* which was an ancient ritual of ascension to heaven. While the verses were not considered as part of the ritual, the entire ritual was placed between several verses. The first was *Iliad* 10.193 which was *"seize any man, lest we become a cause of rejoicing to our foes."* And was used as a spell to get friends. The second verse was the one we mentioned above which was used to escape from danger. The third verse was *"and men gasping out their lives amid the terrible slaughter"*, which comes from *Iliad* 10.52. This was used as a protective spell. While the verses are not connected to the liturgy itself, they are designed to protect and aid the reader in carrying it out. The three verses might make a good mantra before the actual working. After the ritual, the line about the single-hoofed horses, and the other about the men gasping among the slaughter are repeated, along with *Iliad* 10.572 which is another popular magical Homeric protection and victory verse *"And they washed their profuse sweat in the sea."* It is concluded with *Iliad* 8.424 *"You will dare lift up your mighty spear against Zeus"* which was used to restrain the god's anger. This was presumably because the magician had just tried to storm Mount Olympus by performing this ritual and might earn a lightning bolt for their presumption.

The historian Hans Dieter Betz who did tremendously well when translating the *Greek Magical Papyri* hit a rock when it came to the Homeric Verses. While he could understand that they were used for specific magic purposes, he could not work out why whole lines were not used, or why some of the sentences were broken up to obtain their magical effect. The reason might be because the gematria of the sentences required the deletion of some words to make a more significant number.

The vowels and letters of the sentences might have the number of planetary forces in the vowels, or meanings in the consonants to bring about the request's effect. What is more possible is that the verses lines "spoke" to the magician in a personal revelation. When reading Homer images appear as the scene is described and the words can be tied into those meanings. While there might be those who feel it odd that an epic poem should be used as a sacred text in this way, it is exactly the way many monotheists use the *Bible* stories, particularly the Old Testament, which were committed to paper around the same time in human history.

The following exercise is based on a European Rosicrucian technique which also involved placing the Greek letters and associations on the body. It mixes this with a Tantric method and then builds an upper astral body which can be used by the *Higher Genius* to connect to the lower. It also uses the esoteric teaching connected to the *Hanged Man* Tarot card. All this is involved but makes it easier for the *Higher Genius* to awaken in the *Sphere of Sensation*. There are several stages to the exercise and while the early stages are straight forward, particularly if you have experienced Israel Regardie's *Middle Pillar* the latter stages are dissociative and start to split your consciousness into two so that both created bodies are purified and consecrated and then integrated.

The lower body is the *Sphere of Sensation* and is under the rulership of the Moon. The upper created body is solar and is designed to attract the *Higher Genius*. The rarified astral part of the *Higher Genius,* which is outside the body, uses it as a temporary transformer through which it contacts that part of itself which is mostly asleep within the self. When the two bodies are integrated it should provide a spiritual jolt which awakens the *Higher Genius* within the *Sphere of Sensation*. But even if this does not happen, through repetition of the exercise the lunar self becomes aware of the *Higher Genius*'s over shadowing and starts remembering its solar nature. This is the symbolism of the Alchemical Marriage between the Sun and the Moon.

Making this contact is an important part of a magician's life which will help stabilise their magic and life theme. However, the *Sphere of Sensation* is a death trap for many thought-forms having been built from out-of-date thoughts and wrongly interpreted experiences. These can serve to overturn any real ritual experience and replace it with the same pre-initiation universe.

The Indian Tantrics worked their way around this concept by installing the godform of the contact into each energy centre so that it could work on the energy centres to purge the *Sphere of Sensation*. The godform would be an intelligent force which would teach the *Sphere of Sensation* how to use the different energies. Adapting the Tantric technique is not difficult, particularly as the modern western magic already has taken on some of the Tantric attitudes to spiritual energy (Kundalini). The normal technique is to place a different Godform for each of the spheres, but in this one we will use the single godform of the *Higher Genius* as that is the being we wish to make our connection. It is better to rely on it to make the changes it wishes than rely on any correspondence theory.

Western magicians are used to the Kabbalistic Tree of Life to place energy centres in the *Sphere of Sensation* by limiting them to five basic ones (feet, groin, heart and throat and crown). In doing this they lost the alignment with the physical centres and attempts (by the likes of Dion Fortune) to put them back largely failed. This system abandons the Tree of Life attributions completely and returns to the older Tantric positions. It does keep the centre based in the feet, which aligns with the European Rosicrucian teaching and the Western planetary colours. This might alarm the purists of both systems, but as an Indian guru once pointed out to me – the symbols are subjective anyway and it is better to use those which are closer to what you want.

CENTRES

For this system we will use seven energy centres one for each of the planets

The first is the *brow* centre: It is visualised as a pale blue sphere with an orange Conjunctio sign. It is attributed to Jupiter and is your connection to your *Higher Self*. When it is open it allows you to "see" things on the astral. It is the ruler of the mind. It is activated by the Greek Vowel Y. Placing a godform in the centre of this centre allows you to hear your contact. You might experience some visionary experiences while this centre is open.

The second is the *Throat* centre: This is visualised as an orange sphere in a pale blue octagon. It is attributed to Mercury and governs communication. It is through this centre that the *Logos* speaks its creation for the universe. Your universe is built by the words you chose to describe it -- good or bad. The Tantrics say that this force is divine ambrosia and in a normal person it fuels their destructive side. However, it could equally be nectar to help you grow. Placing a godform here starts to build your universe according to what the godform sees as your destiny. It is activated by the Greek vowel E. When this centre is open you are more articulate, but you must be careful about your words. Make sure your sentences are truly what you want.

The third is the *Heart* centre (the upper part of Tiphareth): This is visualised as a red ball with a green six rayed star in the centre. It is attributed to Mars and it brings about what you want. It is here that the desires and thoughts are actualised as actions. This particular thing is a blessing and a curse. It is the place of the "wishing tree" which in Tantric myth was the place where you got what you wanted. In a normal person what they want is what they think they want and is based on the desires and thoughts of their ancestors. It is more likely that a person's fears will manifest here – when someone says with the throat "I knew this would happen" it is the heart centre which has bought it about. Placing a godform here can give you faith that only the right things will happen, it is one of the reasons that this centre has to be opened before a ritual. Note that in Western magic we tie this centre with the Navel centre and open both. It is activated by the Greek vowel O.

The fourth is the **Navel** centre (the lower part of Tiphareth): This is a bright yellow sphere with an equal-armed cross of blue. It is attributed to the Sun and provides the sphere with all the energy of life and power. It is your personal fire and provides you with the energy. It is said that it is this centre provides you with "awakening" which happens when the fires of your *Lower Self* become transformed into those of the higher. Kundalini rises to this centre and takes its throne for ever. Seeing this centre tied to the Heart centre and both being connected to Tiphareth makes a great deal of sense. When opened together they provide you with the desire and the power to make what you want happen. When a godform is installed here, you should experience a balance of your energy, you start to understand how everything is really one thing and there are often feelings of compassion and love. It is activated by the Greek vowel I.

The fifth centre is the **sacred centre** which covers the sexual organs: This is green sphere enclosed with a red ouroboros. It is attributed to Venus and it is the home of the unconscious. This is the intelligence that rules our patterns of behaviour and most of our automatic life. It is the consciousness that most people live in. The Tantrics call it the animal consciousness but it is really all the programming that we have developed over life which is good or bad. Note the association with the sex drive, which predates Freud by 2000 years. One of the things which is supposed to happen when the centre is under control is that fears are overcome. When a godform is installed in this centre it will unpick unconscious association trees at a deep level. This could create some tensions as these associations rise to the surface so that the person becomes aware of them, and then explode. When these associations are removed it is possible that a person loses a lot of things that were dependant on them. It can also assist the person in seeing those things which have been shut down in childhood. So if you have childhood visions you might start experiencing these psychic events again. The centre is activated by the Greek vowel H (like a breath).

The sixth centre is in the *feet*. This centre is violet with a green square in the centre and it is ruled by the planet Saturn. There is some confusion with this centre because it is associated with the anus in Tantra, but as Dion Fortune pointed out, this is because in

Indian Yoga the feet are tucked under the bottom. This represents the physical body, or rather the structure that interfaces between it and the *Sphere of Sensation*. Physical illnesses are often caused by thoughts which existed within the *Sphere of Sensation* which were unresolved and having a physical effect on this sphere (it is one of the reasons that this, with the sexual organs were tied together). This centre is the result of all the others but it also the voice of the psychical body crying out what it needs. The centre is activated by the Greek vowel Ω (Aw).

The crown centre: This is not properly a centre but is the divine spark in human. It is put above the head and is attributed to the Moon. The colour of this sphere is indigo. This might seem odd, particularly as we associate the crown with the highest god and white light. But the *Sphere of Sensation* is astral and sub-lunar. What we are working with is an astral body and this is ruled by the Moon and Hekate. When the centres are fully functioning and balanced they reflect the power of the universe. From the Moon we can look out beyond our limited spiritual understanding and see the chaos from which order was created. This centre connects to the highest mind, the *Higher Self,* and is considered the gate to the void. Occult teaching says that humanity was always meant to be astral and that our *Higher Self* looked at the beauty of the world and decided to play out its story in that. Therefore, when we connect to the crown, we are looking at who we really are, rather than the person who incarnated. Placing a godform in this centre allows us to focus our magic on the contact and allow it to connect to the third eye where it is united with the rest of the *Sphere of Sensation*. The Greek letter associated with the crown is the letter A. (Thus when we vibrate IAO we are stating a mantra to switch on the Sun, then the Moon and then to bring it to earth).

PRACTICE

It takes a few weeks to get each sphere open properly (sometimes longer) but it is possible to get results quite quickly. In your temple space light a single tea light before the picture of your *Higher Genius*.

Start with the feet, move to the sexual centre, the solar plexus, the heart, the throat and then the third eye before moving onto the crown. Focus on one centre a day.

The procedure for each sphere is to breathe in through the nose and visualise the air going to the centre. As you breathe out, you visualise the negative or locked up energy being expelled from the centre. As you do this, vibrate the Greek vowel for the centre. What you are doing is removing the negative energy with a word of power which reflects it

Higher Genius

Letters on the
body

Lower Self

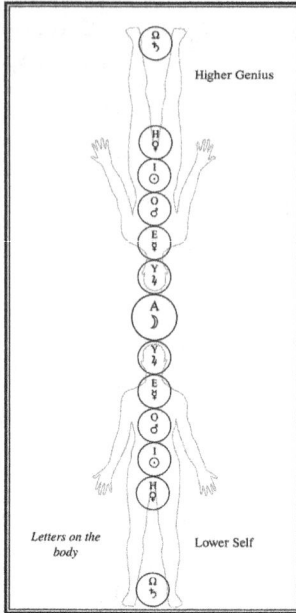

and breathing in new energy to replace it. Do this for five minutes

Do the sign of silence.

Then invoke your *Higher Genius* to dwell in that centre.

I invoke My *Higher Genius* to indwell and take its throne in my [name of centre]. I surrender to its will so that I will find my own.

Breathe in and absorb the image into the centre. Set your timer for 20 minutes

Vibrate **PHÊOUS PHΩOUTH (FE-OOS FAW-OOTH)** [*lotus emerged from the Abyss*] Vibrate the name and see the statue come to life inside the centre. Do this for 30 minutes while focused entirely on the sphere. The goal here is to surrender and accept that the contact is going to help you. As you vibrate you let go a little part of your thinking and allow new ideas to emerge. You might find your Higher Genius talking to you and giving you advice but the real thing here is to feel that centre alive with the energy of the god. You should allow feelings to come up and experience them. You should note any strange ideas you might have. You might experience flashes of power; these are normal. In some cases you will experience negative things like physical pain. These are all the rebellions of the *Lower Self.*

Set your timer for ten minutes and sit for a few moments in silence (if you open your eyes you might experience some interesting psychedelic sensations). The idea is to feel what it is like to have the centre open and commune with the god.

Do the sign of silence and a Greek Cross.

If you want to develop this further you can also pathwork into the centre to further talk to the godform which has now taken up their throne.

STAGE TWO

With the development of Tarot as a magical and mystical tool in the late 19th century attempts were made to interpret the symbols of the major arcana. Ideas were taken from the basic symbolism (or symbolism was added) to fit the various schools of esoteric teaching. One success for this emerged from the European Rosicrucian groups based around Alois Mailander and J. B. Kerning with their interpretation of the Hanged Man[1]. They reasoned that Hanged Man was the *Higher Genius* reversed and suspended into Matter and integrated it into teaching based around placing Greek letters on the body.

The solar body is shaped like the image you have been using of the *Higher Genius*. It is immediately above the lunar body and sharing the same crown (see diagram). You follow the same procedures as you did with the lunar body, only you start with the crown and move upwards to the feet.

Unlike the lunar body the centres are not physical but when you focus on them they resonate to the physical centres. This creates an odd split feeling of consciousness as if you are seeing out of both centres at once. This is to be encouraged but your chief focus should be the centres on the Solar Body.

PRACTICE

Take one centre a day. Start with the crown, move to the throat, heart the solar plexus, groin and then the feet of the Solar form.

The procedure for each sphere is to breathe in through the nose and visualise the air going to the centre. As you breathe out, you visualise the negative or locked up energy being expelled from the centre. As you do this, vibrate the Greek vowel for the centre. Do this for five minutes. Then invoke your contact to dwell in that centre.

I invoke My Higher Genius to indwell and take its throne in this solar body which I have prepared for it. I surrender to its will so that I will find my own.

Breathe in and absorb the image into the centre. Set your timer for 20 minutes.

Vibrate I.A.Ω and see the statue come to life inside the centre. Do this for 30 minutes while focused entirely on the sphere. Set your timer for ten minutes and sit for a few moments in silence contemplating what you have done.

Do the sign of silence and a Greek Cross.

THE MYSTICAL MARRIAGE

The final stage, which is not tried until at least week three, is to slowly draw the image of the *Higher Genius* downward into your lower *Sphere of Sensation*. This is done with visualisation and mantra work based around the Greek vowels.

It is not a straightforward process and takes some serious visualisation.

First slowly vibrate each of the vowels to open the centres. Start with the feet move up the lunar body, and to the feet of the Solar body. (Ω, H, I, O, E, Y, A, Y, E, O, I, H, Ω).

When you have done this allow the crown of the *Higher Genius* to descend to the brow centre and the brow centre of the *Higher Genius* to descend to the crown)

Focus on your brow and vibrate A Y as a mantra. At this point you should be imagining the crown of your *Higher Genius* connecting to your mind. You should do this for five minutes (set the timer), then stop and meditate on the quiet for five minutes.

Then focus on the brow of the *Higher Genius* connected with your crown. Vibrate Y A for five minutes and then spend another five minutes meditating on the voice of the *Higher Genius* working on your crown.

That should be enough for the first day. On the second day vibrate each of the vowels as before. This time allow the crown of the *Higher Genius* to descend to the throat centre, the brow centre of the *Higher Genius* to descend to the lunar body brow and the throat of the *Higher Genius* to become the lunar centre's crown.

Focus on your throat and vibrate A E as a mantra. At this point you should be imagining the crown of your *Higher Genius* connecting to your communication centre. You should do this for five minutes

(set the timer) then stop and meditate on the quiet for five minutes.

Focus on your brow and vibrate Y Y as a mantra. At this point you should be imagining the brow of your *Higher Genius* connecting to your inner vision. You should do this for five minutes (set the timer) then stop and meditate on the quiet for five minutes.

Focus on your crown and vibrate E A as a mantra. At this point you should be imagining the brow of your *Higher Genius* connecting to your spiritual being. You should do this for five minutes (set the timer) then stop and meditate on the quiet for five minutes.

On the third day activate all the centres as before and allow your *Higher Genius* to descend until its crown falls to the heart centre, its brow to your throat, its heart to your crown.

As before vibrate A O and then meditate, Y,E and meditate, E, Y and meditation and O, A and then meditate.

On the fourth day, activate all the centres and allow your *Higher Genius* to descend until its crown falls to the solar plexus centre, its brow to your heart, its throat to your throat, its heart to your brow and its solar plexus to your crown.

Vibrate A I and then meditate, Y,O and meditate, E, E and meditation, O, Y then meditate and I A and then meditate.

On the fifth day, activate all the centres and allow your *Higher Genius* to descend until its crown falls to the groin centre, its brow to your solar plexus, its throat to your heart, its heart to to your throat, its solar plexus to your brow and its groin to your crown.

Vibrate A, H, and then meditate, Y,I and meditate, E, O and meditation, I, Y then meditate and H A and then meditate.

On the sixth day activate all the centres and allow your *Higher Genius* to descend until its crown falls to the feet. Its brow will be on your groin, its throat on your solar plexus, its heart on your heart, its solar plexus on your throat, its groin on your brow and its feet on your crown.

Vibrate A Ω and meditate, Y, H and meditate, E, I and meditate, O,O , then meditate, I, E and meditate. H,Y and Ω, A and meditate.

On the seventh day repeat the exercise and end it by visualising yourself becoming a golden hexagram and chanting the following

A, Ω, Y, H, E, I, O,O, I, E, H,Y, Ω, A

And saying:

As above is below and below is above.

Meditate on this.

Chapter Five
Month Four

The Mysteries of the Seven

Work for this Month

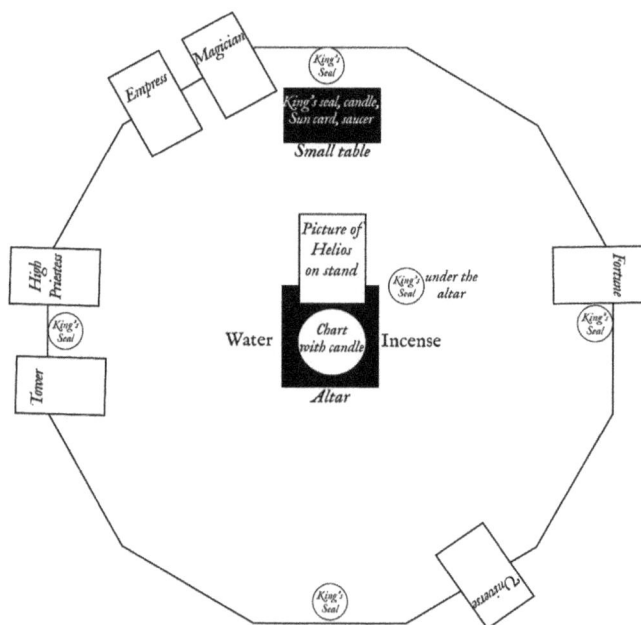

Empress

Magician

King's Seal

King's seal, candle, Sun card, saucer

Small table

High Priestess

King's Seal

Picture of Helios on stand

King's Seal under the altar

Water

Chart with candle

Incense

Altar

Fortune

King's Seal

Tower

King's Seal

Universe

This month is about activating the rays, the planets and the gods connected to your *Sphere of Sensation*, purifying and consecrating them so that they become forces at the disposal of the *Higher Self*.

In addition to your salutations, and *Prima Materia* exercise do the following ritual daily for four days for each of the seven planets.

1. Take an appropriately coloured candle and inscribe it with your name, the name of the god and the names of all the planetary spirits from the *Picatrix*. After you have inscribed it draw a banishing pentagram at it and say, Creature of wax I exorcise and cleanse you for my purpose so that you shall be a perfect sacrifice to the spirits of [name planet] so that I will be a more effective channel for their powers, and those of my *Higher Genius*.

2. Place your astrological chart on the altar (orientated so that your ascendant is in the East) before a statue or picture of the god you are invoking. Place the candle on top of your chart. Place the planetary tarot cards in a circle about the altar where they would be in your chart. Make seven copies of the King's Pentacle for that planet. Place one under the altar, and one in the East, South, West and North of the circle. Make a paper crown and place one pentacle on it. Place the last seal on the small table which you are calling the spirit along with its tarot trump and the court card (which will be either the day or night card depending on the time) Place a saucer on the table, along with a tealight and have a bottle of red wine to hand.

3. Perform the lesser invoking ritual of the pentagram and the solar breath.

4. Say, **I am a creature of chaos searching for meaning in Order. I stand between the Sun and the Moon, the gods and matter, I am balanced and the perfected vehicle for my *Higher Genius*.**

5. Do the invocation to the Sun for that time of day.

6. Visualise your *Higher Self* descending and chant the following A, Ω (feet), Y, H, (Groin) E, I (solar plexus), O,O, (Heart) I, E (Throat) H,Y (Brow), Ω, A (crown). Becoming a golden hexagram and golden light pouring from your heart.

7. Open the quarters and balance the elements.

8. Go to the small altar and draw the planetary hexagram to open a portal for the god to appear.

9. Perform the invocation to the planetary god and light the candle on the central altar. Ask this god that it might open your *Sphere of Sensation* to express its powers better and your destiny following the will of your *Higher Genius*.

10. Assume the godform of the planetary god.

11. Go to the small altar and say,

12. **In the name of [planet god] I invoke you spirits who manifest the powers of [planet] under the Moon and within my *Sphere of Sensation*. I call King [name of planetary spirit] who brings forth the powers of [Planet] within me. Awaken those powers again so that my *Higher Genius* may make use them to achieve its mission on Earth. I offer you flame (light candle) and wine (pour into the saucer) which is a symbol of life blood. Come forth as I chant your holy names.**

13. Circle the altar six times each time chanting the seven names of the king followed by **Egeiro (ἐγείρω)** which means "awake." So, for an invocation for the Sun you would say, **Bandalus Egeiro;**

Dahimas Egeiro; Abadulas Egeiro; Dahifas Egeiro; Atiafas Egeiro; Maganamus Egeiro and Gadis Egeiro.

14. Stop before the small altar see yourself as contained in a cube in the colour of the planet with the King before you. Draw the day or night geomantic symbol (depending on the time) and allow him to form into the image of the tarot court card. Ask him to reveal his part of your destiny. Ask him questions about your chart and finally ask him to help you awaken your *Higher Genius*.

15. Meditate on what you have experienced.

16. Say, **I free all beings seen and unseen who make have been trapped by this ceremony. May you go with the blessing of the [planetary god].**

17. Say, **Janus has closed the Eastern Gate in Peace. Janus has closed the Western Gate in Peace. Janus has closed the Northern Gate in Peace. Janus has closed the Southern Gate in Peace.**

18. Say, **The sky quivers. The Earth quakes before me, for I am a magician and I possess magic.**

Magical systems make a great deal about the seven astrological planets, but few really explain why those energies are so important.

We may assume there is a Neo-Platonic over-god or goddess who is above all things and is so profound it is known only by what it is not. Its roots might be traced to Ancient Egypt where all things were created from a primal chaos god called Nu who was the "father of the gods" which surrounds a bubble of Order in which the sphere of life is encapsulated.

All we can be certain about this god is that it wants to understand itself, and an aspect of itself formed for the creation of the universe. This aspect in various magical, philosophical, and religious traditions was called the *Logos* (λόγος). *Logos* means "word", "speech", "account", "reason", and "proportion,"but it became a technical term in philosophy beginning with Heraclitus (c. 535–475 BCE), who used the term for a principle of order and knowledge. *Logos* is the logic behind an argument and is the persuasive technique often used in writing and rhetoric. From this it came to mean the divine ideas which were spoken by the One Thing to build the universe.

In the Greek magician tradition these words were the seven vowels. These vowels were not just sounds, but the ideas of sounds; in fact they are much closer to light. These are the seven rays which split from the one central light. This has some similarities to an idea suggested by Alice Bailey who suggested a similar concept in her *Treatise on the Seven Rays** as we know them but the seven primal ideas of light.

SEVEN HIDDEN GODS

This created seven hidden gods, which flow throughout the universe. These are seven have never been properly named (the Elohim in *Genesis* is close). For reasons described later, these seven correspond to the seven planets of the ancient solar system and the seven base colours of the spectrum. However, they are more complex than that. They weave themselves throughout creation and build a framework of ideas and a narrative (or stories) upon which creation and things like plots and destiny unfolds. The closest description of these forces occurred during the Middle Ages with the idea of the Olympic Spirits although the concept was a corrupted image. The Olympic Spirit concept recreated the Olympic gods within a Christian framework, but by boiling down such things to seven basic "spirits," the creators mimicked the original concept of the seven hidden gods. The hidden gods encompass the four elemental forces and the concepts of Love and Strife as suggested by Empedocles.

This was mirrored in one of the earliest Zeus myths, in which Zeus takes the bull-form known as Taurus to win the heart of Europa and his face "gleams with seven rays of fire."

The idea of seven rays appears in the Mysteries of Mithras and Dionysus, the *Chaldean Oracles*. The Gnostics and others worshipped a God of Seven Rays. It is not clear what these rays were, and they

---

* Bailey, A. (1993). *A Treatise on the Seven Rays*. New York: Lucis Publishing.

were often seen as an expression of the Sun. In fact, Helios (as pictured) was often crowned with seven rays.

According to the Hermetic work *Sermon of Isis to Horus*:

> *"Seven wandering stars are there which move in the spheres before Olympus' Gate... To these stars' humanity is committed. We have within us Mene, Zeus, Ares, Paphie, Kronos, Helios and Hermes. By this means are we destined to draw from the living Aether of the Kosmos our tears, mirth, anger, our parenthood, our conversation, our sleep and every desire."*

These rays are not gods, but divine forces working throughout creation. If you could reach a state where communication between these forces was possible, they would be abstract, non-negotiable, alien to the human mind – and yet at the same time annoyingly familiar.

THE GODS OF THE SOLAR SYSTEM

The Cosmic Rays might have created the universe, but our solar system is special – life exists here. In some ways, it is best to see it as a big laboratory with the world as its focus. The goal of the experiment is to create a species of life in which the *Logos* could manifest the more complex aspects of itself. The *Logos* chose to manifest through the solar force and each of the seven rays of the planets closest to the Earth and thus influence its fate. Their influence was gradual and at first dominated by the primal gods and gradually the higher aspects of the hidden gods kicked in as life evolved.

The Sun is therefore the chief god of the solar system while the planet called Jupiter is the representative of the chief ruler of humanity. The Moon force dominates humanity, mediates the will of the *Solar Logos*, and brings it down to an acceptable level. The Over Mind has an idea, it passes this idea to the *Cosmic Logos* who transmutes it to the *Solar Logos* who adapts it for its solar system. The Moon then mediates it to the Earth. The descent of the middle pillar on the Kabbalistic Tree of Life shows this process.

Note that the hidden gods are not the planets, just that the planets are symbols of part of them.

Obviously, there are more than seven gods or goddesses, but there are only seven archetypal forces from which the others are derived. We can see them using the above list or build our own based on archetypes. The consort of each god is seen as being an extension of them. So, Zeus and Hera are polarities of each other as the King and Queen archetype.

The Seven are:

The Night/Mother/Alternation (Violet Ray) (Exemplified by Hekate)
The Limiter/Time/ Law giver (Indigo Ray) (Exemplified by Kronos)
The Wise and Knowledgeable, Ruler (Blue Ray) (Exemplified by Athena, and Zeus)
The Trickster/Communicator/Magician/Poet (Orange Ray) (Exemplified by Hermes)
The Lover and Creators (Green Ray) (Exemplified by Aphrodite and the Mother Goddesses)
The Warrior and Destroyer (Red ray) (Exemplified by Aries and Typhon)
The Healer and the Prophet (Yellow Ray) (Exemplified by Apollo and Asklipios)

It can be seen from this list that each of the gods could fit into many different archetypes. This is one of the reasons that the gods were given titles such as Zeus the Destroyer, or Zeus the Wise to tune the energy of the godform to suit the power invoked.

In our solar system the point of contact with these beings was the Sun, Helios or (later) Mithras or the Yellow Ray. The Sun acts as a physical reference point to all those beings who might be cosmic.

These too might normally be too abstract for most humans, so they have another mediator the Moon (Violet Ray).

These find expression in the seven planets in the solar system and the days of the week which is where we see them in magic.

INDIGO RAY (SATURN)
Fate, time, the past, limits and boundaries, form, structures including houses, old age, serious, ambition, bones, knees, skeleton, shins, ankles and circulation, rheumatism, arthritis, envy, suffering, fear, guilt, toxins, repressed aspects of the self, death, vermin and lice, politicians, scientists, architects, teachers, mines, mountains, discipline and wastelands.

BLUE RAY (JUPITER)
Water, lawmaking, opportunity, growth, progress, evolution, money, banks, rulers, royalty, faith, hope, charity, redemption, freedom, spiritual wisdom and development, hypocrisy, hips, thighs, feet,

lawyers, priests, counsellors, actors, open spaces, public places, and panoramic views.

RED RAY (MARS)

Fire, wars, anger, action, sexual desire, physical energy, quarrels, courts, justice, courage, protection, transformation, revenge, destruction, surgery, the head, genitals, excretory system, rashes, red spots, migraine, predators, soldiers, surgeons, athletes, furnaces, foundries, and metal work.

EMERALD RAY (VENUS)

Earth, love, eroticism, desire, pleasure, inspiration, joy, partnerships, peace, laughter, friendship, creativity, the arts, beauty, evaluation, promiscuity, over-indulgence, lewdness, gentle animals, the throat and neck, kidneys, lower back, diplomacy, artists, fashions, bedrooms and gardens.

ORANGE RAY (MERCURY)

Communication, movement, messages, computers, the media, language, trade, theft, magic, skill, learning, intellect, psychology as a science,, rationality, cunning and mischievous animals like monkeys, the digestive system, arms and hands, merchants, clerks, accountants, scholars, universities, examinations, shops, schools, airports and train and bus stations.

PURPLE RAY (MOON)

The unconscious, habits, instinct, sea, rhythm, the astral realm, mysteries, women (particularly their health), mothers, childbirth, psychism, menstruation, mental health, the stomach, breasts, warts, sterility, obsessions, delusions, insanity, cleaners, brewers, midwives, sailors, and harbours.

YELLOW RAY (SUN)

Air, leadership, general health, healing, organisation, arrogance, display, disdain, drama, fathers, power, individualisation, the heart, the back, the lungs, kings, directors, managers, actors, palaces and theatres.

The Yellow, Blue, Red and Green rays are the elemental colours which are used to build creation, and these represent the elements. Yellow is air, Blue is Water, Red is Fire and Green is Earth. Orange is a direct expression of the *Logos* and represents consciousness. The Purple ray represents the force of flux and reflux while the Indigo ray restriction and Time.

Vowel	Sound	Ray/Planet	Day of the Week
A	Ah (as in father)	Violet ☽	Monday
E	E (as in pet)	Orange ☿	Wednesday
H	Breathed out	Emerald ♀	Friday
I	E (as in feed)	Yellow ☉	Sunday
O	O (as in hot)	Red ♂	Tuesday
Y	U (as in rue)	Blue ♃	Thursday
Ω	Aw (as in awe)	indigo ♄	Saturday

With these rays of light, the *Logos* created the four elements of air, water, fire and earth and used them to create Chaotic *Hyle*, which is a form of proto-matter that is behind all change. Its nature is discordant, and it causes expansion and anti-structure. It appears random, but given time, it will eventually form an ordered system from its various parts, which it will act to break down as soon as it formed. This ordering action, which draws together the different chaotic parts into working systems was called Eros. The world of Order formed within the world of Chaos.

THE MASKS

The seven 'gods' might have created humanity, but humanity's first experience was with the primal gods. Primitive humanity moved about the planet trying to survive and it developed relationships based on fear of the natural forces around it. Built from the seven hidden gods, they had the power to create masks for these primal forces. These masks allowed them to understand the forces, build up myths around them, and relate to them. Like many relationships based on fear these were not too successful. Humans created monsters that haunted their nights and needed supplication and sacrifice. Gradually humanity evolved past these fears enough to develop those higher emotions and could slowly replace the primal gods with those more intricately linked to the hidden seven.

The lesson of the masks was still valid. Humanity could not understand the seven forces except through the masks that they created. One man, or culture, might see Venus as a harlot while another would see her as fertility. All gods are an aspect of the seven including those that claim to be monotheist. True monotheism is a difficult concept to imagine. Monotheists might think they are worshipping the One God, but they all give that God different attributes. Jesus can have paradoxical masks of being love and yet being a harsh unsympathetic judge who tortures people for eternity. In terms of the hidden gods, these are two different rays with a similar mask.

The hidden gods have an enormous number of masks in fact every human can create one for all the forces they create. Some are stronger and more important than others. The strongest are those that have the largest number of people who emotionally agree on their composition and over the longest period. A mask might be retired if the religion is extinguished, but its power will simply sleep. It can be reawakened if the circumstances that created it are stirred.

Humanity continues to give masks to gods that are increasingly in their own image. This is not necessarily bad. The masks have power to speak, act and carry out the will of the hidden god they stand for. Built from human minds, they can sometimes act in human ways or have human functions that the hidden god may not express particularly well. Zeus may be the symbol of the perfect ruler, but in the *Iliad*, he makes mistakes particularly in the way he treats Hera. Some gods also feature elements of others – Athena is the Goddess of Wisdom and yet she has a trickster element like Hermes. Athena the trickster (seen as the guide of Odysseus) becomes a different "hidden god." This is one reason why the titles of the gods and goddesses are so important in magic. The titles help us correctly tune the magic so that it reaches the correct hidden god (or group of them). All gods and goddesses fit into one of the seven hidden god or goddess categories even though they might have different names or myths. For example, Vesta is connected to the same hidden god as Vulcan, Mars and Hades.

DÆMONS

The hidden god is the divine force, the mask stands for the best aspect that humanity can make of that force, but neither can work with humanity on a physical level. A hidden god, wearing its mask, stirs up a form within the astral matter which surrounds the Earth.

This is a thought-form or entity that can influence material matters. This thought-form is created in the same way that a human is built, which is why it can influence matter.

A hidden god wishing to create a storm will use a mask of itself in storm god mode. It will form an image of this storm god on the astral and this will attract all the proper elements on the astral plane. Once it has enough momentum in the stirring on the astral, it will start to influence the physical sphere. This image is a *dæmon*. This is an important formula to understand how physical magic works but for now it is important to realise that 99.99 per cent of what a magician works with is an astral *dæmon* and not anything else.

THE CREATION OF HUMANITY

A human is created in the same way as a *dæmon* and they are similar. The *Logos* creates an idea for a human and the hidden gods weave that idea into the life pattern. This divine idea supplies consciousness and a soul for human life. It enters a narrative (or destiny) and experience to help the *Logos* understand some aspect of itself. Most life stories are mundane because the *Logos* needs to understand itself in ordinary contexts far more than it needs to understand itself in special situations. Magicians and philosophers in small numbers aid the process. A trained magician can act like a *dæmon* on Earth by co-operating with the divine forces. It does this to restore a balance and ensure that the narrative does not become too dystopian (or if it does that humanity has the means to move from it).

Trained magicians are rare, and it takes time to work out their role. As *dæmons*, magicians reflect the mask of the god who trains them. Their life in some way follows the path of that god. Thus, those on the path of Thoth tend to be writers or similar communicators; Anubis tends to attract those who have something to do with death; Hekate those who have the job of guiding others; Horus is connected to the military or police; Isis tends to have a path where the mother is dominant. This is complicated by the concept of the "Hero" which may also serve as a trainer and a contact.

THE MAGICIAN AND THE GODS

A magician is not a priest. A priest's role is to mediate the powers of the god or goddess into their community and awaken in that community an understanding of that mask. They may perform miracles in the name of that god, but their goals are one of worship. They look to mobilise humanity to a general evolution through belief in a higher power.

A magician does not need belief in a higher power; they know it is there. Their relationship with their contact means they step outside the norms of society and often must perform magic that is outside what such a community thinks it needs.

When a magician performs magic for someone else, it is not part of a general pious hope but to help him or her towards a specific goal or destiny. A magician is like Thoth, always on the balance point, and sometimes needs to side with Set as often as Osiris. Such a person does not fit with the desires of a community for stability.

A magician may worship a god, but it is something they do in their spare time and part of their own personal devotion. What is more common is that they perform rituals to bring them closer to those gods so that they can help each other. This relationship is precarious, as the chosen mask will only co-operate with the magician while there is work to be performed and there are none of the rewards that the mask offers its worshippers available to the magician.

Another aspect of the relationship is, when working with the *Higher Genius*, the magician uses the power of the god to bring about change either in their own lives or that of the wider world. It is possible because a human is made from combinations of the seven rays and are effectively masks of divine forces themselves. It makes sense then that the *Higher Genius* within the personality should be reminded of its powers under the seven rays as they manifest in the solar system and the sphere of sensation.

A magician can do this by performing planetary attunement rituals which awaken the ray, planet and god within. A ritual will result in a purification and consecration but will mostly remind the *Higher Genius* of its powers.

PLANETS AND DAYS OF THE WEEK

The Greeks and the Romans said that a god ruled each day of the week. It makes sense then that the best days to contact those planetary spirits are on that day.

Luna/Selene ruled Monday
Mars/Aries ruled Tuesday
Mercury/Hermes ruled Wednesday
Jupiter/Zeus ruled Thursday
Venus/Aphrodite ruled Friday
Saturn/Kronos ruled Saturday

Sol/Helios ruled Sunday

The invocations to those spirits are:

SUN

HELIOS*

HEAR golden Titan. King of mental fire.
Ruler of light; to you supreme belongs
The splendid key of life's prolific fount;
And from on high you pour harmonic streams
In rich abundance into matter's worlds.
Hear! for high raised above the aethereal plains,
And in the world's bright middle orb thou reigns,
Whilst all things by your sovereign power are filled
With mind-exciting, providential care.
The starry fires surround your vigorous fire,
And ever in unwearied, ceaseless dance,
Over the wide dew bearing Earth.
By thy perpetual and repeated course,
The hours and seasons in succession rise;
And hostile elements their conflicts cease,
Soon as they view your fearful beams, great king,
From deity ineffable and secret born.
The steady Parcae, at your high command,
The fatal thread of mortal life roll back;
For wide-extended, sovereign sway is yours.
As famed Adonis, delicate and fair.
Ferocious *Dæmons*, noxious to mankind,
Dread the dire anger of thy rapid scourge;
Dæmons, who machinate a thousand ills,
Pregnant with ruin to our wretched souls,
That merged beneath life's dreadful-sounding sea,
In body's chains severely they may toil,
Nor ever remember in the dark abyss
The splendid palace of their fire sublime.
Oh best of gods, blessed *Dæmon* crowned with fire,
Image of nature's all-producing god
And the soul's leader to the realms of light.
Hear! and refine me from the stains of guilt;

---

* Proclus, *Five Hymns* translated by Thomas Taylor.

The supplication of my tears receive,
And heal my wounds defiled with noxious gore;
The punishments remit
And mitigate the swift, sagacious eye
Of sacred justice, boundless in its view.
By thy pure law, dread evil's constant foe,
Direct my steps, and pour thy sacred light
In rich abundance on my clouded soul:
Dispel the dismal and malignant shades
Of darkness, pregnant with poisoned ills,
And to my body proper strength afford,
With health, whose presence splendid gifts imparts.
Give lasting fame; and may the sacred care
With which the fair-haired muses gifts, of old
My pious ancestors preserved, be mine.
Add, if it please thee, all-bestowing god,
Enduring riches, piety's reward;
For power omnipotent invests thy throne,
With strength immense and universal rule.

MOON

HEKATE-SELENE*

Come to me, beloved mistress, Three-faced
Selene; hear my sacred chants;
Night's ornament, young, bringing light to mortals,
Child of dawn who rides upon fierce bulls,
Queen who drives your car on equal book
With Helios, who with the triple forms
Of triple Graces dance in revel with
The stars. You're Justice and the Moira's threads:
Klotho and Lachesis and Atropos.
Three-headed, you're Persephone, Megaira,
Allekto, many-formed, who arm your hands
With dreaded, murky lamps, who shake your locks
Of fearful serpents on your brow, who sound
The roar of bulls out from your mouths, whose womb
Is decked out with the scales of creeping things,
With poisonous rows of serpents down the back,
Bound down your backs with horrifying chains.
Night-Crier, bull-faced, loving solitude,
Bull-headed, you have eyes of bulls, the voice

---

* PGM IV.2785-2890

Of dogs; you hide your forms in shanks of lions,
Your ankle is wolf-shaped, fierce dogs are dear
To you, wherefore they call you Hekate,
Many-named, Mene, cleaving air just like
Dart-shooter Artemis, Persephone,
Shooter of deer, night shining, triple-sounding,
Triple-headed, triple-voiced Selene.
Triple-pointed, triple-faced, triple-necked,
And goddess of the triple ways, who hold
Untiring flaming fire in triple baskets.
And you who oft frequent the triple way
And rule the triple decades, unto me
Whom calling you be gracious and with kindness
Give heed, you who protect the spacious world
At night, before whom Dæmons quake in fear
And gods immortal tremble, goddess who
Exalt men, you of many names, who bear
Fair offspring, bull-eyed, horned, mother of gods
And men, and Nature, Mother of all things,
For you frequent Olympus, and the broad
And boundless chasm you traverse. Beginning
And end are you, and you alone rule all.
For all things are from you, and in you do
All things, Eternal one, come to their end.
As everlasting band around your temples
You wear great Kronos' chains, unbreakable
And unremovable, and you hold in
Your hands a golden sceptre. Letters round
Your sceptre Kronos wrote himself and gave
To you to wear that all things stay steadfast:
Subduer and subdued, mankind's Subduer,
And force-subduer; Chaos, too, you rule.
ΑΡΑΡΑΧΑΡΑ ΗΦΘΙΣΙΚΗΡΕ
[AR-AR-ACH-AR-A 'EF-THEES-EEK-'ER-E]
Hail, goddess, and attend your epithets,
Dart-shooter, heavenly one, goddess of harbours,
Who roams the mountains, goddess of crossroads,
O nether and nocturnal, and infernal,
Goddess of dark, quiet and frightful one.
O you who have your meal amid the graves,
Night, Darkness, broad Chaos: Necessity
Hard to escape are you; you're Moira and

Erinys, torment, Justice and Destroyer,
And you keep Kerberos in chains, with scales
Of serpents. Are you dark, you with hair
Of serpents, serpent-girded, who drink blood,
Who brings death and destruction, and who feasts
On hearts, flesh eater, who devours those dead
Untimely, and you who make grief resound
And spread madness, come to my sacrifices.
Come, Hekate, of flaming council,
I invoke you with these incantations.
ΒΟΥΟΡΦΟΡΒΗ ΠΑΝΦΟΡΒΑ ΦΟΡΒΑΡΑ ἈΚΤΙΩΦΙ ΗΡΕΣΧΙΓΑΛ
ΝΕΒΟΥΤΟΣΟΥΑΛΗΘ
[VOO-OR-FOR-V'E PAN-FOR-VA PHOR-VARA AK-TEEO-FEE
'ERE-SCHI-GAL NEV-OO-TO-SOO-AL-'ETH] (nine times).

MARS
ARES*

Ares, exceeding in strength, chariot-rider, golden-helmed,
Doughty in heart, shield-bearer,
Saviour of cities, harnessed in bronze,
Strong of arm, unwavering, mighty
With the spear, O defence of Olympus,
Father of warlike Victory, ally of Themis,
Stern governor of the rebellious, leader of righteous men,
Sceptred King of manliness, who whirl your fiery sphere
Among the planets in their sevenfold
Courses through the aether,
Wherein your blazing steeds ever bear
You above the third firmament of heaven.

---

* The *Greek Magical Papyri* have few references to Ares (prefering to use
Set-Typhon for the Mars function). I have used the Homeric Hymn to Ares
(Anonymous. *The Homeric Hymns and Homerica* with an English Translation
by Hugh G. Evelyn-White. *Homeric Hymns*. Cambridge, MA.,Harvard
University Press; London, William Heinemann Ltd. 1914.) with the words
of power using PGM IV 850 which was taken from Homer's *Iliad* 5.386. This
means "Ares endured when Otos and mighty Ephialtes … him." Homer
included the world bound but the PGM writer dropped the word in that
spell and in another which uses the same verse. It refers two giants who
bound Ares in a bronze jar until Hermes liberated him. Dropping the word
appeared to be a deliberate use of word magic. Instead of binding Ares (as
this verse would do, the sentence makes him strong in the face of adversity.

Hear me, helper of men, giver of dauntless youth!
Shed down a kindly ray from above upon my life, and strength of
war, that I may be able to drive away
Bitter cowardice from my head and crush
Down the deceitful impulses of my soul.
Restrain also the keen fury of my heart which provokes
me to tread the ways of blood-curdling strife.
Rather, Oh blessed one, give you me boldness to abide
within the harmless laws of peace,
avoiding strife and hatred and the violent death *Dæmons*.
ΤΛΗ ΜΕΝ ΆΡΗΣ ΟΤΕ ΜΙΝ ΩΤΟΣ ΚΡΑΤΕΡΟΣ
Τ ΕΦΙΑΛΤΗΣ
[TL'E MEN AR-'ES O-TE MEEN AW-TOS KRA-TE-ROS T E-FEE-
AL-T'ES]
(Five times.)

MERCURY
THOTH-HERMES

I call upon the great translator of the word from which all creation
was formed. Mind of the One Thing,
Come forth from your home in Mount Kyllene in Arkadia. Be
present amongst your sheep, of which you are the great shepherd.
Come forth Champion of Akakesion, who rules the marketplace
and the crafts. Who teaches the way of business, and upon whom
all fortune rests.
Guide, Minister, Messenger who brings the highest to the lowest,
and the lowest to the throne of the One Thing.
Messenger of the Blessed Ones who holds the map of the universe
in your caduceus and knows all the ways, even to the darkest
Hades.
Guardian of the three-fold cross-roads, Slayer of Argos, the
Trickster, Contriver whose mind and tongue can destroy all. Wily,
Shifting, Many-Turning, is your name, patron of writers and
magicians.
I will invoke thee by thy name ERINNES, the giver of good
fortune for that is what you have done, and I will tell others of
your powers so that they shall lean upon thee as I have.
And they will say, Great are the deeds of Thoth-Hermes.
For you are a god amongst gods, one of the seven mighty ones.
Come forth Pronaos and lead us into the portico of your Mysteries.
For I know your forms. In the East you are an Ibis, in the West you

are a Dog-faced baboon, in the South you are wolf and in the north
you are a serpent.
I know that you come from Hermopolis.
Come to me Thoth-Hermes as I chant the holy name which you
rejoice to hear

ΑΒΕΡΑΜΕΝΘΩ ΩΘΝΕΜΑΡΕΒΑ*
(A-VE-RA-MEN-THAW AWTH-NE-MA-RE-VA)
(Eight Times)

JUPITER†
ZEUS

Most glorious of Immortals, mighty God,
Invoked by many a name, sovereign King
Of universal Nature, piloting
This world so it is in harmony with your Law.
It is good that mortals should invoke you,
For we are your offspring, and souls of all
Created things that live and move on earth
Receive from you the image of the One.
Therefore I praise you, and shall hymn your power
Unceasingly. Thee the wide world obeys,
As onward ever in its book it rolls
Where ever you guide, and rejoices still
Beneath Thy sway: so strong a minister
Is held by your unconquerable hands, —
That two-edged thunderbolt of living fire
That never fails.
Under its dreadful blow
All Nature reels; when you direct it.
The Universal Reason which, with all the greater
 and the lesser lights,
Moves through the Universe.
How Mighty you are,
The Lord supreme for ever
No work is formed apart from you, O God,

---

* This 12-letter word means "Lord of the Waters" and is a reference to
Thoth as the creator. The world of 12 letters is reflected.

† *Hymn to Zeus* by Cleanthes of Assos (330 BCE – 232 BCE), translated by E.
H. Blakeney (1927) and slightly updated by me.

Or in the world, or in the heaven above,
Or on the deep, save only what is done
By sinners in their folly.
You can make the rough smooth,
bring forth wondrous order
From chaos, and in your sight unloveliness
Seems beautiful;
for so you have fitted things
Together, order and chaos, so that there reigns
One everlasting Reason in all.
Most bounteous God that is enthroned
in clouds, the Lord of lightning, save mankind
From grievous ignorance!
Oh, scatter it
Far from their souls, and grant them to achieve
True knowledge, on whose might you rely
To govern all the world in righteousness;
That so, being honoured, we may thee requite
With honour, chanting without pause thy deeds,
As all men should: since greater guerdon ne'er
Befalls or man or god than evermore
Duly to praise the Universal Law.
"I call upon you, master of the gods, high-thundering
 Zeus, sovereign Zeus
AION IAΩ OYEE
AY-ON EE-AH-AW OO-EE
(Vibrate four times.)

VENUS*
APHRODITE-BARZAN

I invoke Golden Aphrodite,
Who wakens with her smile the lulled delight
Of sweet desire, taming the eternal kings
Of Heaven, and men, and all the living things
That fleet along the air, or whom the sea,
Or earth, with her maternal ministry.
I call upon You, the Mother and Mistress of Nymphs.
Foam-born Aphrodite, ethereal and Chthonic mother of gods and
men. All-Mother Nature, goddess unsubdued. You hold together

---

* The first part of the invocation is Percy Bysshe Shelley's (1792 – 1822)
adaption of a Homeric Hymn and the second part is PGM IV 2916

things and cause the Great Fire to revolve and keep the ever-moving BAPZAN (VAR-ZAN*) in its unbroken course.

You accomplish everything from beginning to end.

By your will the holy water is mixed and with your hands POYZΩ (ROO-ZAW)† is moved amid the stars. You control at the world's midpoint and move holy desire into human and draw men and women together and make them desirable.

Through all the days to come, our Goddess Queen. Come to these chants, Mistress

ΑΡΡΩΡΙΦΡΑΣΙ (AR-RAW-REE-FRA-SEE)
ΓΩΘΗΤΙΝΙ (GAW-TH'E-TEENEE)
ΚΥΠΡΟΓΕΝΕΙΑ (KY-PRO-GE-NEE-A)‡
ΣΟΥΙ ΗΣ ΘΝΟΒΟΧΟΥ(SOO-EE 'ES THNO-VO-CHOO)
ΘΟΡΙΘΕ (THO-REE-THE)
ΣΘΕΝΕΠΙΩ (STHE-NE-PEE-AW)

Come in, Holy Light, and give Answer, showing Your Lovely Shape!"

SATURN§
KRONOS

Oh Kronos, you who restrain the thumos of all mortals.

I call you, the great, holy, the one who created the whole inhabited world, against whom transgression was committed by your own son , you whom Helios bound with adamantine fetters lest the universe be mixed together, you hermaphrodite, father of the thunderbolt, you who hold down those under the earth

ΑΙΕ ΟΙ ΠΑΙΔΑΛΙΣ (E-E EE PE-DA-LEES)
ΦΡΕΝΟΤΕΙΧΕΙΔΩΙ (FRE-NO-TEE-CHEE-DAW-EE)
ΣΤΥΓΑΡΔΗΣ (STY-GAR-D'ES)
ΣΑΝΚΛΕΟΝ (SAN-KLE-ON)

---

* Betz drops the v in his edition and writes the word Barza and says it is Old Persian meaning "shining." Preinsendanz keeps the v making BAR-ZAN which is Old Persian and means quarter or street. It came to mean division of a city. This means the word refers to the Zodiac divided into quarters.

† Betz reads the first letters Rh while Preinsendanz just sees an R. POYZΩ could be a corruption of the Persian magic world "Zouro" could mean "purity." None of these words describes anything which can be clearly understood. It could represent the fire of passion.

‡ Word means Cyprus born

§ Adapted from PGM IV 3086

ΓΕΝΕΧΡΟΝΑ (GE-NE-CHRO-NA)
ΚΟΙΡΑΨΑΙ (KEE-RA-PSE)
ΚͪΗΡΙΔΕΥ (K'E-REE-DEF)
ΘΑΛΑΜΝΙΑ (THA-LA-MNEE-A)
Come, master, god, and tell me your mysteries for I am the one
who revolted against you.
Appear before me calm to speak about the things I ask. Help me
to understand your mysteries for I am like unto you part of Aion a
creature of chaos seeking knowledge in Order so that the universe
be maintained.
Be gracious to me lord.

THE SEVEN KINGS OF THE EARTH

The Seven Kings of the Earth are identified by the 16th century
magician Heinrich Cornelius Agrippa in his *Three Books of Occult
Philosophy** (*De Occulta Philosophia libri III*) as the planetary spirits
Zazel, Saturn, Hismael, Jupiter, Bartzabel, (Mars), Sorath, (Sun),
Kedemel, Venus, Taphthartharath, Mercury, and Chashmodai,
(Moon). While most people associate these with being outside the
sphere of the earth, the Key of Solomon makes it clear that they are
"beneath the firmament" and not celestial. The names are Hebrew,
and some seem to be sourced from Paracelsus but there seems to
be some confusion to their nature and some of this was because
Agrippa wanted to create names which fitted into his magic squares
and had to change some of the names to fit into the gematria of each
square.

Zaz, which is a Hebrew name meaning "go away", was part
of the word "Mezuzah" which was what the Israelites put on their
doors in Egypt; "death" (Mavet) "go away" (Mavet and Zaz) The
words appeared on a lot of Hebrew amulets. It is also a variant of the
name of Zeus† with Mount Zeus being Mount Zas‡. The *Grimorium
Verum* uses Zazel as a spirit to torment someone in a love spell. Some
currently think that his name was originally the Azazel who was an
important part of the Hebrew scapegoat ritual, in which the sins of the
people were given to a goat that was run into the wilderness. Bartzabel
is possibility a corruption of *Ba'al Zəbûl*, a Semitic god whose name

---

* Agrippa von Nettesheim, H. (1982). *Three Books of Occult Philosophy or
magic*. New York: AMS Press.

† Mierzwicki, T. (2006). *Graeco-Egyptian magick*. Stafford: Megalithica Books.

‡ Pherecydes (6th century BCE) developed a cosmogony, derived from
three divine principles, Zas (Zeus),[Cthonie (Earth) and Kronos (Time),

means "lord of the dwelling." Hismael is close to a corruption of Ishmael, who was the first son of Abraham, the founder of the Arabian race. Sorath could be a Hebrew transliteration of the Arabic "Surat" (aka "Surah") which is the word for "chapter" in the *Koran*. Kedemel means "East," "ancient" or "old god." Taphthartharath could come from a corruption of Thaphaboath, a gnostic demon whose name was based on the Hebrew name for Tartarus or the place of punishment*. Chashmodai is rather too close to the name of Ashmodai, an important demon who appears to have been the Syrian Hamathites God Ashima, who was based on the Akkadian fate goddess Shimti.

While only some of these "roots" may be accurate it shows that these names come from a variety of different sources, traditions and levels, none of which were especially planetary or natural. I was trained in the Agrippa system and it dovetails nicely into the *Key of Solomon* work, it also has the power that magicians have used it for a few hundred years and thus created an adequate mask for the forces they represent. However for this system it lacks a logical coherence for the nature spirits.

I look to a much older system found in the Arabic *Picatrix*† which may date to the first part of the ninth century and synthesised Sabianism, Ismailism, with Greek Hermetic texts of magic and astrology with more ancient Chaldean systems. Its Latin form was hugely influential on the magical systems of Renaissance. As a source for these spirits *Picatrix* quotes the *Liber Antimaquis* which was a Latin translation of the Arabic Kitab al-Istamatis. This book was important as it proved the survival of a Hermetic Tradition of magic within the Muslim culture‡ based around the mysterious Sabianists. §

It mentions seven planetary spirits, which are made up of six others – one for each direction, North, South, East, West, the sky and

---

* Thaphahaboath appeared in Origen's Contra Celsum which Agrippa quotes from.

† Greer, J. and Warnock, C. (2010). *The Picatrix*. Place of publication not identified: Adocentyn Press.

‡ See Hermann of Carinthia and the Kitāb al-Isṭamāṭīs: *Further Evidence for the Transmission of Hermetic Magic* Charles S. F. Burnett *Journal of the Warburg and Courtauld Institutes Vol.* 44 (1981), pp. 167-169

§ The *Picatrix* quotes ibn Wahshiyya's *The Nabatean Agriculture* which is the chief source for the Sabians, and was translated in 904 in time for it to be an influence on the writer of the *Picatrix*. The Sabians were considered the inheritors of the Ancient Babylonian system of magic along with Hermetic Greek systems.

the Earth. While many might see these as celestial figures there are several reasons to discount that:

Each planetary force is a cube, a symbol of matter.

- They need offerings which implies they are *Dæmons*.
- Their functions are all material.
- They rule the six parts of the seven climes of the Earth which come from the ancient Greek astrologer Ptolemy who listed parallels, starting with the equator, and proceeding north at seven intervals. This system was adopted in Arabo-Persian astronomy and eventually by al-Razi, the author of the 16th-century haft iqlīm ("seven climes"). Ptolemy's work, which was based on half-hour differences in the length of the solstitial day was a development of Aristotle who thought there were five zones (from north to south) Arctic, European (northern temperate) Africa (Equator) Antipodes (southern temperate zone) and Antarctic.
- They are not depicted as being either ordered or chaotic but hold the same balance as humanity and natural forces.
- These are extremely "physical spirits" according to *Liber Antimaquis* from these spirits "a spiritual virtue enters into every part of the world. From them come good and evil, fortune and misfortune to all creatures, as each one (of the spirits) is moved in its sphere, its sign, and its powers. From them come prayers, and by them (the influence of) magical workings are received, and those miracles performed that man can do, and they are assigned to the men of every part of the world, and to every man according to the share of intellect he has, and to the offices that are used by men.*"

To complicate the concept slightly, *Liber Antimaquis* says that none of the spirits are embodied. In fact three of them (above front and behind) have "nothing terrestrial" in their composition but the other spirits do. What this says is that three spirits act as the soul of nature and dwell above the firmament close to their celestial planetary source. While the other three (those of left right and below) are compounded with terrestrial things.

"The superior spirits are above, in front, and behind because the virtues of these spirits foretell the complexion and birth of man.

---

* Renaissanceastrology.com. (2018). *Spirits from the Liber Antimaquis.* [online] Available at: http://www.renaissanceastrology.com/ liberantimaquisspirits.html [Accessed 1 Apr. 2018].

The other three, which are assigned to the right, the left, and below, are embodied and conjoined to diverse bodies and plants in the manner which we have described."

In modern magical terms the spirit above is the Higher Self of the planetary spirit, the spirit before is its direction or fate; the one behind is its memory. The spirit on the right hand is its active force and the one on the left its passive, and the one below is its physical body. These add up to its total identity. In addition, both sources give the name of an eighth spirit which represents the motion of the planet when it interacts with other forces. This name becomes important when we are attempting to transform one element to another.

For example, the spirit of Saturn's name is Barimas. Its *Higher Self* is Tus; the spirit's fate is Tamas; its memory Darus, active force Darjus; passive force Qajus and its body is Harus.

This shows a hexagram of lower and higher forces which can be expressed on the Kabbalistic tree of life and a cube of matter. The name of Barimas in transformation or motion is Tahitus.

The name of the Jupiter spirit is Damahas, its *Higher Self* is Darmas, his body is Matis, its ordering force is Magis, the chaotic self is Daris, its fate is Tamis, and its memory is Farus. The name of Damahas in transformation or motion is Dahidas.

The name of the Mars spirit is Dagdijus, its *Higher Self* is Hagidis, his body is Gidijus, its active force is Magras, the passive self is Ardagus, its fate is Handagijus, and its memory is Mahandas. The name of Dagdijus in transformation or motion is Dahidas.

The name of the Sun spirit is Bandalus, its *Higher Self* is Dahimas, his body is Abadulas, its active force is Dahifas, its passive is Atiafas, its fate is Maganamus, its memory is Gadis. The name of Bandalus in transformation or motion is Tahimaris.

The name of the Venus spirit is Didas, her *Higher Self* is Gilus, her body is Hilus, her active power is Dahifas, her passive power is Ablimas, her fate is Basalmus and her memory is Arhus. The name of Didas in transformation or motion is Dahtaris.

The name of the Mercury spirit is Barhujas, his *Higher Self* is Amiras, his body is Hitis, active power is Sahis, passive power is Daris, his fate is Hilis and memory is Dahdis. The name of Barhujas in transformation or motion is Mahudis.

The name of the Moon spirit is Garnus, her *Higher Self* is Hadis, her body is Maranus, active power is Maltas, passive power is Timas, her fate is Rabis and her memory is Minalus. The name of Garnus in transformation or motion is Dagajus.

These spirits can be made in a pentacle with the names of the seven names in the outer ring with the main name of the spirit along with their sigil drawn on the magic square of the Sun. For the sake of not having to write the letters in Arabic they should be written in Theban (see page 190).

In the *Picatrix* these names are words of power and can be used as such in any magic working. A ritual invoking Garnus could focus on the chanting of her names to raise power from the matter in the immediate environment. The number of times you chant is not fixed and continues until you feel that there is enough energy in the room.

For the activation of a single force, the name of transformation or motion is not required. However, if you want to transform one force into another, perhaps using the geomantic symbols, then you should use the name of transformation or motion of the force which represents the status quo. So if you were feeling blocked or depressed (which is a state caused by Barimas) you would invoke all the names of Barimas but add the spirit which represents its transformation before invoking the names for Jupiter (Joy and expansion) or the Moon (the way forward). You would not have to invoke the eighth name for the second planet because you do not wish it to transform yet.

It is important to remember that these spirits are close to natural forces so in many respects you are speaking to physical objects and drawing the power out of them. That power needs always to be balanced which is why the Kings of the Earth need offerings. The *Picatrix* insists on some particularly unpleasant offerings including monkey brains, leopard's blood, and the occasional burnt human skull, but these can be replaced by similar symbols

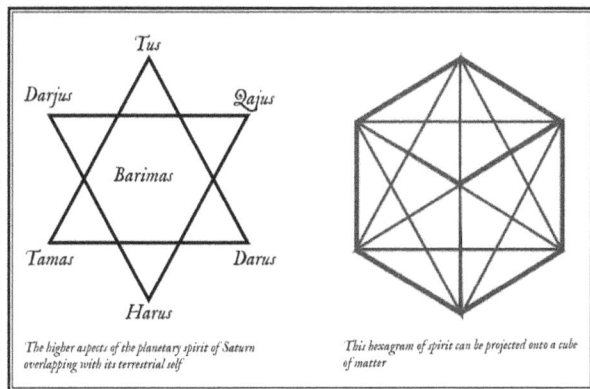

The higher aspects of the planetary spirit of Saturn overlapping with its terrestrial self

This hexagram of spirit can be projected onto a cube of matter

(such as a skull candle, red wine, and figurines of an animal). The offerings should not be given during the first ritual but should be made after the spirits have delivered on your rite's intention (after all if the spirit has ignored you then there is nothing which needs to be balanced).

In the *Picatrix* these names are words of power and can be used as such in any magic working. A ritual invoking Garnus could focus on the chanting of her names to raise power from the matter in the immediate environment. The number of times you chant is not fixed and continues until you feel that there is enough energy in the room.

Being spirits which rule the material level, they are not completely ordered or chaotic. I have a theory that the name of the "active power" is the spirit who orders matter while the "passive spirit" is chaotic, but this needs further experimentation.

In their natural state spirits are not at all anthropomorphic. When they are called, they appear in their positions above, below, left, right behind and before the circle. They appear as a presence rather than using any form and space; vibrate and focus on the centre of the room. When the names are chanted the power is drawn up from the floor into a cone of spiralling energy. It is a good idea to use this centre of power to place your pentacle of the spirit, any candle or offerings. This power can be focused using the geomantic symbols mentioned below. However, it is possible to use forms based on their associated tarot court card if they are used alongside geomantic forces.

In my book *Making Talismans* I say that using planetary Earth spirits is like negotiating with the electricity to turn on an electric light and recommend working with "safer" planetary angels instead. While I still see working with the planetary Earth spirits as harder, working with them sometimes becomes vital. There is a need to "earth" higher workings, particularly those which need a physical effect. The Kings of the Earth can make that happen. Initial offerings should be made during the ritual, particularly wine or meat or incense, to draw the spirit to the ritual. The main offerings should not be given after the spirits have delivered on your rite's intention (after all if the spirit has ignored you then there is nothing which needs to be balanced). Don't make the mistake I did and give the full offering of thanks at the first sign of a result. The Planetary Kings are not angels or gods who will "know what you mean" and automatically continue their work. The spirits have absolutely no sense and will say "thanks every much" and down tools. It is helpful to think of them like computer data which has an on-off switch and controlled by the other beings you invoke.

For the activation of a single force, the name of transformation or motion is not needed. However, if you want to transform one force into another, using the geomantic symbols, then you should use the name of transformation or motion for the force which represents the status quo. So, if you were feeling blocked or depressed (which is a state caused by Barimas) you would invoke all the names of Barimas but add the spirit Tahitus which stands for its transformation before invoking the names for the Jupiter (Joy and expansion) or the Moon (the way forward). You would not have to invoke the eighth name for the second planet because you do not wish it to transform yet.

During any invocation make seven copies of the King's pentacle. Place one under the altar, and one in the East, South, West and North of the circle. Make a paper crown and place one pentacle on it. This will provide you with some protection from the spirit hurting you while at the same time helping your *Sphere of Sensation* adapt to the spirit's force. Place the last seal on the altar which you are calling the spirit.

BANDALUS

Planet: Sun

Divine Names:
Bandalus answers to the divine names of Helios.

Names of Parts:
His *Higher Self* is Dahimas, his body is Abadulas, his active force is Dahifas, his passive is Atiafas, his fate is Maganamus, his memory is Gadis. His name in transformation or motion is Tahimaris.

Names of Power:
Bandalus, Dahimas, Abadulas, Dahifas, Atiafas, Maganamus, Gadis. The other name used to transform or move him is Tahimaris.

Elemental Nature:
Fire.

Gods:
He is a direct reflection of Helios Apollo and the Sun Gods.

Ray:
Yellow.

Tarot:
By day (i.e.a day chart) Bandalus takes the form and nature of the Knight of Wands. By night takes of the form and nature of the Princess of Swords.

Functions and Nature:
Bandalus rules all birds in the earth, Water, Air, Earth or Fire. He is naturally honest, punctual and has a great desire to rule, and

command. He gives great and wise judgement and is hard-working. He speaks slowly, with confidence, and great gravity, but is inclined towards secrets. Bandalus sees what thoughts enters a person's heart and respects honour. He makes humans proud, arrogant, domineering and interested in show. Yet such influenced humans follow Bandalus's lead and believe that everything is ruled by them.

Plants:
Plants attributed to Bandalus are those which smell pleasant or have lots of flavour. They have yellow or reddish colours. He tends to like sweet and sour herbs which are sharp and a little bitter. They have the effect of dissolving malignant magic, clear the eye, strengthen the heart, or resist poison. These include Saffron, Laurel, Pome Citron, Vine, St Johns Wort, Amber, Musk, Ginger, Marigold, Rosemary, Cinnamon, Eyebright, Pyony, Barley, Lignum, and Aloes.

Trees:
Bandalus rules the Ash, Palm, Laurel, Frankincense, Cedar, Heliotrope, Orange, Lemon and Sunflower.

Animals:
Lion, Horse, Ram, Crocodile, Bull, Goat and Glow-worms.

Fish:
Sea calf, Crabs, Starfish.

Birds:
Eagle, Cock, Phoenix, Nightingale, Peacock, Swan, Buzzard, Goshawk and Flies.

Minerals, Metals and Stones:
Gold, Hyacinth, Crisolite, Adamant, Carbuncle, Stones found in Eagle's Nests and Ruby.

Seasonal Associations:
Bandalus can be seen in the spring flowers, in the summer heat, autumn mists and gentle winter rain.

Countries:
He rules Italy and the Czech Republic.

Days and Hours:
Bandalus is strongest in the first and eighth houses of Sunday.

Colours:
He likes the colour of yellow, gold, scarlet and all reddish colours.

Enemy:
Baramus.

DIDAS

Planet:
Venus.

Divine Names:
Didas answers to the divine names Aphrodite, Venus and Hathor.

Names of Parts:

Her *Higher Self* is Gilus, her body is Hilus, her active power is Dahifas, her passive power is Ablimas, her fate is Basalmus and her memory is Arhus. The name of Didas in transformation or motion is Dahtaris.

Names of Power:
Didas, Gilus, Hilus, Dahifas, Ablimas, Basalmus and Arhus. The other name used to transform or move her is Dahtaris.

Elemental Nature:
Earth.

Gods:
She is a direct reflection of Venus and the Love Gods.

Ray:
Green.

Tarot:
By day she takes the form and nature of the Princess of Cups. By night she uses the form and nature of the tarot card King Of Swords

Functions and Nature:
Didas rules the South Wind. She stands for humour, mirth and the mating instinct in nature. She brings a pleasant feeling and calms all quarrels. She is involved in any process which requires the bringing together of people.

In her most earthly aspect, she is dangerous and leads to obsession, but at her highest she brings the highest divine impression to Earth.

Didas brings a love of beauty and sensuality, but situations of jealousy and passion. She has expensive tastes and is the same persistent current which has bought pornography to the world and made prostitution its oldest profession. However, she is the inspiration behind all arts and craft which upholds beauty of form She is the spirit behind the fashion and entertainment subculture with all the depth that entails.

Plants:
Anything which has a sweet flavour, white Flowers, Green Myrtle, Apples, Rose, Fig, White Sycamore, Wild Ash, Turpentine Tree, Olive, Orange, Mug Wort, Ladies Mantle, Balm, Vervain, Walnut, Almonds, Amber, Musk, Peaches, Apricot, Plums and Raisins.

Animals:
Hart, Panther, Small Cattle, Coney, Calf, and Goats.

Birds:
Sparrow, Wagtail, Stockdove, Hen, Nightingale, Thrush, Pelican, Partridge, Wren, Swan, Owl, Blackbird, Parrot, Swallow and Magpie.

Fish:
Dolphin.

Minerals, Metals and Stones:
Copper, White Brass, Cornelian, Sky Sapphire, White and Red Coral, Lapis Lazuli (because it banishes melancholy) and Beryl.

Seasonal Associations:
In summer she manifests as clear weather but in winter rain or snow.

Countries:
Arabia, Austria, Iran, Iraq, Turkey, Cyprus and North Africa.

Days and Hours:
Didas is strongest in the first and eighth houses of Friday.

Enemy:
Baramus.

BARHUJAS

Planet:
Mercury

Divine Names:
Barhujas answers to the divine names Hermes, Mercury and Thoth.

Names of Parts:
His *Higher Self* is Amiras his body is Hitis, his active power is Sahis, his passive power is Daris, his fate is Hilis and memory is Dahdis.

The name of Barhujas in transformation or motion is Mahudis.

Names of Power:
Amiras, Hitis, Sahis, Daris, Hilis Dahdis. The name of Barhujas in transformation or motion is Mahudis.

Elemental Nature:
Air.

Gods:
He is a direct reflection of Thoth, Mercury, and the gods of knowledge

Ray:
Orange.

Tarot:
By day takes the form and nature of the Queen of Swords. By night he uses the form and nature of the tarot card Knight of Disks.

Functions and Nature:
Barhujas is the divine mind in creation. He supplies a subtle mind which is the source of intelligence. He is the force which drove humanity to develop speech, communication, and higher thought. Because of his communicative nature, he also can help with providing the power behind divination, which is a method of communication with the gods. Barhujas rules the marketplace and travel. He is apt to find faults in others and exploit them and he has a strong "trickster" element. He also tends to transform when he is close to other spirits. So if he is used with Didas he will take on a merry nature, but can be heavy and pessimistic if used with Barimas. He controls, merchants, scientists, astrologers, administrators, writers, lawyers and messengers.

Plants:
Any flowering plant which likes sandy barren places. They often bear seeds in pods. They rarely smell and are often connected to the brain. This includes, Walnut, Filbert Tree, Nut, Elder, Adders-Tongue, Dragon-Wort, Lung-Wort, Aniseed and drugs used to aid divination.

Animals:
Hyena, Baboon, Fox, Squirrel, Weasel, Spider And Greyhound, Wolf, and Serpent.

Birds:
Linner, Ibis, Parrot, Jay Swallow, and Crane.

Fish:

DIDAS

King of Venus Didas

BANDALUS

King of the Sun Bandalus

BARIMAS

King of Saturn Barimas

DAMAHAS

King of the Jupiter Damahas

DAGDIJUS

King of Mars Dagdijus

BARHUJAS

King of Mercury Barhujas

GARNUS

Queen of Moon Garnus

Mullet and Forkfish.

Minerals, Metals and Stones
Mercury, Millstone, Firestone, Topaz, and stones with many colours.

Seasonal Associations:
Windy, stormy and violent weather, hail, thunder at any time of the year. In hot countries he is said to cause earthquakes.

Countries:
Southern Greece and Egypt.

Days and Hours:
He is strongest during the first and eighth hours of Wednesday.

Enemies:
Bandalus (the Sun overwhelms him), Garnus (who is too emotional) Dagdijus (who is too violent)

GARNUS

Planet:
Moon.

Divine Names:
Garnus answers to the divine names Hekate, Selene, Artimus, Persephone, Isis and Diana.

Names of Parts:
Her *Higher Self* is Hadis, her body is Maranus, her active power is Maltas, her passive power is Timas, her fate is Rabis and her memory is Minalus. The name of Garnus in transformation or motion is Dagajus.

Names of Power:
Garnus, Hadis, Maranus, Maltas, Timas, Rabis, Minalus. For rituals involving Garnus in transformation or motion add the name Dagajus.

Elemental Nature:
Air/Earth.

Gods:
Hekate, Diana, Artimus, Persephone and all the Moon gods.

Ray:
Violet.

Tarot:
By day Garnus takes the form and nature of the Princess of Cups. By night she uses the form and nature of King of Cups.

Function and Nature:
Garnus is a complex figure in that she is has a double function as the unseen ruler of all the Earth who moves the others. This power can be seen in her two geomantic symbols which are the most important. She delights in new things and is in continual motion. She creates sudden and irrational fear and tends to love peace at all costs. Garnus rules the addictive personality and the metaphorical gypsy who refuses to settle anywhere or with anyone. In modern terms she is the unconscious self. She teaches all skills but to a basic level. She rules all women and the astral shells of the dead. She is the emotional and instinctive nature.

Plants:
Any plant with soft, thick ivory leaves with a watery or slightly sweet taste. Plants which grow in watery places and grow quickly. Or those with shady, great spreading leaves. This includes, Colwort, Cabbage, Melon, Gourd, Onion, Garlic, Mandrake, Poppy, Lettuce, Rape, Lindon and Mushrooms.

Animals:
All fish or creatures that live in the water, Frogs, Otter, Snakes, Dogs, Weasels, and Snails.

Birds:
Seagulls, Gannets, Geese, Ducks, Owls, and Cuckoo.

Fish:
Cockle, Shell-Fish, Crab, Lobster, Tortoise and Eel.

Minerals, Metals and Stones
Silver, Selenite, Soft Stones, and Crystals.

Seasonal Associations:
Garnus works with the different spirits to create different weather patterns. She takes the energy of Mars to create violent wind and red clouds, Venus to create rain, Mercury wind gusts, Saturn dark clouds and cold winds, Jupiter gentle winds and light rain. Garnus works with the Sun to create specific seasonal weather.

Countries:
Holland, Scotland Denmark, Norway, Sweden.

Days and Hours:

He is strongest during the first and eighth hours of Monday.

Enemies:
Barimas (restricts her movement and represents a more celestial rather than "local" time) and Dagdijus (more aggressive and active).

DAGDIJUS

Planet:
Mars.

Divine Names:
Dagdijus answers to the divine names Aries, Mars, Set and Typhon.

Names of Parts:
Dagdijus, his *Higher Self* is Hagidis, his body is Gidijus, his active force is Magras, the passive self is Ardagus, his fate is Handagijus, and his memory is Mahandas. The name of Dagdijus in transformation or motion is Dahidas.

Names of Power:
Dagdijus, Hagidis, Gidijus, Magras, Ardagus, Handagijus, Mahandas. For rituals involving Dagdijus in transformation or motion add the name Dahidas.

Elemental Nature:
Water.

Gods:
Mars, Aries, Hephaestus, the war and metal working gods.

Ray:
Red.

Tarot:
By day Dagdijus takes the form and nature of the King of Wands. By night he uses the form and nature of Knight of Cups.

Functions and Nature:
Dagdijus is masculine, hot, dry and fiery. Be brings everything to conflict and creates quarrels. He is the ultimate warrior and is full of courage and bravery but lacking in reason. He will not obey anyone and is extremely proud. At his best he is a chivalrous knight or honourable Achilles, but at his worst he is a psychopathic thug and a pirate. He is easy to summon but difficult to control. Calm wisdom usually works sometimes summoning Didas. Dagdijus is good for practical assignments than spiritual attainment. That said he has a talent for strategy and dominates other people. Dagdijus is the spirit

of sports.

Dagdijus can be incautious, impulsive, indiscreet, reckless, brutal, jealous, rancorous, and cynical. In nature he is the force which drives conflict which is normally about resources. He is also the natural drives and energy. Dagdijus is action, and desire. It is the survival instinct and is the animal nature. Everything that sticks, cuts or penetrates belongs to Dagdijus, syringes, surgical operations and surgeons. He can be invoked to make a surgeon skilful.

Plants:
Any red, yellow or fiery colours, like Saffron, or whose taste is bitter sharp or burns the tongue, or love to grow in dry places, corrode, or sting such as Nettles, Thistles, Harrow, Cammock, Devils Milk, White And Red Brambles, Onions, Horehound, Leeks, Dittany, Pepper, Mustard Seeds, and Raddish. All prickly trees such as te Thorn and Chestnut.

Animals:
Panther, Tiger, Hunting Dog, Vulture, Fox, Horse, Wolf, Leopard, and Ass.

Birds:
Hawk, Vulture, Kite, Crow, Owl, Raven, Comorant, and Magpie.

Fish:
Pike, Sharks, Forkfish and Jellyfish.

Minerals, Metals and Stones:
Iron, Antimony, Arsenic, Brimstone, Ochre, Adamant, Loadstone, Bloodstone, Jaspar, Touch Stone, and Vermilion.

Seasonal Associations:
Dagdijus creates red clouds, thunder, lightning, hot air, fair weather, and the western winds.

Countries:
Germany, Israel, North Korea, Japan, Mongolia.

Days and Hours:
He is strongest during the first and eighth hours of Tuesday.

Enemies:
All the other Spirits are his enemy other than Didas.

DAMAHAS

Planet:

Jupiter.

Divine Names:
Damahas answers to the divine names Jupiter, Zeus, YHVH, IAO and Amon.

Names of Parts:
Damahas' his *Higher Self* is Darmas, his body is Matis, his active force is Magis, the passive self is Daris, his fate is Tamis, and his memory is Farus. The name of Damahas in transformation or motion is Dahidas.

Names of Power:
Damahas, Darmas, Matis, Magis, Daris, Tamis, Farus. When Damahas in transformation or motion Dahidas.

Elemental Nature:
Water.

Gods:
Jupiter, Zeus, YHVH, IAO and all the lightning gods or rulers of the gods.

Ray:
Blue.

Tarot:
By day Damahas takes the form and power of Queen of Wands. By night he uses the same form and nature of Queen of Cups.

Functions and Nature:
Damahas is an expansive force which looks to rule and dominate. However, unlike Mars it does this by the power of its natural authority. He is a creator and desires to create new forms. He appears as a man in his prime, usually seated on a throne or in a chariot. He has the winged eagle of victory about him and he holds a thunderbolt. Although he is a supreme force in nature, he is still bound to uphold fate. He will supply oracles.

Plants:
The plants of Jupiter include edible fruits and nuts as well as those with a pleasant odour. Agrimony, Alexander, Almond, Anise, Apple Tree, Apricot Tree, Ash Tree, Arnica, Aparagus, Basil, Bay, Beet, Balm, Betony, Blueberry, Borage, Bodhi, Carnation, Chestnut Tree, Chicory, Comfrey, Colstfoot, Current, Clove, Dandelion,

HELIOS UNBOUND

Eglantine, Elecampagne, Endive, Fennel, Fig Tree, Fir Tree, Ginseng, Houseleek, Honeysuckle, Hyssop, Irish Moss, Horse Chestnut, Liverwort, Maple Tree, Masterwort, Meadowsweet, Mistletoe, Mulberry Tree, Myrrh, Nutmeg, Oak Tree, Peppermint, Raspberry, Roses, Sage, Sandalwood Sorrel, Sugar Cane, Sumac, Sycamore Tree, Tomato and Witch Grass.

Animals:
Human, domestic animals and those with cloven hooves such as Sheep, Oxen, Deer, those which are speckled and beautifully coloured, and edible, or speaking, or trained such as Lions, Cheetahs, and Leopards.

Birds:
Birds with straight beaks, grain eating, which are not black, pigeon, Francolin, Peacock, Domestic Fowls, Hoopoe, Lark and Eagle.

Fish:
Anchia or the Sheath fish.

Minerals, Metals and Stones
Marcasite, Tutty, Sulphur, Red Arsenic, All White And Yellow Stones, Stones Found In Ox-Gall. Tin, White Lead, Fine-Brass, and Diamond

Seasonal Associations:
Dagdijus rules July and brings gentle breezes. He can also bring storms which have forked lightning which strikes the ground.

Countries:
Tuscany. France, Spain, Arabia, Turkey, Cilicia, Antalya, Paphlagonia, Central Greece, and Libya.

Days and Hours:
He is strongest during the first and eighth hours of Thursday.

Enemies:
Barimas.

BARIMAS

Planet:
Saturn.

Divine Names:
Barimas answers to the divine names Saturn, and Kronos and YHVH .

Names of His Parts:
Barimas's *Higher Self* is Tus; the spirit's direction Fate is Tamas; its Memory Darus; Active Force Darjus; passive force Qajus and its body is Harus. In transformation his name is Tahitus.

Names of Power:
Barimas, Tus, Tamas, Darus, Darjus, Qajus and Harus. When Damahas in transformation or motion add the name Tahitus.

Elemental Nature:
Earth.

Gods:
Saturn, Kronos and YHVH and all the time gods and Law givers.

Ray:
Indigo.

Tarot:
By day Barimas takes the form and power of Queen of Disks. By night he uses the form and nature of King of Swords.

Functions and Nature
Barimas is a restrictive force behind nature and matter. He expresses most obviously as time and the actual form that life takes around us. As a limiter he is associated with death and is seen as malefic in astrology, but the Romans associated him with agriculture, which has as its function the death of plants. He brings about endings and limits.

Plants:
The plants of Saturn include the Daffodil, Dragonwort, Rue, Cumin, Hellebore, Benzoine, Mandrake, Opium, and any plants which give a "high". Also, any plants which do not require sowing, and never bear fruit. Plants which bring forth dark berries, or black fruit, as the Black Fig-tree, the Pine-tree and Cypress. Yew, or any tree with a rough, or a bitter taste, strong smell, or which has a black sap. Any poisonous plant.

Animals:
Lone, Solitary, Nocturnal Creatures and those which eat their own young. Ape, Cat, Hog, Mule, Camel, Bear, Mole, Asses, Wolf, Hare, Dragon, Basilisk, Toad, Serpents, And Creeping Insects, Scorpions, Pismires, and such things comefrom putrefaction, in water, or in the ruins of houses such as Mice, And Vermin.

Birds:
Birds which have long necks, and harsh voices, as Cranes, Ostriches, and Peacocks, which are dedicated to Saturn, and Juno. The screech-Owl, Horn-Owl, Bat, Lapwing, the Crow and Quail.

Fish:
Eel, Lone Fish, Lamprey, Dog-Fish, Tortoise, Oysters, Cockles, and Sea-Sponges.

Minerals, Metals and Stones:
Lead, and Gold, by reason of its weight, and the Golden Marcasite. Onyx, Sapphire, Brown Jasper, Chalcedon, Loadstone, and all dark, weighty, earthy rocks.

Seasonal Associations.
Dagdijus rules July and brings gentle breezes. He can also bring storms which have forked lightning that strike the ground.

Countries:
Macedonia, Bulgaria, Serbia, India, lesser Asia, Iran, Iraq and Ethiopia.

Days and Hours:
Dagdijus is strongest during the first and eighth hours of Saturday.

Enemies:
Damahas.

GEOMANTIC SYMBOLS

Sigil	Meaning	Planet	Ruling Spirit
⁞	Via (Way)	☽	Garnus
⁙	Puer (Boy)	♂	Dagdijus
⁛	Admissio (Loss)	♀	Didas
⁙	Albus (White)	☿	Barhujas
⁛	Conjunctio (Union)	☿	Barhujas
⁙	Puella (Girl)	♀	Didas
⁛	Rubeus (Red)	♂	Dagdijus
⁙	Aquisitio (Gain)	♃	Damahas
⁙	Carcer (Prison)	♄	Barimas
⁙	Tristitia (Sorrow)	♄	Barimas
⁙	Laetita (Joy)	♃	Damahas
⁙	Cauda Dragonis (Dragon's Tail)	♄	Barimas
⁙	Caput Dragonis (Dragon's Head)	☋ ♃	Damahas
⁙	Fortuna Major (Greater Fortune)	☉	Bandalus
⁙	Fortuna Minor (Lesser Fortune)	☉	Bandalus
⁙	Populus (People)	☽	Garnus

Geomancy is better known as a form of Earth divination, but the magical use of the symbols has been known since the Dark Ages and at various points was integrated with Western alchemical systems and magic. It is included here as a way of working with the planetary Earth spirits mentioned above and although it is much later than the pagan period the astrology it is associated with is more Hellenistic than Modern and it has worked well for me.

Each symbol is created from four binary lines much like lines of a tiny computer code. The Earth spirits are symbolically made up of each of these lines of code which works a ☋ little like DNA.

The Kings of the Earth are built from and focus the magical ideas of these bits of binary code. They are also transformed by interaction with other pieces of binary code to create other patterns.

Each Geomantic sign has four elemental levels which follow the platonic order of Fire, Air, Water and Earth. Each element is present in some form in each. This elemental state can be active

The top line is fire, the second line is Air, the third is water and the fourth is Earth. When there is a single dot, the element is active, but two dots mean that it is passive. Via ( ) with four dots is considered the perfect elemental balance. There is an occult maxim which states when all four elements are in balance then it creates a fifth, that of spirit, which enables movement. Populus ( ) has all the elements passive which means that it is inert. Geomancy says that Populus needs the energy of other symbols to give it any direction. A spirit rules each geomantic symbol. Normally these are the Agrippa spirits but this book uses the names in the *Picatrix* to keep a degree of consistency.

Within the structure of these symbols it is possible to add another to them to transmute them. If we were feeling trapped or stuck in a rut that would be the symbol Carcer ( ). If we wanted a way out we could work with the Conjunctio symbol ( ). The top and bottom lines would be 1+2=3 or an odd number and one. It would leave Carcer's active fire and Earth as it is. But the water and air lines (2+1=3 or one) would be transformed from passive to active. The new symbol which would be created because of work with Conjunctio would result the Via symbol ( ). In this example the action of invoking or contemplating what Conjunctio means suggest the process of uniting opposites, making contact, doing the absolute opposite of whatever you are doing now. Invoking that force would give you the power to do that and create your own way.

You could also do an air and water rite with the intention of flicking the switch on the parts of Carcer (with Tahitus) which are latent. This would transform the natural force you are facing into a different geomantic pattern.

Name	Meaning	Astrology	Element	Court Card	Spirit King
Puer	Boy	Mars in Aries	Fire of Fire	Queen of Wands	Dagdijus

Use:	Symbols of Puer reflect active, raw energy symbolic of the first day of spring. It is the force if initiation when life starts to awaken after winter. It represents male sexual energy and testosterone and activates aggression and general competitive behaviour. It can bring about sudden change, normally through conflict. It can also be used for creativity, energy, enthusiasm, physical prowess and courage. It is a symbol for the enforcement of justice and it can be an effective requirement of a rite to promote leadership qualities (although certainly not on its own as it lacks the power to plan). It is unstable and does not last. It is a perfect energy to invoke before exercise or sport, but it will burn out quite quickly. Most of this energy will be directed to nature rather than the intellect or emotions. Puer insists on a physical result with the least engagement of the brain. The symbol activates the ego, which sometimes can be important, it can be useful at times when you have no personal ability to stand up for yourself. Or if you desperately need to start a project, or end procrastination. It is not compatible with any magic which requires things like reconciliation, or even to get on very well with people. The symbols of Puer have a strong influence over the physical body of a living being, its personality, ego and natural tendencies. However they are weakened by matters which require co-operation with others, partnership or any form of relationship or dependence. This includes enemies or predators where the solitary nature of Puer would be overcome.
Mantra/ Word of Power	OB (Ō B)
Part of the body	Left Shoulder
Ray	Red

Name	Meaning	Astrology	Element	Court Card	Spirit King
Amissio	Loss	Venus in Taurus	Water of earth	King Of Disks	Didas

Use:	This symbol causes anything good or bad to be pushed away or to lose power. It is a good symbol for a banishing or to use in the exorcism of a room. If it is attached to a name it will have the effect of causing that individual to be removed from the person's life. It is also useful to remove negative people or get over a broken relationship.
	
	    In nature it represents any repelling force (such as repelling magnets). It is the force which causes loss – particularly financial loss. It obviously could be used negatively as part of a curse or to attempt to bring another ruin. However it is easy to detect, and counter and it is not so strong at taking things in which you do not have a personal stake. It is good for clearing the ground to allow new growth.
	
	    Magic using amissio must be carefully focused as it is negative. So, while you could use it to banish poverty, what it would do is create a vacuum or limbo when you really wanted wealth.
	
	    Amissio symbols are more powerful in magic focused on making material possessions and objects go away and is less effective at moving things like hate or revenge. It is also weak at banishing the dead or possessions which do not belong to you. While it is good at dealing with a break-up it is not so strong at breaking up existing relationships or dealing with bad sexual habits.

Mantra/ Word of Power	HZ (aspirate z) ('eh z)
Part of the body	Right hand
Ray	Green

Name	Meaning	Astrology	Element	Court Card	Spirit King
Albus	White	Mercury in Gemini	Air of Air	Knight of Swords	Barhujas

Use:	This symbol represents consciousness, which exists in everything in nature. It might be consciousness which works at another level, or slower than humanity but it is still there. Invoking this natural form of consciousness can be used to enhance your own natural intelligence, it can also be used to understand the awareness of your environment. This is not the same as animistic thinking when inanimate objects have a personality. Having consciousness does not mean that your toaster believes in Silicon Heaven, it just means that it is aware and alive at a certain level. 　　　Albus is a good symbol to assist in Psychometry, a form of extrasensory perception which allows you to make relevant associations from an object of unknown history by making physical contact with that object. It is useful in magic which involves communication. As a reversed Rubus it can be used to resolve disputes and conflicts, through communication and diplomacy. 　　　It is stronger when used in magic which involves your immediate surroundings because it enables communication with the spirits behind objects which are close to you. It is strong in magic to help in school – in language and communications. Albus is weakened when attempting to carry out its function over a long distance. You cannot invoke it to aid communication between Israel and Palestine unless you lived in those countries. It is not useful for magic involving the higher human mind aspects such as abstract mathematics, philosophy or general magical practices. This is because Albus comes from a less abstract form of intellect.
Mantra/ Word of Power	EK (ai(r) kay)
Part of the body	Solar Plexus
Ray	Orange

Name	Meaning	Astrology	Element	Court Card	Spirit King
Populus	People	Moon in Cancer	Fire of Water	Queen Of Cups	Garnus
Use:	This symbol represents the lunar memory of the world and is connected with ancestors and the dead. It is a good symbol to use when dealing with ancestors or hero contacts as Populus creates a psychic dial tone which you can use to make a communication. Heroes and ancestors were important contacts for a magician in ancient times, often being the force which was used to deliver the magic to the place it had to go. It has a practical effect on human group-minds. These are powerful elemental collective entities which can build into gods under the right circumstances. The relationship that football fans have with the spirit of their club is a similar concept. Some businesses have attempted to create similar group-minds with their customers or within the company. Populus can be used in magic designed to control group-minds While Albus was the mind of the nature, Populus is the memory of its experiences which is contained in the cells. It might also be the force which causes hauntings and atmospheres in some places. Populus is strong in matters relating to your own family and home because these are the spirits to which you are closest. It is weaker at dealing with problems relating to authorities (such as your boss, or the government) because these automatically control groups of people.				
Mantra/ Word of Power	AL (Ah l)				
Part of the body	Left side of ribs				
Ray	Violet				

Name	Meaning	Astrology	Elemental	Court Card	Spirit King
Fortuna Major	Greater Fortune	Sun in Leo	Water of Fire	King Of Wands	Bandalus
Use:	Symbols of Fortuna Major provide the very important solar force within matter. The Sun is the distributor of spirit and the "Higher Self" for the entire solar system. This symbol has come to be associated with good luck, presumably because of a belief that if you are working with the spirit of the universe not much can go wrong for you. The goddess Fortuna represented fate, or the divine destiny for each person. \n\nThis symbol represents the Wheel of Fortune as it rises and is in your favour. Fortuna Major represented the rising Sun of the new day. Because of this position it means that the magic will start slowly and improve over time as the solar force becomes more powerful. It can be a powerful symbol of invoking spirit or new ideas into life (particularly if you use it alongside a Sunrise ritual). \n\nWhile Acquisitio is where an object is already present and needs to grow and develop. Fortuna Major can be used to make a person "invincible, and honourable". According to Agrippa it can "bring their businesses to a good end, and drive away vain dreams." \n\nFortuna Major is stronger when used in magic connected with anything to do with pleasure and happiness. It is also strong in the creation of life, including children and pregnancy. It is weakened when being used in magic which interactions with other groups of people, friends or to enhance reputation (no-one likes a winner). The power of Fortuna Major is individualised fate and not for groups which would appear to be more fixed.				
Mantra/ Word of Power	IM (ee m)				
Part of the body	Right thigh				
Ray	Yellow				

Name	Meaning	Astrology	Element	Court Card	Spirit King
Conjunctio	Union	Mercury in Virgo	Air of Earth	Knight Of Disks	Barhujas
Use:	Symbols of Conjunctio draws opposites together to create a union. These are objects which are so different they would not otherwise make a connection. This applies to people, places, or material things. This makes Conjunctio useful in relationship magic, although it is important to realise that this sort of union is more one of the head than the heart (which mean Conjunctio is better for a marriage than a passionate fling). It is good at bringing resources for projects or finding the right way to resolve a crisis. Mercury was a god of boundaries, which is the place were two regions connect. In the case of Janus, Conjunctio was the place where past met the future or where inside became outside. The Romans saw it as a destiny point. This makes the symbol important for transmutations where you want one thing to become another. The element of boundaries makes it an ideal symbol for a magic circle, because it draws the opposites of spirit and matter into the ritual. It is useful for alchemical transmutation, or to assist in mystical magic where you are seeking to make a divine connection. Conjunctio is stronger when used in magic connected with anything to do with other people, employees, animals, or situations where contact and interaction is required. It is not so useful in magic where the target is isolated and unable to interact with other people. Something about the magic depends on contact which allows Conjunctio to work. For some reason it is not so good in magic to end debt problems.				
Mantra/ Word of Power	EN (pronounced as you see it)				
Part of the body	Right side of ribs				
Ray	Orange				

Name	Meaning	Astrology	Element	Court Card	Spirit King
Puella	Girl	Venus In Libra	Fire of Air	Queen Of Swords	Didas

Use:	Puella is connected to the feminine power. This is the nurturing nature can be applied in any area of life which supports and assists growth. It has a dark side. Mothering is based on the concept of protecting a child from themselves and this can be controlling, constricting and patronising. Puella is a symbol of passive control. It does not seek to conquer by direct physical means, nor does it come from the head. Loving, sensual, passionate, playful, intense, light, dark, sad, joyful, embracing, connection, love, touch, the senses, merging into life, pleasure and through surrender. This makes it useful for romantic magic, and rituals which work through that emotional state. It can be used to put desires into constructive thought, calling for inspiration or diplomacy. It is good for magic relating to women, divorce, lawsuits and public disputes. It can create a magical glamour or improve a person's beauty. Such a glamour is likely to be an illusion based on the viewer's perception of the person rather than a physical change. Puella finds it difficult to change the personality or the physical body. The energy is instable and fickle and it needs to be linked to other forces to hold for any length of time. It is stronger when used for magic relating to partnerships such as marriage, business relationships, contracts, legalities, negotiations, and agreements. It is a co-dependant energy and is weaker at dealing with situations where someone needs to act independently. This makes it less useful at healing the physical body.
Mantra/ Word of Power	HX (aspirate x) ('ex)
Part of the body	Right thigh
Ray	Green

Name	Meaning	Astrology	Element	Court Card	Spirit King
Rubeus	Red	Mars In Scorpio	Water of Water	King Of Cups	Dagdijus

Use:	Rubeus symbols are connected to the darker side of Mars. On the positive side they can empower someone to do the impossible and allow someone to throw themselves into whatever they decide to do with concentrated energy and awesome willpower. In nature it is represented by violence, or the need to kill and hunt. Although to humans this is considered "wrong", in nature it is just part of life. Rubeus provides the total package behind that energy including the need to dominate the environment, suspicion of others, revolution, removing out-of-date systems. Rubeus symbols are good at manipulation magic or to provide the drives for a person to escape a bad situation, particularly when they are being manipulated. One side effect of Rubeus is addiction; the symbol can be used as part of a cure. It can be used to provide passion, for example, in a relationship where that appears to be lacking. It is a good symbol to use when a creative project becomes hard work and mundane and the drive to finish it is waning. Rubeus symbols are good for talismans to make intuition stronger as they help develop gut feelings. They are useful for those who are working with death magic or helping people make transitions. Their strong Scorpio power means that Rubeus is stronger when used for magic relating to death, sex, and rebirth – anything that propels a person from a safe cocoon. It is weakened in magic involving your personal possessions or money – anything that prevents freedom of movement and action.
Mantra/ Word of Power	ΟΣ (Ō S)
Part of the body	Throat
Ray	Red

Name	Meaning	Astrology	Element	Court Card	Spirit King
Acquisito	Gain	Jupiter In Sagittarius	Air of Fire	Knight Of Wands	Damahas

Use:	Acquisito symbols take objects and draw in substance from the outside environment to make them bigger. It is a material force which expands existing situations for good or bad (imagine a terrible situation extended). With Jupiter in Sagittarius we are talking about good fortune and success. It is a symbol which gives knowledge through experience and often can assist in travel. It can be used to expand outside known limits. Acquisito is a good symbol for gaining knowledge and can be used to assist studies. It can also be used to find a good teacher or obtain skills. Traditionally it is used for material gain, however the structure of Acquisto makes it less useful for this purpose because it is the sort of material gain which does not fulfil desire. The power of the symbol just brings more of the same rather than a lottery win. It can be used to develop good Jupiterian habits such as tolerance or patience. It is stronger for magic relating to philosophy, travel, occultism and finding out answers. It's also good for magic involving your extended family and the Higher Courts. It is less powerful when trying to influence your intellect, being better at subjects requiring natural wisdom rather than clever thinking. It is more high mathematics rather than helping you remember your times table. It is also less effective in magic working with your brothers and sisters or protecting computers.
Mantra/ Word of Power	YT (you T)
Part of the body	Left hand
Ray	Blue

Name	Meaning	Astrology	Element	Court Card	Spirit King
Carcer	Prison	Saturn In Capricorn	Fire of earth	Queen Of Disks	Barimas

Use:	Carcer Symbols confine and limit forces. This can be useful if the magician wants to protect a boundary, such as a magic circle, or to bind or limit a being's actions. It could be used to make a structure more solid, but it might have some restrictive aspects to it. You might use it to prevent your house walls falling, but you might be unable to leave (or sell it).
	The symbol is marked by worldliness and has an impact on your legacy – your enduring impact on society, by your actions and what you create. It could be monuments, books, buildings, theories, or the shaping of young minds (as a teacher).
	It is a symbol to create habits and re-enforce discipline. On the negative side it can create an obsession with ritual, and depression. It is excessively materialistic. Despite being limiting, it can encourage material growth, and money through hard work. However, it can represent a block or barrier which needs to be overcome before any progress can be made. It is stronger when used for magic relating to long-term planning, or something which will take a long time to come to fruition. It is strong in building a public persona (as opposed to your private one). It helps to create a strong focused and disciplined leader. It can be used in magic to work for (or against) authority figures. It is weaker in magic connected to your immediate family and house. It is too cold, damp, austere and autocratic for family life. It can create black mould and damp.
Mantra/ Word of Power	OPh (Oo F)
Part of the body	Chest
Ray	Indigo

Name	Meaning	Astrology	Element	Court Card	Spirit King
Tristitia	Sorrow	Saturn In Aquarius	Water of Air	King Of Swords	Barimas

Use:	Symbols of Tristitia depress and slow natural objects and the force has a greater impact on emotions. While Carcer imprisons, Tristitia is a reaction to limitation. It is related to melancholia which is Saturnian and caused by obsessions, fears, delusions and fixed ideas. It is an important part of intellectual life. The Italian Neo-Platonists Marsilio Ficino wrote a book devoted to the melancholy of a man of genius, suggesting that Saturn imbued those with unusual sensitivity of soul. Tristitia helps counter melancholia, and change its intellectual and creative abilities to become more positive. Tristitia with its Aquarian connection helps face negative situations in creative ways. It is through opposition that we develop and evolve. If carefully used it can be a symbol of positive change, or reverse a bad situation. Normally it has a negative short-term result which forces change. Tristitia has uses in negative magic, where you want someone to react out of fear or delusions or to get caught up in a painful situation and not see what is really happening. It could be a component in an invisibility ritual where you do not want to be noticed by another. It is stronger when used in magic for groups, and friends when we want to create a communal sense of responsibility and seriousness for the work. When we work with others we sacrifice our own aims and goals for something bigger. It is weaker when it is used for magic which will bring personal happiness as its nature is to work through sadness. It will not work on children, or anything to do with non-serious relationships or fun sexual pleasures.
Mantra/ Word of Power	OX (Oo chi)
Part of the body	Genitals
Ray	Indigo

Name	Meaning	Astrology	Element	Court Card	Spirit King
Laetitia	Joy	Jupiter In Pisces	Air of Water	Knight Of Cups	Damahas

Use:	Symbols of Laetitia expand and speed-up slow natural objects, like Tristitia, and the force has a greater impact on emotions. Laetitia was the Roman goddess of gaiety. It brings happiness and mystical and spiritual experiences. The earthy nature of the element suggests a practical and physical joy and happiness. If you are after a job or intellectual satisfaction rather than pure joy for its own sake then this is not the symbol to use.

Laetitia provides mental health when energy levels are low, or snaps a person out of a funk which has kept them from enjoying life. It speeds up situations in a positive direction or for magic related to buildings. It is good for a ritual to do with construction which will bring you joy. It improves self-image and and beauty particularly to the face. Laetitia is changeable and fickle. The symbol often needs to be tied to something else to hold it down. In Ancient Roman society, the goddess was linked to other objects such as the Emperor (Laetitia Augusta), the People (Laetitia Publicae) or the sensible words like *Fundata*, "Established" or "Well-Founded." Laetitia is stronger when used for magic in a limited and focused environment. It is strong when used for depressing subjects such as frustration, anxiety, confinement, slavery, sickness, and imprisonment. It can be used against blind spots in the personality, and poor self-esteem.

It is weaker when used for physical health, or coping with adversity, crises, and reversals of fortune, or employment. It does not mean it does not work; it is just that these things are alien to Laetitia. Laetitia is about the joy of the moment and cannot be applied to long-term important things. |
Mantra/ Word of Power	Υ Ψ (ups)
Part of the body	Head
Ray	Blue

Name	Meaning	Astrology	Element	Court Card	Spirit King
Cauda Draconis	Dragon's Tail	South Node	Earth of Fire	Princess Of Disks	Barimas

Use:	Symbols of Cauda Draconis represent the threshold where one thing moves to another, or out of someone's life. It represents change and transmutation but often does not care if the result is positive. Moon, the force behind Cauda Draconis is fluid. While it can bring destruction and change, the transitions are unlikely to be entirely destructive or to influence every aspect of a person's life. It can be used, normally with other symbols, to bring about a change in one area, particularly if it is part of a person's life which they don't want. It could be a good symbol to bring about the ending of a destructive relationship without damaging the rest of one's life. Some care is required. If you are in a miserable job and you used Cauda Draconis to take you away from it, you are more likely to see yourself fired or resigning.
	Something this destructive could be used for curses, magical defences and protective talismans, if you were being attacked. Its Saturnian nature makes it useful as a barrier protection on boundary. It could stop anything that blocks growth, or prevents things from improving.
	Positively, it can be used to collate experience and remind yourself what you are good at and what you have obtained. It is good for magic which requires you to remember something already learnt.
	It is weaker when it is used for magic connected to family (you cannot really get rid of relatives) or neighbours. It is stronger when used for magic connected to travel, or religion and occult philosophy (things which alter old perceptions).
Mantra/ Word of Power	ΑΤΟΩ (Eh Te ō Oh) (A-TO-AW)
Part of the Body	Right Foot
Ray	Violet

Name	Meaning	Astrology	Element	Court Card	Spirit King
Caput Draconis	Dragon's Head	North Node	Earth of earth	Princess Of Wands	Damahas

Use:	Caput Draconis symbols represent new beginnings, initiations, and concrete starts. The Moon/Jupiter/Venus force behind Caput Draconis suggests material expansion and growth. It is the time when the seeds start to show forth and the strongly earthy nature improves minerals, soils, root crops and anything underground. A good symbol for a baby's cot, or a first day at a school or a new job.

It can be used to increase life powers and fortune (particularly with Fortuna Major). It cancels the drama of the endings started by Caput (although it is not able to undo them). In fact if you want a bad patch to end and a new beginning, magic involving Cauda and Caput would be a good technique.

Caput Draconis is connected to your life destiny and can be used to help get you moving again. In fact, meditating on the symbol and performing the mantra can help keep your life on book. Surprisingly this will take us out of our comfort zone and force us to try new things. It can be used for assisting life changes where we begin new careers or change track after a divorce. Caput and Cauda Draconis bring unpredictable events which force people to learn through them.

It is weaker when it is used for magic connected to anything which is restrictive, or things you cannot see (ie, will not have a tangible result). It is stronger when used for magic connected to health and healing as it provides the energy to start getting better. |
Mantra/ Word of Power	ANHY (Eh eN (aspirate e) uu) sounds like Ah-en-who
Part of the body	Left Foot
Ray	Blue

Name	Meaning	Astrology	Element	Court Card	Spirit King
Fortuna Minor	Lesser Fortune	Sun in Leo	Earth of Air	Princess Of Swords	Bandalus

| Use: | Symbols of Fortuna Minor represent the forces of Sunset. It is a symbol of the beginning of the night, the light shining in the dark. It is the beginning (Genesis counted the day beginning at Sunset) and the end. The Sun is always going to have some protective aspect against darkness, but it is the herald of the dark. The east is where the Sun rises, so this geomantic symbol reverses that idea. It is the process of time as the protector of order (Aion the Roman god of time was lion faced) and the continuation of everything that was.

It provides swiftness, protection, and outside help. It can provide external success and prestige. Fortuna Minor is for cases when you need outside help rather than something that draws on your own reserves and inner power. Anything obtained using Fortuna Major can be easily lost. You should not use it for anything that requires a long-term solution as it is a transient and unstable power. You can use it to achieve a short-term goal.

It is a good symbol to help build teamwork on a short-term project, particularly if used with Populus. It could temporarily resolve a work crisis with a boss, although it might bring in outside powers which put the person in their place (which in the long-term does not resolve anything).

It is weaker when it is used for anything needing a long-term approach, such as major hopes or dreams. It is less successful working directly on large groups of people or friends. Any outside help will have to be for you or no-one else (Leo is a rather egotistical sign). It is stronger when used for magic connected to pleasure and happiness as no-one expects these to last. |
|------|------|
| Mantra/ Word of Power | IM (Ee M) |
| Part of the body | Left Thigh |
| Ray | Yellow |

Name	Meaning	Astrology	Element	Court Card	Spirit King
Via	Way	Moon in Cancer	Earth of Water	Princess Of Cups	Garnus

Use:	Symbols of Via represent life's journey. It can be used when we have somehow lost sight of what we are supposed to be doing and have become bogged down in living life. In nature, it is the driving force which creates movement whether it be for migration patterns or evolution. It can manifest when we desire to leave a house or country and live somewhere new. Via symbols create a natural change or movement. It is good for magic to protect a person while travelling or even when trying to learn something new. It can help in the rehabilitation process following an injury. It can be placed on cars or other means of transport to prevent inconvenient breakdowns. It is a good symbol to use if you are looking for a way through a problem and need ideas. It is associated with the waning Moon. Magically this is normally a time that you do the rituals to make things go away, but Via is the force that makes everything change. It changes anything active to something passive and vice versa It is one of the most dynamic figures as it changes everything around it. It has a lot in common with the chaotic dæmons in that it exists to create change as its main reason for existence. It is always moving to be stable. It can assist in pathworking, and astral projection. It can adapt aspects of yourself to help you move past any restrictions or blocks you might have about such things. It is weaker when it is used for magic connected to social status, establishment or career. This is because wanderers do not really fit into established society and companies do not like people to be constantly moving. It is stronger when used for personal space, your home and immediate family.
	AΛ (Ee L)
Part of the body	Stomach
Ray	Violet

CREATING GEOMANTIC SYMBOLS

When used magically, geomantic symbols are built from the dots which make up the four lines. There are many ways that a symbol can be drawn and in most magical books there is a lack of conformity or much in the way of logic. The rules are:

One dot can be drawn as a small unconnected circle or a small line.
Two dots can be drawn as a line or a crescent.
Three dots can be drawn as a triangle or a V shape in any direction.
Four dots can be drawn as a circle or a square.

These rules give us a wide range of magical symbols which can be used to represent the Earth energy and its pattern. Above is a good diagram below is from a 19th Century book *The Magus* by Francis Barrett*.

Each symbol is a different aspect of the Earth pattern that the hexagram represents. It probably does not matter which one you use as it will ultimately be part of the same geomantic symbol but the symbols each have something subtly different to say about the nature of the geomantic character which needs to be meditated upon. For example, Fortuna Major has one symbol which shows a orb or a cross on top of a circle. This shows Fortuna Major's divine solar nature. However, it can also be a cross over a lunar crescent which emphases its importance revealing the hidden and obscure. Understanding the meaning behind each of

---

* Barrett, F. (n.d.). *The Magus, or Celestial intelligencer.* Wellingborough, England: Thorsons Publishers.

these symbols is the key to unlocking their magical uses.

MAGICAL USES OF GEOMANTIC SYMBOLS

This section is only a summary of the magical meanings based on my own research. It would be better for research if magicians detail their own experiences with each geomantic symbol. The order of the symbols is zodiacal starting with Aries, but in an esoteric sense the symbols should really begin with Via (waxing Moon) and end with Populus (the waning Moon). The reason for this is that all the symbols are aspects of these two lunar symbols. The lunar nature of these planetary energies working in matter is the key to understanding them. The only reason we know that they are not completely lunar is that there are 16 of them which highlights the other symbolism of the elements.

Geomantic symbols are the elemental powers of the spirits of nature. Each geomantic symbol acts as a type of wand for the nature spirit. When a nature spirit takes up a geomantic symbol its nature changes. For a while I could not understand how when I invoked one nature spirit alongside his or her geomantic symbol the form changed. This became more marked when I carried out an added invocation to the Enochian spirit of the symbol. I then realised that the geomantic symbols were in effect turning the spirits into the forms of the court cards in Tarot.

The Tarot and elemental attributions here come from Pat and Christine Zalewski* and interlock nicely with the *Picatrix* and the Golden Dawn system. For example, when Dagdijus controls the Puer (Fire of Fire) symbol he manifests as the Queen of Wands. But when he takes up the (Water of Water) symbol of Rubis and he manifests as the King of Cups.

A name of power or mantra can be developed using the Greek vowel for the planet and the consonant for the zodiac sign and together encapsulate the essence of the geomantic symbol. The attribution of the part of the body (for medical magic) comes from an 18th century Arabic manuscript found in the Bibliotheque National by Stephen Skinner.†

ASTROLOGY IS THE KEY

An astrological chart acts as a blueprint for the personality and maps out its powers and outlines its earthly mission. Its use has been a feature of magic since Hellenistic times. This does not mean

* Zalewski, C. (1994). *Enochian chess of the Golden Dawn*. St. Paul, Minn.: Llewellyn Publications. Zalewski, C&P The Magical Tarot of the Golden Dawn Aeon (2008).

† Skinner, S. (1991). *Terrestrial astrology*. Arkana.

you have to be a great astrologer. Astrology is a specialisation and besides there are lots of great computer programmes out there like Janus to help.

I am a reluctant astrologer in that I have learnt just enough to get by and skip over a lot of detail which a "proper" astrologer uses. This book uses the concepts of Hellenic Astrology as these align best with this type of magic. It does so in a general way as the goal is to invoke your *Higher Genius* and not become the best astrologer in the world. However I recommend going further by reading the large and excellent *Hellenistic Astrology* by Chris Brennan.

It is important to have a computer program draw up your chart. The most useful are *Delphic Oracle* or *Janus* which have most of the settings you need. The chart itself has considerable magical power in that it has all the personal information for you and how the gods are working in your life. We use a copy of your chart as a magical image and place it on the altar so that it takes all the energy from a ritual and places it in your sphere of sensation.

For now we are going to use the astrology fairly basically so that we can work out what the gods are doing with your life.

Decide if you have a day or night time chart.

This is not difficult, if you were born between Sun rise and Sun set you will have a day time chart, which is ruled by the Sun. Otherwise you have a night chart which is ruled by the Moon.

The Ancients called these sects, and the planets and the gods behaved differently depending which one they were in. The Sun and Jupiter bring good things in a day chart, while Saturn brings bad things. Moon and Venus brings good things in a night chart while Mars brings bad. Mercury is neutral in both day and night houses and takes on the nature of those planets and houses it occupies.

Symbol	Sign	Ruling Celestial Body
♈	Aries	Mars
♉	Taurus	Venus
♊	Gemini	Mercury
♋	Cancer	Moon
♌	Leo	Sun
♍	Virgo	Mercury
♎	Libra	Venus

Symbol	Sign	Ruling Celestial Body
♏	Scorpio	Mars
♐	Sagittarius	Jupiter
♑	Capricorn	Saturn
♒	Aquarius	Saturn
♓	Pisces	Jupiter

Divide your chart in two from the ascendant. Anything that is above is connected to the day sect and the Sun while anything below is connected to night. If a planet is in its own sect (For example Jupiter is in the top half of the chart) it is happy and will express its power positively. If it is not it will be unhappy and express its powers less beneficially. If Saturn is in the side of the night, it will be hugely malefic and an important problem for the person. Likewise if Mars is in the side of the day it will cause problems.

Note if any planet is within 16 degrees either side of the Sun. This planet is under the beams of Helios and becomes hidden. This means that some aspect of the person will be hidden. So if this is Mars they might be racked with hidden conflict. If it's Venus their true feelings might never be known. If the planet is moving out of the Sun's rays within seven days then things will get better. However if they are moving into the Sun's rays things will get progressively worse. Porphyry in his Introduction said that this does not apply if the planet is in its own zodiac sign (such as the Sun in Leo), exalted or in bounds. This was called "being in the chariot" which meant you were protected from the Sun's rays.

See the zodiac sign the planet is in and if the planet is happy within it. It will be happy if it has its home there (domicile means home). When a person is at home, they have access to all their resources and are in their own element. When it is not in its home it is the guest of another planet and this might make it stronger or weaker.

According to Firmicus just as you enter the house of a person who has good fortune, so you are blessed. But if the person is suffering from poverty you end up as a partner to their grief. The more planets you have in their right home, the more brilliant your life will be (because it is closer to the archetypal Thema Mundi which was the ideal chart of God)

Note if the planet is exalted or depressed. The Sun is exalted or finds its highest expression in Aries, the Moon in Taurus, Saturn in Libra, Jupiter in Cancer, Mars in Capricorn, Venus in Pisces, and Mercury. The Sun becomes depressed in Libra, the Moon in Scorpio, Saturn in Aries, Jupiter in Capricorn, Mars in Cancer, Venus in Virgo, and Mercury in Pisces. The planet will have more power in your chart when it is exalted and less influenced when it is depressed. Depression means that it has less influence. One ancient source referred to the exalted planets as enthroned, while depressed planets as in prison. If a malefic appears in a sign that entire sign is blighted along with all the planets in it.

Note any conjunctions, oppositions, or sextiles for each planet. A conjunction is a positive union between two planets, an opposition is a conflict, a square is a difficulty and a sextile is an accord or an alliance. When trying to understand aspects it is sometimes better to see them as gods in part of a myth. Sun opposes Jupiter would make a story of Helios standing in the way of Jupiter's plans. Venus squaring (having difficulty) with Mars would be a story of a row between the two lovers (normally about sexual matters). A good planet (such as Saturn and Jupiter in a day chart) will be weakened by being tied to a bad planet such as Mars.

Check if any planet is retrograde. This weakens the planet, making its results illusionary or delayed or otherwise hindered. A person who has Mercury retrograde might not be able to communicate their ideas effectively. A person with Venus retrograde will be too withdrawn and never make the first move to find love. Retrograde hides abilities so it might be that the person needs to discover them. Some research is needed here, because if the planet was retrograde it was technically out of its proper place, so it is important to count forward a few days to see how long it takes to get back to its proper house. In cases of Mercury, that is quite quick, so it will mean that the person will have Mercury issues earlier in life but may overcome them.

THE PLANETS' TRADITIONAL MEANINGS AND IMAGES

THE SUN – HELIOS

The Sun shows a person's authority, mind, intellect, height of fortune, dealings with the gods, judgement, ego, and fame. It also rules the head, the right eye, the heart, life-breath and nerves. He appears as a beautiful naked man holding a staff. By day he has a chariot of fire; by night he sails a golden bowl. His Tarot card is the Sun.

THE MOON - SELENE

The Moon reveals a person's physical life, body, mother, conception, home, fortune, city, possessions, ancestors, expenditures, marriage, travel, way of life. She rules the left eye, stomach, breasts, spleen, membranes, and bone marrow. She appears as a woman with a Moon crown, carrying a bow and flanked by a white and black wolf.

SATURN – KRONOS

Saturn makes people petty, paranoid, and full of anxieties. He creates those who put themselves down and makes them solitary, secretive, and deceitful. Such people can be sullen, miserable but prone to travel, particularly by water. They will meet obstacles and restraints, imprisonment, accusations, tears, being orphaned. However, he makes good farmers and gardeners or those who depend on the soil. He also creates those who acquire great reputation, high status, guardians, and administrators. He is a good father to other people's children. He rules the legs, knees, tendons, watery parts of the body, phlegm, bladder, kidneys and all things hidden. He can bring violent deaths by water or strangulation. He appears as an old man dressed in black sometimes holding a scythe and hour-glass. His Tarot card is the Universe.

JUPITER – ZEUS

Jupiter signifies child-birth, desire, love, alliances, knowledge, abundance, payments, profits, justice, authorities, governments, priests, friendships, freedom, wealth, and inheritances. He rules the outer thighs, the feet, semen, the womb, the liver, the right-hand side of the body. He appears as a fit and strong man in his 40s with a lightning bolt and holding a staff of authority. His Tarot card is the Wheel of Fortune.

MARS – ARES

Mars stands for violence, wars, robbery, insolence, and adultery. theft, banishment, exile, estrangement from parents, rape, abortions, sex, marriages, loss of good things, separations, lawsuits, and hate. However, he is the power to work with one's hands, masons, and engineers. He supplies leadership abilities and rules soldiers and generals and hunting. He rules the head, buttocks and the genitals, blood, seminal passages, bile and excretion. He can create hard and abrupt changes. His tarot card is the Tower. He appears as a muscular soldier in full armour carrying a sword or spear and a shield.

VENUS – APHRODITE

Venus stands for desire and love and can represent the Mother and wet nurse. She creates priesthoods, fashion, friends, decorating, reconciliations, marriages for love, arts, music, singing, beauty, painting, and cleanness. She rules shops, measurements, weights, and games. She supplies help from women, or relatives, and she can supply a good reputation. Her tarot card is the Empress and she appears as a beautiful naked woman wearing a necklace (or girdle) and a crown.

MERCURY – HERMES

Mercury stands for education, writings and learning. He supplies the power to debate issues, use language, mathematics, and geometry. It is the force of commerce, youth, play and theft, commerce, profit, discoveries, messages, hearing. He supplies logical and critical thinking. He creates writers, teachers, doctors, lawyers, philosophers, weavers, and those in charge of strategies and planning. Mercury makes good actors and those who make a living without being stable. They are astrologers and magicians. However, he brings an irregular fortune and distractions. Mercury rules the hands, shoulders, fingers, joints, belly, hearing, intestines, tongue, and windpipe. He appears as a young man with winged sandals, and a caduceus. His tarot card is The Lovers.

EXAMPLE

This is a daytime chart (the person was born at 10.30 am) and most of the planets are in a day sect (only the Moon is not). This means that Mars's malefic power is enhanced but the Sun, Saturn and Jupiter's good sides are emphasised. Venus's power is weakened although the Moon is still strong. Venus

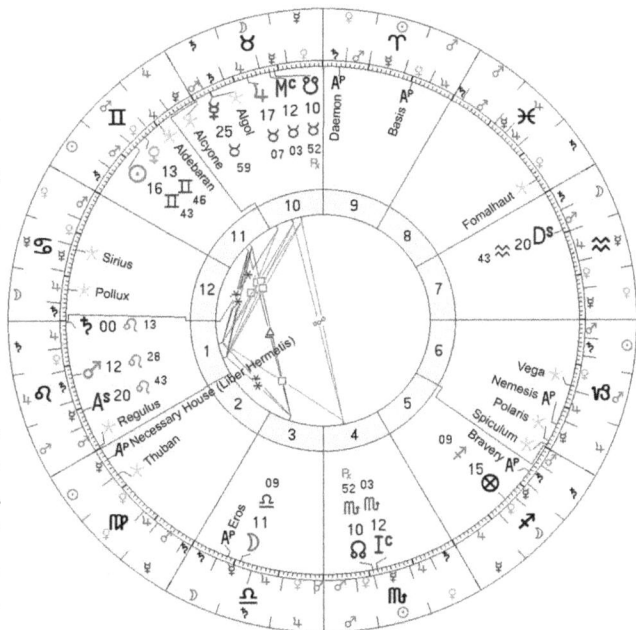

however is under the rays of the Sun. Everything associated with Venus is hidden; it has a weaker connection (a trine) to the Moon which supplies a little respite. Mercury is in its home of Gemini and is safe from the Sun. Meanwhile the Sun is OK in Gemini and in a strong position close to the mid-heaven. The Sun is sextile Mars which as we said before is a malefic and a main problem for the person. Mars is in Leo, which is not a problem for it, so it might be that the sextile might create egotistical outbursts of anger. Saturn is in Leo which is OK and since this is a day chart will express more positive aspects of itself. Jupiter is in Taurus which is OK, and it is close to the mid-heaven and sextile with Mercury. Mercury has become a benefic because it is in an acceptable position (once it escapes the Sun's rays) Meanwhile the Moon is isolated in a strong position in the night side of the chart. It does have a weak trine with Jupiter. Saturn is sextile to Mercury and since this is a day chart is showing his more benign qualities. However, Saturn and Mars are malefic, thus weakening the whole zodiac sign. Fortunately, in this chart they are weakening each other. One person suggested to me that they spend all their time fighting that they have no energy to be nasty to anyone else. In this situation the person's energy and anger might be slowed by Saturnian limitations, but this balances out as Saturn is forced to move.

The person was born with Leo as ascendant, which is ruled by the Sun, and the Sun seems to dominate the person's chart. They will have considerable authority, mind, self-image, and intelligence. This solar self will manifest in the areas of mind and communication often shouting down feelings, love, emotion and creativity. This issue will get worse as time progresses. The person might have anger issues connected to ego which they will find difficult to suppress. They might resolve a lot of their issues by being busy. Their communication skills will come to the fore later in life and become an important part of their life. This means that the person will be a precise communicator and administrator, a little too fussy and anal about their work, but nevertheless a good reliable worker.

From this we can see the roles that the gods play in this person's life and will look at the stage that they will perform on next month. From this we can see the key dynamics in their life. Helios and Hermes dominate their chart with a well-placed Jupiter capable of bringing good fortune. If anything, their Sun is too strong and the person too much in their head, a problem which will get worse as they get older. If Helios could be encouraged to turn down his light just a little, it would allow more of the person's hidden imagination and creativity to show forth. Care would be needed on the Aries/ Helios sextile as the person will aggressively respond to any challenge to their ego. If this were transmuted the same force could be used to create and build.

CHAPTER SIX
MONTH FIVE

MOON MAGIC AND THE DÆMON OF THE SOUL

The Moon was a ghostly galleon tossed upon cloudy seas.
Alfred Noyes *The Highwayman*

TASKS THIS MONTH

The goal this month is to attune to the lunar forces and the relevant mansions of the Moon. Take your chart and place it on the altar with the ascendant orientated towards the east. Take 12 zodiacal tarot cards and place in them a circle around your altar. The cards should be arranged to match the positions on your chart.

A small table or chair should be set aside for the mansion with a tealight which is placed as an offering to the *Dæmon*. There should be a tealight placed on the centre of your chart, you will need consecrated water and myrrh incense. Place a picture or statue of Hekate on the chart and the candle and the key.

Work related to the Moon is normally done at night, so you will have to do this ritual every evening. Normally you would take a year on this one phase and use the mansion of the Moon which was in the night's sky at the time. This is not possible within a six month "boot camp" so what we suggest is that you start with the mansion of the Moon which is in the night's sky now. The next day you move to the next mansion and continue around the zodiacal wheel for the next 28 days. While this will not give you the full impact of the mansions' energy, it will allow you to meet and understand the spirits which guard each one.

You will perform your normal solar invocations and *Prima Materia* exercise as normal.

NIGHT SESSION

1. Face the setting Sun and perform your normal salute to the setting Sun.
2. Perform the cross and the lesser invoking ritual of the pentagram.
3. Perform the confession (this time saying that you are under the wings of Hekate)
4. Purify and consecrate.

5. Depending on the phase of the Moon invoke Hekate (if the Moon is waning use the waning invocation etc) and light her candle.
6. Take the key to the mansion altar. Draw a zodiacal pentagram where the mansion is based. When it is drawn see it dissolve into a whirling vortex. Draw a lunar hexagram and vibrate the name Hekate six times.
7. **In the name of Hekate I invoke the spirit of the [number of the mansion] mansion of the Moon. Come forth [name of spirit] from your abode the [name of mansion]. Bring your powers to me so that I might know you and continue your work on Earth.**
8. Pour a small amount of wine into the dish
9. **I offer you this wine as a symbol of sacrifice to be an offering so that you will help me awaken my lunar self and master it.**
10. Light the tea light
11. **I offer you this flame as a symbol of sacrifice to be an offering so that you will help me awaken my lunar self and master it.**
12. **Come to my offerings [name of spirit] and teach me your mysteries as I chant your name**
13. Chant the name of the spirit for ten minutes watching the vortex over the mansion. Allow the spirit to appear as their magical image. When you have a clear image speak to the spirit and allow it to show you how it impacts on your *Lower Self*. Ask it what it needs to work better in your life where you are strong and where you are weak. You are interested in how you can use that spirit better in the future.
14. When you have finished, thank the spirit and ask it to return if you call it.
15. Say, **"I free all spirits seen or unseen who make have been trapped by this ceremony. Return to your abodes and habitations with the blessing of Hekate."**
16. **I ask the god Janus to close the doors of this ritual in the east, west, north and south and the gates to the [name of the mansion of the moon].**

The Moon is the most important planet for Magic. Much of the press about magic screams "spiritual" when most of the work that happens either takes place on the astral, or physical levels. These are known as the sub-lunar levels and ruled by the Moon. This level has everything that is underworld and above it and it extends to the Moon. The Moon's involvement with magic is so significant that some modern magicians, for whom I have a great respect, such as Jake Stratton-Kent see celestial symbols as derived from the primal and earthly and see the Moon, the four directions, the Earth and the subterranean as making up the original seven main magical forces and the planets being their later reflection.

The Moon was formed when the early universe was formed when a Mars sized planet crashed into the proto-Earth and turned the planet to vapour. As the vapour cooled , a new planet was created and its Moon. The Moon is like the earth's twin which emerged from the underworld and exerts considerable power over both. In late antiquity, it was believed that the spirits of the dead lived on the Moon and the air between the Earth.

There are three goddesses which are important to the Moon. Selene who was the Titan who was the Moon, then there was Artemis, the Hunter Goddess and then there was Hekate. In the Greco-Egyptian texts these three were often compounded and their *dæmons* and imagery confused. However, from our perspective it was Hekate, the Goddess of Magic, who is the most important.

HEKATE

Hekate was one of the "Great Goddesses" who appeared in Anatolia at the dawn of Greek civilisation. Her worship spread to Greece before the eighth century BCE when it was established enough for Hesiod almost to be an evangelist for her. She was goddess of magic, witchcraft, the night, Moon, ghosts and necromancy. She was the only child of the Titans Perses and Asteria from whom she received her power over heaven, earth, and sea.

Hekate assisted Demeter in her search for Persephone, guiding her through the night with flaming torches. After the mother-daughter reunion, Hekate became Persephone's minister and companion in Hades.

Two metamorphosis myths describe the origins of her animal familiars: the black she-dog and the polecat (a house pet kept for hunting vermin). The bitch was originally the Trojan Queen Hecuba, who leapt into the sea after the fall of Troy and was transformed by the goddess into her familiar. The polecat was originally the witch Gale who was transformed to punish her for incontinence. Other say it was Galinthias, the nurse of Alkmene, transformed by the angry Eileithyia, but received by Hekate as her animal.

Hekate was usually depicted in Greek vase painting as a woman holding twin torches. Sometimes she was dressed in a knee-length maiden's skirt and hunting boots, much like Artemis. In statuary Hekate was often depicted in triple form as a goddess of crossroads.

Hekate was identified with a number of other goddesses, including Artemis and Selene (Moon), the Arkadian Despoine, the sea-goddess Krataeis, the goddess of the Taurian Khersonese (of Skythia), the Kolkhian Perseis, and Argive Iphigeneia, the Thracian goddesses Bendis and Kotys, Euboian Maira (the dog-star), Eleusinian Daeira and the Boiotian nymph Herkyna.

Hekate was one of the "old gods" and her parents were Asteria (night) and Perses (Destruction). Unlike the other "old gods" who did not become Olympians, Hekate was respected by the Olympic gods. Hesiod's Theogony said she was favoured by Zeus and retains her sovereignty over the earth, the heavens and the sea even after the Titans are overthrown. What is odd is that all the roles of running the universe were taken by the Olympics and Hesiod implies that all of the other gods' actions must take place according to her will. So in other words if you pray to Hera it is with Hekate's agreement that it happens. All this makes sense when you consider that the other gods are celestial and to make their will happen on Earth they have to manifest through the sub-lunar level, which is ruled by Hekate. It is her who effectively makes the thought forms that their energy must travel.

During the late classical period Hekate becomes more lunar and becomes an underworld goddess of ghosts and magic. She is the goddess of oracles of the dead and the practices of necromancy, psychagogoi and Goetia. Her "old magic" nature started to come to the fore again in the second century of the Christian era. In the *Chaldean Oracles* she becomes a super-cosmic entity who mediates the powers of the One Thing to Earth. She is the ruler of destiny and saviour.

In the *Greek Magical Papyri* Hekate's image is connected to both Céline, Artimus and Persephone. From these three goddesses we can see her being Moon (Selene), hunting and animals (Artimus) and death and the underworld (Persephone).

Hekate was the goddess of crossroads and for this reason was often "married" to Hermes. They make a good couple for both are associated with magic.

Hekate is the great mediator of cosmic forces. She brings all the solar forces to earth, but she also acts as a mediator of the cosmic forces of the planets and the zodiac. There are enough similarities to her and the soul to believe that they are connected. Both:

1.Represent divine forces which are working in matter. In the *Chaldean Oracles* there are two Hekates – one is part of the divine triad and the second is the Queen of Nature. The soul is formed from the *Higher Genius* which is operating in matter through the Soul.

2. Bring higher forces into matter. Hekate draws powers of the Sun and the zodiac while the soul reflects these forces into its life.

3. Hekate is the mistress of beasts and sometimes seen as the force behind all nature. The soul, being the divine force within nature, deals with all those natural forces as part of its destiny.

IMAGERY

Hekate is clad in a long robe, holding burning torches. Hesiod's verses did not contain any allusion to a triple goddess. Her earliest known representation comes from the sixth century BCE where the goddess is seated on a throne with a chaplet bound round her head.

Later she becomes triformis, "triple-formed," (in the 5th century BC) with three bodies standing back to back - corresponding, according to those who regard her as a Moon goddess, to the new, the full and the waning Moon. In her six hands are torches, sometimes a snake, a key, her top, a whip, or a dagger.

The *Magical Papyri* say she has the head of a dog, one serpent, and one horse. In other representations her animal heads include those of a cow and a boar.

INVOCATION TO HEKATE ON A WANING MOON*

This ancient invocation is to be used each time you invoke Hekate from the time of the full Moon to the day before the new Moon. The Waning Moon is used for all magic which requires something to be reduced or banished – bad habits, or destructive people, poverty etc. The invocation involves the darker aspects of Hekate and when used you will find it bringing out the darker aspects of your soul. These are useful for some sorts of magic and should be noted rather than feared or rejected. As they arise you should meditate upon them and allow them to be placed under the control of Hekate. In this way Hekate becomes the goddess of your Lower Genius in the same way that Helios becomes symbolic of your higher. You will

---

* PGM VI 2241-2358

need a candle with the name Ἑκάτη engraved on it and an old ornate house key which you paint silver with Ἑκάτη painted on the shaft. While the titles of Hekate in this invocation might seem strange, or unnecessary, they are actually micro-invocations to the various *dæmons* who serve her.

Hail Holy Light, Ruler of Tartaros,
You who strikes with rays;
Hail, Holy Beam, who whirls up from darkness
and disrupts all things with aimless plans.
I'll invoke and may you hear my holy words
For awesome destiny is always subject to you.
Thrice-bound goddess, set yourself free.
Come and rage against those things which stand in the way of
my destiny.
For Klotho will spin out her threads for you.
Assent, oh blessed one, God in maiden form.
Awaken to me your powers to control my soul
Which is of your nature.
For I know your light in detail,
I am your magician, your minister and fellow witness
Maid.
I now adjure you by this potent night
In which your light is last to fade.
Kerberos opens and does not close its mouth.
The bar of Tartaros is opened.
Raging Kerberos, armed with a thunderbolt, appears.
Stir yourself, Mene,
You who need the Sun,
guard of the dead,
I implore you, Maid, by your strange beams,
You I implore, Oh cunning, lofty, swift,
crested one, by your dæmonic epaulettes of power.
You who draws valiant swords,
Healer, with forethought, far-famed, goading
one,
Swift-footed, brave, Darkness,
Brimo, Immortal, heedful, Persian,
Pastoral, Akyoue, gold-crowned, elder goddess,
Shining, sea-goddess, ghostly, beautiful,
The one who shows, sailer, aimer,
Self-gendered, headband wearing
Glorious, leader of hosts, goddess

of Dodona, and of Ida, with sorrows fresh,
wolf-formed,
Humanity fears you for you have been destructive,
quick, grim-eyed, shrill-screaming,
Thasian, Mene, nethermost one, beam-embracer and saviour,
dog-shaped, spinner of Fate, all-giver,
Long-lasting, glorious, helper, queen, bright, wide-aimer,
vigorous, holy and benign.
You are all these things,
Immortal, shrill-voiced, glossy-locked,
in bloom, divine, with golden face, delighting in humanity,
Minoan, goddess of childbirth, Thuban, long-suffering, astute,
malevolent.
With rays for hair, shooter of arrows,
You are full of cunning and the deliverer from fear;
as Hennes, The Elder, chief of all magicians,
I am Isis' father.
Hear:
ΗΩ ΦΟΡΒΑ ΒΡΙΜΩ ΣΑΧΜΙ ΝΕΒΟΥΤΟ ΣΟΥΑΛΗΘ
'E-AW FOR-VA VRIM-AW SACH-MEE NE-VOO-TO SOO-AL-
'ETH

For I have hidden your magic symbol [hold the candle in left hand]
within myself. I have your key [hold key] and opened the bars of
Kerberos,
the guard of Tartaros and premature night.
I plunged into darkness. I whirl the wheel for you;
Gaze at me as you gaze at yourself:
For I am your mirror, the love
charm of the Nile goddess,
Until you cast the shadowy light from your eyes.
Mare, Kore, dragoness, lamp, lightning, flash, star, lion, she-wolf
I know your good and great majestic names,
Which illuminate the heavens.
The Earth drinks dew and is pregnant;
The universe increases and declines;

ΕΥΦΟΡΒΑ ΦΟΡΒΑ
EY- FOR-VA FOR-VA

ΦΟΡΒΟΡΕΟΥ ΦΟΡΒΑ
FOR-VO-RE-OO FOR-VA
ΦΟΡΒΟΡ ΦΟΡΒΟΡ ΦΟΡΒΟΡ

FOR-VOR FOR-VOR FOR-VOR

ΒΟΡΒΟΡΦΑ ΗΡΦΟΡ
VOR-VOR-FA 'ER-FOR

ΦΟΡΒΑΙΩ ΦΟΡΒΟΡ ΦΟΡΒΟΡ ΒΟΡΟΦ
FOR-VE-AW FOR-VOR FOR-VOR VO-ROF

ΒΟΡ ΦΟΡΒΟΡ ΑΩ ΙΩΗ
VOR FOR-VOR AW EE-AW-'E

ΦΟΡΒΟΡΦΟΡ ΕΥΦΟΡ
FOR-VOR-FOR EY-FOR

ΒΟΦΟΡΕΥΟΙΕΩ ΦΩΘ ΙΩΦΩΘ ΙΩΦΩΘ
VO-FOR-EF-EE-E-AW FAWTH EE-AW-FAWTH EE-AW-FAWTH

ΦΩΘΙΩΦ ΑΩΩΩΘΩ ΩΑΙΩ ΙΩ ΕΩΩΙΩ
FAW-THEE-AWF AH-AW-AW-AW-THAW AW-A-EE-AW EE-AW
E-AW-AW-EE-AW

ΑΑΑ ΕΕ ΗΗ ΙΟΥΥ ΩΩΩ ΟΥΥΥΥ ΑΕΗΙΟΥΩ
AH-AH-AH EE 'E'E EE-OO-Y AW-AW-AW OO-Y-Y-Y AH-E-'E-EE-O-
Y-AW

YYY (UUU) Mistress, Harken-Techtha, who sits beside Lord Osiris,
Michael, Archangel, the god who lights the way,
Awaken my awareness of you within me.
Allow me to speak to your spirits so that they see you in me.

INVOCATION TO HEKATE
ON THE WAXING MOON*

This ancient invocation is to be used each time you invoke Hekate
from the time of the new Moon to the day before the full Moon. The
waxing Moon is used for all magic which requires something to
added into your life. The invocation involves the brighter aspects of
Hekate and this can bring out some of your more positive aspects.
You will need a candle with the name Ἑκάτη engraved on it and an
old ornate house key which you paint silver with Ἑκάτη written on
the shaft.

---

* PGM IV. 2708-2784

Come giant Hekate, Dione's guardian,
Persia, Baubo Phroune, dart-shooter,
Unconquered, Lydian, untamed one
Divinely born, torch-hearing, guide, who bends down proud necks,
Kore, you who've parted
Unbreakable steel gates.
O Artemis, who, too, were once procuress, mighty one,
Mistress, who burst forth from the earth, dog-leader, crossroad goddess, triple-headed,
Bringer of light, august one, virgin,
I call you fawn-slayer, crafty, infernal one,
Many-formed. Come, Hekate, goddess of three ways, who with your fire-breathing phantoms
Rules dreaded roads and harsh magic.
Hekate, I call you with those who have died before their time,
Heroes who have died without a wife and children,
hissing wildly, with yearning in their hearts.
Come forth mighty Hekate and teach me my soul's secrets.
Awaken to me your powers to control my soul,
Which is of your nature.
Hekate, of many names,
Virgin, Kore, Goddess, come, I ask,
guard and shelter of the threshing floor,
Persephone, triple-headed goddess,
You who walk on fire, cow-eyed.

ΒΟΥΟΡΦΟΡΒΗ, ΠΑΝΦΟΡΒΑ ΦΟΡΒΑΡΑ
[VOO-OR-FOR-V'E, PAN-FOR-VA FOR-VA-RA]

ἈΚΤΙΩΦΙ, ἘΡΕΣΧΙΓΑΛ
[AK-TEE-O-FEE ER-ES-CHEE-GAL]

Beside the doors ΝΕΒΟΥΤΟΣΟΥΑΛΗΘ
[NE-VOO-TO-SOO-AL-'ETH]

Gate-breaker ΠΥΠΥΛΗΔΕΔΕΖΩ [PY-PY-L'E-DE-DE-ZAW]

Come Hekate, of fiery counsel, I call you to my sacred chants. You who burst forth from the Earth.

ΜΑΣΚΕΛΛΙ ΜΑΣΚΕΛΛΩ · ΦΝΟΥ ΚΕΝΤΑΒΑΩΘ · ΟΡΕΟΒΑΖΑΓΡΑ ΙΗΞΙΧΘΩΝ
[MAS-KEL-LEE MAS-KEL-LAW FNOO KE-NTA-VA-AWTH O-RE-O-VA-ZA-GRA EE-'E-KSEE-CHTHAWN]

Earth mare ΟΡΕΟΠΗΓΑΝΥΞ · ΜΟΡΜΟΡΟΝ ΤΟΚΟΥΜΒΑΙ
[OR-EO-P'EG-AN-YKS MOR-MOR-ON TO-KOOM-VAEE]

Teach me the powers of the Moon so that I might behold the Sun.
ΘΕΝΩΒ · ΤΙΘΕΛΗΒ · ΗΝΩΡ · ΤΕΝΘΗΝΩΡ
[THEN-AWV TEE-THE-L'EV 'EN-AWR TEN-TH'EN-AWR]

**MANY-NAMED ONE,   ΚΥΖΑΛΕΟΥΣΑ ΠΑΖΑΟΥΣ [KY-ZA-LE-OO-
SA PA-ZA-OOS]**

**KALLIDÊCHMA and PSAB
[ΚΑΛΛΙΔΗΧΜΑ ΚΑΙ ΨΑΒ]
[KAL-LEE-D'ECH-MA KE PSAV]**

**Hekate of the unresting burning fire, awaken within my lower soul the
desire to unite with the higher with ORION [O-REE-ON] and MICHAEL
[MEE-CHA-'EL] who sit on high.**

**You hold the seven waters and the earth, keeping in check the one they call
the great serpent.**

**ΑΚΡΟΚΟΔΗΡΕ   ΜΟΥΪΣΡΩ   ΧΑΡΧΑΡ   ΑΔΩΝΑΪ,   ZEUS   ΔΗ
ΔΑΜΝΑΜΕΝΕΣ ΚΥΝΟΒΙ ΟΥ ΕΖΑΓΡΑ
AK-RO-KOD-'ER-E MOY-EES-RAW CHAR-CHAR AD-AW-NA-EE
ZEFS D'E DAM-NA-MEN-EFS KY-NO-VEE-OO EZ-AG-RA**

ΙΩ [Ee-Aw] **all-powerful goddess and** ΙΩ [Ee-Aw] **all-guarding one;**

ΠΩ [Ee-Ee-Aw], **all-sustaining one.**

ΖΗΛΑΧΝΑ ΚΑΙ ΣΑΑΔ [Z'E-LACH-NA KE SA-AD]

**ΣΑΒΙΩΘΗ · ΝΟΥΜΙΛΛΟΝ · ΝΑΘΟΜΕΙΝΑ
[SA-VEE-AW-TH'E NOO-MEEL-LON NA-THO-MEE-NA]**

Always, ΚΕΙΝΗΘ [KEE-N'ETH]

Stalwart ΘΗΣΥΕΣ ΟΝΥΞ [TH'E-SYES O-NYKS]

Theseus ONYX, {ON-YCH]

Prudent ΔΑΜΝΑΜΕΝΕΎΣ [DAM-NA-ME-NEFS]

**Avenging goddess, strong goddess, rite of ghosts, Persia.
ΣΕΒΑΡΑ, ΑΚΡΑ. [SE-VA-RA AK-RA]**

**Great Hekate, who spins the web of the stars and governs the
spiral of life.**

Guide me through towards pathways of understanding.

I open my mind to thee so that I can learn of your mysteries.
Awaken my lunar soul so that I might behold the solar genius.

EVIL MOON

*"The Moon replenishes the earth; when she approaches it, she fills
all bodies, while, when she recedes, she empties them."*
Pliny the Elder Natural History

What is clear from the ancient Egyptian magical manuscripts is that
there was a certain amount of a love-hate relationship with the Moon.
Much of the imagery associated with the Moon was fearful and there
was an impression given that she was to be avoided if trying to do
some types of magic. The spells within the PGM can be distributed
between Sun and Moon spells. The Sun is seen as a heavenly power
capable of providing the magician with great heavenly wisdom. The
Moon, however is used for curses, sex and working with the dead.
Some of the more dangerous spells involve working when the Moon
is full. Some magic solar magic such as the *Mithras Liturgy* cannot be
performed while the Moon is in the sky.

The reason for this is because while the Moon was powerful,
she was the force which kept nature functioning and spirits within
her orbit. She was the force which bought souls into incarnation.
Since many religions and philosophies of the period saw matter
as something terrible to be ascended away from at the earliest
opportunity then the Moon could be the dweller on the threshold
and the great limiter of spiritual progress. The *Chaldean Oracles* said
that a theurgist should not look upon the face of Physis (the goddess
of nature) and Proclus warned that the face of the Moon was Physis
which should not be gazed upon because she was like Fate. Such
thinking drew a clear line between the theurgists (god workers) and
the goetics (*dæmon* workers) which still exists today.

However, the division is based on a pessimistic dualistic
philosophy which does not reconcile matter and spirit and falls into
the trap of believing all matter is evil and spirit is good. If this duality
is removed and a middle path taken, then both philosophies work
side-by-side. The Moon can still be the force which drives souls into
manifestation; it is just that this is an important part of the process of
the one thing trying to understand itself rather than torturing poor
souls with a punishment of incarnation. The Sun is not a superior
state to the Moon, just spirit working at a different level, which is
closer to the divine connection that the soul still craves.

The Moon is also a symbol of our soul – the spirit of the *Higher Genius* which is lost in the illusion of matter. Rejecting it is rejecting the destiny that our Divine Genius wanted. Fleeing from nature is trying to escape our destiny and ultimately counter-productive. By working with the Moon, and our *"Lower Self"* we are following the pattern that our *Higher Genius* wanted to investigate when it chose to incarnate. The more we respect our natural and lunar selves, the more we start to see it as a reflection of spirit.

DÆMON OF THE SOUL

While the focus of our concentrated programme is to awaken the *Higher Genius*, it needs us to understand the *Dæmon* of the Soul which rules our life while we are in incarnation. It is the same solar spirit but has been transformed through the actions of incarnation and is effectively a lunar (astral) spirit attached to a physical body. As such it takes on characteristics of the person's Moon sign. Each Soul *Dæmon* is different as it holds the influence of the solar self, but all of them have an archetypal source based on the stars which were connected to the Moon when it was passing through that part of the night's sky.

By communicating with that archetypal source, we can connect and communicate with our soul and find out our mission on Earth and help to awaken it to its solar genius. The soul *Dæmon* has powers of its own and remembers much about the *Higher Genius*. It acts as its ambassador gathers information and experience from the material world. However, it is lost inside that material world at least until death.

THE GHOSTLY GALLEON

One of the stranger attributions of Hekate was as a protector of sailors and while the sea was important to Mediterranean culture it does not explain why her mysteries were so important to people who had little to do with the ocean. More recent research has suggested that the ancients saw the ocean as both a metaphor for the night's sky and life itself. This has opened a deeper level of meaning to those who read Homeric works, such as the *Iliad* and *Odyssey*, where sea journeys can be understood as astrological events in the night's sky and by default events and aspects of our life. There are moments when our life is tranquil and other moments when we fear that life's waves crush us. It made sense to understand the mysteries of the Moon as the boat which sails through the skies and to pray to it for protection and safe keeping. The Mysteries of Samothrace appear to have centred on this allegory and the freeing of the chains of destiny*.

The Moon was an important time-keeper. Most ancient civilisations used the Moon as the basis for the calendar. Thoth, the Egyptian god of magic was also a Moon god and one of the Lords of Time. While the solar clocks were ruled by zodiac and the decans, the Moon's path was measured in 28 stations (later called mansions by the Muslims who preserved and developed this tradition). They were important in magical timing to make sure that a person's rituals were correctly aligned to the Moon. This was because the mansions related the Moon's position compared to different important stars. These stars, such as Regulus and Aldebaran, are rarely are looked at in modern magic but were an important part of the ancient systems. This is because are the highest aspect of the rays having been stepped down and transformed by the Moon. As the Moon journeys through the night's sky she takes the star's energy and mediates it in a way that creates another family of *Dæmons* unique to that mansion and reflecting its influence on that time. These *Dæmons* have an influence on our personalities and life. By opening a form of communication with them though Hekate we not only understand their powers but can negotiate with them to ward off some of life's lessons before we need to experience them physically.

The Greco-Egyptian ancient names of these mansion *Dæmons* have been lost, but names of the *Dæmons* were preserved by the same people who created the *Picatrix* along with the magical images. In addition to that we can find some remains of their meaning from the Greek magical Papryi and the powers of the stars they reflect. Other details were fleshed out by going on the astral and seeing them in action. They are soul spirits and guides who not only have magical powers but also guide the soul through the difficult aspects of their destiny. The soul becomes heavily influenced for good or bad by its Moon *Dæmon*.

Because the position of the fixed stars has changed over the centuries the degree which represents the mansions has changed. So, a star which was once in Aries is now in Taurus. The attributions are still the same; it is just that working out which mansion of the Moon is working at a time is different. Normally I don't bother with using a corrected or sidereal time (which represents the night sky as it is now rather than tradition) for the zodiac, but in the case of the mansions of the Moon they are connected to specific stars and

---

* RUCK, C. (2018). *Great Gods Of Samothrace And The Cult Of The Little People.* [S.l.]: REGENT PRESS.

supposed to be a clock. It is therefore important that have them set right. I have supplied both degree settings and I suggest you pick one and stick to it.

To find the *Dæmon* for your own mansion of the Moon look at the exact degree the Moon is in your chart. You could also use Christopher Warnock's Mansion Tracker, Lunar Mansions Software *The traditional meanings for these mansions are hints and starting points and not meant to be taken literally. Their powers are those of a soul and need to be understood in the widest possible sense. For example, Enedil is traditionally said to find treasures and underground streams which is a reference to it being a teaching spirit who helps find patterns and information which is hidden from sight. His power to "destroy buildings being constructed" is a reference to breaking down false thought patterns and bogus thinking. The danger is that he upsets the status quo and relationships (no one likes a smart-arse). While he could be magically used for traditional literal things, it limits the powers of these *Dæmons*.

FIRST MANSION: ALNATH (TWO HORNS)

Zodiac degree: Traditional 0° Aries 00' - 12° Aries 51' Sidereal 3° Taurus to 18° Taurus.

Alnath means "the two butting horns" which refers to the stars Sheratan and Mesarthim which are the head of Aries.

Stars: Sheratan and Mesarthim.
Mesarthim is a binary star in the northern constellation of Aries and the first horn of the Ram.
Sheratan is a star system and the second-brightest star in the constellation of Aries is the second horn of the Ram. According to Ptolemy, Sheratan merges the powers of the two malefic Mars and Saturn; it causes bodily injuries, defeat, destruction by fire, war and earthquakes. Mesarthim is the opposite order of Saturn and Mars which means the power of Mars is constrained and protective by a more powerful malefic.

Ruled by the *Dæmon*: Geriz. Depicted as a dark man with red-orange eyes and an iron helmet. He has a spear in his right hand and his left a crescent shield with the symbol of Saturn on it and a cloak of sheep's fleece. His boots are of sheepskin.

---

* https://www.renaissanceastrology.com/mansiontracker.html

Elections: When the Moon is in this sign it is the right time to begin a journey, buy livestock, create discord between individuals, and imprison someone. It is bad for marriage, partnerships, or the foundation of a meaningful friendship or alliance.

Magical Powers: Curses, black magic, crimes of violence, overcoming depression and a lack of motivation, finishing projects, protection from violence and travel. He is the root to break up couples and set friends and allies against each other.

Note: this mansion is dual in nature alternating between extreme violence and murder and positive defence. Its power is hard to balance once invoked. A person born when the Moon is in this mansion will have much energy but be prone to outbursts of aggression. They will however be protective of people with whom they are attached. Geriz can show those under his protection when it is good to strike and when it is important to defend. His soul follows the way of the warrior.

SECOND MANSION: ALBOTAYN (BELLY)
Zodiac degree: 12° Aries 51' - 25° Aries 42' 18° Taurus to 29° Taurus

Star: Botein

Botein is the tail or flank of the Ram. It is about 170 light-years from the Sun. It has a Martian nature but is more of a natural energy and drive – much in the same way as libido. Ptolemy considered the mansion to be connected more to Venus. This energy is less likely to attack someone else, but more likely to want sex no matter what.

Ruled by the *Dæmon:* Enedil appears as a crowned and armoured king, with long red hair in a scarlet robe holding the sceptre of Agamemnon. He has a golden sheep skin shield with a shield boss with a symbol of a dove upon it. He is seated on a Throne.

Elections: the proper time for planting and journeys, but bad for marriages and keeping movable property.

Magical Powers: Enedil's power is to drive away anger at all costs. This might not be the desired result unless you want to stop someone being angry at you (normally you want them to stop being angry and do something else). However, if you wanted to stop someone beating their partner Enedil might help or might just split the relationship up to avoid any more conflict. Traditionally Enedil can find treasures and underground streams, destroy buildings, wheat planting, end all building work (i.e. causing a collapse during construction), cause strife in relationships, enrage a person against another and to keep people prisoner.

Notes: There is an unpredictable nature to this force as Enedil like a barbarian king, in that it will manifest its force in its own unique (and potentially destructive way). A person born under Enedil will be full of sexual energy and drive. They might have difficulty in monogamy and might encourage break ups in other relationships through their actions. Many old-style politicians and diplomats would have an Endedil soul as it is intricately connected to power. Endedil also creates the souls of successful lawyers.

THIRD MANSION: AZORAYE (PLEIADES)
Zodiac degree: Traditional 25° Aries 42' - 8° Taurus 34' 29° Sidereal Taurus to 10° Gemini.

Star: Alcyone.
Alcyone is a multiple star system in the constellation of Taurus. It is 440 light years from the Sun, it is the brightest star in the Pleiades open cluster. The Pleiades were the seven daughters of Atlas turned into a group of stars. Alcyone was their leader. Plotinus said that their role, then, is to help seekers become consciously aware of Divine Knowledge and Wisdom. The Pleiades are a spiritual "station" where the *Higher Genus* is energised and awakens on Earth. Venus strongly influences the Alcyone energy. Ptolemy attributed them to Moon and Mars.

Ruled by the *Dæmon*: Annuncia is depicted as a beautiful woman holding a book in her left hand, dressed in red with an emerald green cloak. She is seated on a golden sheepskin and holds her hand above her head and often appears to be holding a lit torch. Around her are seven asps and four pillars.*

Elections:
A time to buy animals, travel (but not by sea), hunting, alchemical works, and doing good. It is a tough time for marriage as partnerships will be between unequals and more about romantic love and physical attraction than anything which can last. A time for planting.

Magical Powers: Annuncia protects a person on the sea (in other

---

* These are taken from the PGM refer to the seven fates, which were attributed to the Pleiades.

words life in general) , she imprisons captives, teaches magic and alchemy and "all works connected to fire." She is also an expert on hunting and can help a man and a woman fall in love. Acquisition of all good things. Safe travel or holding individuals captive, success in hunting and alchemical experiments. She brings abundance in all things and the flowering of art, creativity, wealth, and beauty.

Notes: This is a particularly lucky and talented soul who can have what they want and will be extremely lucky in anything they do. It would make for a soul of a magician, artist or writer. But Annuncia does have her darker side. Just because you have those natural abilities, it does not mean that you will bring them to light or be able to exploit them. If you are lucky enough to have an Annuncia soul, it is imperative that you work with her to obtain advice on how to fulfil this destiny. The *Higher Genius* will be expecting a lot from this person and their life might be hard but interesting. This might be why they are said to make their natives wanton, ambitious, turbulent, optimistic and peaceful; to give many journeys and voyages (experiences), success in agriculture and through active intelligence but to cause blindness, disgrace and a violent death.

Fourth mansion Aldebaran (follower)
Zodiac degree : Traditional 8° Taurus 35' - 21° Taurus 25' Sidereal 10° Gemini to 24° Gemini.

Star: Aldebaran.

Aldebaran is an orange giant star found about 65 light-years from the Sun, it is the bull's eye of Taurus. It is a fortunate star portending riches and honour particularly from war and conflict. It was one of the four Royal Stars, or Guardians of the Sky. Ptolemy connected the star with Mars which makes it good for generals and war. Maternus writes that Aldebaran "...when aspected by a malefic portends sudden and unexpected involvement in riots and sedition resulting in justly being condemned by the people."

Ruled by the *Dæmon:* Assarez appears as an armoured horse-rider with black hair and red eyes. He holds a serpent in his right hand. He has a round red shield with the head of a bull upon it. He has a flame coloured cloak and a gold crown. His horse is chestnut brown and has golden chest armour.

Elections: good for employing others, building, investing, and obtaining offices. Bad for marriage and makes traveling difficult and potentially dangerous.

Magical Powers: destruction, creation of enmity, eradication of pests. He causes the destruction and hindrances of buildings, fountains, wells, gold mines, the flight of creeping things, and begets discord.

Notes: Some of the magical material tend to emphasize the malefic side of this mansion at the expense of its positive side. As a Persian royal star it was protector and bought considerable good luck through activity such as war. A soul influenced by Assarez will be defensive, always on guard and under stress and in a constant state of anxiety, but their ability to concentrate and get up and move makes them successful in making money. Assarez souls are potentially charismatic and charming. Aldebaran comes across as the knight in shining armour even when they do not earn the title. The darker side of Assarez is his need for sacrifice which, because he is a soldier's *Dæmon*, can mean loss of life. The Greco-Romans associated the horse with war and attributed it to symbolism such as power, victory, honour, domination and virility.

THE FIFTH MANSION ALMIZEN (CROWN)
Zodiac degree: Traditional 21° Taurus 26' - 4° Gemini 17' Sidereal 24° Gemini to 9° Cancer.

Star: Meissa (Al Hakah).

Almizen is formed by three small stars from the head of Orion which are close together that they look like one nebula. According to Ptolemy it has the nature of Jupiter and Saturn. With gives a strong and dignified nature, self-confidence, inconstancy, arrogance, violence, impiety, prosperity in trade and particularly by voyages or abroad, but danger of treachery and poison. Meissa is one name given to this star another (more interesting) was Al Hakah (which in Arabic means "White Spot" but could be derived from the name of the Ancient Egyptian god of magic Heka). Orion was Osiris to the Ancient Egyptians and it makes sense that he was crowned with Heka.

Ruled by the *Dæmon*: Cabil appears as a floating crowned disembodied head surrounded by stars. On his forehead is a white star. He is a teaching spirit and favours those who want to learn magic, philosophy or trade skills. He speaks to people in their dreams and often helps review situations.

Elections: good for marriage, education, making medicine, travel, employment, building, getting your hair cut, and washing your hair. Bad for business partnerships.

Magical Powers: Learning, healing and love magic which is designed to bring a couple together permanently.

Notes: This mansion is very much focused on the head and intellect in the widest sense. A person who has this as their personal mansion has a natural inner contact and access to information. They should pick up information quickly and understand it, due mostly to their inner voice explaining information to them in a manner they can understand. One danger is that such a person might not have a practical bone in their body being too much in their head. In fact their life destiny might be to take the intellectual knowledge they have and make it practically work. Their Higher Genius might have entered into incarnation to test some theories out.

THE SIXTH MANSION ACHAYA (MARK)

Zodiac degree : 4° Gemini 18' - 17° gemini 08' Sidereal 9 Cancer to 20 Cancer.

Star: Alhena.
Alhena is a brilliant white star located on the left foot of the Twin Pollux. Castor and Pollux (Dioskouroi) were twins and while Castor was mortal, Pollux was immortal. This makes them another excellent symbol for the Higher Self. Alhena then can be seen as the foot of the Higher Genius. Ptolemy said that Alhena was a peaceable Mercury with a slight influence of Venus, and the Picatrix uses it for love magic.

Ruled by the *Dæmon:* Nedeyrahe appears as two people embracing. The Picatrix suggests that it should be a man and a woman and that a person should make two talismans, one for the man and one for the woman and attach them for love magic. The more ancient sources hint that Pollux would make a better image for non-romantic magic. Nedeyrahe would then appear as a young man holding a club and riding a horse with his twin shown behind him (once Castor appeared as Pollux's shadow). Double symbolism tends to appear (two snakes, two vases and cross beams) in any visions.

Elections: good for actions of war and seeking justice ("pursuing enemies and evildoers"), travel, forming partnerships, and hunting. Bad for planting and agricultural work, borrowing money, or depositing something for safekeeping, also bad for taking medicines and treating injuries.

Magical Powers: Love and attraction.

Notes: The Arabic interpretation of the mansion suggests more romantic magic while the imagery of Castor and Pollux suggests a deeper sort of love built on dedication and commitment. Manilius said that a person born under this star will have an easier life. "Those so endowed find even work a pleasure. They would banish war, the trumpet's call, and the gloom of old age: theirs is a life of ease and unfading youth spent in the arms of love. They discover paths to the skies, complete a survey of the heavens with numbers and measurements, and outstrip the flight of the stars: nature yields to their genius, which it serves in all things. So many are the accomplishments of which the Twins are fruitful."

SEVENTH MANSION: ALDHIRA (FOREARM)
Zodiac degree: 17° Gemini 09' - 0° cancer 00' Sidereal 20° Cancer 7° Leo.

Star: Castor.
Castor is a bright white binary star and is on the head of the Northern Twin. Castor was the mortal twin, famous for his skill in taming and managing horses. There are some differences between the sixth and seventh mansion even if they are "twins." Ptolemy said that Castor was more influenced by Mercury. This means that it gives distinction, a keen intellect, success in law and many travels, fondness for horses, sudden fame and honour but often followed by loss of fortune and disgrace, sickness, trouble, and great affliction. Its natives are said to be mischievous and prone to violence.

Ruled by the *Dæmon*: Siely appears as a robed man, praying with his arms up-stretched to heaven. However this image is inconsistent with the meaning of the star, its location, myth and meaning. A better magical image would be of a youth holding a bow in his right hand and a lyre in his left with his arms outstretched to heaven. Behind him is a horse. Like his brother, double symbolism tends to appear (two snakes, two vases and cross beams) in any visions.

Elections: this mansion is good for agricultural pursuits, and for making peace with enemies should one choose to do so (it's good for getting an advantage on them). Siely is bad for buying property although good for selling it. (Siely is the archetypal Estate Agent.) He is not good at healing the sick. He is favourable for gain, friendship and for lovers, however he undermines the law and establishment.

Magical Powers: abundance and acquiring good things

Notes: Arabic and modern astrology has ignored a lot about the Castor legend associated with this mansion and its connections to the last one. In some ways Castor is the dark twin in that he is more influenced by the needs of Earth and is more equipped to survive within it. He is the archetype for a perfected soul. While his brother expresses perfect love, Castor is more pragmatic and earthier. He has to be, as he is mortal and is prone to suffering and death. Someone born with the Moon in this mansion will be successful, particularly in business. It can be an indicator of wealth and abundance, but it might come at a personal cost. Mercury is also the god of magic so the image of him lifting arms above his head is a form of invocation.

Eighth mansion Alnathra (Gap)

Zodiac degree: 0° cancer 00' - 12° cancer 51'. Sidereal 7° Leo to 18° Leo.

Star: Praesepe.
Praesepe is a star cluster with the nickname of the Crib. It has the nature of Mars and the Moon, and causes disease, disgrace, adventure, insolence, wantonness, brutality, blindness, and industry. It makes its natives fortunate, but liable to loss through others. It can help them to be founders of large businesses.

Ruled by the *Dæmon:* Annediex appears as an eagle with the bearded face of a man. This is the Ancient Egyptian symbol for the Ba which was the personified impression that individuals make on the world around them or their effect on others. It was like the person's mana and it had a life which was separate from the physical body. This explains why, while the Star's attributions are a little bleak, the meanings of the mansion are positive with Annediex being invoked for victory. Annediex also rules the longest day of the year when the Sun is at its strongest.

Elections: good for healing, buying new goods, and travel. Bad for marriage, partnerships, and employment.

Magical Powers: love and friendship, forging alliances and military success.

Notes: Alnathra is the force which shows a person's reputation and personal power. It is the drive to carry a person through their life and striving for success. A person born with the Moon in this mansion will have considerable drive to succeed and will be status orientated. They should also have considerable personal power and charisma. If these things are lacking then it is vital to awaken them as part of the Higher Genius's life plan. There are many risks following the path of Alnathra as shown by the meanings of Praesepe and it is easy to see why. A person who looks for victory, prestige and power for their personality is going to run into trouble occasionally.

NINTH MANSION ALTARF (LION'S GLANCE)

Zodiac degree: 12° Cancer 51' - 25° Cancer 42' Sidereal 18° Leo to 28° Leo.

Star: Alterf.
Alterf is an orange to red giant star. Ptolemy said that the star was a mix of the malefic planets Mars and Saturn. It brings misfortunes and tragedies and was a portent of earthquakes, landslides, and famine. There is not a lot of good which comes from this star, but a lot of death and war. Warnock suggests that after the victory and success of the last mansion, the Moon is moving to a phase of defeat and illness.

Ruled by the *Dæmon*: Raubel appears as a eunuch with his hands over his eyes in terror. This is a cryptic symbol to modern minds as eunuchs, while reviled in Rome, were trusted advisors throughout the rest of the Middle East. Eunuchs served Hekate in her most important sanctuary, Llagina, which was a theocratic city-state in what is now modern Turkey. They are mostly a symbol of devotion (in Llagina to the goddess) but to government administration as most courts were based around a bureaucracy of eunuchs. Raubel is the established order breaking down.

Elections: do not try to construct or plant anything. There might be deceit in partnerships during this time, and it's not safe for journeys or inflicting evil on others. Good for capturing individuals to have them languish in captivity and good for fortifying gates.

Magical Powers: curses, particularly for sickness and bringing down divine wrath.

Notes: The mansion is a period where the established order has become sick and fearful and is collapsing in on itself. This may be a good thing except when it is looked at through the eyes of the existing order. On the plus side Raubel can show how to handle such crisis and to go with the flow. A person born with the Moon in Altarf can find negativity in their most joyful moments. As a result they often create their own woe even when the universe is not flinging bad experiences at them. That is not to say that the universe does not send an unfair amount of rubbish their way. They might be born into an environment which is corrupt or weak which needs to be reformed or to be escaped. Much of their happiness depends on them either doing or accepting good things and finding a mental balance.

TENTH MANSION ALJABHA

Zodiac degree: 25° cancer 42' - 8° Leo 34' Sidereal 28° Leo to 12° Virgo.

Star: Regulus.
Regulus is one of the brightest stars in the night sky and is a multiple star system composed of four stars that are organised into two pairs. One of the Persian Royal Stars it is one of the protective forces in the universe and is the Watcher of the North. Ptolemy said that Regulus has the nature of Mars and Jupiter. Which means its energy brings power, prestige, strength, and the ability to rule and lead.

Ruled by the *Dæmon:* Aredafir who appears with the head of a Lion and he is the solar force of healing. It supplies natural strength and power to lead and take control. Aredafir presides over curing infirmities and easing childbirth, placing love between man and wife, strengthening, and completing buildings, and to obtain the love of allies and mutual help. However, since he is still a guardian, Aredafir destroys enemies, and incarcerates captives so they cannot escape.

Elections: A good time for healing, marriage, partnerships and construction. Not a good time for travel or lending.

Magical Powers: Leadership, self confidence, desire of the heart. Starting projects.

Notes: Those who are born under this mansion are high spirited and articulate. They are good leaders, but also practical natural healers. Their methods are of healing, although not that of the surgeon but more homoeopathic in their approach. They have a wicked sense of humour and the nature of a trickster. They are loyal and protective to those under their protection.

ELEVENTH MANSION ALZUBRA (LION'S MANE)
Zodiac degree: 8° Leo 35' - 21° Leo 25' sidereal 12 Virgo – 22 Virgo.

Star: Zosma (Delta Leonis).

Zosma is 58.4 light-years from the Sun and the word is Greek for girdle. Ptolemy said that the star is a negative Saturn-Venus mix. It causes selfishness, immorality, meanness, melancholy and gives an unreasonable and shameless egotism. On the plus side it does give an alert mind and the ability to prophesy. (The Sumerians called the star Kakkab Kua, the constellation of the God Kua, the Oracle.) In medieval times this star portended many problems connected with the planetary Venus.

Ruled by the *Dæmon:* Necol appears as a man riding a lion with a spear in his right hand while his left holds the lion's ear. The lion is riding over a corpse. It is a form of the god Abraxas and the Higher Genius of a dead person wafting away from the Earth on his way to a higher life.

Elections: good for planting, building, partnerships, and battle, mediocre for journeys and trade.

Magical Powers: to be feared and yet to receive good things, having requests made to authority figures answered favourably, increased wealth, fortifying buildings, assisting in battle, rescuing captives, and profit in trade.

Notes: This mansion brings power and respect. A person who is born with the Moon in this mansion tends to manifest the more aggressive and egotistical sides of the Sun. They have great courage but will often ride over the top of people without thinking. They also have profound magical abilities to connect and channel the gods and are natural oracles. They tend to present this message too bluntly and are often ignored because of their lack of tact. They can become depressed because they are ignored and that makes the issue worse. Once they have integrated their powers, they can guide and protect people.

TWELFTH MANSION ALSARFAH (TRANSFORMER)

Zodiac degree: 21° Leo 26' - 04° Virgo 17' Sidereal 22° Virgo to 27° Virgo.

Star: Denebola.

Denebola is second-brightest star in Leo and is a blue double star which appears as one to the naked eye. The Greek name for the star was Alkaia, who was one of Queen Andromache's Amazon generals. Her name means, "Mighty One." Denebola was unlucky in astrology, portending misfortune and disgrace. Ptolemy said that the star was a Saturn and Venus mix. It gives swift judgment, despair, regrets, public disgrace, misfortune from the elements of nature, and happiness turned to anger, and makes its natives noble, daring, self-controlled, generous, and busy with other people's affairs.

Ruled by the *Dæmon*: Abdizu who appears as a Dragon which can be seen fighting a man. While some books tend emphasis the "man" in this image it is the Dragon which is the active symbol. She is likely to be Scylla the daughter of Hekate who was turned into dragon (Hesiodic Megalai Ehoiai says she was the daughter of Hekate and Phoebus Apollo). Scylla was a tragic romantic hero who who was claimed by Poseidon, but the jealous sea goddess, Amphitrite turned her into a monster by poisoning the spring where she bathed. She became a force which sank ships and was killed by Hercules (and resurrected by Phorcys).

Elections: good for building, renting lands, agriculture, marriage, and putting on new garments. Bad for travel and employment.

Magical Powers: separation of two lovers, increases harvest and causes plants to prosper, destruction of riches, destroying ships and reinforcing the loyalty of allies, employees, and captives.

Notes: The *Picatrix* sees this mansion as highly dangerous and Christopher Warnock says that it causes a person to projecting their evils outward. In the *Odyssey* though, Odysseus when sailing in the Straits of Messina between Scylla and her counterpart Charybdis was recommended to steer towards Scylla. The reason was Scylla would only kill six sailors while Charybdis would sink the whole boat. She represents a life misfortune which does not end in destruction. A person born with the Moon in this mansion will be strong and dangerous and with a tendency toward chaos and destruction. They will be great undoers of the established order and can bring about change, but not in a comfortable way.

THIRTEENTH MANSION ALAWWA (HOWLER)
Zodiac degree: 4° Virgo 18' - 17° Virgo 08' Sidereal 27° Virgo 24° Libra.

Star: Zavijava.

Zavijava is a pale-yellow star on the Wings of Virgo. Its name means either the corner or the dog's kennel. A barking dog was considered a good omen of Hekate, but in this case it might have something to do with the naturalistic sex drive of dogs on heat. According to Ptolemy it had the powers of Mars and Mercury which implies a more Leonine nature. It would create a person who has intelligence and energy to be sent out and work under his own authority. This can create a formidable force of character with a competitive nature.

Ruled by the *Dæmon*: Azerut is a form of Priapus, the son of Aphrodite by Dionysus, and he appears as a man (sometimes as a gnome) with a huge erection. He holds a scythe in his right hand which is used to threaten thieves with castration. He was sometimes equated with Hermes and could carry a caduceus. He was a rustic fertility god, protector of livestock, fruit plants, gardens, and male genitalia. Priapus was also the patron god for merchant sailors and was supposed to assist in navigation.

Elections: good for planting and tilling, journeys, marriage, taking medicine, employment, petitioning authority, and cutting hair.

Magic Powers: creating love between two people, increase of trade and profit, assisting with crops, good and safe journeys, completing buildings, protecting property, curing sexual dysfunction and freeing captives.

Notes: This mansion stands for sexual desire and lust, while this might have symbolically been a "male thing" Priapus is not fussy. It is pure libido and it does not matter what form it takes. In fact, one of the traditional meanings of this mansion in a natal chart is that the native has an almost "feminine nature", mostly based on the ancient prejudice that women were prone to giving in to their sexual desires more than men. It supplies a considerable amount of drive to a person with the Moon in this house. This can be extremely negative if repressed (or over expressed) but when controlled can produce an extremely passionate and protective individual.

FOURTEENTH MANSION ALSIMAK (UNARMED)

Zodiac degree: 17° Virgo 08' - 00° Libra 00' Sidereal 24° Libra 4° Scorpio.

Star: Spica.

Spica is the brightest star in Virgo and is a whirling double star in the virgin's wheat. Ptolemy said it had the nature of Venus and Mars. It was the star of the grain harvest and the provider of material needs. Spica is also noted for its spiritual and religious qualities and psychic awareness. It gives honours and fame. Spica is of marked good fortune for scientists, writers, artist-painters, sculptors, and musicians.

Ruled by the *Dæmon*: Erdegel appears as a dog with its tail in its mouth which has a similar meaning to Ouroboros. It is a spirit which shows the cyclic nature of life, it brings beginnings and endings. With the power of Spica it brings the harvest which is a reward to the person who grew the wheat, the ending of one cycle and the beginning of the next.

Elections: good for marriage, healing, agriculture, employment, partnerships, and traveling by ship.

Magical Powers: Trade and profit, increase in harvests, completion of buildings, travel, driving people apart, creating love between spouses, destroying lust, harming crops, assaulting travellers, helping kings, and developing goodwill between allies.

Notes: Alsimak is called "unarmed" because it is a star that is out on its own and lacking any others which would form "weapons." The Picatrix emphasises this mansion's ability to create endings and uses it to break a couple up. However, the implication is that such an ending will create a new beginning. This mansion is really about that critical part of a cycle where the dog (or snake) bites its own tail, enabling the cycle to begin again. A person who is born with the Moon in this mansion should strongly feel the cycles in their life. They might experience extremes of fortune and can notice what stage a cycle is at. They might have the natural ability to predict the consequences of action and even have a natural oracular nature. They might also be creatures of routine.

Fifteenth mansion Alghafr (Covering)

Zodiac degree: 00° Libra 00' - 12° Libra 51' Sidereal 4° to 15° Scorpio.

Star: Syrma.
This is a binary star in the train of the Virgo's dress. The name refers to the covering of nature and was said to represent occult sciences, secret wisdom, and a sharp, penetrating mind that can

extract hidden truths. Ptolemy said the star was like Mercury, and moderately Mars and it was considered a fortunate star.

Ruled by the *Dæmon*: Achalich appears as a young man seated at a library desk reading scrolls and books. He makes a good contact for understanding magical knowledge, divination, or seeing what is not obvious. He is useful for concealing things and invisibility magic. Outside of that he teaches business, writing and the Mercurial arts. He has proved useful at manipulating public opinion and being the guiding force behind Public Relations and Marketing often at the expense of another's reputation.

Elections: Good for all sorts of business, commerce and studying. Favourable for illnesses caused by windiness, employment, moving to a new house, and buying and selling. Bad for journeys, partnerships, and marriage.

Magical Powers: Magic to increase the success of finding material or intellectual treasures and working spells to protect friends and injure enemies' acquisition of friendship and good will. Also, digging of wells, finding buried treasure, impeding travellers, separating spouses, and destroying the reputation of enemies.

Notes: A person born with the Moon in Alghafr was said to be well mannered and know the right things to say. They are aware of the forms of approach that people find pleasing and project them. Such people are natural academics and intellectuals in their approach, but do not really live in an ivory tower. The dark side of this personality is that it often lacks a moral code and will deceive to improve their own (or other's) reputation. It is a position for a researcher, scientist, PR or marketer.

THE SIXTEENTH MANSION ALZUBANA (SCORPION'S CLAWS)

Zodiac degree: 12° libra 51' - 25° libra 42' sidereal 15° Scorpio 3° Sagittarius.

Stars: Zubenelgenubi and Zubeneschalami.
Libra was not considered a separate constellation by the ancients and was called Chelae, or the Claws of Scorpio. Zubenelgenubi was

called the Insufficient Price and Ptolemy said it had the nature of Saturn and Mars. It causes malevolence, obstruction, an unforgiving character, violence, disease, lying, crime, disgrace, and danger of poison. The stars at the points of the claws of Scorpio work like Jupiter and Mercury. Zubeneschamali, or the Northern Scale, was considered a fruitful star. The Chaldeans believed that when this star was clear the crops would be good. It gives riches, honour, and good fortune. It had the power of the two benefits Jupiter and Venus. When the Moon is in this mansion it unites these two stars.

Ruled by the _Dæmon:_ Azeruch appears as a man seated on a throne holding a scale in his hands and he is a good figure to explain economics and business. He brings wealth, normally through investment and banking. The scales here have nothing to do with justice but were an ancient symbol of the merchant in the marketplace. He is a good financial advisor, however a love of money is inauspicious for love. The scales here are more symbols of the balance that a person must have when working with this mansion. Azeruch is really good at showing them how to find this balance so that they do not blight themselves with too much Zubenelgenubi.

Elections: bad for travel, healing, making deals, planting crops, marriage, and partnerships. Good for employment.

Magical Powers: making money, destruction of merchandise and crops, causing hostilities in relationships, impeding travellers, and freeing captives.

Notes: This mansion is bad for anything other than making money. The claws of a scorpion are not a good place to be and lead to anger and conflict. This is the concept of "competition."

THE SEVENTEENTH MANSION ALIKLIL (SCORPION'S CROWN)

Zodiac degree: 25° Libra 42' - 08° Scorpio 34' Sidereal 3 Sagittarius to 10° Sagittarius.

Stars: Acrab and Deschubba.
Acrab and Dschubba are the two stars on the forehead of the scorpion. Ptolemy thought that both stars had the nature of Mars

and Saturn and caused sudden assaults, malevolence, immorality, and shamelessness. These stars were the brains of the scorpion and said to create a fighter of great skill who had a patient and wary approach to any situation, but this will belie their skilled determination. Scorpio is famous for the surgeons born in it and this star shows up just the qualities which they need to have. The same applies to generals, police officers, private investigators, and secret agents.

Ruled by the *Dæmon*: Adrieb appears as a dog-faced baboon which is a form of Thoth-Hermes. He has his arms above his head as if he is worshipping the Sun. The ancient Egyptians observed that baboons would bark at the rising Sun, and this was turned into images of baboons with raised arms in the act of worshipping the Sun. The Egyptians trained baboons to catch thieves and shoplifters, making Adrieb a protective force, especially for property, shops, and material goods. He can advise when there is the possibility of loss and how to avoid it.

Elections: good to buy livestock, besiege estates, put on new clothes, building, love, medicine, and travel, even though the traveller will be anxious. Bad for partnerships, haircuts, and employment.

Magical Powers: keeping thieves from entering a home, committing deceptions, besieging cities, reinforcing buildings, protecting travellers, creating lasting love and friendship.

Notes: Warnock notes that seen in the light of the earlier mansions, in which material wealth is gathered, Aliklil shows it being protected. Aliklil is a disciplined and intelligent force defending the soul. It was said that a person with the Moon in this mansion will do great evil deeds, which ties in with the "secret agent" symbolism associated with this mansion. However, this is a protective force; unbalanced it might create a miserly ultra-conservative person who never takes any risks. Or someone who enforces rules long after they have stopped being valid.

EIGHTEENTH MANSION ALQALB (SCORPION'S HEART)

Zodiac degree: 08° Scorpio 34' - 21° Scorpio 25' sidereal 10° Sagittarius to 24° Sagittarius.

Star: Antares.
Antares is a red super-giant star that is nearing the end of its life.

The word "Antares" means "anti-Ares" or "anti-Mars," because the reddish star looked similar to the red planet. In Persia it was named one of four royal stars in the sky. In Egypt, Antares was a symbol of the scorpion goddess Selkit. In her *Fixed Stars and Constellations in Astrology*, Vivian E. Robson says: "It causes malevolence, destructiveness, liberality, broad-mindedness, evil presages and danger of fatality and makes its natives rash, ravenous, headstrong and destructive to themselves by their own obstinacy." As a royal star, Antares gives worldly success with a ruthless ambition. It is prone to obsession.

Ruled by the *Dæmon*: Egrebel appears as cobra with its tail above its head, its head like a scorpion. In one of humankind's earliest temples, Göbekli Tepe (10th–8th millennium BCE) the snake was depicted in this way to indicate falling rain and fertility. But the associations of death and poison to this mansion show Egrebel as a rather darker *Dæmon* of destruction similar in concept to the tarot key Death. Snakes are symbols of renewal due to the shedding of their skin. Egrebel is also a healer but more surgical, which consumes (or cuts out) the source of the illness. Egrebel has a strong guardian role particularly in keeping evil out of the house. He can also warn of danger and show us how to take precautions.

Elections: good for building, renting and purchasing land, getting promoted, useful for journeys where the destination is to the east, good for planting, and taking medication. Bad for partnerships and employment.

Magical Powers: relieving fevers and diseases of the stomach, conspiring against kings, vengeance against enemies, reinforcing buildings, freeing prisoners, and separating friends.

Notes: Alqalb is a complex force which can be rough for those who expect everything spiritual to be sweetness and light. It is a positive force, which can be obsessive and nasty in its methods. A person who has an Egrebel *Dæmon* as a house guardian is not messing around and does not care if someone gets hurt. It is said that great light casts the greatest shadows, and a person who is born with the Moon in Alqalb was destined to do great deeds and help a great many. Warnock says that the anger of Scorpio will be present in this person, but it will be turned inward. The fact that they express a Royal Star means that they will be fated to have a certain amount of protection and guardianship. They would make good surgeons.

NINETEENTH MANSION: ALSHAULA (STINGER)

Zodiac degree: 21° Scorpio 25' - 04° Sagittarius 17' Sidereal 24° Sagittarius 13° Capricorn.

Star: Shaula.
This star is made up of two to three stars which appear as a single sting in the tail of Scorpio. It was considered unlucky. Ptolemy said that it had nature of Mercury and Mars. It gives danger, desperation, immorality, and malevolence, and relates to acid poisons.

Spirit Annucel appears as a woman with her hands over her eyes and she appeared to me as a Dæmon of Ishtar. The connection appears to be with the hand of Fatima which is a hand with an eye the centre, used to ward off evil. It was based on the hand of Ishtar which lacked the eye. Ishtar was a Mesopotamian goddess associated with love, beauty, sex, desire, fertility, war, justice, and political power While her hand was an auspicious symbol it was used to see off negativity. Annucel's image is both the cause and the cure of the problem. She can show how to conduct conflict profitably and with the minimum of fuss. She will be better in conflict which requires a long-term game.

Elections: good for sieges, litigation, journeys by land, and planting trees. Bad for partnerships, employment, and travel by sea. It is bad for anything that needs a liberation or ships.

Magical Powers: restoring uterine health, protection during pregnancy and childbirth, besieging cities, destroying wealth, expelling people from a place, cursing travellers, and increasing harvests. Talismans made with her image are useful in long term magical attacks, when defences need to be overcome or long-term defences are required against a tenacious attacker.

Notes: The traditional attributions of this mansion focus on protecting women and ensuring childbirth goes smoothly, but it is popular in the manufacture of Scorpio-based curses. The fact that it is good at battles and sieges is symbolic for the arguments and conflicts that come from this mansion. To be fair these things are necessary and inevitable in life and it is better to have a plan to deal with them. Traditionally a person who was born with the Moon in Alshaula will cause their parents great evil and while it is true they can cause much pain, they have a function of preventing harm coming to others.

THE TWENTIETH MANSION AL-NA'AM (BEAM) *

Zodiac degrees: 04° Sagittarius 17' - 17° Sagittarius 08. Sidereal 13°-16 °Capricorn.

Star: Ascella.
This is a binary star in the armpit of the Archer, constellation Sagittarius. The name Ascella is from a late Latin word meaning armpit. However, while you might expect it to be malefic, Agrippa said it had the nature of Jupiter and Mercury and created a religious and thoughtful mind and those born under its influence tended to be philosophical and writers on religious or similar subjects. It gives good fortune and happiness.

Ruled by the *Dæmon*: Queyhuc appears as a centaur holding a bow. While the *Picatrix* says the figure should be the traditional centaur with the head and arms of a man, body of a horse with four feet, Queyhuc may be another name (or a Dæmon of) Chiron the wounded healer. Older depictions of Chiron gave him a front part that was human with a horse's body and hindquarters. Chiron was the spiritual teacher to heroes. His students included Asclepius, Aristaeus, Ajax, Aeneas, Actaeon, Caeneus, Theseus, Achilles, Jason, Peleus, Telamon, Perseus, sometimes Heracles, Oileus, and Phoenix. While Centaurs were normally violent and bestial, Chiron's bow was only used for hunting and there are no signs of savage behaviour. Queyhuc is a gentle guide and inner teacher. He has a specific interest in taming animals (a teaching role) and can teach how to handle animal passions.

Elections: Taming wild beasts, travelling, networking of people, trapping enemies and keeping them locked up, and bringing evil to your enemies.

Magical Powers: Inner plane guidance and wisdom, rituals where passions must be controlled, hunting magic, in its widest terms. It is also useful in magic where you need to learn a useful piece of information. It is suitable for healing, love, and reconciliation magic.

Notes: The medieval manuscripts say that this mansion creates a strong person who can do great deeds for good or for evil. It is the classic description of a hero or anti-hero. It implies that a person

---

* Now seen as the bow of Sagittarius.

born under this mansion is naturally connected to forces of wisdom and can be a guide for others. They will always be tempted to use this natural wisdom for self-gain. Like Chiron's bow, wisdom can be used to put food on the table or to kill. This mansion is useful for figurative and literal hunting and for attaining goals.

THE TWENTY-FIRST MANSION: ALBALDAH (BRIGHTEST OF THE TOWN.)

Zodiac degrees: 17° Sagittarius 08' - 00° Capricorn sidereal 00' 16° Capricorn - 4° Aquarius.

Star: Albaldah.
This is a triple star system in the zodiac constellation of Sagittarius. It is the archer's head. Manilius said that "He will give birth to hearts renowned in war and will conduct the conqueror, celebrating great triumphs in the sight of all, to his country's citadels. Such a one will build high walls one moment and pull them down the next. But if Fortune favours them too generously with success, the mark of her envy is to be seen on their faces, for she works cruel havoc upon their features. So was it that a dread warrior (Hannibal) paid for his victories at the Trebia, Cannae, and the Lake, even before the hour of his retreat, with such disfigurement." Albaldah is a double-sided force which brings about good and bad luck in equal proportion.

Ruled by the *Dæmon:* Bectue appears as a Janus figure with two faces; one facing forward and the other behind. He is the moment of chaos between past and future - the chaotic now. Unlike Janus, Bectue is a force of cosmic balance, bringing good and evil depending on what is deserved. Warnock points out that his position in the mansion cycle is as the herald of the "beginning of the end" however that does not fit with his traditional functions.

Elections: good for building, planting, and making big purchases or investments, however not good for employment.

Magical Powers: causing destruction, strengthening buildings, increasing harvests, making a profit, and separating lovers.

Notes: There is some confusion as to the meaning of this mansion as while some handbooks say that it causes destruction, electional functions suggest it is the right time to build, plant or make big investments. If the "beginning of the end" is starting, none of the above things should be done. However, the mansion is in the Jupiter ruled part of Sagittarius and is benefic and expansive. What is suggested is the Janus point, the delicate balance between where things are still good but distant storm clouds are rising. So, in other words, things are good now but winter is coming. A person born under this mansion will be a "problem to their father" which means that they will not be as successful or lack their good business sense or will coast on their father's fortune. They were also said to be an alcoholic, which was symbolic of general Jupiter over-indulgence. President Donald Trump was born under this mansion.

THE TWENTY-SECOND MANSION AL SAD AL-DHABIH (LUCKY SACRIFICER)

Zodiac degrees: 00° - 12° Capricorn 51' Sidereal 4°-12°Aquarius.

Star: Prima Giedi.

This is two stars which are four minutes apart, in the Goat's right horn. They have been separating since ancient times but during the Babylonian period were thought to be a single star. Ptolemy said that the stars in the horns of Capricorn are partly Venus, and part Mars in their influence. He said that it gives beneficence, sacrifice and offering. The Arabs saw the star as a sheep suitable for sacrifice (which was why the sacrifice was considered lucky).

Ruled by the *Dæmon*: Geliel is a Dæmon of Hermes Kriophoros and appears with winged sandals, wearing a helmet and carrying a ram. Hermes Kriophoros was the "good shepherd" who protected his flock. The image was later co-opted into Christianity. Geliel is a liberator, protector, and healer. He brings about change for those who have been come too set in their ways.

Elections: good for healing, journeys, partnerships, if caught a captive will quickly escape. Bad for marriage and employment.

Magical Powers: to suppress rumours, free captives, cure illness, create hostilities or goodwill between individuals.

Note: One of the important aspects of this mansion is the concept of sacrifice bringing about liberation. While some think this is a Christian concept it was typical of ancient religious thought. Hesiod's idea that the gods smelled the smoke of the sacrifice and were somehow appeased had been developed into an idea of redemption through the religious act. The belief that this mansion was bad for marriage came about probably because estrangement from a partner was one of the sorts of things which was a sacrifice to more important concerns. The mansion does bring the luck of Hermes as a trade-off for any sacrifice you might make. A person born with their Moon in this mansion was said to have a balanced life with good and bad happening to them.

TWENTY-THIRD MANSION SA'D BULA (SWALLOWER'S LUCK)

Zodiac degrees: 12° Capricorn 51' - 25° Capricorn 42' Sidereal 12-23 Aquarius.

Star: Al Bali.
This is a star in the left hand of the Water Bearer, Aquarius. It was said to give good fortune but warn of impending danger. Ptolemy said the star operates like Saturn and Mercury. It earnt its name the Swallower, according to the 13th century Persian astronomical writer Al Kazwini, because the stars seemed to swallow, or absorb, the light of the other.

Ruled by the *Dæmon*: Zequebin appears as a cat with the head of a dog. Symbolically he is a force of destruction which can be directed but is difficult to control when released. He brings about population decrease and destruction over a wide area. He destroys things which promote stability, such as marriage, and will actively make sick people sicker.

Elections: good for putting on new clothes, forming partnerships, taking medicine, and ensures quick escape for those caught. Bad for marriage as it implies abuse, journeys, and depositing something with someone for safekeeping.

Magical Powers: destruction and devastation, healing illness, improving friendship, ruining marriages, and freeing captives.

Notes: This mansion was said to create a person who was moderate between all things good and evil. This would appear to be at odds with the magical meanings of both the star and Zequebin. But the magical image supplies a clue to this paradox. It is a destructive power of a cat under the head of a loyal dog. It chooses to be either, but its default state is to be neither. What it can't do is build something new -- it can only destroy. A person who knows that they have this ability swiftly learns that using it is a bad idea and since they find building difficult they usually follow a path of temperance instead. This mansion can be used to destroy bad things such as an illness but some care is needed here. It is a heavy-handed force which could make the patent sicker.

TWENTY-FOURTH MANSION SA'D AL SU'UD (LUCKIEST OF THE LUCKY)

Zodiac degrees: 25° Capricorn 42' - 8° Aquarius 34' Sidereal 23 Aquarius to 4 Pisces.

Star: Sadalsuud.
This is a pale-yellow double star in the left shoulder of Aquarius. Ptolemy said that it had the nature of the nature of Saturn and Mercury. The fact it was yellow suggested a solar nature and was the star of "mighty destiny" bringing great honour and riches.

Ruled by the *Dæmon*: Abrine appears as a woman breastfeeding a child. She brings fulfilment and tranquillity. She nurtures and supports. Abrine will not provide you with the winning lottery numbers but will make sure you receive what you need. She is useful to invoke when you are beginning a new project and it needs backing. She can also help with fertility issues.

Elections: an appropriate time to take medicine, dispatch troops, employment, and free captives. Not so good for travel, marriage or partnerships.

Magical Powers: abundance, fertility, support, and motherhood.

Notes: This mansion focuses on increase and multiplication. While this is seen as positive it is possible to use this force to increase problems and nurture neurosis. Unbalanced it can create a "mother complex" which is one of the reasons it is not a good mansion to be married under. It enforces fourth house matters and makes travel away from a base less successful. Those born under this mansion were said to be well mannered and have a natural luck. The French emperor Napoleon had his mansion here and he was said to be one of the luckiest of generals who cared for his troops, bringing about considerable loyalty from them.

TWENTY-FIFTH MANSION SA'D AL-AKHBIYAH (LUCK OF HIDDEN THINGS)

Zodiac degree: 8° Aquarius 34' - 21° Aquarius 25' Sidereal 4-23° Pisces.

Star: Sadalbachia.
Sadalachbia, is a greenish star in the right arm of Aquarius, and the westernmost star, at the inner edge of the jar he carries. The name

has been translated as the Lucky Star of Hidden Things or Hiding-Places. This was said to be because when it appeared from the Sun's rays all worms and reptiles, buried during the preceding cold, creep out of their holes. The world is a plural of H'iba' which means Tent. It could also mean that star was named from its spring rising when nomads' tents were pitched on new pastures. Ptolemy was not specific on the value of this particular star but it would appear to be strongly Saturnian with a general hint of Mercury

Ruled by the *Dæmon*: Aziel appears as a man planting trees which is part of Saturn's strong agricultural role. However, the name was that of an angel associated with the Jewish scapegoat rite. In Leviticus 16, two male goats were to be sacrificed for the sins of the people. One goat is selected by lot and sent into the wilderness as a sacrifice to Azazel taking the sins of the people with it. Azazel occurs in the Ancient Book of Giants, which was found at Qumran. In this legend Azazel is one of the Watchers who taught men the art of warfare, of making swords, knives, shields, and coats of mail, and taught women the art of deception by ornamenting the body, dyeing the hair, and painting the face and the eyebrows, and also revealed to the people the secrets of witchcraft and corrupted their manners, leading them into wickedness and impurity. It seems that Azazel was a pre-Jewish god of the Earth and nature which distracted humanity from their heavenly god.

Elections: good for sieges, seeking fights, taking revenge on enemies, good for safety in travel but causes delays, also good for fortifying buildings. Bad for marriage, planting, partnerships, purchasing animals and employment.

Magical Powers: protection of crops, attacking enemies, cursing the body, destroying harvests, protecting messengers on their travels, and separating spouses.

Notes: This mansion shows the problems that ancient societies had with Saturn. He could be a great god of nature and agriculture, but he was also the force which "ate its own children" and an astrological malefic. Modern astrology has tried to downplay this malefic influence, making Saturn a teacher of sometimes unpleasant lessons, but this is missing an important aspect of nature and its relationship with ancient civilisation. Nature obeys rules and if these rules are not followed then people died of starvation. This mansion focuses on the more destructive aspects of Saturn. Warnock points out that the mansion is a force of isolation and solitude which makes it bad for relationships. Traditionally a person born under this mansion was said to be good-natured, presumably because they follow their own rules which are benign.

TWENTY-SIXTH MANSION ALFARGH ALAWWAL (FIRST SPOUT)

Zodiac degrees: 21° Aquarius 25' - 04° Pisces 17' Sidereal 23 Pieces to 9° Aries.

Star: Markab.
This is a white star on the wing of the Winged Horse. The word means anything which is ridden upon and was used to mean saddle, ship or vehicle. According to Ptolemy it had the nature of Mars and Mercury. It portended events concerning ships and the ocean and weather changes (which as I have said before was used as an ancient symbol of emotions).

Ruled by the *Dæmon:* Tagriel appears as woman in a red dress washing her hair and mixing it with perfumes. The name was used by a Kabbalistic angel, was one of the guardians of the second palace of heaven, but I am not convinced she is the same being. She is more of a force of Platonic love which involves rising through levels of closeness to wisdom and true beauty. Although she can be used for love magic hers is the sort of magic which creates deeper loving relationships rather than anything physical, which is why the elections suggested that it is difficult for marriage as it would lead to one which was deeply committed but too idealistic.

Elections: good for employment, building, and journeys. Difficult for marriage.

Magical Powers: creation of love, protection for travellers, strengthening buildings, and holding people in prison.

Notes: Medieval astrology said that people born under this mansion were good and well mannered. One of the difficulties understanding this mansion is because of the change in attitude about the nature of romantic relationships. The Ancient Greeks considered romantic love between a man and woman superficial insanity and preferred a higher love (normally between men) as a better goal to strive for. It is this higher love which is being suggested in this mansion which may or may not work in a relationship. This mansion supplies a deeper form of love for established relationships which is unshakeable, but it is less hearts and flowers and pet-names.

TWENTY-SEVENTH MANSION ALFARGH ALMUAKHKHAR (NEXT SPOUT)

Zodiac degrees: 04° Pisces 17′ - 17° Pisces 08′ Sidereal 9° Aries 0° Taurus.

Star: Algenib and Alpheratz.
These are stars in Andromeda's head. According to Ptolemy the constellation is like that of Venus and it was said to bestow purity of thought, virtue, honour and dignity upon its natives, but to cause battle with chimerical (wildly fanciful, highly improbable) fears and a tendency to become easily discouraged. It gives love between husband and wife and reconciles adulterers. It gives independence, freedom, love, riches, honour, and a keen intellect.

Ruled by the *Dæmon*: Abliemel appears as a winged man holding an empty perforated dish and raising it towards his mouth. He is good for business but will use any means to obtain this success. The magic associated with him includes poisoning the spring of a rival's well. He helps to obtain benefit at the expense of another. In fact his aid is dependant on doing that as he cannot interfere with the balance too much and will ruin to the same measure that someone else will gain. Some of this will always backfire on the person who sends him so that in some way the suffering ends up shared with the victim.

Elections: good for planting, business, and marriage. Bad for travel, employment, and giving or taking loans.

Magical Powers: destroying springs and wells, increasing merchandise, acquiring profit, increasing harvest, healing illness, impeding buildings, harming resources and curses.

Notes: The darker side of material Venus, this mansion is two-faced bringing great good or evil to a person. A person born under this mansion will do evil according to the medieval manuscripts. They will have a narcissistic view of the universe, which means it does not matter if they hurt another, just that they benefit. Manilius in his *Astronomica* said that a person born under this star "will prove merciless, a dispenser of punishment, a warder of dungeon dire; he will stand arrogantly by while the mothers of wretched prisoners lie prostrate on his threshold, and the fathers wait all night to catch the last kisses of their sons and receive into their inmost being the dying breath. From the same constellation comes the figure of the

executioner, ready to take money for a speedy death and the rites of
a funeral pyre. For him execution means profit, and oft will he bare
his axe; in short, he is a man who could have looked unmoved on
Andromeda herself fettered to the rock. Governor of the imprisoned
he occasionally becomes a fellow convict, chained to criminals so as
to save them for execution."

  While this over dramatic, however looking at the list of people
who have the Moon in this mansion, they do tend to feature those
who see the end justifying the means or who obtain success or
fame at a cost. For example, Benjamin Franklyn who once said "A
full belly is the Mother of all Evil" neglected his wife, Deborah,
estranged himself from his illegitimate son, William and negotiated
deals with the hated French to win the American revolution. His
writings, too, have been derided for what critics consider their
strait-laced Puritanism and materialism. His almanacs are all about
getting money or saving it.

TWENTY-EIGHTH MANSION BATN ALHUT (FISH'S BELLY)

Zodiac degrees: 17° Pisces 08' - 00° Aries 00' Sidereal 0-3 degrees
Taurus.

Star: Mirach.
This is a yellow star in the left hip, or girdle of Andromeda. The
traditional name Mirach is a corruption of (Mīzar) which means
girdle. Mirach is of the nature of Venus. It gives beauty, a brilliant
mind, a love of home, great devotion, beneficence, forgiveness, love,
overcoming by kindness, renown, and good fortune in marriage.

Ruled by the *Dæmon:* Anuxi appears as a fish or a man with a fish
face wearing a cloak of many assorted colours. He teaches how to
read dreams, prophecies, and how to develop empathy. He is the
opposite of Abliemel in that he always sees the other's perspective
and invoking him will result in a personal sacrifice (normally this
is harmless, such as the loss of a point of view but it can also bring
pain). He can be a useful contact for exploring the mystical path.

Elections: good for trade, planting, healing, and marriage. Bad for
lending or taking loans. Mediocre for travel. Partnerships begun
here start well but end poorly.

Magical Powers: bringing fish together in one place, inflicting
damage on sailors at sea, increasing merchandise, besieging cities,

increasing harvests, causing things to become lost, destroying areas, bringing safety to travellers, mystical understanding, increasing love between spouses, and keeping captives imprisoned.

Notes: Water is symbolic of resources, wealth, emotions and growth and the symbol of the fish/man/god such as Dagon were important in ancient civilisations. A person born in this mansion might suffer in life, but they will also be a great emphatic teacher. Warnock suggests that this mansion is a force which brings things together. However my view of this mansion is that it is more passive and brings great things but they exist in a raw state and need effort to harvest them. It might show you a good business idea, but you must act to take advantage of it.

For ALL ACTIONS UNDER THE MOON it is better to follow these rules where possible:

When you wish for something to go away from you or someone else, then use the WANING MOON.
When you wish something to come to you, then do the work on the WAXING MOON.
Make offerings to Hekate on the NEW MOON and important rituals that need considerable energy and effort, anything that requires a physical manifestation or similar effect on the FULL MOON.
Make all equipment as close to the NEW MOON as possible.
All rituals that have a sub-lunar or underworld effect must, by necessity, invoke Hekate to bring them to fruition.

CHAPTER SEVEN
MONTH SIX

THE MYSTERIES OF THE 12

RITUAL WORK THIS MONTH

Your rituals will be longer. The goal is to attune to the zodiacal forces and the relevant decan *Dæmons* in your chart. Take your chart and place it on the altar with the ascendant orientated towards the east. Take 12 zodiacal tarot cards and place them in a circle around your altar. The cards should be arranged to match the positions on your chart. Place the card for the decan you are about to invoke on a small table or chair with a tealight which is placed as an offering to the *Dæmon.* There should be a tealight placed on the centre of your chart. You will need consecrated water and incense (use the incense for the planet which rules the decan).

STAGE ONE: THE CENTREPINS

Over the next 12 days you should invoke the four *Dæmons* who make up your centrepins devoting three days to each, starting with Horoskopis, then the underground, then the setting Sun and finally the mid-heaven. The ritual is the same for all of them although the names change. You must spend some time before each rite studying your chart and thinking about how you either express or do not express this power in your life. If you have any planets in those centrepins think about how the decan *Dæmons* are influencing them.

1. Perform the *Lesser Ritual of the Pentagram*.
2. Invoke the Sun for that time of day (and light the centre tealight).
3. Say, **I purify and consecrate my** *Sphere of Sensation* **to liberate it from all the mistakes and misunderstandings caused by me failing to understand my true self. I clear the way so that I will truly express my ascendant in the manner that my Higher Genius wishes.**
4. Go to the east and draw a large zodiacal pentagram with the planetary symbol and invoke the *Dæmon* of the zodiac saying:
5. **"In the name IAΩ I invoke you [name of the Dæmon of the zodiac] you who are the ruler of the sign of [zodiac sign of your**

Asc] Come forth and lend your power to this rite. I open my *Sphere of Sensation* to your power so that you might purify and consecrate the forces under the rule of the Lord of my Horizon so that I might better express the life that my Higher Genius wishes. Come forth as I chant your secret and sacred name.

6. Chant the name of the zodiacal *Dæmon* for five minutes.
7. Pause and briefly meditate on meaning of the zodiac *Dæmon* and its influence on your life.
8. Circumambulate three times and return to the station of the ascendant.
9. Draw a hexagram of the planet which rules the decan of your ascendant.
10. Invoke the *Dæmon* of the decan for the centrepin being aware that you are aligning yourself to it. Say three times **"In the name of [zodiacal spirit] invoke [name of decan Dæmon], revered god, decan of the sign of [zodiac name] bring your influence upon the world of necessity. Come to me in this very hour and very moment to orientate my** *Sphere of Sensation* **to the will of my Higher Genius so that I might better express its will in my life. Go swiftly and quickly [name of Dæmon] for I am like you, an off-spring of the immortal Aion, a being of chaos searching for wisdom in order."**
11. Vibrate the name of your Decan *Dæmon* for ten minutes.

Pause and meditate on the symbolism of your centrepin and see the *Dæmon* being properly expressed. Ask it how you can express its powers better and what you need to do. Ask it to help you transform so that you will be a better expression of your *Higher Genius* and ask it to help you remember who you really are.

STAGE TWO: THE HERMETIC LOTS

Set up your sacred space as before with the small table before the *Dæmon* of the Hermetic Lot you intend to call in the place in which it is in chart. The ritual is identical until point 10.

10. Vibrate the name of your Decan *Dæmon* for five minutes.

11. Invoke the god of the Lot using one of the planetary invocations for basis.

DÆMON

I invoke you mighty ruling Dæmon.

I invoke you MURAI, MURIBI, BABĒL, BAOTH, BAMWI, the great Agathos Dæmon , MURATHO, the form of soul that rests above in the heaven of heavens.

TATOT, BOUEL, MOUIHTAHI, LAHI, BOLBOĒL, I, AA, TAT, BOUĒL and YOHĒL. You are the first servant of the great God, he who giveth light exceedingly, the companion of the flame. You in whose mouth is the fire that is not quenched, the great God who is seated in the fire, he who is in the midst of the fire which is in the lake of heaven, in whose hand is the greatness and the power of God.

Reveal thyself to me here today for I will glorify thee in Abydos, I will glorify thee in heaven before Prē, I will glorify thee before the Moon, I will glorify thee before him who is upon the throne, who is not destroyed, he (= thou) of the great glory, PETER, PATĒR, ENPHE, O God who is above heaven, in whose hand is the beautiful staff, who created deity, and whom a deity did not create.

Come down (in) to me into the midst of this flame that is here before thee, thou of BOĒL. Let me see it, let me hear it, O great God SISIHŌOUT, otherwise said ARMIŌOUTH, come in before me.

Help me to understand you and to express the powers of my Higher Genius which are yours.

FORTUNA*

I invoke you strong Tykhe. Come forth with your auspicious mind and rich abundance.

Never have sceptres obtained calm peace or certainty; care on care weighs them down, and ever do fresh storms vex their souls. Great kingdoms sink of their own weight, and Fortune gives way beneath the burden of herself. Sails swollen with favouring breezes fear blasts too strongly theirs.

The tower which rears its head to the clouds is beaten by rain storms. Whatever you raise you bring low.

The ordinary human has a longer life and is content with the common lot, with safe breeze hugs the shore, and, fearing to trust his skiff to the wider sea, with unambitious oar keeps close to land.

In you, our mortal life is found, and you copious wealth;

---

* A mixture of the Homeric *Hymn to Tchke* and Seneca's chorus to Fortuna in his tragedy *Agamemnon*,

While others mourn thy hand averse to bless, in all the bitterness of deep distress.
Help me to understand you and to express the powers of my Higher Genius which are yours.

NECESSITY

I invoke you Ananke mighty Necessity for you are the great goddess who I cannot refuse.
Like a fish on your line I might resist, but in the end I must surrender.
You bring all the sweetness and the bitter in your wreathed spindle spinning my fate with spider threads of iron. No god can fight you, for you declare what they must do.
By your law, the immemorial ordinance of the gods made fast for ever, bravely sworn and sealed that should any human, daemon, or god, born to enduring life stray from your path, you can punish it with the sea, the earth, cast it into the Sun and fling it into the heavens to fall by all abhorred.
Writer of the story of my life show me what I must to fulfil my destiny. Bind me to a fate where I can be the perfect vessel for my Higher Genius.
Help me to understand you and to express the powers of my Higher Genius which are yours.

COURAGE

I invoke Aretê, which mortals win only through great suffering.
You are life's most beautiful reward of life.
Because of your radiance, oh young woman,
It is enviable to die for you
and, in so doing, to suffer furious, ceaseless labours.
For you inspire such courage within us,
Your fruit is godlike and greater value than gold
or children and leisurely sleep.
Because of you, Iraklís and the sons of Zefs and Lída
Endured difficult labours to acquire your strength.
Yearning for you, Akhilléfs and Aias
Journeyed to the house of the dead.
And on account of your friendly form, this great one from the city of Atarnéfs forsook the light of the Sun.
Come forth, power of Archilles,
May I express your powers in my life, may I aid your mission on

Earth. Help me to understand you and to express the powers of my Higher Genius which are yours.

EROS*

I invoke the author of all creation, who spread your own wings over the universe. You, the unapproachable and unmeasurable who breathe into every soul life-giving reasoning, who fitted all things together by your power, first-born, founder of the universe, golden-winged, whose light is darkness. You who shroud reasonable thoughts and breathe forth dark frenzy, clandestine one who secretly inhabit every soul.

You engender an unseen fire as you carry off every living thing without growing weary of torturing it, having with pleasure delighted in pain from the time when the world came into being.

You also come and bring pain, who are sometimes reasonable, sometimes irrational, because of whom men dare beyond what is fitting and take refuge in your light which is darkness. Most headstrong, lawless, implacable, inexorable, invisible, bodiless, generator of frenzy, archer, torch-carrier, master of all living sensation and of everything clandestine, dispenser of forgetfulness, creator of silence, through whom the light and to whom the light travels, infantile when you have been engendered within the heart, wisest when you have succeeded;

I call upon you, unmoved by prayer, by your great name:

AZARACHTHARAZA LATHA IATHAL Y Y Y LATHAI ATHA LLALAPH IOIOIO AI AI AI OUERIEU OIAI LEGETA RAMAI AMA RATAGEL.

May I express your powers in my life, may I aid your mission on Earth. Help me to understand you and to express the powers of my Higher Genius which are yours.

VICTORY

I invoke the daughter of Night and Doom and mother to human Helen to reveal her mysteries.

Eternal, much revered, you alone rejoice in what is just and right. You influence every mortal and tie us with chains of righteous bondage.

I invoke you, oh Powerful Nike, you who are desired by all

---

* Papyri graecae magicae IV.1716-1870

humanity with fire in their hearts towards adversity.

I invoke whose name quells contending rage, violence, and harm.

It is you who confers the crown amid battle, you who

Distributes the victor's prize.

You rule all things, Nike divine whether it be strife,

or joyful shouts.

Come, mighty Goddess and bring me success

May my deeds be under the shadow of your wings, may I claim, and find your immortal Fame.

May I express your powers in my life, may I aid your mission on Earth. Help me to understand you and to express the powers of my Higher Genius which are yours.

NEMESIS

I invoke the goddess who enacts retribution against those who succumb to hubris. Come forth Nemesis, daughter of Nyx, and implacable justice.

You supply aid to those in need and

Abundant strength to the reasoning power;

And far avert the dire, unfriendly race of counsels impious, arrogant, and base.

Oh Nemesis, and your deep-roaring thunderclaps. Vengeance, justice, outrage, divine jealousy, fortune. You are executioner of braggarts, who pursued them with justice.

Nemesis who opposes the arrogant and watches the things of the Earth. Nemesis the overseer, chastising proud and disdainful ways.'

Unnoticed you snap the haughty neck of the proud, and hold sway over my sustenance.

May I express your powers in my life, may I aid your mission on Earth. Help me to understand you and to express the powers of my Higher Genius Which are yours.

STAGE THREE: THE DÆMONS OF THE PLANETS.

Find the *Dæmons* of the decans for each of the planets. Starting on the day ruled by that planet invoke the *Dæmon* with the intention of understanding how it modifies the power of the planet in your chart. Set up your sacred space as before with the small table before the *Dæmon* of the Hermetic Lot you intend to call in the place in which it is in chart. The ritual is identical until point 8.

Draw a hexagram of the planet which rules the decan of the invoked planet.

Invoke the *Dæmon* of the decan for the decan being aware that you are aligning yourself to it. Say three times **In the name of [zodiacal spirit] invoke [name of decan Dæmon], revered god, decan of the sign of [zodiac name] bring your influence upon the world of necessity. Come to me in this very hour and very moment to orientate my Sphere of Sensation to the will of my Higher Genius so that I might better express its will in my life. Go swiftly and quickly [name of Dæmon] for I am like you, an off-spring of the immortal Aion, a being of chaos searching for wisdom in order.**

Vibrate the name of your Decan *Dæmon* for ten minutes.

Pause and meditate on the symbolism of your decan daemon and see the *Dæmon* being properly expressed. Ask it how you can express its powers better and what you need to do. Ask it to help you transform so that you will be a better expression of your *Higher Genius* and ask it to help you remember who you really are.

WEEK FOUR

It is necessary to strengthen and protect the *Sphere of Sensation* using the arrows of Apollo. Consult your chart and find the decan where your Sun is based. That will be your first and most important arrow. The next day you will involve the *Dæmon* ruling the third decan away from that centre to the left. The next the second and finally the decan on the left of the Sun. Next day start with the decan of the right of the Sun, the day after the second decan on the right of the Sun and then the third. You might have called these decans before but on this occasion, you are activating them for protection. Perform the rituals as normal to point eight.

9. Draw a hexagram of the planet which rules the decan of the invoked arrow *Dæmon*.

Invoke the Arrow *Dæmon* of the decan. Say three times **In the name of [zodiacal spirit] invoke [name of decan Dæmon], revered god, decan of the sign of [zodiac name] bring your influence upon the world of necessity. Come to me in this very hour and very moment to stand guard on my Sphere of Sensation so that no being seen, or unseen may violate my holy sphere of the mysteries. Let those who would do me harm be cut down by your arrows of light from the Sun itself.**

For the mightiest cannot stand against Apollo's swift arrows.

They who fight me fights with Apollo.

His golden bow strikes them from afar.
One swift arrow after another.
The star's cry Hie hie Paian! Shoot the arrow!
For I know Thee and I know Thy secret name:
(Name of decan)
I know your symbols and that you appear as (describe symbols).
I ask you to stand your watch on my Sphere of Sensation so that
all harmful forces may kept away from me.
For your powers are my powers,
For I am like you an off-spring of the immortal Aion, a being of
chaos searching for wisdom in order.
Take your station in my Sphere of Sensation as I vibrate your holy
name.

9. Vibrate the name of your Decan *Dæmon* for ten minutes.
10. Pause and meditate on the symbolism of your decan *Dæmon* and
see the *Dæmon* in the form of an archer in your *Sphere of Sensation*.

The *Odyssey* and the *Iliad* were treated as sacred texts by
the ancients and the stories studied for arcane secrets. The
second poem of Homer, the *Odyssey* tells the story of the
Greek hero, Odysseus returning to his kingdom, Ithaca, after
the destruction of Troy.

Odysseus left the nymph Calypso (Καλυψώ) on a raft and
followed her instructions to "navigate by the stars". Poseidon
sent a storm and Odysseus was shipwrecked on the island of the
Phaeacians, (Φαίακες), Skheria (Σχερία). It was a happy land where
nature always produced flowers and fruits, much like the Elysian
Fields. Twelve kings ruled the island, and a thirteenth one reined
over all of them. It was in a Phaeacian ship Odysseus finally landed
at Ithaca*.

The number 12 was associated with the signs of the zodiac, so
it becomes important that we work with them as part of our path of
return. The Phaeacians say of themselves: " No living person ever
born would come to our Phaecia with a hostile mind, since we are
much beloved by the gods. Our island is remote, washed around by
sea; we have no human contact."† which sums up the signs of the
zodiac and their distance from Earth. The Greek name Φαίακες is
derived from *phaiós* (φαιός "gray") so from this we can read that the

---

* See *Odyssey* book six.
† Homer, *Odyssey*, 6.200-205

Dæmons of the zodiac are neither good nor evil but a mix of both*.

Skheria means "sea coast" which poetically means the rim of the cosmic ocean. The "zodiac" is ruled by the thirteenth king Alcinous (Ἀλκίνοος) whose name means "mighty mind" which is a reference to the *Logos* and Odysseus's way into it is through his daughter Nausicaa Ναυσικάα (whose name means to burn a boat, which could be both be a reference to the stars or a magical technique to approach them).

Thanks to popular astrology most people are familiar with the signs of the zodiac. These are the division of the ecliptic in twelve equal sectors. Each of the parts of the sky have certain patterns of stars associated with different myths which tune the planetary energy when each of these planets moves through them. Zodiac signs originated in Babylonia. The Greeks first adapted the concept and it was fused with Egyptian ideas. The zodiac is divided into twelve signs, each occupying 30° of celestial longitude and corresponding to the constellations Aries, Taurus, Gemini, Cancer, Leo, Virgo, Libra, Scorpio, Sagittarius, Capricorn, Aquarius, and Pisces.

Each human has elements of all the 12 signs, yet some powers are stronger and more obvious than others because they are enhanced by the presence of the planets and the decans.

In PGM VII.795—845 GM VII.795—845 we find a list of magical names of the zodiac and the *Dæmons* which are associated with them. Handily it also supplies some sigils which we can use to access some of this zodiacal power. Each name and sign is written on a laurel leaf as part of the ritual

On his research blog†, Sam Block points out that this attribution of magical names and characters to the zodiac signs is unlike anything else in the PGM. Normally in the PGM the zodiac is mentioned in a direct and non-magical about it (much like astrology).

"To have a magical approach to these signs with barbarous words and characters would be a massive boon for deploying other kinds of zodiacal invocations or conjurations in the style of the PGM," Block wrote.

---

* Magically we will use part of the above verse "οἰκέομεν δ' ἀπάνευθε πολυκλύστῳ ἐνὶ πόντῳ, ἔσχατοι, οὐδέ τις ἄμμι βροτῶν ἐπιμίσγεται ἄλλος." As part of our quest.

† On the Zodiacal Names and Characters of PGM VII.795—845 https://digitalambler.com/2018/05/31/on-the-zodiacal-names-and-characters-of-pgm-vii-795-845/

Unfortunately, the papyrus had been misinterpreted by the scholars who had translated it up to that point. As a result, the list of characters didn't make sense. Some signs had several characters, others none, and some seemed to be clustered together in weird ways. Block went back to the original manuscript and came up with the following list:

Sign	*MAGICAL NAMES*	
Aries	ΑΡΜΟΝΘΑΡΘΩΧΕ	Harmontharthōkhe (Armontharthawche)
Taurus	ΝΕΟΦΟΞΩΘΑ ΘΟΨ	Neophoksōtha Thops (Neophoksawtha Thops
Gemini	ΑΡΙΣΤΑΝΑΒΑ ΖΑΩ	Aristanaba Zaō (Areestanava Zaaw)
Cancer	ΠΧΟΡΒΑΖΑΝΑΧΟΥ	PkhorbazanakhŪ- (Pchorvazanachoo)
Leo	ΖΑΛΑΜΟΙΡΛΑΛΙΘ	Zalamoirlalith (Zalameerlaleeth)
Virgo	ΕΙΛΕΣΙΛΑΡΜΟΥ ΦΑΙ	Eilesilarmū Phai (Eeleseelarmoo Faee)
Libra	ΤΑΝΤΙΝΟΥΡΑΧΘ	Tantinūrakhth (Tanteenūrachth)
Scorpio	ΧΟΡΧΟΡΝΑΘΙ	Ckhorkhornath (Chorchornathee)
Sagittarius	ΦΑΝΘΕΝΦΥΦΛΙΑ ΞΥΥ	Phanthenphyphlia (Phanthenphyphleea) Ksyy (Ksyy)
Capricorn	ΑΖΑΖΑΕΙΣΘΑΙΛΙΧ	Azazaeisthailikh (Azazaeesthelich)
Aquarius	ΜΕΝΝΥΘΥΘ ΙΑΩ	Mennythyth IaŌ (Mennythyth Eeaaw)
Pisces	ΣΕΡΥΧΑΡΡΑΛΜΙΩ	Serycharralmiō (Serycharralmeeaw)

The sigils of the Zodiac are as follows:

ARIES	LIBRA
TAURUS	SCORPIO
GEMINI	SAGITTARIUS
CANCER	CAPRICORN
LEO	AQUARIUS
VIRGO	PISCES

ZODIAC TAROT CARDS

Although there is absolutely no evidence for Tarot cards before the middle ages and no link to them for esoteric purposes before the 18th, they remain a good symbolic focus for different forces. If you want a good primer into the magical use of Tarot look at either Paul Case's *Tarot* or Pat and Christine Zalewski's *Magical Tarot of the Golden Dawn*. Tarot cards can be placed on an altar during a ritual to aid magical focus and meditation. In my view they create a better effect than using the traditional zodiacal images.

The tarot cards which rule the different zodiac signs are:

Zodiac sign	Tarot Card
Aries	The Emperor
Taurus	The Hierophant
Gemini	The Lovers
Cancer	The Chariot
Leo	Strength
Virgo	Hermit
Libra	Justice

Scorpio	Death
Sagittarius	Temperance
Capricorn	Devil
Aquarius	Star
Pisces	Moon

REFINING ASTROLOGICAL IMPACT

Last month you looked at the effects of the planetary powers in isolation. They were effectively how strong the seven rays were in your life. However, this is a little like watching actors perform in front of a black screen. We might know who or what they are, but we have little idea of the context in which they are working. We also do not know how that scenery influences their acting choices – if the backdrop were an office it would provide a different context for our script than being on top of Mount Everest. Our lives have 12 Places or scenes. The ancients realised that the seven planetary powers operate differently in each scene.

In some scenes they found that their powers flowed better than normal and the ancients called these joys. The Sun is at its happiest in the Ninth House which is the house of spirit and magic, while the

Moon finds its joy in the third which is the house of relatives.

The Ancient Place meanings are a little different from modern astrology which has simply added more meanings to its houses, often losing the original point.

FIRST PLACE

This place is called the Hour-Marker and the Helm. The Helm is the command section of a ship. Proclus said that when the *Higher Genius* decided to incarnate into matter it chose the Helm as the place to enter the personality. The Helm is the place which is closely related to who you are. Mercury has its joy here because it is the place of the dawn and the boundary where sky means the Earth. It was also known as the place of life and signifies your body, health, and constitution. It was sometimes believed to reveal appearance. It is the total of the *Lower Self* and the contents of the *Sphere of Sensation*. It can represent the beginning of a person's life.

SECOND PLACE

The Second Place was called the Gates of Hades and there is some esoteric ideas in this title. It is the last house which the planets must pass through before they rise into the heavens. This station was also mentioned in Ancient Egypt in the Book of the Dead. From a human perspective it shows a descent into the material world. It's what happens after your soul as been made and you enter matter at birth. It covers issues like livelihood and the resources you need to live. Money and resources that a person will have are dealt with in this place. Hades was the god of riches and wealth so it makes sense that this is where the association with money came from.

THIRD PLACE

The Third place was called the "Goddess" and the Moon has its joy here. It was said to represent brothers and sisters, friends, short distance travel and the extended family. An important association was religious observance (which modern astrology tends to place in the ninth house). This means worship, sacred places, temples, and priests and priestesses. Malefic signs here would often mean that the person would blaspheme against the gods (and suffer punishment for their efforts). This is more of the administration of worship (the ninth is more the spiritual nature of it all).

The third place indicated power over cities or people. This meant governors, queens and administrators. These are people with followers.

FOURTH PLACE

The fourth place was called the underground because it represented the lowest part of the chart which was under the Earth. This is the place where the person has their roots and their foundation. Like the underworld it is intricately connected to the ancestors and the dead. For this reason, it was said to represent a person's parents and inheritance.

Because it is the most hidden and private part of the chart it came to be associated with the home, the house in which you were born and private property. It also shows a person's sense of permanence. A logical extension of this can be the secrets a person might have.

Unlike modern astrology it is connected to death and funerals. Some ancient astrologers (such as Ptolemy) say this place is connected to children.

FIFTH PLACE

The Fifth Place is the place of good fortune and is the joy of Venus. It is associated with increases, particularly of material wealth. It shows how successful you are going to be. Historically success was often your "genetic success" so the house began to be associated with children.

The house makes benefics even better and reduces the negative effect of malefic planets. However negative placements can show a loss of personal assets through misfortune. Vettius Valens says that the house relates to any good act including generosity or friendship.

SIXTH PLACE

The Sixth place is the place of bad fortune and it is the joy of Mars. It is associated with injury and sickness and troubles. It shows enemies, plots and wars. Travel is sometimes shown but it is not the sort of trip you would voluntarily do. It can cause someone to be born disabled, low-born or naturally unlucky. It is the house of the oppressed.

SEVENTH PLACE

This is called the house of setting and it is connected to things outside you. The most obvious of these are relationships, sex, and marriage. It is another house which is to do with death, but in this case the quality of death normally in old age. Valens tells us it indicates long periods travelling too. Rhetorius the Egyptian said that if there are malefics in this house there could be injury, or a violent death but good planets here suggest inheritance and acquiring the property of others.

EIGHTH PLACE

The Eighth Place is called the idle place. Some astrologers said that this was the place of death and anything that could be derived from things such as inheritance. Valens suggested that it represented the livelihood of the marriage partner.

Generally, it was associated with idleness and weaknesses, inactivity and wasted opportunities. Valens adds that it might also be the place of punishment or Justice.

NINTH PLACE

The Ninth Place was the place of God and it was the joy of the Sun. It was associated with travel and foreigners and journeys. It was associated with philosophical ideas, mysticism, magic, astrology, piousness, oracles and prophets. There are similarities with the third house in that this house represents status, kings and authorities. In my belief, the third represented the form while the tenth represents actual temporal and spiritual authority. An armchair occultist would be third house while the working magician would be in the ninth.

TENTH PLACE

The tenth place is called the mid-heaven and shows the peak of your life and career. It is often used to mean your occupation. It shows your reputation and rank, advancement, change and improvements. It shows how effective you are.

ELEVENTH PLACE

The eleventh place is the place of the good *Dæmon* and it is the joy of Jupiter. It is associated with friendship but this is more to do with the ancient idea of patronage (so these are friends which are useful to your life goals). It is also connected to hopes, desires and expectations. It can be what you see for yourself and therefore bring future benefits. This is also the house of the *Higher Genius* so this can represent some important parts of your destiny.

TWELFTH PLACE

The Twelfth Place is called the house of the evil spirit and it is the joy of Saturn. It stands for everything that happened before birth both for the mother and the child during pregnancy. It is a half-way house between different cycles, but it also shows a degree of weakness. For this reason, it is associated with sickness, death, injuries and other trouble.

It relates to confinement or restraint. Ancient societies did not have a prison system so confinement was less of an option. There are however elements of justice and punishment connected to this place.

CENTREPINS

The centrepins are the main orientating houses and are known as the cardinal points in modern astrology. The first one (in the first house) is called the Horoskopis or the hour-marker. In modern astrology it is called the ascendant). It defines the life of a person. It stands for your starting point where you took your first breath. It is said to represent the vital energy that you put out into the world. Ancient astrologers said that if the planetary ruler of the house of the ascendant was in the 2nd, 6th, 8th or 12th houses the person lacked a clear sense of direction. The Lord of the Ascendant was said to be your advocate when talking to the gods so having it away from the ascendant was a terrible thing. Things are much better if the Lord of the Ascendant is exalted because it would have more power to direct the person's life.

The other centrepins fourth house was known as the "underground" because this is the place closest to the Earth and is where things most naturally come to rest. It symbolises burial and what we leave behind when we die. It is old age, ancestors, and our security.

The seventh was the house of the "setting Sun" It gives signs for the quality of death, wedding preparations, long terms abroad and the elderly age. However, it was associated with long journeys. Some of this might be down to the fact that the seventh house is the furthest from the ascendant and therefore life and your "self." The association with partnerships and romance arrived later but it makes sense in a Hellenic system because it was also a place of confrontation with our darker sides. Most relationships are about projection and the resulting confrontation is how relationships become friendship, partnership, and marriage.

The last is the mid-heaven or work. It stands for authority and practical hierarchy. It is our highest potential, and our best achievements. It was associated with fame, social responsibility, status, and character. The lord of the 10th show the person's honour and reputation, the native and the nature of their work or profession. It will be the public perception of them rather than what they really are.

If the lord of the mid-heaven happens to be in the fourth house and a malefic should be present with it, or make a diameter (opposition), it creates evil-doers.

Invoking the *Dæmons* of these places, along with any attendant planets orientates the *Sphere of Sensation* to its correct pattern.

In the last month you attuned yourself to the planets and their *Dæmon* s, but the ancients considered the *Dæmons* which ruled the decans vital. It is my personal belief that it is these that became the demons of the grimoire tradition, mostly because of their multi-part symbolic nature and division of function.

DECANS

The decans are 36 groups of stars (small constellations) used in the Ancient Egyptian astronomy. Each rising marked the beginning of a new decanal "hour" (Greek hōra) of the night for the ancient Egyptians, and they were used as a sidereal star clock beginning by at least the 9th or 10th Dynasty (c. 2100 BCE). A different decan in the eastern sky at dawn right before the Sun rises, the ancient Greeks called them dekanoi (δεκανοί; pl. of δεκανός dekanos) or "tenths."

Originally, they had their basis in the Ancient Egyptian calendar with each decan under the name of a god. When the Greeks arrived, the decans were incorporated into astrology and the names of the rulers became more mysterious *Dæmons*.

As we have seen each star was a physical manifestation of a god, so the knowledge of the decans could name the gods which were a major influence on your life. The *Dæmons* tune the zodiacal influence so that it becomes something slightly different. A person might be a light-hearted Sagittarius but the influence of a Saturnian *Dæmon* of the third degree might turn that force into a more rigid and disciplined format. The *Dæmon* will take the Sagittarian energy and create a set of ethical rules that the person will live by. However rather than being a fundamentalist neo-biblical approach they will be open to review. When faced by a crisis the *Dæmon* will force the person to follow the most honourable book. They will take Jupiterian issues like law, race, culture, religion, education, spirituality, and philosophy very seriously and approach them with a certain discipline that a normal Sagittarian lack.

The decans and their rulers are assigned as follows:

Sign	0-10 degrees	10-20 degrees	20-30 degrees
Aries	Mars	Sun	Venus
Taurus	Mercury	Moon	Saturn
Gemini	Jupiter	Mars	Sun
Cancer	Venus	Mercury	Moon
Leo	Saturn	Jupiter	Mars
Virgo	Sun	Venus	Mercury
Libra	Moon	Saturn	Jupiter
Scorpio	Mars	Sun	Venus
Sagittarius	Mercury	Moon	Saturn
Aquarius	Venus	Mercury	Moon
Pisces	Saturn	Jupiter	Mars

The names of the *Dæmons* of the decans were found in the *Sacred Book of Hermes to Asclepius* which survived in medieval manuscripts but dates to the 1st to 4th centuries CE. The book gave the names of the *Dæmons* of the decans, their magical images and plants and stones attributed to them. The version I consulted was translated by Joao Pedro Feliciano.* This supplies the secret names of the *Dæmons* which rule each decan and appear closer to the names of the Egyptian gods. These forces are extremely useful when it comes to understanding the self and healing. Jake Stratton-Kent, in his *Testament of Cyprian the Mage,* has managed to find the modern names for the stones and plants. Although this information is less useful to this work, it is important for any future planetary work involving these spirits.

I have expanded the meaning of each based on the symbol of the planet and the symbolism of the *Dæmon*. Some of the associations such as the Tarot cards and the titles are based on the Shem Angels

---

* *The Hermetic Tablet: Journal of Western Ritual Magic* Winter Solstice 2016.

which fulfil a similar function.* The specific Tarot titles come from my *Shem Grimoire* book and are based on my own Tarot researches.

ARIES

First decan of Aries is ruled by the *Dæmon* KHENLAKHÔRI and it is a messenger for the God. It has the face of a young child with hands raised upward. He bears a sceptre, holding it above his head. His feet are wrapped to his knees. He rules illnesses that afflict the head. KHENLAKHÔRI's Tarot card is the Two of Wands and he is the Lord of Resolution and Belligerence. The stone sacred to him was the Babylonian Stone† and the plant was an Isophrus.‡

Khenlakhôri creates a more active, longer lasting and sometimes aggressive form of Aries. The person will have a lot of energy but be inclined to rage when things go wrong. In many ways they will be more childlike – prone to temper tantrums and sulking. They are extremely stubborn.

The Second decan is ruled by the *Dæmon* KONTARET or KAÙ and he has a dog's face. He holds a sceptre in his right hand and a disk in his left. He is covered in wrappings down to his ankles. He governs the temples and the nose. Its Tarot card is the Three of Wands the Lord of Initiation and Intimidation. His stone is a Siderite, and plant is Wild Rue.

Kontaret encourages those under his power to start something new and makes it difficult for them to stay still. He inspires pioneers in whatever they do and press on taking risks where others would not. Those influenced by Kontaret might have less long-term staying power and are more ego driven. They can be forceful guides and at times intimidating. Kontaret-influenced people can be the scary teacher at school who some people learn the most from, while others were paralysed with fear.

The Third decan is ruled by the *Dæmon* SIKET and is depicted as a woman with a drum on her head and a sceptre in her right hand, with a flask in her left. She is covered in wrappings down to her ankles. She rules over the ear, uvula, and teeth. The Tarot card is the Four of Wands, the Lord of Perfected Work and Insensitivity. Her stone was a bostrychite§ and plant Plantain.

---

* *The Shem Grimoire* by Nick Farrell

† A Bloodstone according to Stratton-Kent.

‡ A Heliotrope according to Stratton-Kent

§ Either Iron alum or satin asbestos according to Stratton-Kent.

Siket makes Aries more childlike, fun-loving and a little self-centred. She causes them to hate vagueness and prefer people to be direct and blunt with them. They crave novelty and thrive on competition. In relationships Siket influenced people need to take the lead but also crave dynamism in a partner.

TAURUS

The first decan of Taurus is ruled the *Dæmon* SÔOU, who looks like a man with the head of a ram. He wears a Syrian robe down to his feet and holds in both hands sceptres which he rests on his shoulders. This decan governs the neck. Its Tarot card is the five of pentacles and he is the Lord of Convention and Mental Inertia. Its stone is a Selenite* and plant is a Spherical Cypress†.

Sôou encourages Taurus towards practical and rational thought. He might help a person focus on the material and be clever in business. But he does not encourage original thought. Sôou's ideas and communication may lack innovation, but they will be more practical. Sôou influenced people avoid conflict and want peace and harmony in their dealings. They are slow to make decisions or change their minds. They are mentally conservative and can sometimes be lazy. As a force, Sôou sometimes tries to stop intellectual systems breaking down before they have time to be tested.

The second decan of Taurus is ruled by the *Dæmon* ARÔN who looks like a woman holding a sceptre with both hands, standing upright, her feet together, covered with wrappings down to her feet like Osiris. She governs the tonsils and the neck. Her Tarot card is the Six of Pentacles, the Lord of Security and Greed. Arôn's stone is Aphrodite's Stone‡, and her plant is Dittany.

Arôn encourages a focus on the home and comfort. She creates people with a strong conservative streak who avoid "messy" or unpredictable situations, crises, and emotional displays. Arôn can cause a lack of understanding for a partner's need for change, growth, or emotional stimulation. Arôn can make a person desire to own wealth and goods, without giving them any satisfaction.

The Third decan of Taurus is ruled by the *Dæmon* HRÔMENÔS. He appears as a dog-headed man with curls on his head. In his right hand he holds a sceptre and his left hand touches his buttocks. He

---

* Gypsum according to Jake Stratton-Kent

† Based on the original Greek, Jake Stratton-Kent believes this to be a citrus fruit.

‡ Yellow zircon, according to Stratton-Kent

wears a belt that falls at his knees. It rules the mouth and throat. Hrômenôs' stone is a Hyacinth and his plant is a Bugloss. His Tarot card is the Seven of Pentacles which is the Lord of Limitation and Materialism.

Hrômenôs makes Taurians even more conservative and restricted. He can make a person feel less secure or make security a high priority. Hrômenôs will make someone hardworking and reliable, but it will only provide them with limited success. If they succeed it will be because they have worked hard rather than come up with something new. Hrômenôs-influenced people are preoccupied with the physical and tend not to believe in anything they cannot see. They can lack creativity, but Hrômenôs makes people humble, grounded, and unaffected by celebrity or social status. While they are obsessed with money the Hrômenôs-influenced are more interested in what it does for them rather than showing it off.

GEMINI

The first decan of Gemini is ruled by the *Dæmon* XOKHÁ who is a messenger for the god Set. which looks like a man with the head of a donkey. He holds a small key in his right hand, and his left is dropped. He is covered in wrappings down to his knees. He governs the shoulders. His stone is a Diamond and plant is an Orchid. His Tarot card is the Eight of Swords, which is the Lord of Words and Stress.

Xokhá aids people attract the most good fortune through wit and ingeniousness. He makes Gemini people even more versatile, sociable, curious, and able to put others at ease with friendliness and sincere curiosity. They become more mentally adventurous, ready and willing to learn, into "mind expansion", and less attached to their own values than others because they are impartial and open-minded. Xokhá encourages expression through written communication and has a connection to the Egyptian god Thoth. His force creates stress to enable performance under pressure.

The second decan of Gemini is ruled by the *Dæmon* OUARÍ who looks like a man with the head of a goat. He holds a stick (or staff) in his right hand, and his left hangs over his thigh. He is covered in wrappings down to the knees. He governs the arms. His stone is a Pankhrous* stone and his plant is Cinquefoil. Ouarí's Tarot card is the Nine of Swords, which is the Lord of Analysis and Interrogation.

---

* Opal, according to Stratton-Kent

Ouarí encourages intellectual genius and enables skill planning and strategising. This means a person can take a nebulous idea and see the steps they must take to bring it about. Innovation and creation come easy to them when they set their mind to it. The down side is Ouarí creates frustration in routine and a constant quest for new things. Ouarí-influenced people can be fun and social and need something going on in their lives. He creates good journalists and barristers who use their skills to obtain information from people.

The third decan of Gemini is ruled by the *Dæmon* PEPISÔTH. It has the form of a woman holding thunder(bolts) in her right hand and a flask in her left. She has wings which go from the middle of her body to her feet and has a crown on her head. She governs the hands. Her stone is a Heliotrope and her plant is Rosemary. Her Tarot card is the 10 of swords which is the Lord of Mutability and superficiality.

Pepisôth creates a person who strongly needs to express themselves. She encourages people to collect and distribute information. It emphases flexibility and evolution which enables a quick adaption to any situation. Such people enjoy intellectual conversations but become bored if they are not getting enough mental stimulation. However, there is a lack of specialisation or depth to this *Dæmon* due to Ouarí's short attention span.

CANCER

The first decan of Cancer is ruled by the *Dæmon* SÔTHEÍR. It looks like a man with the head of a dog; his whole body has a spiral shape like that of a serpent. He is seated on a pedesta and governs illnesses that manifest in the sides of the trunk. Its stone is a Dryite and plant is Artemisia*. Sôtheír's Tarot card is the Two of Cups which is the Lord of Love and Vulnerability.

Sôtheír transforms Cancer people making them more emotional and home focused. He makes love incredibly important and romance everything. This means sentimentally looking for that mythical "One" who you will settle down with and live happily ever after. This makes a person incredibly vulnerable. This means that the person is often hurt. This emotional sensitivity does help magically, making a person intuitive with the instinctual ability to work out others' needs.

The second decan of Cancer is ruled by the *Dæmon* OUPHISIT. This spirit looks like a woman with the body of a bird. Her wings are outstretched as if she was about to take flight. She has a tress on her

---

* Mugwort, according to Stratton-Kent

head. this decan governs afflictions of the lung. Her stone is Green Jasper and its plant is Selenogone.* Her Tarot card is the Three of Cups which is the Lord of Expression and Fulfilment.

Ouphisit gives people good minds, which are sometimes too influenced by their emotions. It creates a situation where someone thinks about something and feels another way about it. The mind is overwhelmed by unconscious desires which biases any objective thinking. This may cause a person to look at some facts but ignore others just because they lack appeal. This *Dæmon* supplies a great intense memory and the ability to subliminally absorb and learn. The Ouphisi-influenced have a good psychic ability because of those mental processes, however they must express what they feel. This is because Ouphisit is a *Dæmon* of Abundance who brings ideas into matter.

The third decan of Cancer is ruled by the *Dæmon* KHNOUPHOS who has two female heads turned away from each other. One wears a small hat, the other a diadem. Dragons surround her neck. Her whole torso is set on a pedestal. She governs the spleen and her stone is Eukhaitê† and plant is a Spherite.‡ Her tarot card is the Four of Cups which is the Lord of Sensitivity and Emotion.

Khnouphos creates a version of Cancer which is even more psychic than normal, although it can be more obsessed with the past. It will cause someone to hang onto pain for decades. There is a complete inability to detach from people or places and there will be a tendency to accumulate objects or emotionally manipulate to feel secure. The Khnouphos-influenced can be victims of habit. It creates a moody person with a baffling sense of humour.

LEO

The first decan of Leo is ruled by the *Dæmon* KHNOUMOS. He has the head of a lion, from which issues seven solar rays. His whole body is that of a spiralling serpent, going upwards. He rules over afflictions of the heart. His stone is Agate and the plant is Edelweiss§. Its Tarot card is the Five of Wands, which is the Lord of Animal Power and Ego. Its name was associated with healing (often of digestion) and appears on lots of different talismans — particularly outside Egypt.

---

* Peony, according to Stratton-Kent

† Eagle Stone, according to Stratton-Kent

‡ Citrus fruit, according to Stratton-Kent

§ Alchemilla, according to Stratton-Kent.

Khnoumos creates some difficulty for Leonine energy as it creates challenges and opportunities throughout life. These challenges are not meant to defeat a person – but help create opportunities. Khnoumos makes Leos more authoritarian and autocratic. It creates a more egotistical form of Leo, but one with focused energy and drive. The image is one of a running lion and Khnoumos appears to influence the animal drives and cause strife through competition.

The second decan of Leo is ruled by the *Dæmon* IPI and looks like a naked man with a sceptre in his right hand, a whip in his left, and a lunar crescent (selênên) on his head. He governs the upper back. His stone is a Selenite and plant is a Chrysogone*. His Tarot card is the Six of Wands which is the Lord of Success and Excess.

Ipi is a protective *Dæmon* who aids success through organisational skills, he can equally resolve a situation by overdoing it in terms of strength and drama. He brings good fortune through magnanimity and inspiring confidence in others. Success can be found in creative areas such as entertainment, children, and recreation. Ipi makes Leo more optimistic, pragmatic, practical, calm, loyal, and thanks to Jupiter—feel hopeful and re-energised. However, they have issues with those who do not recognise their abilities and need praise.

The third decan of Leo is ruled by the *Dæmon* PHÁTITI. It looks like a wild faced man with his right hand held up in a greeting position. He holds a flask in his left. He governs the liver. Its stone is a Helite†, and there was no ancient attribution for his plant. Phátiti's Tarot card is the Seven of Wands which is Lord of War and Violence.

Phátiti is a *Dæmon* who destroys old and outworn structures with little subtlety. It tends towards violence to justify any solution. Sometimes this is good, when it comes to destroying something seriously rotten, but it can also be the mindless thug, genocide, or total war. Passions and desire run high and this *Dæmon* creates a strong willpower. Phátiti creates a sense of a "calling" and forces people to act with authority, power, and their personal magnetism.

VIRGO

The first decan of Virgo is ruled by the *Dæmon* ATHOUM. Its face is that of a dog with a crest on his head. His body is red and fiery and stands on a pedestal. and governs the belly. Athoum's stone is

---

* Chrysanthemum, according to Stratton-Kent

† Halite, according to Stratton-Kent

a Corallite* and his plant is Weasel Eye. Athoum's Tarot card is the Eight of Pentacles which is the Lord of Practicality and Pedantry.

Athoum brings about material wealth and happiness through hard work. Virgo becomes more methodical and pickier. On the plus side it becomes more patient and gets results by doing things properly. It can force Virgo to hang onto projects when they should be abandoned. Athoum creates is a pedantic force which enables a person to see details but sometimes at the expense of the bigger picture. He brings practical skills, talents and abilities, with an emphasis on being useful. Athoum makes Virgo more self-effacing and discriminating. He creates a need to be useful rather than the need to be recognised.

The second decan of Virgo is ruled by the *Dæmon* called BRUSOUS and looks like a man with a horned goat's head, dressed down to his heels, bearing a sceptre in his right hand and a flask in his left. It governs illnesses of the bowels. Brusous' stone is a Dendrite† and its plant is Liquorice. Its Tarot card is Nine of Pentacles which has the titles Lord of Material Gain and Criticism.

Brusous-influenced people take an analytical, reserved and practical approach to relationships. Brusous creates is the form of love that listens and sees. Brusous does not like show-offs and know-it-alls. He can brings material gain, although any result goes as fast as it arrives. Brusous influences Virgo to be is hyper-critical which can be useful in some environments. When he is critical Brusous is truly trying to help but sometimes they come across as being negative, particularly if another person is hanging onto delusions. Brusous can see a person in their true colours.

The third decan of Virgo is ruled by the *Dæmon* AMPHATHÁM, and looks like an standing man, covered chest to feet in wrappings, bearing a sceptre with both hands, and having a small hat on his head. He governs the navel and his stone is an Euthlizouti and his plant is a Katanankê‡. Amphathám's Tarot card is the Ten of Pentacles which is the Lord of Established Wealth and Intellectualisation.

Amphathám influences Virgo to keep wealth and protect material possessions. He defends against material curses and genetic illnesses. Amphathám's is a force that can abstract anything which is not the truth. He is a great revealer and intellectual, creating sharp minds that can easily understand complex patterns, processes, and problems.

---

* Could be Coral.

† Dendrite Agate, according to Stratton-Kent

‡ Vetch, according to Stratton-Kent

Communication tends to be direct and focused rather than creative. It is force of a journalist rather than a novelist. There might be a struggle with perfectionism. Amphathám's is serious when he speaks but can have a great wit with dry or sarcastic humour.

LIBRA

The first decan of Libra is ruled by the *Dæmon* SPHOUKOU. He looks like an old man with a belt, his left hand raised as if to receive something, the right hand hanging down. He holds a flask. Sphoukou governs the buttocks and rectum. Its stone is Jasper-Agate and its plant is a Polium.* His Tarot card is the Two of Swords which is the Lord of Peace and Indecision.

Sphoukou is a great reconciler and bringer of peace. He transforms Libra into a peace-keeper and a diplomat between warring parties. Because he demands peace at all costs it can make those under his influence indecisive, vague, or confused. However, they are focused on the truth. Sphoukou creates a strong need for partnership mostly because he draws out the need for security through others. Sphoukou teaches charm and manners. It is an idealistic force which sees flaws in their environment and their relationships and seeks to change them.

The second decan of Libra is ruled by the *Dæmon* NEPHTHIMÊS. He looks like a man standing on a fountain from which issue streams which unite into one. He is covered from his chest to his ankles in wrappings. He has a curl in his beard and holds a flask. Nephthimês governs the urethra, bladder, and the urinary tract. His stone is a Red Onyx and his plant is Vervain. His Tarot card is the Three of Swords which is the Lord of Sorrow and Bureaucracy.

Nephthimês rules all laws created by humanity and the ties that hold human societies together. While these are shadows of the laws of creation they are key factors in humankind's evolution. This *Dæmon* insists that the rules are followed, and those under his influence are either law-abiding citizens or those who end up being caught by their own unconscious sense of Justice. Nephthimês creates a sense of struggle, particularly in relationships, and will create life lessons through relationship choices. Nephthimês creates fears of rejection however he can stabilise Libran characteristics, making them more decisive and constant.

The third decan of Libra is ruled by the *Dæmon* PHOU. He has the

---

* Felty Germander according to Stratton-Kent

face of a serpent with a man's body. He bears a crown on his head and stands upright in wrapped trousers. He governs illnesses that afflict the anus, like haemorrhoids, calluses, and fissures. Phou's stone is an emerald and its plant is Vervain. His Tarot card is the Four of Swords which is the Lord of Liberty and Chaos.

Phou is a much more liberated active form of Libra. It overthrows tyranny and destroys old and outworn systems. He appears the opposite of much of Libra force but is really the balancing nature of the sign and the desire to restore harmony. If systems become too corrupt Phou desires to destroy them so that they can be rebuilt. It can be a more idealist drive than something which is practical. It might believe in a revolution but will only do so if people are not going to get hurt (which limits options). Phou influenced people have an intense sense of justice and the ability to mobilise others.

Scorpio

The first decan of Scorpio is ruled by the *Dæmon* BÔS. He looks like a man with the head of a bull and has four wings. He has a belt, holds a flask in his right hand and a sceptre in his left. Bôs relieves pains that afflict the penile orifice and inflammatory oedemas. His stone is Hematite, and he is connected to any mercurial plant. Its Tarot card is the Five of Cups which is the Lord of Intensity and Revenge.

Bôs brings out the intense and violent nature of Scorpio. He can bring intense mystical experiences, but often acts like a Fury. Bôs provides focus which can be an obsession. There is no forgiveness only revenge with this *Dæmon*. On the positive side Bôs forces a person to challenge themselves to do the impossible and supplies concentrated energy and willpower. It will use its powers to see through others to exploit them. It is a strongly sexual force, which is strongly part of its power complex. Bôs is a dangerous force for those with low self-esteem as they can project their self-loathing outward and end up manipulating others and feeling resentful.

The second decan of Scorpio is ruled by the *Dæmon* OUSTIKHOS. He looks like a man standing in a robe atop a scorpion. Oustikhos rules over warts and infections of the genitals. His stone is a Pyrite and his plant is a Sunflower. His Tarot card is the Six of Cups which is the Lord of Desire and Manipulation.

Oustikhos supplies the energy to pursue goals, particularly those which are based on sensual needs and pleasures. On the positive side this provides drives for spiritual goals, but it can turn

Scorpio into an extremely controlling and manipulative force. It is a useful force to use against slander. While not as aggressive as Bôs, Oustikhos' actions are more ego driven and arrogant. He emphases the subtle and the profound and is motivated by a need to create emotional closeness with others. Oustikhos influenced people penetrate the core of reality, to see things and others as they truly are. This *Dæmon* rules crisis, life and death decisions and emergency services. Oustikhos is also *Dæmon* of liars, back-stabbers, traitors, thieves, and sexual criminals. It builds impenetrable defences and can beguile opponents into underestimating their resilience.

The third decan of Scorpio is ruled by the *Dæmon* APHÊBIS. He has the body of a man with the head of a goat. He holds reins with both hands and is covered in wrappings from chest to heels. He governs the testicles and heals inflammation in the area, whether in one or both. Aphêbis's stone is the Egyptian Sardonyx and his plant is Liquorice. Its Tarot card is the Seven of Cups which is the Lord of Attraction and Obsession.

Aphêbis emphasises the attractive and obsessive side of Scorpio and it finds its greatest power in relationships. It is a charismatic and magnetic force which draws a person towards their heart's desire. Its power is to take a form and make someone want it. On the negative side Aphêbis creates compulsive desires and he could be the *Dæmon* behind drug or alcohol addiction. Aphêbis takes love seriously and it is extremely picky and sceptical of others at first. Aphêbis influenced people are good at unlocking a person's secrets and getting them to talk about their issues. He creates an aura of mystery that other people can't help but be attracted to.

SAGITTARIUS

The first decan of Sagittarius is ruled by the *Dæmon* SEBOS. He looks like a clothed man, his left hand open and lowered, bearing a needle in his right. Next to him are several spears. Sebose is covered in a net from chest to feet, and his head is wrapped. It governs sores that afflict the thighs. His stone is Phrygian,*his plant is Sage. Its Tarot card is the Eight of Wands which is the Lord of Swiftness and Inconsistency.

Sebos creates flexibility by quickly moving from one thing to another. Sebos can make things happen but tends to be inconsistent. Sebos breaks unhealthy habits and intransient thinking and can be a

---

* Alunite according to Stratton-Kent

great catalyst for change. Sebos can be a *Dæmon* of intellect and trade, data and communication and transport. But his Mercury nature makes him prone to lies, swindling and theft. Sebos influenced people have a curious nature, as the individual is always ready to receive information and learn foreign languages. Sebos causes Sagittarius to amass information and sometimes embrace junk data. It blocks filters when absorbing information and they will often do not check if something is correct or true.

The second decan of Sagittarius is ruled by the *Dæmon* TEUKHMOS. He has the head of an Ichneumon bird, and a man's body. He holds a flask in his right hand and a sceptre in his left. Teukhmos governs the bones and sends the fractures that afflict them. His stone is an Amethyst and his plant is a Adraktitalos.* Teukhmos' Tarot card is the Nine of Wands which is the Lord of Adventure and Impulsiveness.

Teukhmos creates change by introducing an element of risk and he needs people to have a sense of adventure. Teukhmos-influenced people are obsessed with travel and could be entrepreneurs and other risk takers.. Teukhmos-influenced people are always upbeat but inconsistent, and competitive. They are usually natural athletes, or if not, they appreciate athleticism in others. Teukhmos rejects routine and does not tend to be there if anything gets too dull. It can make Sagittarius optimistic and less likely to make detailed plans.

The third decan of Sagittarius is ruled by KHTHISAR who appears as an old man with a crown on his head, covered in wrappings from chest to heels, holding a flask in his right hand and a sceptre in his left. Khthisar governs the thighs where he sends pain and corrosion. His stone is an Aerizon and his plant is Centaury. His Tarot card is the Ten of Wands which is the Lord of Disciple and Oppression.

Khthisar tames Sagittarius by forcing it into a discipline which gives a positive way forward. It is a philosopher *Dæmon* which whispers truth when the natural Sagittarian way is to accept all ideas however stupid. It helps in times of trouble and oppression, but often causes a form of self-martyrdom by hanging onto situations which should be abandoned. Khthisar creates ethical rules that those under his influence person will follow. Rather than having a fundamentalist neo-biblical approach Khthisar-influenced people will review these codes. When faced by a crisis the *Dæmon* will force the person to follow the most honourable course. It takes Jupiterian issues like law, race, culture, religion, education, spirituality, and philosophy seriously and approaches them with a discipline that

* Dracunculus vularis according to Stratton-Kent

a normal Sagittarian lacks. Sometimes Khthisar's Saturnian nature will oppress that Sagittarian energy which will still wonder why it cannot be free and innocent all the time.

CAPRICORN

The first decan of Capricorn is ruled by the *Dæmon* TAIR. He is headless with a man's body. Around his chest is a girdle made from scarab shells. In his right hand he has a flask and his left is extended on his thigh. Tair rules the knees and the illnesses that affect them. Its stone is an Ophite and its plant is a Delphinium. Tair's Tarot card is the Two of Pentacles which is the Lord of Harmonious Change.

Tair is a force which brings about slow and gradual change. It is a spirit of diplomacy which is effective at dealing with authority. It teaches how to fix mistakes through the correct use of control. Tair creates workaholics who find a great deal of joy from work. It is orderly and subdued and likes to be in control of things. Tair creates planners and goal-setters who might be ambitious but need security. Tair influenced people can be extremely materialistic, conservative, and sceptical of innovative ideas. It is difficult for it to break old habits. He makes Capricorns pessimistic and too serious. While they are extremely sexual, if they are too career focused they can suppress their sexual drive completely. Tair-influenced people have a lot of endurance.

The second decan of Capricorn is ruled by the *Dæmon* EPITEK. He has the head of a pig, and his body is like that of the first (decan). Epitek has a belt; a flask in his right hand and a sword in his left. It rules the back of the knees. Its stone is a Karkhedonios (chalcedony) and its plant is an Anemone. Epitek's Tarot card is the Three of Pentacles which is the Lord of Material Works and Debauchery.

Epitek makes things happen, particularly for work and business. Everything he does is mostly work related and those he influences can be perfectionists and natural materialists. That said Epitek is more interested in a job well done, than the money made. The overbalance towards the material can create an excessive over indulgence in sensual pleasures and material wealth. Epitek sometimes becomes bogged down and isolated in a material world which offers no depth or spirituality. Epitek-influenced people can become lazy and hope that someone else will bail them out of their problems. This is rare, though, as generally there is powerful need to stay in control. Epitek-influenced people express anger in a cool, level-headed way. They fear disorder and "letting go".

The third decan of Capricorn is ruled by the *Dæmon* EPIKHNAUS. He wears a mask, holds a flask in his right hand and a needle in his left. He wears a belt. Epikhnaus governs the same areas as previously shown in the second decan. His stone is an Anankite and his plant is a Thistle. Epikhnaus' Tarot card is the Four of Pentacles which is the *Dæmon* of Earthly Power and Depression.

Epikhnaus controls material things, people, relationships, money, health, or situations. He tends to hang onto old, outdated states longer than it should. Epikhnaus-influenced people are conservative and like things the way they are. It can lead to a form of melancholia in which the world seems superficial. This is difficult for Epikhnaus-influenced as they are rubbishing their own Capricorn material worlds and leads to depression. Epikhnaus creates practical Capricorns in life and at work which usually brings success in career. A serious approach towards their duties usually reduces the fun they might have. Epikhnaus is far less able to have fun as the other *Dæmons* of Capricorn and wants a structured reality rather than a chaotic one.

AQUARIUS

The first decan of Aquarius is ruled by the *Dæmon* ISU, or THRÔ*. He is a dog-headed man, covered in wrappings from the chest to heels. Isu rules over tibias and all abscesses and lesions found there. Its stone is a Knêkitê†, its plant is an Asar‡. His Tarot card is the Five of Swords which is the Lord of Revolution and Neophilia (change for its own sake).

Isu overthrows old systems so that they can be replaced with new ones. It does so violently and without subtlety. Whatever happens though Isu brings about a defeat the status quo or ends the revolutionary. Isu creates conflict which is sometimes unnecessary and can force Aquarius to be too distant and idealistic. Other times it is a force which insists on novelty or change for its own sake. This can help adaption to change but can be a killer for traditions and routines. It is a good force to call on if you are blocked creatively. Isu makes Aquarians have an original, independent outlook on relationships. It likes to break boundaries and tends to see others as souls rather than a being who has a gender. It might make relationships which concentrate less on the carnal level and sex, and more on the intellectual level.

---

* In this case pick one and stick to it. Personally, I would use ISU.

† Grey porphyry according Stratton-Kent

‡Asurum, Hazel wood and Wild Spikenard according to Stratton-Kent

The second decan of Aquarius is ruled by the *Dæmon* SOSOMNÔ. He looks like a man covered in wrappings from chest to heels. He bears an agkhia (which is likely to be an Egyptian ankh) in his hands and wears a crown. He governs the knees and leg fat. Sosomnô's stone is a Lodestone, and its plant is a Gladiolus. His Tarot card is the Six of Swords and which is the Lord of Science and Intellectual Arrogance.

Sosomnô is a healing spirit who is focused on material science. It enables an open mind to deeper areas of study. He is the *Dæmon* of the scientific method which desires proof for theories based on evidence. Sosomnô's downside is that sometimes those he influences can assume that whatever treasured theory they hold is correct. He sometimes activates the mad scientist view that the ends justify the means and encourage all sorts of atrocities. Sosomnô brings out the intellectual qualities of the Aquarian, making them less idealistic and more logical. He still inspires unconventional ideas, but these will be more rational. Sosomnô provides detachment and the grace of objectivity. He is more interested in facts than feelings, and those under his influence come across as aloof or unemotional.

The third decan of Aquarius is ruled by the *Dæmon* KHONOUMOUS. He looks like a man covered in wrappings from chest to heels. He wears a crown and holds a flask in his right hand and a sceptre in his left. He governs the same parts of the body as Sosomnô. His stone is a Median* and his plant is a Catananche. Khonoumous' Tarot card is the Seven of Swords which is the Lord of Intuition and Impracticability.

Khonoumous obtains information without logic or reason and supplies an inner perception about any given situation. His psychism is no that of feelings masquerading as intuition. Khonoumous-influenced people need logical thought before arriving at any conclusion. When his force is unbalanced it creates an internal faith which is less reliable. Khonoumous-influenced Aquarians are not in touch with their physical reality, who will come up with great ideas which are unworkable. Khonoumous-influenced people are outsiders who feel "different" and are loners. They might have strong egos and defence mechanisms. While they have a broad compassionate philosophy their kindness and concern for others is at odds with their drive for independence.

PISCES

The first decan of Pisces is ruled by the *Dæmon* TETIMÔ. He looks like a man dressed in a dark blue robe. He's covered in wrappings from

* Ink stone, according to Stratton-Kent

chest to heels. In his right hand he holds a flask, while the left hangs beside his thigh. Tetimô rules the feet and sends them abscesses. Its stone is Beryl and his plant is Vervain. His Tarot card is the Eight of Cups which is the Lord Dissolution and Depersonalisation.

Tetimô breaks down artificial structures within the psyche by a total immersion in the unconscious. It is a force without ego which allows the gradual surfacing of buried unconscious material. This lack of ego causes the loss of personal identity to a bigger force. While this is important in mystical work, where the personality can act like an anchor, it is less useful in mundane existence. Tetimô-influenced people seeks isolation to avoid the pain of interacting with others because of their sensitivity. They often feel defenceless, vulnerable, and paranoid. Tetimô makes victims or martyrs who are compassionate and pragmatic. They can be artistic, spiritual, or psychic. It is found in those who need religion to provide them with structure and security.

The second decan of Pisces is ruled by the *Dæmon* SOPPHI. He looks like a man, naked, but bearing a coat on his shoulders, thrown behind him. He holds a flask in the right hand, his left index finger is raised to his mouth, and he wears a crown on his head. Sopphi's stone is a Perileukios Onyx and its plant is a Libanotis. His Tarot card is the Nine of Cups which is the Lord of Happiness and Escapism.

Sopphi is a Jupiterian force which produces happiness. It is also the Greek concept of *Eudaimonia* which means a good life or flourishing rather than just emotion. The word means good *Dæmon* which makes Sopphi one of the more obvious gifts of your *Higher Genius.* It can produce escapism to avoid pain. If true *Eudaimonia* is unavailable, a Sopphi-influenced person will look towards shallow pleasure as a compensation. Sopphi attracts good luck when they are tender, devoted, giving and compassionate. It creates a love for the less fortunate. Sopphi is an empathic force which feels the world's pain and provides a desire to do all they can to relieve this pain and make it better. Sopphi draws people to spiritual matters. It makes Pisceans under his influence kinder and provides psychic abilities. Negatively, they may drift into fantasy or drugs to escape reality.

The third decan of Pisces is ruled by an *Dæmon* called SURÔ. He is called the coiling dragon. He has a beard and a crown on his head. His stone is a Hyacinth and its plant is a Chamomile. Surô's Tarot card is the Ten of Cups which is the Lord of Perfected Success and Stillness.

Surô concludes all projects perfectly even when they look a mess to start with. Perfect completion often does not mean that it finishes as it is intended (other than by hindsight). Surô encourages some perfectionism. He suggests not acting when no action is needed when stillness obtains the most positive outcome. Surô-influenced people are likely to have feelings of guilt about their anger, and difficulties with asserting themselves, preferring to "go with the flow." The danger is that if creative expression for this energy is bottled up it can create indirect aggression and game playing. Surô is happiest when creatively expressing desires, compassion, and anger freely and imaginatively.

THE ARROWS OF APOLLO

The Ancient Egyptian decan system had the concept of arrows which were the seven decans closest to the Sun. They have been found on the bracelet of Prince Harnakhte and the tomb of Osokon II*. Magically they were the arrows of protection sent by the gods to protect the Pharaoh but there is no reason why they would not do the same thing to any human.

Based on the *Sacred Book* meanings above, the seven *Dæmonic* forces could stand for and could cause illnesses and be asked to prevent it. This system appears to have fallen out of use in magic, perhaps because it was lost when the Egyptian temples closed. Its elite nature might have been the reason as the only proof we have of it being used is for the Royal Family. However, it is an elegant system which unlocks many issues connected to the *Higher Genius*. I have called them the arrows of Apollo.

It worked in the following way. Note the Sun sign and the *Dæmon* which rules that decan. Then do the same for each of the three decans on either side of it. That should give you the names and planetary spirits who oversee your protection (or who will make you sick).

If a person has their Ascendant in Leo, and their Sun in the middle decan of Leo, the arrows of Apollo, that means they will have the following *Dæmons* Ipi (Jupiter), Khnouphos (Saturn), Ouphisit (Moon), Sotheir (Mercury),Phatiti (Mars), Athoum (Sun) and Brusous (Venus).

Another who has their Ascendant in Leo and their Sun in the 4th degree of Gemini has the following *Dæmons* acting as Arrows of Apollo. Xokha (Jupiter), Horomenos (Saturn), Aron (Moon), Soou

---

* Here they are shown as serpents with lion's heads and the gods which rule the planets.

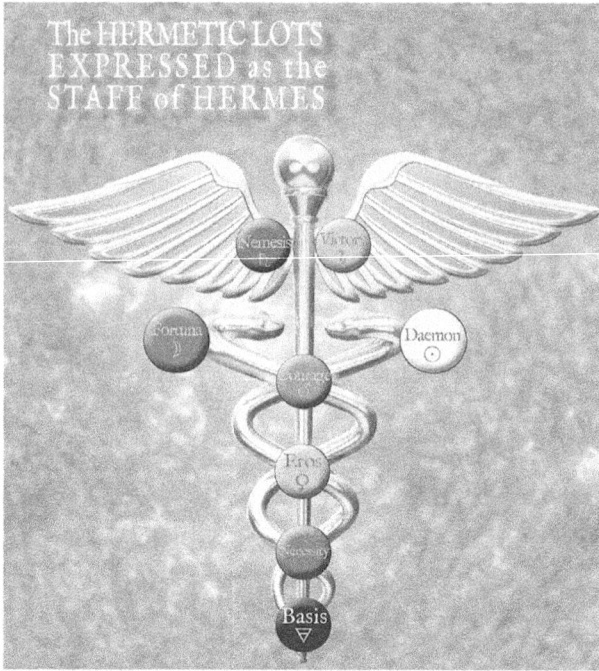

This shows the Seven Hermetic Lots as an interaction between the Moon (Fortuna) and the Sun (Dæmon). It shows their ruling planets (and gods) with their roots on Basis.

(Mercury), Ouari (Mars), Pepisoth (Sun) and Sotheir (Venus).

The Arrows would have several functions. Collectively they supply protection (see below) and may be invoked during times of crisis. Individually they are an aspect of the seven rays and their role changes for each person. In the example given above, the same *Dæmon* brings one person the powers of Venus and the other Mercury because they were both born at separate times of the year. They might encourage the first person to express its powers intellectually and through communication and the other through creativity or relationships. It will also defend that person differently. For the first person it would protect the mind and for the second it would protect their creativity. In this role they are more specific and personal than the planetary spirits of Agrippa.

EXAMPLE OF A USE FOR THE ARROWS

To use them to protect you from any form of attack buy seven wooden arrows with sharp metal tips. They can be bought from any re-enactment equipment maker and should not have any branding on them. Each arrow will represent one of the decan *Dæmons*.

For each arrow, either with a wood burner or an indelible marker, print the sigil of the zodiac sign, the secret name of the zodiac, your name, and the *Dæmon*'s name on each of them and finally a symbol of the Sun and the name Apollo (Ἀπόλλων).

Perform the *Lesser Ritual of the Pentagram* and purify and consecrate the space. Then invoke Helios-Apollo depending on the time of day. Sprinkle each candle saying:

In the name of Apollo, I purify you weapon of air so that you will defend me from my enemies from afar. For as even as the greatest hero can be despatched by a single arrow so shall my seen and unseen enemies fall.

Pass each arrow through the flame and say,

In the name of Apollo, I consecrate you, weapon of air, so that you will defend me from my enemies from afar. For even as the greatest hero can be despatched by a single arrow so shall my seen and unseen enemies fall.

Pause.

A beggar, that came on his wanderings, easily strung the bow, and shot through the iron.*

Hold each arrow in your left hand and say,

Apollo expresses his power through [astrological name] and [decan name] so that this arrow shall defend me against my seen and unseen enemies. Awaken [decan name] to bring this arrow to life.

Chant the name of the *Dæmon* while visualising it taking its position with a bow and arrow to protect you. Do this for five minutes (the longer the better). After doing this for all seven arrows lash them into a heptagon with yellow or gold thread. All the arrows should point the same way.

Lay the arrows on your altar and place a statue or picture of Apollo in the centre and light a tealight as an offering to him and say,

How Apollo's laurel sapling shakes!†
The temple shakes. Away, away with the profane!
For the bow is the weapon of Lycoreian Phoebus.

---

* This is a magical phrase taken from the *Odyssey*.

† This is a paraphrase from the Homeric Hymn number two to Apollo.

Thetis mournfully laments Achilles
If she hears, "Hie Paian, Hie Paian."
For the mightiest cannot stand against Apollo's swift arrows.
They who fight me fights with Apollo.
His golden bow strikes them from afar.
One swift arrow after another.
The star's cry "Hie hie Paian! Shoot the arrow!"
With my chant I place myself under the project of the arrows of
Apollo so that those who strike me shall be struck by his Dæmons.
Let no sickness touch me for I am under the protection of Apollo's
arrows

Create a chant built from the following: Apollo, [zodiac name], [the name of one of the seven], [the decan *Dæmons*] and Henosis*

Chant for ten minutes during which you should see yourself and Helios in the centre of the heptagon protected by the *Dæmons* (who might be coloured in planetary colours). The scene should be full of Sunlight with rays from Apollo's head binding and uniting them. You should visualise the arrows glowing with power.

When you have finished, thank the gods and the *Dæmons*, and close your temple normally. The arrows should be placed under your bed. Once a year the arrows should be recharged.

USING THE DECAN DÆMONS FOR HEALING

This method is an adaptation of was taught to me by Joao Pedro Feliciano and is highly effective for healing work.

First work out which *Dæmon* is causing the illness. Take a candle and write the patient's name, the secret name and sigil of the zodiac sign, and the name of the decan *Dæmon*. When the decan is rising† place a picture the person (or their astrology chart) on the altar with a magnet on top. Then place the candle on top of that.

Prepare your ritual space with the *Lesser Ritual of the Pentagram* and the opening of the gates. Open all four elemental gates with their normal elements.

Purify and consecrate the candle and say,

Creature of Wax I purify and Consecrate you so that you will

---

* A word which means to unite, but to the Neo-platonic it also meant a uniting with God.

† You will need to use a computer programme to find out when this is. It is important that the invocations are performed while the decan is rising so might need to open your temple a ten minutes earlier so that you reach that point when the decan is rising.

be a perfect sacrifice to appease [name of decan Dæmon] so that rather than harming [name of patent] it shall heal them instead.

After a moment's pause, say the following three times:

In the name of [zodiacal spirit] invoke [name of decan Dæmon], revered god, decan of the sign of [zodiac name] bring your influence upon the world of necessity. Come to me in this very hour and very moment to send a healing to [patent name] to heal his/her, so that (s)he may swiftly recover and be healed of all pain and suffering. Go swiftly and quickly [name of Dæmon] for I am like you, an off-spring of the immortal Aion, a being of chaos searching for wisdom in Order.

Visualise the person you want to heal and then slowly vibrate the name of the decan *Dæmon* 365 times. This should take you about 40 minutes.

When you have finished, thank the *Dæmon* , let the candle burn down.

The most important decan *Dæmons* are those which rule houses which contain the seven planets, the four centrepins and the seven Hermetic lots.

GOOD DÆMON AND GOOD FORTUNE

The Place of the Good *Dæmon* (which is the 11th house) and the place of Good Fortune (fifth house) is influenced by the decan and any planets that are in them. Invoking these provides the *Sphere of Sensation* with the best spiritually and materially fortunate path in life.

THE LOT OF THE DÆMON

The decan *Dæmon* influences the nature of the lot of the *Dæmon* and takes on many of the powers being expressed by it. In this system it is invoked to unite the entire chart and therefore important and done last.

THE DÆMONS OF THE HERMETIC LOTS

The ancients squeezed more information from astrological charts by seeing the influence of planets as part of a mathematical formula which could generate added information to unlock a person's destiny. These were preserved and extended by the Arabs in their Arabic parts, but in Hellenistic times the most important were the Hermetic lots. The lots are theoretical points in a chart which are derived by synthesising the zodiacal positions of planets or points to highlight another part of the chart which focuses on a topic. To do this you need to know if your astrological chart is a nocturnal (night) or a diurnal (day) chart. This is based on if you were born during the day or the night.

The most exact way* to calculate a lot is to take the longitude of the ascendant (A) which is then added to the longitude of a planet (B). A longitude of a second planet (C) is subtracted from that number to determine the specific position of the lot in the chart. (Lot = A + B − C).

In 378 AD in his Astrological primer *Introduction*, Paul of Alexandria cites a Hermetic work on the seven lots called Panaretus (Πανάρετος). He wrote:

> *The First is the lot of Fortune which, for those born by day, it will be necessary to count from the solar degree to the lunar degree, and one must cast out the collected number from the degree number of the ascendant, giving 30 degrees to each sign. And where the collected number leaves off, that place is the lot of Fortune. For those at night, the reverse, that is from the lunar degree to the solar. And likewise, one must cast out the rest from the degree of the ascendant.*

> *Second is the lot of Dæmon. You will count for a diurnal birth from the Moon's degree to the Sun's degree, and one must cast out the collected number from the degree of the ascendant, again likewise apportioning up to 30 degrees from each sign. And where the number leaves off, there will be the lot of Spirit. Thus, by day, but the reverse by night.*

> *Third is the lot of Eros. You will count for those born by day from the Lot of Dæmon to the degree of Venus and an equal amount from the ascendant, but the reverse for those at night.*

> *Fourth is the lot of Necessity. You will calculate it for those born by day from the degree of Mercury to the lot of Fortune, and an equal amount from the ascendant, but the reverse for those at night.*

> *Fifth is the lot of Courage, which you will work out from the*

---

* It is the most accurate but it was not the way the ancients did it. In a diurnal (day) chart measure the distance from the Sun to the Moon, and then measure the same distance from the ascendant. In a nocturnal (night) chart measure the distance from the Moon to the Sun, and then measure the same distance from the ascendant. Most modern magicians will use a computer program, such as Janus to do it, so knowing how is not exactly that important.

degree of Mars to the lot of Fortune, and an equal amount from the ascendant for those born by day, but the reverse for those at night.

Sixth is the lot of Victory. You will count for those born by day from the lot of Spirit to the degree of Jupiter, and an equal amount from the ascendant, but the reverse for those at night.

Seventh is the lot of Nemesis. You will count for diurnal births from Saturn to the lot of Fortune, and an equal amount from the ascendant, but by night the reverse.

In an astrological sense, it is possible to see how the interactions of the planets create these different points. The lot of Eros for example includes a relationship between the ascendant, the *Dæmon* and Venus. However, a magical approach reveals the interaction between the Sun (*Higher Genius*) and the Moon (Fortune) to create the structures upon which a life is made. While an astrologer might see these as points on a chart, a magician would see them as planetary *Dæmons* connected to a person's fate.

The most important are the lot of Fortune which is ruled by the Moon and based on the goddess Fortuna. The next most important is the lot of the *Dæmon* , ruled by the Sun and the *Higher Genius* because through them the others are calculated. From this we can see that our life is a complex reaction between what the *Higher Genius* wants, and what Fortune provides.

Lot of Fortune: [Day] Fortune = Ascendant + Moon – Sun, [Night] Fortune = Ascendant + Sun - Moon.

Fortuna is the story that the fates and your *Higher Genius* have planned for you in this life. This includes money, and the way that an individual physically reacts to the surrounding environment, the body, health and general vitality. It stands for what is the result of your actions.

Paulus Alexandrinus wrote that fortune "signifies everything that concerns the body, and what one does through the book of life. It becomes indicative of possessions, reputation and privilege."

Fortuna

The goddess connected to this lot is Fortuna or Tyche. She was associated with the Moon because she waxed and waned. She appeared as a woman holding a cornucopia in her right hand and a ship's rudder, a ball or a wheel in her right.

Lot of *Dæmon* : Day Spirit = Ascendant + Sun – Moon Night Spirit = Ascendant + Moon - Sun

We met the lot of *Dæmon* in the earlier chapter. The Hermetic lot however is more about how our *Higher Genius* is focused in the world. It shows intentions, and gives signs related to career. He will appear in whatever form you have selected for your *Higher Genius*.

Paulus wrote: "*Dæmon* is the lord of soul, temper, mindfulness, and every power; and sometimes it cooperates in the determination concerning what one does."

Lot of Basis: Day Lot = Ascendant + Fortune – Dæmon Night Lot = Ascendant + Spirit - Fortune

Lot of Necessity: Day Lot = Ascendant + Fortune – Mercury and Night Lot = Ascendant + Mercury – Fortune.

This lot is based upon Mercury. Paulus wrote: "Necessity signifies constraints, submissions, struggles, and wars, and makes enmities,

hatreds, condemnations, all the other restrictive things befalling men as a result of their birth."

This lot is a *Dæmon* of the goddess of Necessity or Ananke. Homer said that she was the force which needed events to happen, compulsion and inevitability. In his *Fragments* Empedocles wrote that Ananke (Necessity) wrote laws that even the gods must obey. She was depicted as a winged woman holding a spindle and a whip.

She was the bringer of experiences which cannot be avoided. 2nd-

Necessity

century Hellenistic astrologer Vettius Valens said Necessity revealed the enemies a person would have in their life. If it is near a malefic it creates lawsuits, deaths, trials, and condemnations. She could also be what you must sacrifice.

She shows what your *Higher Genius* needs in this life and can outline the story we want to follow. The connection to Mercury is a little odd, but if you remember that Mercury, as the protective god of boundaries, had a Saturnian side it starts to make sense.

Lot of Eros: Day Lot = Ascendant + Venus – Spirit and Night Lot = Ascendant + Spirit - Venus

This lot is based upon Venus. Paulus wrote: "Eros signifies the appetites and the desires. It becomes a contributing cause of friendship and mutual favour."

He was depicted as a winged youth holding a bow, or whip, and sometimes riding a dolphin.

This Lot reveals and enables what we desire. It is not just about love and sex but what we are drawn to. It can encourage a good moral purpose and a love of beauty. If the person has a planet near this lot, you can say that person has a love of that god and what it represents. Mercury would mean a love of words and communication (or more negatively thievery), while Mars would love fighting and conflict. Venus can unbalance it

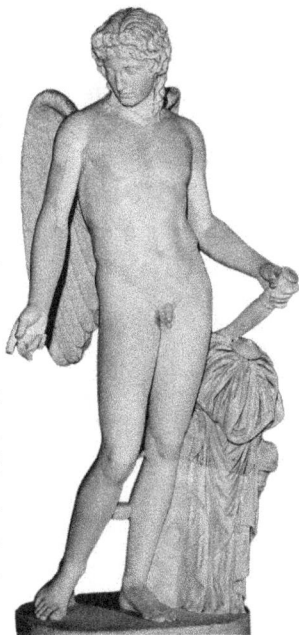

Eros

the person a poisoner, adulterer, and murderer. The lot can show friends. Eros is the polarity of Necessity because he represents choice and the things we can do something about.

Lot of Bravery (Virtus): Day Lot = Ascendant + Fortune – Mars Night Lot = Ascendant + Mars - Fortune

This lot is based upon Mars and so far, it seems to gives signs for the natives fortitude and actions. Where this lot is placed by house seems to show what you must face and what you most fear. But it also shows how bravery enables you to overcome the challenges your *Higher Genius* wants you to experience Paulus wrote:

> "*Bravery becomes a contributing cause of boldness, treachery, might, and every villainy.*"

This lot was a *Dæmon* of the god Virtus who involves all the abilities and potentialities available to humans. In Homer's *Iliad* and *Odyssey*, "arete" is used to describe heroes and nobles and their mobile dexterity, and especially their strength and courage. Penelope's arete, for example, relates to co-operation.

Virtus appears as a beautiful naked man or woman wearing nothing but a scarlet cloak, a helmet and carrying a spear or sword. (S)he teaches you what you have to overcome and in a manner which will not harm your honour.

Lot of Victory: Day Lot = Ascendant + Jupiter – Spirit. Night Lot = Ascendant + Spirit - Jupiter

This lot is based upon Jupiter. Paulus said:

> "*Victory becomes a contributing cause of trust, good expectation, contest, and every association; but sometimes it contributes to penalties and rewards.*"

This lot shows fame and eminence. Often however it shows what a person is happy doing or areas in which they find it easy to be successful.

Victoria was shown as a beautiful winged goddess holding a victory wreath, sometimes standing on a globe. Her Greek form was Nike the goddess of strength, speed, and victory. Victoria was a symbol of victory over death and decided who would be successful during war. She can show you how to overcome problems, particularly conflicts.

Lot of Nemesis: Day Lot = Ascendant + Fortune – Saturn. Night Lot = Ascendant + Saturn - Fortune

This lot is based upon Saturn. It shows what is most likely to bring the native down. Paulus wrote: "Nemesis becomes a contributing cause of subterranean fates and of everything which is ice-cold, of demonstration, impotence, exile, destruction, grief, and quality of death."

It was said that where Nemesis falls would be the native's undoing and these are the negative qualities of the zodiac sign. In Aries it would be death in battle, or through anger or impatience; Taurus will be undone through the love of money or material possessions; Gemini: slander, communication or duplicity; Cancer will be undone by insecurity or attachment, or their family; Leo:

pride, arrogance, and excessive visibility; Virgo: lack of faith, jumping to conclusions; Libra: legal matters, divorce; Scorpio: through murder, jealousy, scheming, lack of trust; Sagittarius: intemperance, intolerance, entrapment; Capricorn: sexual illnesses, carelessness, neglect; Aquarius: isolation, disconnection from others; Pisces: indiscretion and gullibility.

Nemesis was the goddess who enacts retribution against those who succumb to hubris. She was the winged balancer of life and a daughter of Justice who restrained mortals' frivolous insolences with her adamantine chains.

She appears as a beautiful woman dressed in black and carries either a measuring rod, scales, a sword, and a scourge. She rides in a chariot drawn by griffins. She is the equaliser and can help fight against those who are otherwise untouchable.

The Lot of Basis: Day Lot = Ascendant + Fortune – *Dæmon* (or) Lot = Ascendant + *Dæmon* – Fortune so that it always falls below the horizon.

The lot of Basis was not one of the seven Hermetic lots but was an important one for Hellenic Astrologers and it fits well as a lot which "earths" the chart. It is the god which gives breath to the body and signifies long journeys. It a *Dæmon* of the same god as the ascendant. So, if your ascendant is the second decan of Leo it is a *Dæmon* of Jupiter. It is the entire result of the movement of your *Higher Genius* and fortune as it relates to your material world.

Using the *Dæmons* of the Decans we can understand these issues in considerable clarity and so invoking them and meditating upon them becomes part of trying to understand our *Higher Genius*. The seven Hermetic lots along with the centrepins will build a *Sphere of Sensation* which is closer to what the *Higher Genius* wants.

EXAMPLE

Using the example from last month we can see how these houses set the stage for the planetary forces.

A person has Leo as their ascendant in the third decan and the *Dæmon* PHÁTITI who gives her a strong willpower and aggression. She will act with authority, power, and their personal magnetism and be a little bit scary. This Ascendant is sextile to the Sun which means that her personality is even stronger. This means that they could make good friendships and suggests that the Sun in Gemini is a hugely important part of their chart. The Sun is in the second decan of Gemini ruled by the *Dæmon* OUARÍ who encourages intellectual genius and enables skill, planning and strategising. This makes them a good organiser and manager and inquisitor.

The ascendant is sextile the Moon which is in the middle decan under the influence of NEPHTHIMÊS, who will insist on rules being followed and provides an unconscious sense of Justice. He tends to create a sense of struggle, particularly in relationships. In fact, it will tend to create life lessons through relationship choices. The sextile between the Leo ascendant makes this aspect of the person stronger and a good part of their character. They will follow the rules of a religion and it will give them the friends and recognition they want.

The Sun's rays will prevent the good aspects of Venus helping the person. Venus would normally be strong in this position but in this case the Sun overwhelms it, making any serious romance be more like friendship and a meeting of minds more than anything else. The ascendant is sextile to beleaguered Venus, which is damaged by the Sun's rays. However, it is important that, in this case, this person is prevented from being from being turned into a loveless robot by the fact that both the Sun and Venus share the same bounds. In this case Venus is sheltering from the Sun. The ancients called this a chariot and says that the person is protected from the Sun's rays if it is in its own domicile, exaltation, or bounds. This means that they do not lose the power to express themselves creatively. It can also enable them to project beauty and elegance. It is possible that if the person "becomes too Sun Gemini" they will lose their Venus side, and it might be useful for the person to work with OUARÍ to get a balance.

Mercury is strongly placed in the tenth house but not early in life. Jupiter in the 10th makes the person respected and well known (even famous); however it is square Mars. While it is in such a strong position it limits Mars' negative aspects. It will mean that the person works hard and will be rewarded and recognised. They will do well in the communications industry, writing or talking. The sextile of Mars and the Sun might mean that Gemini energy will help relieve some of the sickness which the malefic will bring to the 12th house. Since a sextile is rarely bad, it is possible that Mars will provide her with internalised energy reserves, but it might lead to bursts of egotistical anger and a more masculine approach. Mars and Saturn in the 12th meant that there would have been difficulty during the pregnancy and the person or the mother would be lucky to survive. Saturn will bring the person internal pains.

The Moon is in her joy in the third house in Libra, sextile Mars, trine the Sun and Venus. This means that there is an appearance of sexuality and confidence and assertion. While this is not enough to save Venus, it might mean that there is a need to find a stable relationship (something the burnt-out Venus in Gemini would not bother with) and hang onto it once they have it. The emotions and the will are at peace with one another, suggesting a balanced personality. Normally they will put others before themselves, unless (as is the case here) they have a strong personality.

Based on this positioning we see that the person's Sun is extremely powerful but is much more balanced by the Moon, Mercury and Jupiter. Their *Higher Genius* clearly wants them to communicate and be up front. They might suffer from sickness, and a lack of romantic connection or imagination. There might be a tendency to be too concerned with form rather than feeling in their magical life. However, there is a lot of opportunity for success.

CHAPTER EIGHT
MONTH SEVEN

MYSTERIES OF THE HIGHER GENIUS

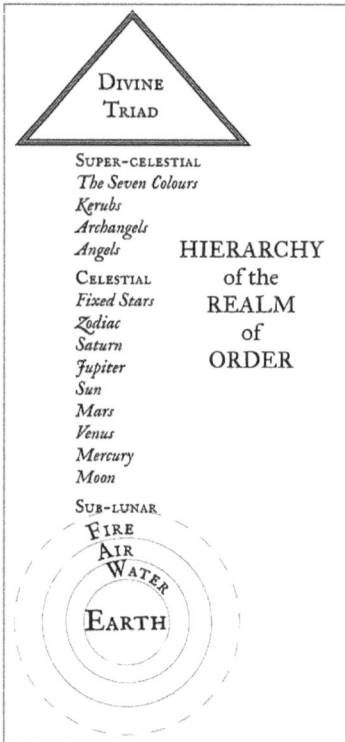

DIVINE
TRIAD

SUPER-CELESTIAL
The Seven Colours
Kerubs
Archangels
Angels   HIERARCHY
CELESTIAL   of the
Fixed Stars REALM
Zodiac   of
Saturn   ORDER
Jupiter
Sun
Mars
Venus
Mercury
Moon

SUB-LUNAR
FIRE
AIR
WATER
EARTH

This is the last month of the seven-month programme, which ends with a weekend retreat when you are cut off from the rest of the world to await the arrival of your *Higher Genius*.

During the month leading up to the retreat you should be as isolated from the world as possible in the 21st century. This means no television or social media. Conversations should be limited only to what is considered necessary. While it is OK to go to work you should consciously restrict conversations, to avoid talking about trivia. You should also avoid stress at all costs. If these things are impossible then you should take time to perform the emptying of the cup exercise. When you get spare moments the Sun breath is also an asset. You should abstain from all forms of intoxicants and eat lightly. You should also not eat red meat or pork during this month.

The first three weeks of this month you should do your usual solar rituals during the day. Then in the main session:

1. Perform the *Lesser Ritual of the Pentagram*.
2. The correct invocation of the Sun for that time of day.
3. The headless ritual.
4. The elemental pentagrams and balance them.
5. Purify and consecrate.
6. And then perform the Activation of Divine Love (below)

The last week involves three days of preparation and then the three days of retreat.

Rising through the levels

I n the last few months, you will be aware that at different times you experience different states of consciousness. Before going on it is important to explain these as this month you are going to enter another level.

Traditionally, when you look a theosophical or Neoplatonic philosophy, they became unnecessarily complicated so what follows below is a simplification.

The One Thing's mind is split in three divisions: the conscious, the unconscious and matter. The matter level is what we see with our senses while the divine unconscious is depicted in concepts like the underworld. The conscious mind is the animating force, which unites creation. It brings new ideas into being. This conscious mind is divided into four levels. None of these levels are more important or superior to the other. They are what they are. No one says the brain is a superior organ to the heart – they have different functions and without either the human would die.

The sub-lunar level

The sub-lunar level encompasses matter and the astral and the lowest level of the underworld. It is the realm the Goetic magician who uses magic drawn from nature, the elementals, the dead and terrestrial *Dæmons*. They also take power from the symbolism of the Moon gods such as Hekate and Diana. These channel celestial and divine power into the material and astral realm.

Note the word Goetia does not just mean demonic magic. It is the most common form of magic as its function is to affect the material plane, the thoughts and minds of people, and the *Dæmons* of the gods and work with the dead. Although many magicians claim to aspire to celestial, or divine forms of magic, the bulk of their work is Goetia.

It needs little in the way of purification. Sub-lunar magic is powered by elemental energy from below, or from "the Moon." Its rituals often feature calls to nature or the elements to bring about their goals. Its magic depends on some form of sacrifice to transmute one type of energy to another. It is enhanced by repetition and chanting. Its rituals are best conducted at night according to the waxing and waning of the Moon. The magical use of pathworking or astral takes place at the highest aspect of the sub-lunar level, where it can influence the celestial or divine level closer to their source.

THE CELESTIAL LEVEL

The celestial level is the realm of the divine gods or archangels. They have their foot on the lunar levels but are divided into seven broad categories as expressed by the planetary forces. The celestial forces manifest in the upper parts of the sub-lunar level as the different masks of god. At this level, they are closer to their energetic and functional nature. It is their job to bring the divine ideas from above so that Hekate can properly experience them in the sub-lunar realm. Magic at this level is the work of the theurgist or god worker. It has been the level we have been working at throughout this book.

To achieve the levels of consciousness necessary, the theurgist must separate their soul from matter and purify it so that it may respond to the energy of at least one of the seven energies found on this level. Rituals seeking to attain this level are called ascensions and through periods of attunement to the divine energy the theurgist starts to embody that divine energy.

Such rites might start on the sub-lunar level, which provides a bedrock for an astral ascension. Symbolically this level is under the control of the Sun, although others see it under the rule of Jupiter or its equivalents such as YHVH. Note the purity required to attain this level is not the sort of purity demanded by religious abstinence, fasting or other taboos. These are symbolic of the true purity, which is the adoption of a mindset that operates at the celestial level and not at the material. The work of the theurgist is to provide a conduit for these powers into the astral and then use them to ascend still higher into the super-celestial level.

SUPER-CELESTIAL LEVEL

This is the level we will attempt to work at now. This realm is the closest that a human mind can go to entering the mind of the one thing. It is not something that can be managed all the time, but it can be glimpsed. This is a world without form, from which the seeds of reality are formed. Attaining it requires another change of mindset from Microcosmic to Macrocosmic and it is the realm of the mystic. Stepping into this world requires the aid of the celestial forces and further purity.

There is no ritual that will help, other than working at the celestial level and having its forces aid you. As in the celestial level you should become more like the one mind to truly understand it. This level is symbolically controlled by the stars, which in ancient times meant the fixed stars. Realistically they are far above that and is the place where the ideas come from. Stepping into this divine mind is what is meant by crossing the abyss.

What is important is that this level is much more abstract than those previously. It is less personal and harder to put your finger on and be definite about. It is more mystical and means attempting to connect to concepts rather than things.

PAGAN ANGELS AND DÆMONS

The beings identified in later Christian magic as angels and Demons are more abstract understandings of divine force. Angels represent the pinnacle of abstract divine order while demons take on the role of the chaotic shadows. This process can be seen in the *Testament of Solomon,* where demons are invoked but angels control them.

What I might say next will anger those who reject symbolism which is considered "Christian" or Jewish within a neo-pagan context. In Rome, during the first and second century, it was common for "pagans" to adopt Christian and Jewish religious symbols in their altars. Cynics have said that they were hedging their bets, but the reality is that they felt free to worship those similar pantheons alongside their own.

Some of this was because of the eclectic nature of the pagan religion. The Hellenes, which broadly covered the Romans and Greeks and all they conquered, saw all religions as aspects of their own. So, Amon in Egypt was Jupiter, as was YHVH of the Jews (although some Romans thought they worshipped Saturn). Jesus could be Osiris, Adonis, Antonis or any number of redemptive gods, just as the Christians worshipped him. Rome was full of these cults, and they only ever fell foul of the authorities if they advocated illegal acts.

In antiquity, pagan writers moaned that Christianity had taken the best bits of their religion and merged it into their own. They are not difficult to spot, and not even the Protestant and Catholic counter-reformations thought to remove these pagan elements which had become the cornerstone of their religion. Sharing went both ways. Between the first and fifth century, there was a move to incorporate Jewish angels into the Greco-Egyptian magical system. This coincided with a more monotheistic approach amongst pagans. The idea, following neo-platonic lines, was that there was a central unity which expressed itself through many different gods. What I am describing is not One God in the Christian, Jewish or Muslim sense.

There was a monotheistic cult of Theos or Zeus Hypsistos, which was a pagan version of Judaism. However, the pagans of the time had a more sophisticated way of reconciling all their pagan gods with a more abstract unifying being. Plutarch's teacher, Ammonius, equates God with Being and says it lives in instant eternity, ruling, and conserving the world. Ammonius saw traditional Apollo as a shadow or image of this reality. In Plutarch's Essay *On Isis and Osiris* Osiris is an image of the true God, identified with Plato's Good and Beautiful, and as the destiny of the soul. This god, too, rules the world through his powers (dynameis, δυνάμεις) which include traditional gods.

In the *Greek Magical Papyri*, we can see these monotheistic deities being formed by merging or promoting gods like Phanes-Aeon, Helios, Set-Typhon, and Thoth-Hermes. These entities stood for the Transcendental One Thing who is unknowable but must be sought; it is that which is the creator, or the divine spark within humanity. The *Chaldean Oracles* even suggested the One Thing had three aspects, much like the Christian idea of a trinity.

Such an abstract divine being created a problem for existing religions, which saw their gods as having forms and human personalities and able to work within matter. While it was possible to abstract this One Thing, it created a substantial philosophical gap between the gods and the One Thing*, something vital if you were going to follow the Neo-Platonic ideas of emanation. The

---

* In Kabbalistic view is that there are four broad states; God at the top (Atzaluth), then the archetypal world (Briah), the World of Formation (Yetzirah) and the matter (Assiah). The gods had a form and therefore were attributed to Yetzirah. This left a gap in Briah between the highest unknowable God and the gods.

magicians who wrote the PGM filled this gap with the concept of angels. Angels had the advantage that they did not have a function rather than a myth and lacked an agreed form. While it is clear from some of the Roman curse tablets that in popular magic angels were already being used magically, their nature was like those "unnamed gods" in that you invoked them because you wanted abstract power untainted by perception and form.

They were powerful beings who were manipulated to carry out the request. Greek versions of the Jewish names of God became useful in this sub-set of pagan magic. IAO SABAŌTH (ΙΑΩ ΣΑΒΑΩΘ) for example was a name of the abstract One Thing which was called to invoke angels and control the gods. By the second century, pagan intellectuals were seeing angels as celestial * and abstract. One has to remember that there was never any organised "church" for the idea nor any real universal or central doctrine. Some pagan magicians sometimes treated angels as gods or had Pagan gods send angels (although these might be lesser angels), but to an ancient Pagan, the use of Judeo-Christian angels was not a problem. In fact, a tomb of a priest of Sabazios Vincintius in Rome has a depiction of the dead person being led to a post-mortem banquet by an angel. He is shown in other scenes as being accompanied by Mercury. Sabazios is equated with Jove and mentioned with Mercury.

PAGAN ANGELS

Modern magicians who follow the Abramelin system (or have read about it) mistakenly tend to equate the *Holy Guardian Angel* with their *Higher Self* or what the ancients called their *Higher Genius*. In doing so, they make this angel into something much more important than it is. That is not saying that it is not a great spirit, but it is not your real higher spiritual self. Another mistake associated with the *Guardian Angel* is that it is a Christian (or at least Jewish) concept.

Ancient pagans used angels to fill a gap between *Dæmons* or gods and matter. They acknowledged that *Dæmons* and gods were different, operating on different levels; it was just that a spirit of the rarefied aether had no chance of influencing an object of dense matter. What was needed was a half-way spirit which could be the "messenger" of the god. The name of the angel was unimportant as it was the "hand of the god." Ancient Alexandrian magicians sometimes borrowed Hebrew names for pagan angels (which has

---

* See *Ancient Angels: Conceptualising Angeloi in the Roman Empire* By Rangar Cline

in my view led to some confusion of the nature of some of the Kabbalistic angels, such as Uriel).

The concept of a *guardian angel,* or a spirit assigned to you at birth to protect you is connected to the idea of fate and destiny. If the *guardian angel* had a function, it was to ensure that you lived out your fate and did not suffer from accidental death before your time. Knowledge and conversation with the *Guardian Angel* were largely unnecessary as you could see its activity through what was happening in your life. If you could speak to it, the Angel would tell you that it had intervened to stop something happening, which would have prevented an essential part of your story unfolding.

There were moves to develop the "theology" of *guardian angels.* On the island of Santorini, graves had a circled cross and the first name of each person prefixed with the word "Angelos." For centuries the graves were considered to be Christian, but the discovery that one grave dated from the first century and the last was in the fifth seemed to suggest that they were part of a pagan cult. The circled cross once thought to be a Christian sign was more likely to be a stylised rosette which appears on many pagan tombs.

Understanding that the graves were pagan gave rise to a few other assumptions. The reason that names and details were put on gravestones by pagans was so that people would read them out loud and give the dead person a new life. Other reasons to do so was to establish them as heroes in the underworld where they would lead a blessed life between human and divine. So a person reading the Santorini graves was declaring that the person was an angel.

In his book *Ancient Angels,* Ragar Cline points out that there was an ancient belief that you were your *guardian angel.* In Acts 12, people surprised to see that Peter had escaped from prison, mistook him for his *Guardian Angel.*

> *"The guardian angel could be seen as anything from the manifestation of the individual, to the point that the identity of the soul and guardian angel were merged, and in the case of Peter, the individual's angel could be mistaken for the individual."*

This was not the *Higher Genius* because it was too close to matter – an expression of the soul.

The question then remains as to why the people of Santorini wanted identification with their *guardian angels* after death.

Guardian angels had the roles of psychopomps after death, which explains some of this, but gravestones were for long after this process was over. Placing the world Angelos on the tomb suggest that in some form the *Guardian Angel* guarded the dead body. We know of invocations in Melos and Thessaly where the Angelos was called upon as a tomb guardian. If the *guardian angel* was part of the self which aligned a person to their destiny, it seems unfair to have the spirit guarding a tomb for eternity.

One answer to this could be the following scenario: when a person incarnates the part of them that keeps them on the mission of their destiny is angelic. By the time they die, they have fulfilled whatever fate the gods required and have become their angel. That destiny takes them to whatever part of the afterlife their story needs. However, the physical part of that angel (remember *guardian angels* are supposed to operate at a physical level) remains attached to the dead body until it is decomposed and forgotten. This would explain why the ground around graves was sacred as it was full of the energy of what was left of *guardian angels*.

Because the *guardian angel* is so bound up with you and your fate, and you eventually become it, it is unlikely that knowledge and conversation is that necessary. Your spiritual path would be looking for your Higher Genius.

The angels used by pagans were part of a dissimilar system and had a different flavour to Jewish or Christian angels. The name might have been the same, but they were nor propping up the same theology. This is one of the reasons I have recommended using the ancient Greek pronunciation of their names so that they have a slightly different feel.

ANGELIC AND DÆMONIC SYSTEMS

Unfortunately, the ancient systems connected to angelics were not as thorough and complete as later systems. Ancient magicians have used archangels and angels without much thought of hierarchy or function which are so loved by modern" Kabbalistic" magicians. In PGM angelic names often appear for effect without much logic. It took 1000 years of Judaeo-Christian magic to create the elaborate system of archangel, angel, intelligence and spirit described by Agrippa. It is possible to see the roots of the system in some of the early proto-grimoires such as the *Testament of Solomon* or the writings of Pseudo-Dionysus and they were just as useful to the pagan magician.

Looking at the diagram which starts this chapter, we see the unknowable divine triad at the top and emerging from these the seven primal colours or energy rays. These are the most abstract forces in the universe and provide power for the rest.

FOUR HOLY CREATURES

The next level are the kerubs. In the *Bible*, these appeared in Ezekiel, Isaiah and Revelations. They were described as the four holy creatures – additionally, they are seen as Bull, Lion, Eagle and Human. Sometimes they have wings.

The assumption in modern magic is that they were Jewish angels from which all the other angels derived, but they were much older than the *Bible* and appeared to have a place in many non-Jewish cultures. In Vietnam they are known as "Tu Linh", and are named Long – Lan – Quy – Phung, four sacred animals representing the tremendous power of the universe. Four gods at world-quarters have similar roles in Indian, Aztec, Chinese, Japanese and Icelandic religion. They might not have the same responsibly given to the Four Holy Creatures, but their archetypal presence is there.

They arrive in European systems from Persian and Babylonian star lore. The iconography if the Hebrew kerubs was made during the time of the Babylonian captivity around 600 – 560 BCE. In Babylonia, they were known as the Watchers of the Directions and were connected to different constellations. The image of the Great God on his throne often had the title "lord of the four creations."*

The importance of these four stars and their constellations comes from the fact that they were marking points of the solar year and the dominant constellation in the sky. The symbolic animals represented the constellations. People could look at them and know the season.

---

* For the last four centuries it had been believed that the Babylonians borrowed the idea from the Indo-Iranians who settled in the area between 2000 – 1500 BCE. Around 3000 BCE they decided that there were Four Royal Stars or Watchers of the four directions or the Persian Royal Stars which were Aldebaran (Tascheter) – Vernal equinox (Watcher of the East): Regulus (Venant) – summer solstice (Watcher of the South): Antares (Satevis) – autumn equinox (Watcher of the West): Fomalhaut (Haftorang) – winter solstice (Watcher of the North). The symbols of these were: Aldebaran – Bull, Regulus – Lion, Antares – Scorpion, Fomalhaut – Southern fish (Aquarius). However, the Babylons tended to associate the equinoxes etc more with the fixed constellations and the winds rather than one star. In 1945 George Davis in a *Popular Astronomy* article pointed out that there was no proof of Persian Royal Stars or watchers in any historical text. Stars that important should rate a mention in the MUL.APIN astrological tablets, but they do not. It would appear that Davis found the much repeated concept was an invention.

The magical obsession with directions, and seasons, and winds is somewhat confusing for modern magicians. For the ancients the move through the seasons was a vital part of life, and the forces directing this ticking astral clock were logically the most important. The ancient myths show the gods expressing these forces and trying to explain their mysterious actions. The myth of Demeter and Persephone tells the cycle of seasons and planting, but they are effectively giving form to a more powerful force, which is the season itself.

The four kerubs are the four primal directing forces for all life. The four great coordinators wield tremendous archetypal powers to direct form and create order. To them are attributed the ideas of the elements, directions, and seasons, and the four of them contain the totality of the directing force of the divine triad throughout all levels. They use and focus the powers of the seven rays.

In the mysteries of Hermopolis in Ancient Egypt, the four were even more abstract and divided into their male and female polarities making eight. The ancient Egyptians considered the universe to be made from chaos by four gods and their consorts (the number four was supposed to represent completeness). Each pair represented the male and female aspects of the four creative powers or sources. Nun and Naunet represented the primaeval waters of chaos (which would later become water); Huh and Hauhet represented the currents of these waters of chaos (the energy which will manifest as fire); Kuk and Kuaket represented darkness itself (which would later manifest as earth); and Amun and Amunet represented air (or "that which is hidden"). These eight elements interacted causing an explosion, and the burst of energy which was released caused the Primaeval Mound (located at Hermopolis, but also known as the "Isle of Flame") to rise from the waters of Chaos.

From this act of creation order (Maat) was established within the sea of chaos. This chaos was always trying to undo the rule of Maat and needed to be fought by the gods. This chaos became personified by the great serpent Apep who fights a night-time battle with most of the gods. If Ra loses then chaos swallows creation.

The names of the four Holy Creatures, according to an Ancient Coptic text* are Paramara (earth) (Ⲣⲁⲣⲁⲙⲁⲣⲁ), Zorothion (fire) (Ⲍⲟⲣⲟⲑⲓⲟⲛ), Periton (water) (Ⲡⲉⲣⲓⲧⲟⲛ) and Akramata (air) (Ⲁⲕⲣⲁⲙⲁⲧⲁ). These spirits are rarely invoked because their powers are too close to the One Thing for a magician to get a handle on them. They can be used to provide background energy to a working. More understandable versions of these beings exist on each of the five levels. The four "creatures" exist in the realms of order and chaos and appear to be the forces which bring about order from chaos and return it to chaos to complete the cycle.

ARCHANGELS

Archangel comes from the words *archon* (ἄρχων) and *aggelos* (ἄγγελος). *Archon* means *ruler, commander, chief, leader*†. The word *aggelos* means *messenger*‡, and it comes from the verb *aggelo* (ἀγγέλλω) which means *announce, report, bring news, bring the message*§. *Aggelo* derives from the verb *ago* (ἄγω) which means *lead, carry, fetch, bring*¶, *convey***, and in another form *anagomai* (ἀνάγομαι) which means *I lead up from the lower to the higher, raise, ascend to, bring up*††

The idea for them probably comes from Zoroastrian Amesha Spentas. These were seven beings who inhabit immortal bodies that operate in the physical world to protect, guide and inspire humanity and the spirit world. They represented a stepped down power of the light god Ahura Mazda so that it could manifest in the denser levels of creation. Amesha means" eternal"and "spenta" means brilliance. There were seven, and they were the attributes of the single god itself:

Spenta Mainyu (Bountiful Spirit), Asha Vahishta (Highest Truth), Vohu Mano (Righteous Mind), Khshathra Vairya (Desirable Kingdom), Spenta Armaiti (Holy Devotion), Haurvatat (Perfection) and Ameretat (Immortality).

Despite there being a dearth of biblical mentions for archangels,

---

*A spell to protect a mother and child, Berlin11347, published in Meyer, M. and Smith, R. (1994). *Ancient Christian Magic*. San Francisco, Ca: Harper San Francisco.

† Liddell-Scott, ἄρχων,

‡ Liddell-Scott, ἄγγελος

§ Liddell-Scott, ἀγγέλλω

¶ Etymologicum Magnum, *ἄγγελος*

** Hesychii Alexandrini Lexicon, ἄγει

†† Liddell-Scott, ἀνάγομαι

there was a detailed tradition for them among Alexandria's Jewish community. This filtered into the magical community and found its way into the *Greek Magical Papyri*. Unlike modern occultists who knock themselves out using Hebrew lettering, the Alexandrian magicians used the Greek version of the archangelic names. The pronunciation is slightly different from traditional Kabbalah Hebrew. In Greek, the letters are all pronounced, and we have the written versions of the words to work it out. The el is spelt with a ή (eta), which is breathed out and not transposed to an «e «, so the vowel sounds a bit like the word air. This means that the el sound at the end of each name would sound like "il" when said quickly. The "a" sound in Greek is short like "up" or "aha." Raphael would sound like Ra-fa-il instead of the longer sounding Rah-fay-el of the Golden Dawn.

There was some argument in antiquity about who the seven archangels were. While most agreed that Michael, Raphael, Gabriel and Uriel were the basic four, there was an extensive body of opinion about the other three. The *Book of Enoch* says that the seven were Michael, Raphael, Gabriel, Uriel, Saraqael, Raguel, and Remiel.

The Eastern Orthodox Tradition believed the other three were most often named Selaphiel, Jegudiel, and Barachiel. The Coptic Church called Uriel Suriel, and the other three were Zedekiel, Sarathiel and Ananiel. Closer to the pagan/Christian magical tradition, Pseudo-Dionysius gives them as Michael, Gabriel, Raphael, Uriel, Camael, Jophiel, and Zadkiel.

PGM X 36-50 gives the following list Michael, Raphael, Gabriel, Souriel (Uriel), Zaziel, Badakiel, and Syliel.

> Michael (Μιχαήλ)(Mee-ha-'el) "Who is like God?"
> Raphael, (Ραφαήλ) (Ra-fa-'el) "God's medicine."
> Gabriel (Γαβριήλ) (Wa-vree-'el*) "God's strength."
> Souriel (Σουριήλ) (Soo-ree-'el†) "God's light."
> Zaziel (Ζαζιήλ) (Za-zee-'el) "Hidden God."
> Badakiel (Βαδακιήλ) (Va-tha-kee-'el‡) "God Plans."
> Syliel (Συλιήλ) (Sy-lee-'el) "God's Throne."

The PGM list provides a list of God names, barbaric names of power, and their associated vowels. The vowels begin with the planetary vowel associated with each. It is possible to see what planetary force

---

* Here the sounds are soft which means that it sounds like Wa-vri-il with the W like w in what, womb, were, was and v like v in very, victim etc.

† The oo like oo in book, look, and cook.

‡ With th like th in that, there, then, and though.

the Alexandrian magicians' ancients associated these angels with and make some logical assumptions. For example, Syliel (of whom we know little about), is connected to the divine name Adonai (Lord) (Ἀδωναι) A-tho-ne), and responds to the vowel string ΩΑΕΗΙΟΥ and the barbaric name of power has a long series of omega vowels in the middle. Everything about him suggests Saturn and the archangel of materiality. Less obvious is the association of Michael with the Moon, instead of the Sun and Zaziel who was always associated with the mysteries being connected to Mars. This implies that the "pagan" magician view of these archangels was different from conventional Jewish thinking. The planetary attribution to the archangels has always been weak with little reason to attribute them to any. Like the colours, their powers are considered too wide to be planetary. Any planetary attribution can be included as part of their abilities and not their totality.

In the PGM X structure, Michael is an angel who stands between the sub-lunar world and the celestial. His role is a guardian to keep the darker and unbalanced forces rising into the more purified realms of spirit. His name "Who is like God?" is like a question which everything must answer before he lets them journey. Raphael maintains his traditional role as communicator and healer. Gabriel becomes a love angel, which is appropriate when you remember he was the "messenger" for the birth of Jesus. Souriel, is an extended version of the name of the archangel Uriel and is a good choice for the solar angel. According to the *Jewish Encyclopaedia**, Jewish tradition made Uriel "as the source of the heat of the day in winter" and the Angel of Sunday, suggesting that the myth that "Michael was always the Jewish angel of the Sun" is incorrect. Uriel means "God's fire" and the Sun is a good symbol. Zaziel is better known for his demoted role as a spirit of Saturn in later occultism and is associated with the Kabbalistic sphere of Binah. The word could be derived from *Zaza* which means "brightness" which works well as a meaning for a "Mars" angel. It would mean that he is a polar opposite of Gabriel in terms of Archangelic physics.

Badakiel means "God checks" or "God plans" so is the creative force which sets long term goals for the universe and makes sure they happen. The administrative role makes a great deal of sense when you consider similarities to Jupiter.

All seven angels answer to the God Abrasax who is invoked using the Barbaric Name of Power IΩXYX

* Roth, C. and Wigoder, G. (1970). *The new standard Jewish encyclopedia [encyclopedia]*. Jerusalem: Massada.

Archangel	Vowel String	Divine Name	Planet	Name of Power
Michael (Μιχαήλ) Mi-ha-il	ΑΕΗΙΟΥΩ	Nyseu (Νυσευ) (Ny-sef)	Moon	Χυχ Chych
Raphael (Ραφαήλ) Ra-fa-il	ΕΗΙΟΥΩΑ	Nychieu (Νυχιευ) Ny-chee-ef	Mercury	Χυβαχυχ Chyvachych
Gabriel (Γαβριήλ) Wa-vre-il	ΗΙΟΥΩΑΕ	Aōche (Αωχη) A-aw-ch'e	Venus	Βαχαχυχ Vachachych
Souriel (Σουριήλ) Soo-re-il	ΙΟΥΩΑΕΗ	Mecheu (Μεχευ) Me-chef	Sun	Βακαζιχυχ Vakazeechych
Zaziel (Ζαζιήλ) Za-ze-il	ΟΥΩΑΕΗΙ	IAO (ΙΑΩ) EE-A-AW	Mars	Βαζαβαχυχ Vazavachych
Badakiel (Βαδακιήλ) Va-da-ke-il	ΥΩΑΕΗΙΟ	Sabvaōth (ΣαβαωΘ) Sa-va-awth	Jupiter	Βαδητοφϖϑ Vad'etop-thawth
Syliel (Συλιήλ) Si-li-il	ΩΑΕΗΙΟΥ	Adonai (Ἀδωναι) A-tho-ne	Saturn	Βαινχωωωχ Vaeencha-wawawch

Each Angel is ruled by a divine name and is drawn towards you by vibrating the barbaric name of power and the vowel string. If we wanted to invoke Michael we would write the words:

Abrasax IO-Chych Michael (Μιχαήλ) ΑΕΗΙΟΥΩ Nysef (Νυσευ) Chych (Χυχ) on a white or violet candle.

After opening the temple, you would say, **I invoke you Abrasax who unites the seven by the powers of your name.**

I conjure thee by the name ΙΩΧΥΧ (Ee-aw-chych) so that you will awaken to me the mighty Archangel Michael.

Light the candle and say,

In the name of Ny-sef, I invoke the Archangel Michael, who is the guardian between the world and the celestial world. Come forth mighty Michael, for I know your secret barbaric name of power which you rejoice to hear.

Vibrate the name Chych for five minutes.

I invoke you by the arrangement of the sacred word which was spoken by Thoth to create you and the celestial realm. Awaken to me, Michael, in a manner I can comprehend.

Slowly vibrate AEHIOYΩ for five minutes.

The appearance of Michael will not be a form, or, if it is it is, not something with which you can communicate. Archangelic forms tend to be swirling energy patterns and an overall presence. Sometimes, you get hit by a force or emotion which is so strong it stays with you for days. However, the effect is more mystical, and words don't seem to do much. If you wish to frame a question, meditate on it in the presence of the archangel and allow all the images you can associate with the question to be broadcasting it. It will reply but it will not be in words. Sometimes you will see a picture or a scene, but the image will be cryptic and impossible to decode straight away, but you will know that you have received it. Communication between you might take place, but often it will take days or weeks for the message to get through – either through dreams or just real life events explaining them.

THE RULES OF WORKING AT THIS LEVEL

Just because you are trying to work at a higher level does not mean you are. Many people have come off the rails working at this point because they end up tricked into thinking that their *Higher Genius* is telling them something that it is not. At this point, your *Higher Genius* is not an entity; it is part of everything else.

1. If you see a form, it is sublunar and not super-celestial. The real thing is the above form. Any connection you get at this level is going to be difficult to understand intellectually. Once in desperation to explain something, the supercelestial entity played a movie. It said, "it is like this." All it was the image of a bird landing on a river. That was the form, which intellectually had no meaning; it arrived with a wave of feeling and understanding, which still shakes me 15 years later.

2. If a being tells you that you are important it is not your *Higher Genius*; it is likely to be your *Lower Self*. The same thing applies if something tells you that you are destined to be a great prophet or found a new religion. When I first entered a *Higher Genius* state, I asked, "what do you want me to do?" hoping to get some specific life direction. I got two words "live" and "experience." Sure, you can make a religion around those two words, and you would be missing the point.
3. You may not get a message, visions, or any astral fireworks. What you should receive is a presence which brings with it those effects.

ACTIVATION OF DIVINE LOVE

ΑΧΜΑΓΕ ΡΑΡΠΕΨΕΙ

One of the most notable features of the divine self is love. Romantic love is a shadow of the sort of love which is needed in this operation. The ancient Greeks saw erotic love as a form of madness. In the *Phaedrus* Socrates says that although this madness can be an illness, it can also be the source of man's greatest blessings.

Socrates listed four types of 'divine madness.' There was a prophecy from Apollo, holy prayers and mystic rites from Dionysus and Muse-inspired poetry. However the highest form of madness was

ΣΣΣΣ ΗΗΗΗ
ΣΣΣΣ ΗΗΗΗ

love from Aphrodite and Eros. This sort of love arises from seeing the earth's beauty and remembering the true and universal harmony.

He said that most earthly souls are so corrupted by the body that they lose all memory of the universal beauty. When their eyes fall upon the beauty of the earth, they are merely given over to pleasure.

When love becomes spiritual and "Platonic," it helps the soul as it gazes upon the universe as a lover looks into the eyes of his beloved and reverence it.

> "The parts of the soul out of which the wings grew, and which had hitherto been closed and rigid, begin to melt open, and small wings begin to swell and grow from the root upwards."

Symposium, Socrates argues that love must not be confused with the object of love, which, in contrast to love itself, is perfectly beautiful and good. A person who understands this is not a god but an angel who intermediates between gods and men.

> *"As such, he is neither mortal nor immortal, neither wise nor ignorant, but a lover of wisdom (philosophos, φιλόσοφος)."*

The PGM contains a ritual initiation into this concept called the Sword of Dardanos. The spell has been twisted into a love spell which "immediately bends and attracts the soul of whomever you wish." While there is no doubt that while it could have such a use, it is a sledgehammer to crack a nut as the imagery is cosmic rather than individual.

The rite requires the use of a magical image of Aphrodite as a dove. Above her head is writing "ACHMAGE RARPEPSEE (ΑΧΜΑΓΕ ΡΑΡΠΕΨΕΙ)." Below are Psyche and Eros embracing one another and beneath Eros's feet these letters: "SSSSSSSS (ΣΣΣΣΣΣΣΣ)," and beneath Psyche's feet: "EEEEEEEE (ΗΗΗΗΗΗΗΗ)."

THE LOVERS.

The image is then of the Goddess of Love acting as the *Higher Genius* and her messenger Eros setting the person's Psyche on fire with the result that Psyche and Eros unite. The image described is different from the legend of Psyche and Eros as it was written in *Metamorphoses* in the 2nd century AD by Lucius Apuleius Madaurensis. The first image is not part of the myth (where Eros never burns Psyche, but it is her fire which reveals him). Both images are implied in Rider-Waite *Lovers* Tarot card with the Angel above being Venus with flames of desire (encoded in the symbol of the Sun) radiating from her with Eros and Psyche below. The Christian Waite would never show Adam (Eros) and Eve (Psyche) embracing, but he would have been aware of the Golden Dawn association of a different part of the myth to this tarot card.

After making the image, invoke Eros:

I call upon you, author of all creation, who spread your wings over the whole world, you, the unapproachable and unmeasurable, who breathe into every soul life-giving reasoning. You who fitted all things together by your power, first-born, founder of the universe, golden-winged, whose light is darkness, who shroud reasonable thoughts and breathe forth dark frenzy, clandestine one who secretly inhabits every soul. You engender an unseen fire as you carry off every living thing without growing weary of torturing it, having with pleasure delighted in pain from the time when the world came into being. You come and bring pain, which is sometimes reasonable, sometimes irrational, because of whom men dare beyond what is fitting and take refuge in your light which is darkness. Most headstrong, lawless, implacable, inexorable, invisible, bodiless, generator of frenzy, archer, torch-carrier, master of all living sensation and of everything clandestine, dispenser of forgetfulness, creator of silence, through whom the light and to whom the light travels, infantile when you have been engendered within the heart, wisest when you have succeeded.

I call upon you who is unmoved by prayer, by your great name: AZARACHTHARAZA LATHA EEATHAL Y Y Y LATHAEE ATHA LLALAPH OIOIO AI AI AI* OOEREEEF OEEAEE LEGETA RAMAEE AMA RATAGEL, (ΑΖΑΡΑΧΘΑΡΑΖΑ ΛΑΘΑ ΙΑΘΑΛ ΥΥΥ ΛΑΘΑΪ ΑΘΑΛΛΑΛΑΦ ΙΟΙΟΙΟ ΑΪ ΑΪ ΑΪ ΑΪ ΟΥΕΡΙΕΥ ΟΙΑΪ ΛΕΓΕΤΑ ΡΑΜΑΪ ΑΜΑ ΡΑΤΑΓΕΛ)

First-shining, night-shining, night rejoicing, night-engendering, witness.

ER'EKEESEETHPH'E ARARACHARARA 'EPHTHEESIK'ERE EEAVEZEVYTH EEAW
(ΕΡΗΚΙΣΙΘΦΗ ΑΡΑΡΑΧΑΡΑΡΑ ΗΦΘΣΙΚΗΡΕ ΙΑΒΕΖΕΒΥΘ ΙΩ)

You in the deep:VREEAMVRAW VEREEAMVEVAW
(ΒΡΙΑΜΒΡΩ ΒΕΡΙΑΜΒΕΒΩ),

You in the sea, MERMERGOO (ΜΕΡΜΕΡΓΟΥ).

Clandestine and wise, ACHAPA ADAWNE-E VASMA CHARAKAW EEAKAWV EEAAW CHAROO'ER AROO'ER LAEELAM SEMESEELAM SOOMARTA MARVA KARVA MENAVAWTH 'E-EE-EE-A
(ΑΧΑΠΑ ΑΔΩΝΑΙΕ ΒΑΣΜΑ ΧΑΡΑΚΩ ΙΑΚΩΒ ΙΑΩ ΧΑΡΟΥΗΡ ΑΡΟΥΗΡ ΛΑΪΛΑΜ ΣΕΜΕΣΙΛΑΜ ΣΟΥΜΑΡΤΑ ΜΑΡΒΑ ΚΑΡΒΑ ΜΕΝΑΒΩΘ ΗΙΑ).

---

* Betz has the "AI" three times while some other writers have it four times.

The next phase is to involve the soul of the person you want to fall in love with you, but the following invocation turns the intention towards your higher.

Burn me, oh Eros, oh Dæmon of Venus, so that I might love my Higher Genius and attract it to my conscious mind.
Love creates order from chaos.

By love we are united and separate we have become lost. Awaken to me the passion and desire so that we shall be mystically married. Awake this to me as I chant your great name born by the Archangels* of the Holy Triad MICHAEL, GABRIEL, RAPHIEL, URIEL, CAMAEL, JOPHIEL, ZADKIEL
NEPHERIERI (for seven minutes)

I summon the immortal and infallible strength and love of God. I submit my soul to Divine love.

Chant **NEPHERIERI** (seven times) *while imagining Venus above you and Eros flying from her and touching you with a torch. You should see yourself on fire with love and passion. It brings pain and desire but much more. You should see Venus descend and merge with you. Allow plenty of time to meditate on this.*

THE THREE DAYS OF PREPARATION

In the three days leading up to the retreat, you should restrict your activities considerably and avoid contact with others at all. At this point, it does not matter if you have to talk to people you live with, but even this should be limited. You should sleep separately and abstain from sex. You should drink only water and certainly not eat heavily.

After you have done your Divine Love ritual, you should add the following invocation.
"I call you, who is higher than all, the creator of all, you, the self-begotten who sees all but is unseen. You gave Helios the glory and the power, Selene the privilege to wax and wane and have fixed courses. You took nothing from the earlier-born darkness

---

* The writer used corrupted names of Jewish archangels which I have clarified using the contemporary Pseudo-Dionysius. The writer clearly wanted to raise the level of the ritual from the world of form to the more abstract forms of Jewish archangels. Many modern pagans might consider this too Christian (something their ancient counterparts did not). If you wish to avoid this you can chant the seven vowels instead.

but apportioned things so that they should be equal. When you appeared, order and light arose. All things are subject to you, whose true form none of the Gods can see. You change into all things, and yet you are invisible, Aion of Aion.

I call you Lord, to appear unto me in good form, for under your orders I serve your angel,

VEEATHEEARVAR VERVEER SCHEELATOOR VOOPHROOMTROM (ΒΙΑΘΙΑΡΒΑΡ ΒΕΡΒΙΡ ΣΧΙΛΑΤΟΥΡ ΒΟΥΦΡΟΥΜΤΡΟΜ) , and your fear, DANOOPH CHRATOR VELVALEE VALVEETH EEAAW (ΔΑΝΟΥΦ ΧΡΑΤΟΡ ΒΕΛΒΑΛΙ ΒΑΛΒΙΘ ΙΑΩ).

Through you arose the celestial pole and the Earth. I call you Lord, as do the Gods who appeared under your order, that they may have power, ECHEVYKRAWM (ΕΧΕΒΥΚΡΩΜ) of Helios, to whom belongs the glory, AAA EEE OOO III AAA 000 SAVAAWTH ARVATHEEAAW ZAGOOR'E (ΑΑΑ ΗΗΗ ΩΩΩ III ΑΑΑ ΩΩΩ ΣΑΒΑΩΘ ΑΡΒΑΘΙΑΩ ΖΑΓΟΥΡΗ), the god ARATHY ADONE-E (ΑΡΑΘΥ ΑΔΩΝΑΙΕ).

I call you in the secret languages
In 'birdglyphic', ARE (ΑΡΑΙ);
In hieroglyphic, LAEELAM (ΛΑΪΛΑΜ);
In Hebrew, ANOCH VEEATHEEARVATH VERVEER ECHEELATOOR (ΑΝΟΧ ΒΙΑΘΙΑΡΒΑΘ ΒΕΡΒΙΡ ΕΧΙΛΑΤΟΥΡ) VOOPHOOTROM (ΒΟΥΦΟΥΤΡΟΜ); in Egyptian, ALDAVAEEM (ΑΛΔΑΒΑΕΙΜ);
In baboon, AVRASAX (ΑΒΡΑΣΑΞ);
In falcon, CHEE CHEE CHEE CHEE CHEE CHEE CHEE TEEPH TEEPH TEEPH (ΧΙ ΧΙ ΧΙ ΧΙ ΧΙ ΧΙ ΧΙ ΤΙΦ ΤΙΦ ΤΙΦ);
In hieratic, MENEPHAE-EEPHAWTH CHA CHA CHA CHA CHA CHA CHA. (ΜΕΝΕΦΩΙΦΩΘ ΧΑ ΧΑ ΧΑ ΧΑ ΧΑ ΧΑ ΧΑ)»

Clap your hands three times. Say 'pop pop pop' 33 times and then take a deep breath and hiss.

Serapis "Come to me Lord, faultless and unflawed, who pollute no place, for I have been initiated into your Name."

CHAPTER NINE
THE RETREAT

The retreat begins at Sunrise on Friday and ends on Sunday night. During which there should be no contact with the outside world. Neither should you speak other than to perform the invocations. You should also have sorted out your practice room and made sure it is cleaned thoroughly.

FRIDAY

Awaken 15 minutes before Sunrise wash and say the following Ancient Egyptian Temple purification prayer*:

Oh Water may you remove all my impurities.
Oh inundation, may you wash off my errant Dæmons.
May you wash the face of Apollo, may you rub the face of Typhon,
May you wash the face of Persephone, may you rub the face of the spinners of fate,
May you rub my face as I invoke my crown
Loosened are my bonds through Apollo
Opened are my bonds through Typhon
My purity is the purity of God.
I shall not fall on some evil obstacle. I am pure.

Put on your white robe and go to the temple door.

THE SPEECH BEFORE THE DOOR

Walk to your temple room door and visualise Hermanubis standing before it and holding a sword. Say the following to him

Doorkeepers of the gateway,
Secret Great Gods who separate the God in his chapel,
Who strike upon his offering altar,
Make way for me so that I can enter the holiest of places,
For I am one of you, I am Serapis, and I have entered the underworld and risen with the Sun.

---

* It comes from an unusual copy of the *Book of the Dead* which was for a priestess in the Temple of Dendra see J.-Cl. *Goyon, Confirmation* du pouvoir royalau Nouvel An, BdE 52, Le Caire 1972

Here me, for I am on the path of return.
For I follow the Supereme Triad*
I respect the gods.
I respect my ancestors.
I am fair.
I know what I have learnt.
I understand what I have heard.
I know myself .

See Hermanubis stand aside and enter your temple.

THE FIRST RITE

The purpose of this rite is to kindle the flame of your *Higher Self.* For this you will need a large thick candle which will burn for at least three days. On it you should print your full name along it and the following words and symbols.

At the top (near the wick) draw this symbol (left) of the Solar spirit†

Then below it draw a snake with ἀγαθοδαίμων (Agathos Daemon) and NXΘANXΘΩΛEKPO (N C H T H A N C H T H A W L E K R O) ANOKΛEPΦPOEPAI (ANOKLERFROERE) along its body. ANOK appears in the beginning of a lot of Magic Words and correspond to the Copitc word meaning "I AM." Homer describes Φηραὶ as a Holy City belonging to Agamemnon. During the period that the ball was made it was famous for its temple of Tyche and it had always been that way. Certainly "I am Fortune" makes sense in association with with *Agathos Dæmon* (Αγαθός Δαίμων).

Along the length write the following:
A Δ A Ξ A Ξ B E N B E N B Λ Ω Θ N Ω M A Z O M O H P (ADAXAXVENVENVLAWTHNAWMAZOMO'ER).

Benben was one of the most potent symbols of ancient Egypt symbolizing the primeval *mound* and housed the spirit of the Sun god Ra. The word is ancient Egyptian. Adaxax (Αδαξας) might

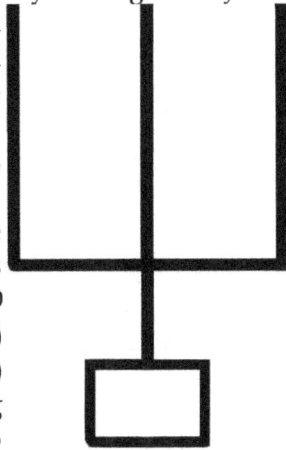

---

* What follows are some of the Delphic Maxims.

† Although this is the symbol for the Olympic Spirit of the Sun (Och) it also was used to represent Helios on ancient talismans. The most dramatic is found on the Magic Ball of Apollo found near the Theatre of Dionysus on the Acropolis.

be a fusion of the Greek words ADA (AΔA) means "virgin" or "untouched" and AXAX (AΞAΞ) meaning "dry heat." Blawthnawm (BΛΩΘNΩM)[but the word is blothnom] is Semitic, possibly corrupted Hebrew, the word appears to be connected to drying out through age although it could also be a root word for "lord. Azomo'er (Aζoµoηρ), Azo is "dry." This would mean that the magic word is about Ra, the Lord of the Benben drying out the waters of creation in the Ancient Egyptian myth. This idea is to invoke the powers of your *Higher Genius* to bring about a new order for your life.

Finally place these symbols on what is left of the candle.

These are symbols associated with Helios Apollo.
Draw an invoking pentagram at the candle and say,

Creature of Wax I exorcise you in the name of Helios, so that you will be a perfect sacrifice to my *Higher Genius* and the light of your sacrifice will guide me to it.

Purify the candle with water saying:

Creature of Wax I purify you with water you in the name of Helios, so that you will be a perfect sacrifice to my *Higher Genius* and the light of your sacrifice will guide me to it.

Place some laurel leaves on your burner and pass the candle through the smoke saying:

Creature of Wax I consecrate you with fire you in the name of Helios, so that you will be a perfect sacrifice to my *Higher Genius* and the light of your sacrifice will guide me to it.

Anoint the candle with Oil of Abramelin saying:

Creature of Wax I anoint with the oil of the holy, setting you aside from the mundane. so that you will be a perfect sacrifice to my *Higher Genius* and the light of your sacrifice will guide me to it.

Place the candle in the east.

Say your morning prayer to Helios.

Say the following prayer seven times:

I call on thee who surround all things. I call in every language and in every dialect, as he first hymned thee, who was by thee appointed and entrusted with all authorities, Helios ACHEVYKRAWM (ΑΧΕΒΥΚΡΩΜ), whose is the glory, AAA EEE OOO (AAA HHH ΩΩΩ) because he was glorified by thee, thou who set the winds in then places and then, likewise, the stars of glittering forms, and who, in divine light, created the Universe,

EE EE EE AAA AW AW AW (III AAA ΩΩΩ) in which thou hast set in order all things.

SAVAAWTH, ARVATHEEAAW, ZAGOOR'E
(ΣΑΒΑΩΘ, ΑΡΒΑΘΙΑΩ, ΖΑΓΟΥΡΗ)
(These are the angels who first appeared.)

ARAGA ARATH ADONE VAS'EM EEAAW
(ΑΡΑΓΑ ΑΡΑΘ ΑΔΩΝΑΙ ΒΑΣΗΜ ΙΑΩ).

I call thee Helios to reveal to me the secrets of the universe
I call thee by your ancient name LAEELAM (ΛΑΪΛΑΜ),
and in Hebrew by your own Name,

ANAG VEEATHEEARVAR VERVEER SVHEE LA TOORVOOPHROOMTRAWM (36 letters);
(ΑΝΑΓ ΒΙΑΘΙΑΡΒΑΡ ΒΕΡΒΙ ΣΧΙ ΛΑ ΤΟΥΡΒΟΥΦΡΟΥΜΤΡΩΜ)

Come forth and show me creation. I kindle this flame.
(light the candle).
Say, Behold that light which shines in the darkness, the lamp of Hermanubis which guides me to my true self.

Perform the LVX formula on the candle and meditate on the flame.
Face east and invoke Serapis:

I invoke You, the Greatest God, Eternal Lord, World Ruler, who are over the World and under the World, Mighty Ruler of the Sea, rising at dawn, shining from the east for the whole world, setting in the west.

Come to me, Thou who risest from the Four Winds, benevolent and lucky Agathos Daemon, for whom Heaven has become the Processional Way. I call upon Your Holy and Great and Hidden Names which You rejoice to hear. The Earth flourished when You shone forth, and the plants became fruitful when you laughed;

the animals begat their young when You permitted.

Illuminate me this day with a vision from the Underworld which will show me the way to unite with my *Higher Genius..*

I invoke You, the greatest in Heaven, E'I LANCHYCH AKA RE'N BAL MISTHRE'N MARTA MATHATH LAILAM
('e-ee Lan-chych A-ka-r'en Val Mees-thr'n mar-ta ma-thath la-ee-lam)

(ΗΙ ΛΑΝΧΥΧ ΑΚΑΡΗΝ ΒΑΛ ΜΙΣΘΡΗΝ ΜΑΡΤΑ ΜΑΘΑΘ ΛΑΪΛΑΜ)
MOUSOUTHI SIETHO' BATHABATHI IATMO'N ALEI IABATH ABAO'TH
(Moo-soo-thee see-e-thaw va-tha-va-thee ee-at-mawn al-e-ee ee-a-vath A-va-awth)

(ΜΟΥΣΟΥΘΙ ΣΙΕΘΩ ΒΑΘΑΒΑΘΙ ΙΑΤΜΩΝ ΑΛΕΪ ΙΑΒΑΘ ΑΒΑΩΘ)
SABAO'TH ADO'NAI
(Sa-va-awth A-daw-na-ee)

(ΣΑΒΑΩΘ ΑΔΩΝΑΙ), the Great God,
ORSENOPHRE' ORGEATE'S TOTHORNATE'SA KRITHI BIO'THI IADMO'
(Or-se-no-fr'e or-ge-a-t'es to-thor-na-t'e-sa kree-thee vee-aw-thee ee-a-dmaw)

(ΟΡΣΕΝΟΦΡΗ ΟΡΓΕΑΤΗΣ ΤΟΘΟΡΝΑΤΗΣΑ ΚΡΙΘΙ ΒΙΩΘΙ ΙΑΔΜΩ)
IATMO'MI METHIE'I LONCHOO' AKARE' BAL MINTHRE' BANE

(Ee-at-maw-mee me-thee-'e-ee lon-cho-aw a-ka-r'e val meen-thr'e vane)
(ΙΑΤΜΩΜΙ ΜΕΘΙΗΙ ΛΟΝΧΟΩ ΑΚΑΡΗ ΒΑΛ ΜΙΝΘΡΗ ΒΑΝΕ)
BAINCHCHYCH CHOUPHRI NOTHEOUSI THRAI ARSIOUTH ERO'NERTHER,

(Va-eech-chych choo-free no-the-oo-see thra-ee ar-see-ooth e-raw-ner-ther)
(ΒΑΙΧΧΥΧ ΧΟΥΦΡΙ ΝΟΘΕΟΥΣΙ ΘΡΑΪ ΑΡΣΙΟΥΘ ΕΡΩΝΕΡΘΕΡ)

You are the Shining Helios, giving light throughout the whole world. You are the Great Serpent, Leader of all the Gods, who control the Beginning of Egypt and the end of the whole inhabited world, who mate in the ocean.

PSOI PHNOUTHI NINTHE'R
(pso-ee fnoo-thee neen-th'er)
(ΨΟΪ ΦΝΟΥΘΙ ΝΙΝΘΗΡ).

You are He who becomes visible each day and sets in the northwest of Heaven, and rises in the southeast.

You who have set at evening as an old man, who are over the world and under the world, Mighty Ruler of the Sea, hear my voice in this present day, in this night, in these holy hours, and illuminate me this day with a vision from the underworld Illuminate me this day with a vision from the underworld which will show me the way to unite with my *Higher Genius*.

Please, Lord KME'PH LOUTHEOUTH OR PHOICHE ORTILIBECHOUCH.
(Kmeef Loo-the-oo-th Or Fee-che Or-tee-lee-ve-chooch)
(ΚΜΗΦ ΛΟΥΘΕΟΥΘ ΟΡ ΦΟΙΧΕ ΟΡΤΙΛΙΒΕΧΟΥΧ)
ΙΕΡΧΕ ΡΟΥΜ ΙΠΕΡΙΤΑΩ ΥΑΪ
(Ee-er-Che Room Ee-pe-ree-ta-aq Y-a-ee)

I conjure Earth and Heaven and Light and Darkness and the Great God who created All, (SA-ROO-SEEN) (ΣΑΡΟΥΣΙΝ), You, Agathon Daimonion the Helper, to accomplish for me everything done by the Use of Vision.

"The one Zeus is Serapis!"

Hail Osiris, King of the Underworld, Lord of Burial, whose head is in Thinis, whose feet are in Thebes, the one who gives answer in Abydos and whose glory is in Pshilom. You are in the nub tree in Meroe, you are in the mountain of Pora Nous , you are upon my house forever. You whose face is the face of a hawk, whose tail is serpents and his back is that of a dragon. You have the hand of a man who is covered in the bandages of death and resurrection. You hold the palm staff of command.
Hail IAHO SABAHO ATONAI MISTEMY IAYIY
(EE-AR-HO SAR-BAH-HO Ah-TON-AI MIS-TEM-EE EE-AH-YAY-EE)

Hail MICHAEL SABAEL, Hail Anubis in the nome of the dog faces, he to whom the Earth

belongs, who strides upright. Hide the darkness in the deep. Bring in the light for me. Come into me, tell me the answer to that about which I am inquiring here today.

Repeat these nine times or until a bright light appears in the east. Sit down and allow the light to begin to instruct you.

NOON RITUAL

The purpose of this ritual is to awaken the forces of destruction and death so that you are purged of anything that might prevent you from attaining your *Higher Genius*. It calls the god Typhon who was the god of destruction.

Perform the *Lesser Ritual of the Pentagram* and the *lesser ritual of the hexagram*.
Perform the noon rite to the Sun.
Perform the Headless Ritual.
Purify and consecrate.

Take off your robe. Wrap yourself in the white sheet as if you were a corpse with your arms crossed, as if you were an Egyptian mummy. Your head should be in the north and feet south so that you are facing the Sun as it approaches mid-heaven (northern hemisphere). Centre yourself in the darkness and when ready, recite the invocation three times.

Mighty Typhon, sceptre-bearing almighty power and sovereign, god of gods; Lord

ABERAMENTHOOU
(ΑΒΕΡΑΜΕΝΘΩΟΥ)
(A-VE-RA-MEN-THAW-OO)

Disturber of the dark, bringer of thunder, sender of storms, lighting flasher of the night, You are the one who exhaled the cold and the heat. Stone-shaker, wall-breaker earth-quaker, boiler of the waters. You are the one who stirs the depths to motion,

IÔERBÊT AU TAUI MÊNI
(EE-ER-V'ET A-Y TAV-EE M'E-NEE)
(ΙΩΕΡΒΗΤ ΑΥ ΤΑΥΙ ΜΗΝΙ)

I am he who searched the entire world to find the great Osiris, whom I brought to you bound. I am he who together with you allied with the gods (others say against the gods); I am he who shut heaven's double door and put to sleep the unseen serpent, who at the edge of your kingdom stopped the sea, the streams, and

the flowing rivers. But, as your soldier, I was defeated by the gods and was cast face down on account of empty wrath. Awaken me, I beseech you, I implore you, friend; do not leave me here cast upon the earth, oh lord of gods:

AEMINAEBARÔThERREThÔRABEANIMEA
(A-E-MEE-NA-E-VA-RAW-THER-RE-THAW-R
A-VE-A-NEE-ME-A)
(ΑΕΜΙΝΑΕΒΑΡΩΘΕΡΡΕΘΩΡΑΒΕΑΝΙΜΕΑ)

Destroy that which is within me which prevents me linking to my Higher Genius. Fill me with power, I beg you, grant me this grace, that whenever I call upon any one of the gods, they come to me swiftly and appear visibly before me. Send me a guide through the valley of my fears so that I shall become fearless like you.

AINE BASANAPTATOU EAPTOU MÊNÔPhAESMÊ PAPTOU MÊNÔPh · [NA-EE-NE VA-SA-NA-PTA-TOO E-A-PTOO M'E-NAW-FA-E-SM'E PA-PTOO M'E-NAWF

(ΝΑΪΝΕ ΒΑΣΑΝΑΠΤΑΤΟΥ ΕΑΠΤΟΥ ΜΗΝΩΦΑΕΣΜΗ ΠΑΠΤΟΥ ΜΗΝΩΦ)

ΑΕΣΙΜΗ ΤΡΑΥΑΠΤΙ ΠΕΥΧΡΗ ΤΡΑΥΑΡΑ ΠΤΟΥΜΗΦ ΜΟΥΡΑΙ ΑΝΧΟΥΧΑΦΑΠΤΑ
(AESIMÊ · TRAUAPTI · PEUChRÊ · TRAUARA · PTOUMÊPh · MOURAI · ANChOUChAPhAPTA)

MOURSA · ARAMEI · IAÔ · AThThARAUI MÊNOKER BORO PTOUMÊTh · AT TAUI MÊNI ChARChARA
(ΜΟΥΡΣΑ ΑΡΑΜΕΙ ΙΑΩ ΑΘΘΑΡΑΫΪ ΜΗΝΟΚΕΡ ΒΟΡΟ ΠΤΟΥΜΗΘ ΑΤ ΤΑΥΪ ΜΗΝΙ ΧΑΡΧΑΡΑ)

ΠΤΟΥΜΑΥ ΛΑΛΑΨΑ ΤΡΑΥΪ ΤΡΑΥΕΨΕ ΜΑΜΩ ΦΟΡΤΟΥΧΑ
(PTOUMAU · LALAPsA · TRAUI TRAUEPsE MAMÔ PhORTOUChA) ·

ΑΕΗΙΟ ΪΟΥ ΟΗΩΑ ΕΑΪ ΑΕΗΙ ΩΙ ΙΑΩ ΑΗΙ ΑΙ ΙΑΩ
(ΑΕΕΙΟ ΙΟΥ ΟΕΟΑ · ΕΑΙ ΑΕΕΙ ΟΙ ΙΑΟ ΑΕΙ ΑΙ ΙΑΟ)

After you have said these three times put on your blindfold and lie down. Allow yourself to become a corpse. You might feel physical pain, but you must relax through it. You are dying to your old self. This process should take at least an hour. But you should preoccupy yourself with scenes of your own death such as imagining your own funeral and what you think others would say about your life. Have you managed to achieve what you wanted? Or was there more? Think about what you think death will be like.

After an hour or so the meditation will change direction. You will find yourself in a landscape and before you will be a *Dæmon* of Typhon. It will guide you through images which are associated with your weaknesses. They could be scary fragmented dreams. In death you must face your inner demons. What Typhon reveals, you can stand and can destroy. You can ask your guide to help you obliterate each complex or situation or show you how to deal with it. Take your time over this. It will be time to stand up only when you have a vision of a sea falcon flying down and striking you on the body with its wings.

Slowly arise and put on your white robes burn frankincense on a censer while saying this:

Mighty Typhon have been attached to your holy form. I have been given power by your holy name. I have acquired your emanation of the goods, Lord, god of gods, master, Dæmon.

ΑΘΘΟΥЇΝ ΘΟΥΘΟΥЇ ΤΑΥΑΝΤΙ ΛΑΩ ΑΠΤΑΤΩ
AThThOUIN ThOUThOUI TAUANTI LAÔ APTATÔ.

Now considering what the *Dæmon* of Typhon showed you, visualise each weakness that was presented to you and visualise it as a living being which has weakened your life.
Say to it:

In the name of the Hekate who is below the seven, who is within the seven. In the name Iao Sabaoth may your power issue forth from me and drive away this Dæmon which is in me, I adjure you, Dæmon , whoever you are, by this god Sabarbarbathioth Sabarbarbathiouth Sababarbathioneht Sabarbarbaphai

(ΣΑΒΑΡΒΑΡΒΑΘΙΩΘ ΣΑΒΑΡ ΒΑΡΒΑΘΙΟΥΘ
ΣΑΒΑΡΒΑΡΒΑΘΙΩΝΗΘ ΣΑΒΑΡΒΑΡΒΑΦΑЇ)
SA-VAR-VAR-VA-THEE-AWTH SA-VAR- VARVA-THEEOOTH
SA-VAR-VA-THEE-AW-N'ETH SA-VAR-VAR-VA-FA-EE).

Come out, demon, whoever you are, and stay away from me, hurry, hurry, now, now, Come out, Dæmon , since I bind you with unbreakable adamantine fetters, and I deliver you into the black chaos in perdition.

See the image being cast from your *Sphere of Sensation*. Do this for each thing that the *Dæmon* of Typhon showed you. When you have finished, perform your confession and then a lesser banishing ritual of the pentagram and purify and consecrate.

Having done this, meditate on it until noon. If you find yourself unable to meditate further and have time write down your experiences and realisations.

Noon:

Perform the Noon prayer followed by the solar breath.

NIGHT

Perform the *Lesser Ritual of the Pentagram* and then the night time prayer to Helios. Then:

PATHWORKING INTO LANDS OF THE NIGHT

The purpose of this pathworking is to enter the underworld, experience the *Dæmon* which might be there and have the first division of your *Higher Genius*. It is based on the ancient Egyptian *Book of Breathing* and takes you through the 12 hours of night. The imagery shows a Greek influence – especially the influence of Hekate as the ruler of the sub-lunar world. While Hades and Serapis are the kings of the underworld, they are a subset of her*.

In an ideal world you would start doing the pathworking at the setting Sun. You would then take one hour for each section. It is too much to expect a person who has technically six months of magical experience to be able to manage such a long pathworking at night. As it is there would be a danger of falling asleep and never completing the pathworking.

I would suggest recording the pathworking and playing it back while you listen. You can turn it off to allow 10 to 15 minutes to explore each stage of the pathworking you can set your alarm to prevent you from falling asleep.

Each stage of all gates will introduce you to the *Dæmon* that rules that part of the underworld. There will be a certain amount of testing of your personality. The *Dæmon* might want you to understand something that you would otherwise have repressed. This is important because it will be something that prevents you from making a good solid connection with your *Higher Genius*. You should not fear these *Dæmons* if they will work to help you beyond whatever limitations you have set yourself. However, it is important

---

* This pathworking is syncretic and parts of it are based on my own visionary experience of the particularly inner landscape.

to realise that they are not psychological functions but very real spiritual forces deep within the unconscious mind. This pathworking supplies a processing of a person's life up to this point and follows Greco-Egyptian approaches to the afterlife. It is important that you take your time and think hard about the challenges that these forces give you.

THE PATHWORKING

Perform the following invocation to Selene-Hekate as the Goddess of the Underworld.

I call upon you, Mistress of the World, ruler of the cosmic system, powerful goddess, gracious dæmon, Lady of Night, who travels through the air,

PHEROPHOIRĒ ANATHRA REŪTHRA
(ΦΕΡΕΦΟΡΗ ΑΝΑΘΡΑ ΟΥΘΡΑ)

Help me this night as I enter your kingdom with the setting Sun. Open the ways for me that I might not get lost in the underworld and might awaken my Higher Genius within the deepest recesses of myself.

Heed your sacred symbols and give a rustling sound and give a sacred angel or a holy assistant who serves this very night, in this very hour, PROKYNĒ BAUBŌ PHOBEIŪS MĒHE to help me find my Higher Genius in your kingdom.

Lie down and play pathworking tape:

FIRST HOUR

You stand facing the west toward the setting Sun. Before you is the desert and to your right hand is the god Hermanubis. He holds in his left hand the ankh cross and, in his right, a winged caduceus.

"Know this," he says. "You are about to enter into the lands of the dead in what will be a trial for you. You have experienced many deaths in your life and each one has led to a new awakening. This is no different, but you will find it harder... Are you ready to proceed?"

You agree, and the scene changes. You are bound like a mummy strapped to a throne on a boat which hovers above the desert sands. You are aware of dark figures moving around the boat – preparing for its departure.

Hermanubis stands in front of you, holding a large heliotrope flower.

"This is symbolic of your life and personality," Hermanubis says. "For the last six months, you have turned to follow Helios as he rode his chariot through the sky. Through repetition, you have tuned yourself to him, and now it is time to begin the dissolution of all that stands in the way. "

As he speaks the heliotrope bursts into flames and dissolves into dust. You feel your life force bleeding away.

"The Sun has set. You are ashes. What you were is no longer. Who you were is irrelevant. You are the corpse of Serapis mourned by Black Isis sailing towards the west, toward the setting Sun. "

The boat begins to move deep into the desert following Helios as he sets in the west. After a few moments, you see a range of hills as the boat floats towards it. In the centre of one of the hills is The Horn of the West. It is a colossal cave through which your boat sails.

Images of your life flash by you. You acknowledge them, but they are passed. There is a song as if the gods of this realm are singing your praises. For you are the dying Sun and you are still very much in charge.

You hear a voice of challenge.

"Where are you?"

You reply: "I am in the Waters of Helios and the first realm of the underworld. I am the dying Sun who seeks his awakening as Helios. I am the magician in search of the Higher Genius."

Before you emerges from the darkness and the waters, a vast armoured Gorgon, whose hair is all snakes.

"You cannot pass through the waters of the underworld unless you can tell me my name," she says.

You reply

"Smashing the foreheads of Helios' enemies" is your name. You are MENEBAIN the first goddess of the hour of the night. You are my defender and guide."

"Open your gates for me. Open wide your gateways for me.

Illuminate for me what I have made. I commended you to my corpse.

Guide me as I enter the underworld. For I am the creator lost in his creation.

I made a soul and set myself under the spinners of destiny.

I created you for my magic power.

I have come that I may greet myself with myself.

Let my limbs breathe when they rise.

I exterminate him who acts against it.

I am the foremost of the Westerners and cause my image to breathe."

You are aware that the boat is full of Baboons – Dæmons of Thoth-Hermes.

MENEBAIN tells you that these are the images by which you have lived your life so far. Each baboon is a word within your *Sphere of Sensation* which dictates your life. These need to be examined to see if they are relevant. For even at the earliest part of this quest, a new person is being formed.

Now it is time to pause and review each of these images with MENEBAIN's help.

(pause)

SECOND HOUR

The boat sails on. You hear a voice of challenge.
"Where are you?"

"I am in the Place of the Soul of the underworld and the second realm of the underworld. I am the dying Sun who seeks his awakening as Helios. I am the magician in search of the Higher Genius."

A vast armoured coiled snake emerges from the darkness and the water. Everything goes quiet.

"You cannot enter the Place of the Souls of the Underworld unless you can tell me my name," she says.

You reply:

"The wise who protects her master" is your name. You are NEBŪN (NEBOYN) the goddess of the second hour of the night, and you are a defender and guide to me.

Lining the river are the gods. They are here to see your fading light. Around you are the shells of the dead. They are the workers of Wernes and the souls of the underworld who are here to receive the food from your boat. You know their names for you have lived amongst them; shone down on them. You have awarded them fields in the afterlife. They sing to you:

"O appear, great soul. The underworld has received the flesh belonging to heaven. You are now living flesh and the Earth is protected for You. Come indeed, Helios, that You live in your name of "Living One." You traverse the fields, protector. You bind the serpent of Chaos (Χάος), and You strike "Horrible of Face". Joy and jubilation are in the Earth to (You) who reveals his corpse. Shine, great illuminator. Be radiant, uraeus-serpent on the head of Helios. Drive away the darkness in the hidden realm in your name "He who chases him away with the secret arm". Illuminate thick darkness, that the flesh may live and be renewed by it. "

The light around you glows brightly and casts light into the darkness of this place. It lights up the underworld with a warm fluorescence.

You feel at peace and calm. NEBŪN tells you that in this place, the dead are at peace. Here are shades of your ancestors and those in your life who have already died. There are some here who wish to talk to you to process those things which were not dealt with life that can be dealt with now. These dead are now bought before you so that you can talk.

THIRD HOUR

The boat sails on and you find yourself in a canal lined on both sides by beautiful temples to the various gods. You see shades of the dead moving within these temples. You can also make out that these temples have the divine presence within them. This part of the underworld is where those who were devout meet their gods. For many devout shades, this is heaven. The shades of the heroes who loved the gods and were loved by them.

You hear a voice of challenge.

"Where are you?"

"I am in the Place of the Water of the Unique Master, which brings forth offerings and in the third realm of the underworld. I am the dying Sun who seeks his awakening as Helios. I am the magician in search of the Higher Genius."

Before you, another armoured woman emerges from the darkness and the waters.

You cannot enter the Place of the Water of the Unique Master, which brings forth offerings unless you can tell me my name.

"She who cuts Souls" is your name. You are LĒMNEI (ΛHMNEI) the goddess of the third hour of the night, and you are a defender and guide to me.

The gods of the underworld surround your boat. They sing to you.

"Come to us, you whose flesh is being towed, and who is guided by his own body, interpreter of the underworld, Lord of Breath, whose body speaks, who supports his life.

Your soul appears, and your power flourishes.

The sky belongs to your soul, the Earth to your corpse. The unique one rises for You,

Alone at the two-ropes which the jackals moor.

The arms of the Westerners receive You in your protected form of 'Old Man'.

How beautiful is it, that the Westerners can see.

How satisfying it is, when those of the Underworld can hear Serapis, when he sets in the West, when his light is put into the region of dark images.

Come indeed to us, Helios of the horizon, gold beetle, seed of the gods. You sail by the banks of the underworld. You traverse your hidden fields, and you make transformations in Earth. "

You are aware that you are fragmented. Instead of one boat, you are shining weakly on four. You feel fragmented and out of focus. It is as if you want to fall asleep.

LĒMNEI (ΛΗΜΝΕΙ) (L'EM-NEE) speaks to you: "this place contains the images of what you offered others in your life. It is the place where you can see how much difference it made the universe. Here you meet your perception of God, however obscure it might be. Here is made an offering to you. Allow these images to come before you so that you might understand them."

FOURTH HOUR

The boat sails on. Now you are aware, through the fading in and out of your vision, that you are in a cavern and rooted in the world of dreams. Here you start to become aware of how close you are to the God Chaos and how difficult it is to hold together any sense of order. Chaos is not evil, but all you know depends on order. As the Sun gets weaker, Chaos is more likely to assert itself. The Egyptians considered the state of chaos the end of all things and equated it to the most terrible of gods, Apophis, and they feared that one day the serpent of chaos would swallow the Sun, and all would fall into chaos from which it sprang.

You hear a voice of challenge.

"Where are you?"

"I am in the cavern with living forms. I have passed through the Gate of That which Hides the Towing. I am in the fourth realm of the underworld. I am the dying Sun who seeks his awakening as Helios. I am the magician in search of the Higher Genius."

From the darkness and the waters emerges a huge armoured woman. She has in her hand a staff of dominion which has power over the creatures of the underworld. On her arm is a shield with a serpent shaped in the form of the North Node ☊∴. This shows the connection to Isis Renenutet, the great protector.

You cannot enter this cavern with living forms unless you can tell me my name.

MORMOTH (ΜΟΡΜΟΘ) "The Great One of Hades" is your name. You are "She who is mighty in her power." You are the goddess of the fourth hour of the night, and you are a defender and guide to me.

Lying back in your boat, you see that it is being towed through a vast dry cavern of sand. Your boat transforms into a huge snake which sails through the cavern. You can see the people on the boat move around you, and they appear to be caring for you. But you are invisible to them. They continue to care for you out of habit, knowing that one day you will be reborn.

You raise your hand weakly. In it, you are holding a serpent wand. Snakes rise and fall in the narrow water, and you are aware that the river has become dangerous.

MORMOTH says you: "These paths here are in confusion. Every one of them is opposed to one another. Those who know them who will find their paths. They are as high as the flint walls of Memphis, which are on water and land."

As you sail, you find huge knives block your way and chop the path into different ways. There is no right path, just your path, but it is possible for you to choose the wrong one. As each new path opens you say the following spell

"I open the path of the underworld that I may ease the suffering of Serapis."

MORMOTH says to you: "For the light of Serapis is hidden in darkness with fire about it. It fell from him was lost in the desert sand. And now it has been placed within the dark place."

The stress of all this has caused you to be awake. You realise that you have become black and without any solar power. You know that you are safe and protected by MORMOTH (MOPMOΘ). But you also know that you are close to the merging with chaos.

FIFTH HOUR

The boat sails on. In your weakness you are starting to feel an awareness of a dark but not unfriendly presence. You become aware of the various aspects of your life as a story made from threads of destiny that you decided at a point before you were born. You feel that cord in your left hand. This was your old story of everything that is passed up until this moment. The last six months are woven into the final stages of that rope and now instinctively you know it is time to let it go. Your story has carried you to this point, and now it is time for a new story. Sure, it will contain elements of the old one. But the central theme of your future life will not be represented by your back story. Think about the things that make you hold on to that thread. Are there people you think you will lose? Have you hung on to a career because you fear to rely on your skills? Are there people who are of no use to you who you hang onto out of fear of being alone? At this point, where order and chaos are balanced, it is time to let go of all the things you no longer need or want. When you are ready to let go of the rope in your left hand, you will then become aware of the rope in your right hand, which is slowly beginning to form. A new story free from the limits of your past.

You hear a voice of challenge.

"Where are you?"

"I am in the Cavern of the West. I have passed through the gate of the "station of the god"." I am in the fifth realm of the underworld. I am the dying Sun who seeks his awakening as Helios. I am the magician in search of the Higher Genius."

From the darkness emerges an armoured woman. She has three heads, and she holds the tools of a weaver.

You cannot enter Cavern of the West unless you can tell me my name.

"She who Guides in her Bark" is your name. You are NŪPHIĒR (NOYΦIHP) (NOO-FEE-'ER), and you are the goddess of the fifth hour of the night, and you are a defender and guide to me.

"In the greatest darkness of Chaos, fate and destiny are formed," NŪPHIĒR says: "The ancient Egyptians considered this place the temple of the invisible god Sokar. He was the god of death and oblivion. He was more ancient than Hades, and he sleeps within the heart of Serapis."

You are now travelling on the secret way, the way of destruction and Typhon. It is the darkest winter, the coldest death, before you notice that the cavern has taken on a reddish glow flickering darkly.

Before you, it opens out into a lake of fire. You can see burning in the flames millions of souls. This is the basis behind the Christian concept of hell.

NŪPHIĒR says: "the ancient Egyptians said the Lake of Fire was a fiery punishment for the damned but cryptically added that the blessed dead drink from it as if it were icy water. These fires are the alchemical fires of transformation and regeneration. You are about to regenerate entirely in the deepest layers of the underworld, in the thick darkness of the sinister land of Sokar so that you can awaken to a new destiny.

The flames engulf the boat, burning everything mortal, but since the boat and its passengers are gods the flames do no damage. The fire causes your sphere to tingle, but you are aware at a profound level something is burned away from you.

NŪPHIĒR says: "I am a Dæmon of the forces of fate. I grant you this vision of what you will become. "

You have the flash of an image of a golden child with the face of a lion.

The gods sing their magic.

"This image is like this in the thick darkness. The cavern belonging to Sokar is illuminated by the two eyes of the heads of the great god serpent. His two feet shine in the coils of the great God while he protects his image.

A noise is heard in this cave after this great God has passed by them, like the thundering ground of the sky in a storm."

You are aware that the bark is protected by the Uraeus snake, which guarantees the endurance of your rule. It rears up to strike with fire any of your enemies. This cobra-goddess was also called "Wadjet."

SIXTH HOUR

The boat sails on. You hear a voice of challenge.

"Where are you?"

"I am at the depths, in waterhole of the Underworld. The name of this Cavern is West. I have passed through the Gate of the "sharp knives"." I am in the Sixth realm of the Underworld. I am the dying Sun who seeks his awakening as Helios. I am the magician in search of the Higher Genius."

A huge armoured woman with the head of a crocodile appears from the darkness and the waters.

You cannot enter Cavern of West unless you can tell me my name.

"She who arrives "is your name. You are KHORBORBATH (ΧΟΡΒΟΡΒΑΘ) (CHOR-VOR-VATH) the "Arrival that shows the right way". You are the sixth hour of the night, and you are a defender and guide to me.

This cavern is dark. The dark in which the universe was born. All around you are the waters of Nun, the primordial ocean. It is the waters of potentiality which hold regenerative powers heated by the fires you lit in the earlier cavern.

You are now the corpse of Serapis, you are the dead heliotrope plant in the clay. Unable to move or feel.

The gods of this Cavern sing their spells

"This great God travels in this region on the water. He rows through this field to the place of the corpse of Serapis. This great God addresses the gods who are in the fields. He moors at these mysterious tombs which contain the image of Serapis. This God calls out above these mysterious tombs, and it is his voice which this God hears. Then he passes on after he has called out."

You are back in time to the beginning, before creation was formed. In the darkness, you see the god Thoth. He is forming a word. It is the word of creation, a world of destiny, and it is the word of your primal idea. It awakens within your corpse your True Soul, your fiery and solar self. The word is:

HELIOROS

As the name is vibrated, the infinite darkness creates the form of a new soul and a new life. It lightens the chamber. You see the form hovering above you. It is an image of a serpent eating his tail. The gods sing the spell.

"This is the body of Helios as his flesh. 'Many Faces' guards him. His tail is in his mouth; he is stretched out beneath this image of the body of Helios. All the gods of the Underworld come to him without him going to any other place in the Underworld and lend him their power. The voice of Helios is what comes to the image."

Within the serpent is formed a young man with the face of a golden lion. The eyes of the lion are like Suns, and his mane is of fire. He has in his right hand a whip which he uses to shape the universe, and in his left, he holds the globe of the world. He is the ruler and the shaper. He turns to lie on his back and sinks slowly into you.

You have within you an image of the universe, of the underworld and Re. You are reborn from the holy waters of Nun, from the first time, deep in the darkness of the underworld. You are the fiery "Atum-Kheperer" and Helioros.

SEVENTH HOUR

The boat moves on. You hear a voice of challenge.

"Where are you?"

"I am in the Mysterious Cavern. I have passed through the Gate of Serapis. I am in the seventh realm of the underworld. I am Helios awakening in the body of the magician. I am the magician in search of the Higher Genius."

From the darkness and the waters, a vast serpent emerges. She speaks with the voice of a woman.

You cannot enter Mysterious Cavern unless you can tell me my name.

"She who repels the gangs of Seth" is your name. You are ORBEËTH (OPBEHΘ) "She who repels the Evil One and slaughters 'Horrible of Face". You are the goddess of the seventh hour of the night, and you are a defender and guide to me.

ORBEĒTH coils around you and protects the boat.

The boat is in a sea of darkness. The only light comes from your glow. There are things in the darkness. You can hear something massive, moving, like a trillion scales rubbing on each other. The Wamemty-serpent spits a tongue of fire and then rearing before the boat is the colossal serpent of Chaos Apep.

His mouth opens and becomes a black hole, sucking in the river and drawing all matter into his jaws.

The gods spring to attention. Isis and Thoth are on the prow of the boat casting magic at Apep. The Wamemty-serpent spits fire at the snake. All this magic binds the snake, and it snaps its jaws shut. Typhon hurls his spear at it, and it falls back wounded.

You are transformed into a giant cat. You are the god Mau. Bigger than the serpent you stride towards it with a giant knife in your hands and slice it into many pieces. The pieces writhe and twist and then sink into the darkness of Nun.

You return to your bark and shapeshift into Helios. The light shines in the darkness because the darkness could not overcome it.

EIGHTH HOUR

The boat moves on. This symbolises that, with the defeat of Apophis in the previous hour, Chaos is left behind and the order of creation has been reinstated. You are starting to feel your powers return, and you can now stand. About you, you see gods moving and starting to use their powers to bring about a new creation or, more specifically in this instance, re-creation.

You hear a voice of challenge.

"Where are you?"

"I am at the "Sarcophagus of her gods". I have passed through the Gate of "Standing without getting tired". I am in the eighth realm of the underworld. I am Helios awakening in the body of the magician. I am the magician in search of the Higher Genius."

Before you, a huge armoured woman emerges from the darkness and the waters.

You cannot enter "Sarcophagus of her gods" unless you can tell me my name.

"She of the midnight" or "Mistress of the deep night" is your name. You are PANMŌTH (ΠΑΝΜΩΘ) (PAN-MAWTH) You are the goddess of the eighth hour of the night, and you are a defender and guide to me.

You see before you that the boat is being towed through the

night's sky. In front is the god Apis and behind him come the Fiery Serpents. On the ship are Typhon, Horus, Isis, Thoth and legions of the followers. There are righteous ancestors and souls and magicians. The universe is pulling you into manifestation and power. You raise your arms, and they are all transformed by your light. They have new clothes, and their powers are refreshed as yours have been. In this place, everything receives its power for the day from Helios.

NINETH HOUR

The boat moves on. You hear a voice of challenge.
"Where are you?"

"I am at the "Place where the Images Flow". I have passed through the Gate of "Guardian of the flood". I am in the ninth realm of the underworld. I am Helios awakening in the body of the magician. I am the magician in search of the Higher Genius."

Before you from the darkness and the waters appears a huge woman in armour made from seashells. She is dressed in gold and pale white light, and she has blue butterfly wings.

You cannot enter "Place where the Images Flow" unless you can tell me my name.

"Protector of her eye" is your name. You are THYMENPHRI (ΘYMENΦPI) (THY-MEN-FREE) "She who adores and protects her Lord". You are the goddess of the ninth hour of the night, and you are a defender and guide to me.

There is a new determination. You now have twelve oarsmen and a new power to journey through the underworld. You are lighting up the whole underworld now. The gods are distributing food to the dead, and you have the feeling of a seed which is burst into the Sunlight for the first time. You notice flying above the boat is a star. You ask THYMENPHRI who it is, and she says:

"All ideas are born at this hour. This is the idea of you being connected and working with your Higher Genius. It is the united spirit of what is to come, and your power to manifest magic in the realm of the living. Here it is an idea, becoming born deep inside your unconscious, but it is due to happen in another place and time, for it is an idea which may not dwell in the land of night."

Around you see Thoth's baboons once more, creating more images of what will become in the coming day.

TENTH HOUR

The boat moves on, and you are transformed into a hawk-headed snake. Above you is the scarab of regeneration.

You hear a voice of challenge.

"Where are you?"

"I am at the "With deep water and high banks". I have passed through the Gate of Great Manifestations, giving birth to forms". I am in the tenth realm of the underworld. I am Helios awakening in the body of the magician. I am the magician in search of the Higher Genius."

Before you from the darkness and the waters emerges a huge armoured woman. She has the face of a lioness.

You cannot enter "With deep water and high banks" unless you can tell me my name.

"She who rages" is your name. You are SARNOCKOIBAL (ΣΑΡΝΟΧΟΙΒΑΛ) (SAR-NO-CHEE-VAL) You are the goddess of the tenth hour of the night, and you are a defender and guide to me.

SARNOKHOIBAL stands before you, and she holds in her hand a caduceus. He places it on your left eye, and it is regenerated. This is symbolic of your magical power. She then touches your right eye so that it too is completely restored.

She says: "Your eyes are the givers of forms and you place them in the sky and the world of the living. You are the creator; you are the form maker."

You look up, and you see the star still following you. In its centre is a lion-headed god holding a whip and a globe. You realise that it is an embodiment of your power and that of something else.

The Gods sing to you:

"They are like this in the Underworld as forms and shapes of Khepri when he carries his oval to this place to go forth afterwards to the eastern horizon of the sky."

ELEVENTH HOUR

The boat moves on. You are feeling now fully restored and ready for your new life, but you lack focus. Images come and go; they have emerged from the chaotic sea but lack any central coordination. You realise that the act of creation is bringing about Order. Chaos is too abstract to be useful. It is helpful to know that these things are going on behind what we do even if we do not need to be entirely aware of it Chaos is not just the infinity of the universe; it is also beyond time and space. God before anything we can understand as God.

This cavern is where, ultimately, all human memories end up. Swimming in a sea of Chaos in God's unconscious. The divine part has returned to its awakened conscious. Swimming in this chaotic memory will be parts of the entire memory of nature, of every human, each atom which has ended its story – resting for eternity while the universe's true self understands others.

You hear a voice of challenge.

"Where are you?"

"I am at the "Mouth of the cavern which examines the corpses". I have passed through the Gate of "Resting place of those of the Underworld". I am in the eleventh realm of the underworld. I am Helios awakening in the body of the magician. I am the magician in search of the Higher Genius."

Before you from the darkness and the waters emerges a huge armoured woman.

You cannot enter "Mouth of the cavern which examines the corpses" unless you can tell me my name.

"The starry one" is your name. You are BATHIABĒL (ΒΑΘΙΑΒΗΛ) (VA-THEE-A-V'EL) You are the starry lady of the boat, who repels the enemy when he appears. You are the goddess of the eleventh hour of the night, and you are a defender and guide to me.

BATHIABĒL turns to you and gives you a crown and an ankh cross and says:

"I give you control over the Aion. You are the Lord of Time."

The gods sing the spell:

"Time swallows her images in front of the seer who is in this place. She gives them (back) afterwards for the birth of Khepri in the Earth.

"Time is she who takes away the hours She is upon 'He who takes away the hours'. What she has to do: To live through the voice of Re, day after day. She swallows her images at this place."

Thoth says: "At this place, the ideas for the new day take form and are placed into time. The Sun has nearly risen, and in the morning, those ideas will be born in time."

A colossal serpent "World-encircler" is carried in front of the Sun boat in anticipation of the final rejuvenation of Helios.

You notice that around you are countless burning bodies. BATHIABĒL tells you that these are the bodies of those ideas which do not survive the test of time. They are the followers of Typhon which are destroyed every night so that they do not impede the ascent of Helios.

The gods sing the spell that destroys them.

You look up and the star, which is the assistant, is still following the bark. It has survived the test of Time and will move on to manifestation.

TWELFTH HOUR

This is the last hour of your underworld journey, where Helios will emerge renewed and visible again to all. Around you, the colours of the dawn gather. They have become more fixed and stable. There is a feeling of anticipation.

The boat moves on. You hear a voice of challenge.

"Where are you?"

"I am at the "Place with emerging darkness and appearing births" in the Cavern of the End of thick darkness". I have passed through the gate of "That which raises the gods". I am in the twelfth realm of the underworld. I am Helios awakening in the body of the magician. I am the magician in search of the Higher Genius."

Before you, a huge armoured woman emerges from the darkness and the waters. You cannot enter "Place with emerging darkness and appearing births" in the Cavern of the End of thick darkness" unless you can tell me my name.

"She who beholds the perfection of her Lord" is your name. You are ABRATHIABRI (ΑΒΡΑΘΙΑΒΡΙ) (A-VRA-THEE-A-VREE)

You are the goddess of the twelfth hour of the night, and you are a defender and guide to me.

Although you have your powers, you must leave what you were in the underworld to be reborn. Part of you lies back on the bark and takes the form of the dead Serapis. You have freed yourself from it, and you look back at your body with detachment. This was the total of what you were before you began this journey, and now you feel you are something different. Thank the old self. It is battered and decayed by the events that shaped it, but it carried you to this point where your new self will arise. Your solar self is liberated from the past, and you see that the mighty world serpent has formed an ellipse above your head.

ABRATHIABRI takes you by the shoulders and lifts you through the serpent ellipse and into the sky. You hear the gods and goddesses sing their morning spells.

"We worship this great God at dawn when he rests in the eastern gateway of the sky. "Born is he, who is born, who has emerged, has emerged venerated of the Earth, soul of the Lord of Heaven. The sky belongs to your soul that it may rest in it. The Earth belongs to your corpse, Lord of Veneration. You have seized the horizon, that you may rest in your shrine, the two goddesses raise you with their bodies. Acclamation to you, the soul which is in heaven. The beginning is light, and the end is thick darkness. The star flies with you, through the ellipse and into this time and place."

Arise as your holy solar self to the dawn of a new day. Now you may meditate on your journey and allow yourself to sleep.

SATURDAY

MORNING

EKKLESIA OF THE ARCHANGELS

The Ekklesia was the assembly of a Greek city-state, and the function of this ritual is to create a similar a meeting of the seven Archangels in your *Sphere of Sensation*. This will help you ascend to your *Higher Genius*. You should make or copy the Ekkliesia seal. The Seal is a complex symbol which brings the forces we have been discussing into one place.

Carefully draw the seal (or simply photocopy it) and sign your name in the centre of the pentagram. If you want to be a real drama queen, you can sign your name in blood, but the result will be the same. You are identifying the seal with you and your *Sphere of Sensation*. The next stage is to ritually awaken it.

This ritual is performed in the morning of the second day of your retreat. After you have awoken and eaten something, perform your ritual ablutions and enter your sacred space. Place the signed seal on the altar and the three-day *Higher Genius* candle on it.

Take a red, black, yellow and blue candle. Write the names of the four holy creature on the appropriate candle, and your name and place them in their correct positions.

Paramara (earth) (Ραράμάρά), (North), Zorothion (fire) (Zuruwyun), (South), Periton (water) (Perytun) (West)and Akramata (air) ('Akramata), (East).

Take seven white candles and write the name of each Archangel in Greek, along with the divine name and the Barbaric name of power. So for Michael, you would write Μιχαήλ, ΑΕΗΙΟΥΩ, Νυσευ and Χυχ. Place each candle on the boundaries of your circle so that they match the position of the seal.

1. Perform the lesser invoking ritual of the pentagram and the *Lesser Banishing Ritual of the Hexagram* (with the IAO formula).
2. Perform the *Prima Material* exercise, the solar breath extension and then the Genius Abiding exercise.
3. Purify and consecrate the space.
4. Do your ritual to the Sun rising.
5. Invoke Abrasax*

ARNEBOUAT, BOLLOCH, BARBARICH, B, BAALSAMEN, PTIDAIOY, AR-NEBOUAT

(ΑΡΝΕΒΟΥΑΤ ΒΟΛΛΟΧ ΒΑΡΒΑΡΙΧ Β ΒΑΑΛΣΑΜΗΝ ΠΤΙΔΑΙΟΥ ΑΡΝΕΒΟΥΑΤ)

(AR-NE-VOO-AT VOL-LOCH VAR-VAR-REECH V VA-AL-SA-M'EN PTEE-DE-OO AR-NE-VOO-AT

Come to me, you from the four winds, ruler of all, who breathed spirit into men for life, whose is the hidden and unspeakable name, unutterable by human mouth, at whose name even the *dæmons* are terrified when they hear it! You whose right eye is the Sun,

---

* This is taken from PGM 13 760-790

ARNEBOUAT, BOLLOCH, BARBARICH, B, BAALSAMEN, PTIDAIOY, AR-NEBOUT

and left eye is the Moon

ARSENPENPROOUTH BARBARAIONE OSRAR MEMPSECHEI

(ΑΡΣΕΝΠΕΝΠΡΩΟΥΘ ΒΑΡΒΑΡΑΙΩΝΗ ΟΣΡΑΡ ΜΕΜΨΕΧΕΙ)
(AR-SEN-PEN-PRAW-OOTH　VAR-VA-RE-AW-N'E　OS-RAR MEM-PSE-CHEE)

They are ever watching eyes shining in the pupils of humanity. Heaven is your head, aether the body, Earth the feet, and environment the water, for you are all things Agathos Daemon.
You are the ocean, begetter of good things and feeder of the civilized world. Yours is the eternal processional way in which your seven-lettered name is established for the harmony of the seven sounds of the planets which utter their voices according to the 28 forms of the Moon,

SAR APHARA ARAPH A I ABRAARM ARAPHA ABRAACH PERTAOMECH AKMECH

IAO　OYEH　IAO　OYE　EIOY　AHO　EHOY　IAO

(ΣΑΡ ΑΦΑΡΑ ΑΡΑΦ Α Ι ΑΒΡΑΑΡΜ ΑΡΑΦΑ ΑΒΡΑΑΧ ΠΕΡΤΑΩΜΗΧ ΑΚΜΗΧ ΙΑΩ ΟΥΕΗ ΙΑΩ ΟΥΕ ΕΙΟΥ ΑΗΩ ΕΗΟΥ ΙΑΩ)

SAR A-FA-RA A-RAF A EE AV-RA-ARM A-RA-FA A-VRA-ACH PER-TA-AW-M'ECH　AK-M'ECH I-A-AW OO-E-'H EE-A-AW OO-E E-EE-OO A-'H-AW E-'H-OO EE-A-AW

Yours are the beneficent coming forth of the stars, *Dæmons*, and Fortune and Fates, by whom is given wealth, right old age, good children, good luck, a proper burial.

Lord of Life, king of the heavens and the Earth and all living things in them, you whose justice is not turned aside, you whose glorious name the Muses sing, you whom the eight guards attend who are

E AW CHO CHOUCH NOUN NAUNI AMOUN AMAUNI
Η Ω ΧΩ ΧΟΥΧ ΝΟΥΝ ΝΑΥΝΙ ΑΜΟΥΝ ΑΜΑΥΝΙ)
'Η AW CHAW CHOOCH NOON NAV-NEE A-MOON A-MAV-NEE

You who have a truth that never lies. You who are the seven made as one. I ask that you reveal to me* your four incorporeal creatures, with four faces and six wings.

Alpha, Leon, Phone, Aner,

Paramara Zorothion Periton Akramata,

So that they may stretch out their four spiritual fingers and awaken their presence in my seal and the *Sphere of Sensation* so that I might be uplifted to my Higher Genius.

Go to the East and light the yellow candle saying ALPHA. *When it is lit, vibrate* AKRAMATA *eight times while visualising an octahedron† made from bright yellow light.*

Go to the South and light the red candle saying LEON. *When it is lit, vibrate* ZOROTHION *eight times while visualising a tetrahedron pyramid made from bright red flame.*

Go to the West and light the blue candle while saying PHONE. *When it is lit vibrate* PERITON *eight times while visualising a hexagon in blue light.*

Go to the North and light the black candle while saying ANER. *When it is lit vibrate* PARAMARA *eight times while visualising a black cube.*

Go to the centre and see the energy form at the four quarters and draw an opening sign over the seal (like drawing back curtains). Allow yourself to feel the energy created by the four holy creatures.

You who have a truth that never lies. You who are the seven made as one. I ask that you reveal to me your seven Archangels Michael, Raphael, Gabriel, Souriel (Uriel), Zaziel, Badakiel, and Syliel. So that they may stretch out their four spiritual fingers and awaken their presence in my seal and the *Sphere of Sensation* so that I might be uplifted to my Higher Genius.

Light the Michael candle and say,

In the name of NYSEU (Ny-Sef), I invoke the Archangel MICHAEL (Mee-cha-'el), who is the guardian between the world and the celestial world. Come forth, mighty Michael, for I know your secret barbaric name of power which you rejoice to hear.

Vibrate the name CHYCH (chych) for five minutes.

---

* The invocation fo the four holy creatures is taken from Berlin 11347

† The use of platonic solids for the four holy creatures is taken from the practical work of adept Jane Gibson

I invoke you by the arrangement of the sacred word which was spoken by Thoth to create you and the celestial realm. Awaken to me Michael in a manner I can comprehend.

Slowly vibrate **AEHIOYΩ** for five minutes. When you have finished, allow yourself to be more sensitive to the Michael force. Light the Raphael candle and say,

In the name of NYCHIEU (Ny-chee-ef), I invoke the Archangel RAPHAEL (Ra-fa-'el), who is the communicator of the divine word. Come forth, mighty Raphael, for I know your secret barbaric name of power which you rejoice to hear.

Vibrate the name **CHYBACHYCH** (Chy-va-chych) for five minutes.

I invoke you by the arrangement of the sacred word which was spoken by Thoth to create you and the celestial realm. Awaken to me Raphael in a manner I can comprehend.

Slowly vibrate **EHIOYΩA** for five minutes. When you have finished, allow yourself to be more sensitive to the Raphael force.

Light the Gabriel candle and say,

In the name of AŌCHE (A-o-hi), I invoke the Archangel GABRIEL (Wa-vree-'el), who is the embodiment of the love which unites all things. Come forth, mighty Gabriel, for I know your secret barbaric name of power which you rejoice to hear.

Vibrate the name *BACHACHYCH* (Va-Cha-chych) for five minutes.

I invoke you by the arrangement of the sacred word which was spoken by Thoth to create you and the celestial realm. Awaken to me Gabriel in a manner I can comprehend.

Slowly vibrate **HIOYΩAE** for five minutes. When you have finished, allow yourself to be more sensitive to the Gabriel force. Light the Souriel candle and say,

In the name of MECHEU (M'e-chef), I invoke the Archangel SOURIEL (Soo-ree-'el), who is the divine energy linking the universe. Come forth, mighty Souriel, for I know your secret barbaric name of power which you rejoice to hear.

Vibrate the name **BAKAXICHYCH** (Va-kazi-hih) for five minutes.

I invoke you by the arrangement of the sacred word which was spoken by Thoth to create you and the celestial realm. Awaken to me Souriel in a manner I can comprehend.

Slowly vibrate **IOYΩAEH** for five minutes. When you have finished, allow yourself to be more sensitive to the Souriel force.

Light the Zaziel candle and say,

In the name of IAO, I invoke the Archangel ZAZIEL (Za-zee-'el), who the brilliant light of the holiest. Come forth, mighty Zaziel, for I know your secret barbaric name of power which you rejoice to hear.

Vibrate the name BAZABACHYCH (Va-za-va-chych)for five minutes.

I invoke you by the arrangement of the sacred word which was spoken by Thoth to create you and the celestial realm. Awaken to me Zaziel in a manner I can comprehend.

Slowly vibrate OYΩAEHI for five minutes. When you have finished, allow yourself to be more sensitive to the Zaziel force.
Light the Badakiel candle and say,

In the name of SABVAŌTH (Sa-va-awth), I invoke the Archangel BADAKIEL (Va-da-kee-'el), who the brilliant light of the holiest. Come forth, mighty Badakiel, for I know your secret barbaric name of power which you rejoice to hear.

Vibrate the name BADETOPTHŌTH (Va-d'e-to-fawth)for five minutes.

I invoke you by the arrangement of the sacred word which was spoken by Thoth to create you and the celestial realm. Awaken to me Badakiel in a manner I can comprehend.

Slowly vibrate YΩAEHIO for five minutes. When you have finished, allow yourself to be more sensitive to the Badakiel force.
Light the Syliel candle and say,

In the name of SABVAŌTH (Sa-va-awth), I invoke the Archangel SYLIEL (Sy-lee-'el), who the mystery of the limits. Come forth, mighty Syliel, for I know your secret barbaric name of power which you rejoice to hear.

Vibrate the name BAINCHŌŌŌCH (Va-een-chaw-aw-awch) for five minutes.

I invoke you by the arrangement of the sacred word which was spoken by Thoth to create you and the celestial realm. Awaken to

me Syliel in a manner I can comprehend.

Slowly vibrate ΩAEHIOY (AW-A-E-'E-EE-OO) for five minutes. When you have finished, allow yourself to be more sensitive to the Syliel force. Return to the centre relax and see the archangelic forces around you.

In the name of Abrasax, I allow the seven holy archangels and the four sacred creatures of the word, to enter my *Sphere of Sensation* **and transform me so that I might ascend to my Higher Self.**

Sit and wait and open yourself to the invoked energies. Whatever happens, will be unique to you and mystical.

SATURDAY AFTERNOON

THE SEVEN RAYS

After working with the seven archangels, it is time to rise still further to the more abstract level of the seven rays and the vowels. It is important to remember that these seven rays are not the same 19th-century theosophical concept as espoused by Helena Petrovna Blavatsky and Alice A. Bailey, although they could be a development of the ancient ideas. Nor should the fact that there are seven rays being looked at, that their powers are planetary or that because they are represented by a colour, they are the literal power of that colour Those forces are simply expressions of those rays (in fact in ancient gem talismans and art they are not given any colours). The *Chaldean Oracles* of the 2nd century CE feature the seven rays as purifying agents of Helios and they do have that function, but not just that. They are the primal divine energy which is behind the universe and are united by the One Thing. They are closer to the concept of the vowels. Vowels give "life" to a word and enable it to be pronounced. Until a vowel is added a word is dead clay.

They appear as we get close to an understanding of our *Higher Genius.* They give us the final purification before the vision of the *Higher Genius* and the discovery of our divine self.

What this exercise does is open your *Sphere of Sensation* to those powers of life. When they are correctly approached, they will resonate with the corresponding parts of your *Sphere of Sensation* and transform them.

You might see forms while doing this exercise, but you should try and push past them as they are not really the ray. You might have feelings about each colour, but you should try to push past these too. You will know when you have reached the power of the ray when you become it, and it is hard to explain unless you have experienced it. It is worth pointing out that each of these rays was said to represent a "heaven", which can be seen to mean the progressively rarefied states of holiness.

This level of consciousness is not easily obtained, and for the purposes of this experience, you do not have to – you just must do the process and achieve to your highest level you can. The work of the last six months has been to build your ladder upwards, continually refining your *Sphere of Sensation* and giving your *Higher Genius* a stronger foothold in your awareness.

THE EXERCISE

1. Perform the lesser invoking ritual of the pentagram and the *Lesser Banishing Ritual of the Hexagram* (with the IAO formula).
2. Perform the *Prima Materia* exercise, the solar breath extension and then the **Genius Abiding** exercise.
3. Purify and consecrate the space.
4. Do your ritual to the Sun at noon.
5. You could prepare seven coloured cards to help you visualise. They should be marked with the following vowels

Violet	∀
Indigo	Ω
Blue	﬩
Green	H
Yellow	⅃
Orange	Ǝ
Red	O

4. Set your timer for half an hour.
5. Light a single white candle marked with the name Abrasax and say the following invocation.

I invoke you Abrasax who unites the seven by the powers of your name. I conjure thee by the name IΩXYX (E-Aw-hih) so that you will awaken to me the mighty the powers of the seven rays

which emerge from your head. So that I will experience the seven heavens behind all things.

Look at each card or just shut your eyes and visualise yourself swimming in a sea of that colour. Vibrate the vowel for half an hour as a mantra. As you do, you allow yourself to become lighter, so you appear to be floating upward. Feel yourself dissolving into the colour. Take your time, but you should start to feel infinite and sensitive. Then other forces and ideas will arrive; note these but remain passive. This mission is not to gather intellectual information but tune yourself to the ray. Once your timer has bleeped move on to the next ray in sequence. Each one will get harder, but the more you leave behind in terms of thinking and feeling, the easier it will become. The order of the rays is Violet, Orange, Emerald, Yellow, Red, Blue, and lastly Indigo. You can stop chanting when you have reached a deep enough state, but if you lose focus, you should return to the chant.

SATURDAY NIGHT IMMORTALISATION

This ritual uses the *Mithras Liturgy* from the *Great Magical Papyri of Paris*. To fit this book's magical goals, I changed some aspects and expanded some of the prayers to make the symbols more more obvious to modern magicians. In this, I was aided by Hans Deiter Betz's book* which is an extensive academic study on the ritual.

The ritual immortalises or deifies the magician by showing them a vision of their relationship with the Sun. It mixes many different ideas, including Platonism, Stoicism, and the mystery cults. The Roman Philosopher Emperor Julian, who was an initiate of Mithras, wrote of a similar structure in his *Hymn to King Helios*. Julian mentioned three levels of creation – the physical, which is ruled by the visible Sun, a middle world, governed by the spiritual Sun Mithras, and the intelligible world of perfection, ruled by the supreme Helios. Mithras acts as a mediator between this remote divine world and the physical. *The Great Magical Papyri of Paris* ritual was not as concise as Julian's and was based on an earlier, less elegant idea involving a hybrid god Helios-Mithras. Since it makes

---

* Betz, H. D., 2003. *The Mithras Liturgy*. Tubingen: Mohr Seibeck.

no odds magically, I have opted for Julian's system.

The original ritual was built around a formula from another mystery religion or cult and had enough similarities to suggest it originates from parts of a Roman Mithras ritual. It is like the Golden Dawn's Z *documents* which use the formula of the 0=0 initiation to perform other magical rituals. In the *Great Magical Papyri of Paris*, the ritual immortalises the person so they can receive an oracle from the Sun (gods are more likely to talk to immortals rather than humans). However, it can be used to immortalise the magician to build and strengthen the links to their *Higher Genius* in its solar form.

The rite is a mixture of ritual and pathworking and alternating between the two techniques. This will take time but be aware there is no hurry.

THE RITE

Inscribe a white candle with your name and ΑΠΑΘΑΝΑΤΙΣΜΟΣ (Apathanatismos) (which means immortalisation). Place this on your altar and place a chair before it. Evenly space seven tealights in a line behind and another in front of your ritual space. These should be arranged, so you have a capital letter H (lying on its side) of candles. Take your lit Higher Genius candle and carefully place it east of the altar. You should be holding your astrological chart*.

1. Perform the lesser invoking pentagram.
2. Perform your prayer to the Sun at his setting.
3. Perform the third Sun breath process.
4. Open the quarters and purify and consecrate the space.

Facing east say,

Be gracious to me, Oh Providentia† and Psyche for as a child of the mysteries I request immortality which is granted to initiates

---

* In the original ritual, this chart was for the date and time of the ritual. In this case it is the date and time of birth of the person conducting the ritual.

† The original invocation addressed Providentia and Psyche to ask them to overlook the fact that he has written down the mysteries (something which was forbidden). Providentia was the embodiment of foresight. This might because the ritual had been tuned to obtain an oracle and if he misused the mysteries by writing them down, she would not only stop the rite working, but punish him. Psyche was a goddess who represented life and the Soul who might have featured in his initiation. Although it was not part of the actual ritual, the call to Providentia and Psyche as the goddesses of vision and the soul provides an opportunity to state the ritual's intention.

so that they may ascend into heaven as an inquirer, behold the universe and see the Sun behind the Sun – my Divine Genius and thus, better fulfil my destiny.

Look up:
I invoke that which was the origin of my origin, ΑΕΗΙΟΥΩ
I invoke that which was the beginning of my beginning,

(Make a popping sound by smacking your lips three times, hiss three times, and spit out the sound fuh.)
Go to the east and draw an invoking active spirit pentagram Ý vibrating the name Zeus. Then draw an invoking Air pentagram ☆ Vibrate (MMM) for a full breath. Visualise divine air pouring from the pentagram and flooding your Sphere of Sensation. Then say,

Air given to me by Zeus, which mixed within me. You are the supreme breath within me.

Go to the south and face south. Draw an invoking active spirit pentagram ☆ vibrating the name **Hades***. Draw an invoking fire pentagram ☆ and vibrate* **HY HIA EH***. Visualise divine fire pouring from the pentagram and flooding your Sphere of Sensation. Then say,*

Fire given to me by Hades, which mixed within me. You are the supreme fire within me.

Go to the west and face west. Draw an invoking active spirit pentagram ☆ vibrating the name Persephone ☆. Draw an invoking water pentagram. Vibrate ΩΩΩ AAA EEE and visualise divine water pouring from the pentagram and flooding your Sphere of Sensation. Then say

Water is given to me by Persephone, which mixed within me. You are the supreme water within me.

Go to the north and face north. Draw an invoking active spirit pentagram ☆ vibrating the name Hera. Draw an invoking Earth pentagram ☆ Vibrate YH YΩH and visualise the Earth element pouring from the pentagram and connecting your Sphere of Sensation. Then say

Earthy substance, given to me by Hera. You are the supreme earthy substance in me.

Return to the altar and face east.

Oh you divine gods of the elements make a perfect body for me (your name) whose mother is (your mother's name), transform me by a divine arm and an eternal right hand as you did at my birth to exist in a world without light and yet radiant a world which

appears soulless and however is alive and divine. For the world is comprised of the soulless and ensouled and I unify opposites.

Be aware of your body and carry out the first exercise of divine awareness.

Balance the elements within you and feel the light start to glow within your body while chanting YHI AYI EYΩIE seven times: *(pause, then look to the East and say,)*
METERTA PHOTH* (ΜΕΤΕΡΤΑ ΦΩΘ) (ME-TER-TA FAWTH) if it is your will, Give me an immortal rebirth which transforms my underlying nature so that I can unite with my Higher Genius IEREZATH (ΙΕΡΕΖΑΘ) (EE-E-RE-ZATH).

Enable me to gaze upon the immortal beginning with an immortal spirit, ANCHREPHRENESOYPHIRIGCH (ΑΝΧΡΕΦΡΕΝΕΣΟΥΦΙΡΙΓΧ) (AN-CHRE-FRE-NE-SOO-FEE-REEGCH),

With the immortal water, ERONOYI PARAKOYNETH (ΕΡΟΝΟΥΪ ΠΑΡΑΚΟΥΝΗΘ) (E-RO-NOO-EE PA-RA-KOO-N'ETH),

With the most steadfast air, EIOAE PSENABOTH (ΕΪΟΑΗ ΨΕΝΑΒΩΘ) (E-EE-O-A-'E PSE-NA-VAWTH);
that I may be born again in thought, KRAOCHRAX R OIM ENARCHOMAI (ΚΡΑΟΧΡΑΞ Ρ ΟΙΜ ΕΝΑΡΧΟΜΑΙ) (KRA-O-CHRAKS R O-EEM E-NAR-CHO-ME), and the sacred spirit may breathe in me,

NECHTHEN APOTOY NECHTHIN ARPI ETH (ΝΕΧΘΕΝ ΑΠΟΤΟΥ ΝΕΧΘΙΝ ΑΡΠΙ ΗΘ)

NECH-THEN A-PO-TOO NECH-THEEN AR-PEE 'ETH)

Let me wonder at the sacred fire, KYPHE (ΚΥΦΕ);

Gaze upon the unfathomable, terrifying waters at the dawn of time,

NYAW THESAW ECHAW OOCHEEECHAWA (ΝΥΩ ΘΕΣΩ ΕΧΩ ΟΥΧΙΕΧΩΑ)

And the life-giving, and encircling Aether may hear me, ARNOM'ETHF (ΑΡΝΟΜΗΘΦ);

---

* The original manuscript uses Meterta Photh (Μετερτα Φωϑ) and gives alternative spelling Methartha Pherie (Μεθαρθα Φεριε) intead of Φηρıη. The second version of the words are similar and might be an attempt to provide a clearer pronunciation. In context Meterta Photh is likely to be a magical name connected to Mithras-Helios.

For today I am about to see with immortal inner vision.

I was born mortal from a mortal womb but improved by an exceedingly powerful and an eternal right hand and by the immortal spirit of the immortal Aion and Master of the fiery diadems.

I, (your name) whose mother is (your mother's name) have been sanctified through holy consecrations through rituals and initiations and for a short time a holy power supports my psyche* after Ananke, the bitter and relentless *Dæmon* of material life, has pressed down upon me.

According to the immutable decree of God, EYE YIA EEI AO EIAY IYA IEO it is out of the reach of a mortal, to ascend with the golden radiance of immortal brilliance. We are too weak to open our mind's eyes and look on that incorruptible beauty. OEY AEO EYA EOE YAE SIAE illuminates all my mind, kindles my whole soul and draws it upward, and this beauty transforms me into an essence†.

For I am Mithras'son (or daughter).‡
I am [insert the name you are known in magic]

(Sit in the chair with your astrological chart on your lap and carry out the stage three version of the solar breath. Then relax and play the following pathworking on your recorder.)

THE PATHWORKING

Perform the Sun breath for ten minutes, or until you feel light and imagine yourself rising into the clouds on the dust of gold.

You rise into the darkness of space. You see before you the Sun

---

* This statement about magic is important and often overlooked. All this work you have done will allow you to connect to your Higher Genius which will support you but after a while it will fade as life real life gets in the way. Connecting to your Higher Genius requires a continual recharge which is provided by a new consecration.

† This clarifies a passage in the original and is taken from Hermetica 31, translation by Copenhaver.

‡ I have provided a missing mystery name which has been left off the manuscript. It would be the magician's own divine parent which would be the god that they have the greatest connection. This ritual worked fine for those who did not have that sort of connection by using Mithras-Helios. Betz said the magical words here are most likely to be a code for the original magician's secret name. It would be better if you used your magical name or Motto.

glowing bright and orange and the planets in their dance through the vacuum of space at this moment.

Then before your eyes, the physical melts away, and you see the divine forms of the planets. Below you is Hera, the Earth goddess. Nearest to you is Hekate-Selene. In the distance, you see Aphrodite and Aries. In the far distance, you see Zeus with his father Kronos far into the icy void. Close to the Sun is Mercury and before him is the vast and radiant disk of the Sun being pulled through space by four horses.

Below the Sun you will see a vortex of power which radiates a divine power, just as the Sun disk shines with light. The ancients called this vortex a pipe and believed it influenced the winds. However, it is the way that the Sun controls life in the whole solar system.

Suddenly you feel like you are being watched. All the gods are staring at you. It is not right that a mortal should seek to be in the same spheres as the gods — Bellerophon who was the greatest hero before Hercules was struck down for trying to fly to Mount Olympus. The gods hate the noise of humanity. They start to turn towards you.

Put your right finger on your mouth* and say, "**Harpokrates bring forth silence, Symbol of the living, imperishable god! Guard me in Silence Harpokrates.**

NECHTHEIR THANMELOY
(ΝΕΧΘΕΙΡ ΘΑΝΜΕΛΟΥ)
(NECH-THEER THAN-ME-LOO)!"

Then make a long hissing sound, next make a popping sound.

The say, **PROPROPHEGGE MORIOS PROPHYR PROPHEGGE NEMETHIRE ARPSENTEN PITETMI MEOY ENARTH PHYRKECHO PSYRIDARIO TYRE PHILBA."**

(ΠΡΟΠΡΟΦΕΓΓΗ ΜΟΡΙΟΣ ΠΡΟΦΕΓΓΗ ΝΕΜΕΘΙΡΕ ΑΡΨΕΝΤΕΝ ΠΙΤΗΤΜΙ ΜΕΩΥ ΕΝΑΡΘ ΦΥΡΚΕΧΩ ΨΥΡΙΔΑΡΙΩ ΤΥΡΗ ΦΙΛΒΑ)

(PROPROFEGG'E MOREEOS PROSFEGG'E NEMETHEERE ARPSENTEN PEET'ETMEE MEAWOO ENARTH FYRKECHAW PSYREEDAREEAW TYR'E FEELVA)

---

* This is the sign of the Egyptian God of Science Harpokrates. Harpokrates was also a protective god. The sign is used by the Golden Dawn and its descendants. The original ritual did not name the god, but instead gave his titles.

With those words you sense yourself covered in a shroud of darkness and silence. The godform of Harpokrates settles around you and the gods no longer see you, but instead the god of silence.

After a while, you see that the world above is transparent and circling and that none of the gods or angels is threatening you.

You hear a great crash of thunder. It is as if nature is trying to shock you back into your body. However, you resist and say,

As the God form of Harpokrates, you say, "Silence! Silence! I am a star, wandering about the heavens with the gods, and shining forth out of the deep, OXY O XERTHEYTH (ΟΞΥ Ο ΞΕΡΘΕΥΘ) (OKSY O KSERTHEFTH)

You look at the Sun and notice it has become more significant. Pentagrams stream forth from the brightness. It is as if the universe is full of them.

You make a hissing sound twice and a popping sound twice. Then say again: "Silence! Silence!"

In the Sun's centre, you see a darker place, and you head towards it. Closer and closer to the Sun you go. Fortunately, you have not got a psychical body because the heat would have turned you dust ages ago.

In the centre of the Sun, the darker place is two fiery doors shut tight. Recite the following prayer.

I invoke thee, mighty Aion

"Hear me I(your name) 1 whose mother is (your mother's name), Oh Lord, you who have bound together the fiery bars of the four roots of the elements which lock the doors of the Sun,

O Firewalker, PENTITEROYNI (ΠΕΝΤΙΤΕΡΟΥΝΙ) (PE-NTEE-TE-ROO-NEE),

Light-Maker and Light Encloser, SEMESILAM (ΣΕΜΕΣΙΛΑΜ) (SE-ME-SEE-LAM),

Fire-Breather, PSYRINPHEY (ΨΥΡΙΝΦΕΥ) (PSY-REEN-FEF)

Fire-Spirited, IAO (ΙΑΩ) (EE-A-AW),

Shining Spirit, OAI (ΩΑΪ) (AW-A-EE)

Rejoicing in fire, ELOYRE (ΕΛΟΥΡΕ) (E-LOO-RE),

Beautiful Light, AZAI (ΑΖΑΪ) (A-ZA-EE),

Aion, ACHBA (ΑΧΒΑ)* (ACH-VA),
Ruler of Light, PEPPER PREPEMPIPI (ΠΕΠΠΕΡ ΠΡΕΠΕΜΠΙΠΙ) (PEP-PER PRE-PE-MPEE-PEE),

Fire-Bodied, PHNOYENIOCH (ΦΝΟΥΗΝΙΟΧ) (FNOO-'E-NEE-OCH),

Light-Giver, Fire-Sower, AREI EIKITA (ΑΡΕΙ ΕΪΚΙΤΑ) (A-REE E-EE-KEE-TA),

Fire-gatherer, GALLABALBA (ΓΑΛΛΑΒΑΛΒΑ) (GAL-LA-VAL-VA),

Powerful Light, AIO (ΑΙΩ) (A-EE-AW)

Fire-Whirler, PYRICHIBOOSEIA (ΠΥΡΙΧΙΒΟΟΣΗΙΑ) (PY-REE-CHEE-VO-O-S'E-EE-A),

Light-Mover, SANCHEROB (ΣΑΝΧΕΡΩΒ) (SAN-CHE-RAWV)

Lightning-Shaker, IE OE IOEIO (ΙΗ ΩΗ ΙΩΗΙΩ) (EE-E O-E EE-O-E-EE-O),

Life creator, BEEGENETE (ΒΕΕΓΕΝΗΤΕ) (VE-E-GE-N'E-TE),

Light-Increaser, SOYSINEPHIEN (ΣΟΥΣΙΝΕΦΙΕΝ) (SOO-SEE-NE-FEE-EN)

Fire-Light-Maintainer, SOYSINEPHI ARENBARAZEI MARMARENTEY (ΣΟΥΣΙΝΕΦΙ ΑΡΕΝΒΑΡΑΖΕΙ ΜΑΡΜΑΡΕΝΤΕΥ) (SOO-SEE-NE-FEE A-REN-VA-RA-ZEE MAR-MA-RE-NTEF),
Subduer of the stars, open for me,

PROPROPHEGGE EMETHEIRE ORIOMOTYREPHILBA, (ΠΡΟΠΡΟΦΕΓΓΗ ΕΜΕΘΕΙΡΕ ΜΟΡΙΟΜΟΤΥΡΗΦΙΛΒΑ)

(PRO-PRO-FE-GG'E E-ME-THEE-RE MO-REE-O-MO-TY-R'E-FEEL-VA)

Open for me the closed doors of the Sun because of the pressing and bitter and inexorable necessity I face. I wish to reflect my spiritual self, my holy guardian genius so that I can fulfil my life's purpose.

I invoke the seven immortal names, of the seven gods living and honoured, which never pass into mortal nature and cannot be

---

* The great PGM translator Karl Preisendanz reads this as AH-BA instead of ACHBA believing it to be a combination of the Egyptian Ah (shining)-Ba(soul)

named in the human tongue or mortal speech or mortal sound, but only through sacred vowels. Draw nigh, O Lord!

Open your eyes and carefully and slowly read out the following vowel strings severn times, one for each of the seven immortal gods of the world.

ΗΕΩ ΟΗΗΩ ΙΩΩ ΟΗ ΗΕΩ ΗΕΩ ΟΗ ΗΩ ΙΩΩ ΟΗΗΕ ΩΗΕ
ΗΕΩ ΟΗΗΩ ΙΩΩ
ΟΗ ΗΕΩ ΗΕΩ **ΟΗ ΕΩ ΙΩΩ ΟΗΗΕ ΩΗΕ** ·

ΩΟΗ ΙΗ ΗΩ ΟΩ ΟΗ ΙΕΩ ΟΗ ΩΟΗ ΙΕΩ ΟΗ ·ΙΕΕΩ
ΕΗ ΙΩ ΟΗ ΙΟΗ ΩΗΩ ΕΟΗ ΟΕΩ ΩΙΗ ΩΙΗ ΕΩ
ΟΗ ΙΙΙ ΗΟΗ ΩΥΗ ΗΩΟΗΕ ΕΩΗΙΑ ΑΗΑΕΗΑ
ΗΕΕΗ ΕΕΗ ΕΕΗ ΙΕΩ ΗΕΩ ΟΗΕΕΟΗ ΗΕΩ
ΕΥΩ ΟΗ ΕΙΩ ΗΩ ΩΗ ΩΗ ΩΗ ΕΕ ΟΟΟ ΥΙΩΗ

Shut your eyes and return to the place you were before the Sun's gates.

Open your mind's eye, and you will hear thundering and shaking in the surrounding realm, and you will likewise feel yourself being shaken. This is the last test before entering the heavens. You must let go all of your thoughts and feelings and allow your personality-free "I" to go forward. Take some time at this; cast everything off slowly. You will feel calm even if you see the storm clouds of this test buffet you. When you are in the correct state, as the god form of Harpokrates you say, "Silence! Silence! I am a star, wandering about the heavens with the Gods, and shining forth out of the deep,

OXY O XERTHEYTH (ΟΞΥ Ο ΞΕΡΘΕΥΘ) **(O-KSY O KSER-THEFTH)."**

The doors of the Sun open, and this reveals the world of the gods. There is a feeling of pleasure and joy of the sight. You step in and enter the spiritual world.

Draw breath from the spiritual world into yourself several times. You will feel refreshed and restored. Inside this Sun is another Sun. This Sun is Helios-Mithras.

Look towards it and say, **"Come, Lord, ARCHANDARA PHOTAZA PYRIPHOTA ZABYTHIX ETIMENMERO PHORATHEN ERIE PROTHRI PHORATHI."**
(ΑΡΧΑΝΔΑΡΑ ΦΩΤΑΖΑ ΠΥΡΙΦΩΤΑ ΖΑΒΥΘΙΞ ΕΤΙΜΕΝΜΕΡΟ ΦΟΡΑΘΗΝ ΕΡΙΗ ΠΡΟ ΘΡΙ ΦΟΡΑΘΙ)
(AR-CHAN-DA-RA   FAW-TA-ZA   PY-REE-FAW-TA   ZA-VY-

THEEKS E-TEE-MEN-ME-RO FO-RA-TH'EN E-REE-'E PRO THREE FO-RA-THEE)

When you have said this, the rays of the Sun will turn toward you; look at the centre of them. For when you have done this, you will see a youthful god, beautiful in appearance, with fiery hair, and in a white tunic and a scarlet cloak, and wearing a fiery crown.

Raise your two hands towards him touching your thumbs and index fingers together to form a fire triangle.

"Hail, O Lord, Great Power, Great Might, King, Greatest of Gods, Mithras, the Lord of heaven and earth, God of gods: mighty is your breath; mighty is your strength, O Lord. If it is your will, announce me to the supreme god, the one who has begotten and made you."

Help me (your name) who was born from the mortal womb of (your mother's name) and the fluid of semen, and who, since he has been born again from you today, has become immortal out according to the wish of God the exceedingly good.

I give you all my human power (place your hand on the horoscope) so that I will know you.

You will feel his power. Look intently and breathe hard out of your nose and release all your breath.

Kiss your horoscope and say to your right hand: **"Protect me, PROSYMERE."**
(ΠΡΟΣΥΜΗΡΙ)
(PRO-SY-M'E-REE)

Above and behind Mithras a door opens in the spiritual Sun.

Seven women* come from deep within the Sun disk, dressed in

---

* These are a syncretic from of the Seven Hathors, the fates, the Pleiades and the seven fixed stars in the constellation of the Ursa Major. The Seven Hathors are the seven cows who follow the celestial bull Osiris-Apis, Bull of the West (Ursa Minor), and have a calendar role. They were musical goddesses depicted with tambourines and sistra, sometimes they hold a notched palm branch known as "the Year-staff" and were said to oversee a person's destiny. They were hugely important at the birth of a divine child and they are depicted on the pylon in the Isis Temple at Philae at the entrance to the birth house. They can either suckle the Pharoah or give him life by pressing the Ankh cross to his lips. The reason you are invoking these forces is to work out your destiny and co-operate with it. The names of the Seven Hathors are known from the tomb of Queen Nefertari; Lady of

linen garments, and with the faces of asps. They are the Fates of heaven and wield golden wands. When you see them, you say,
"Hail, Oh seven fates of heaven, You who are noble and good, Oh sacred ones and companions of MINIMIRROPHOR* (ΜΙΝΙΜΙΡΡΟΦΟΡ) (MEE-NEE-MEER-RO-FOR) Oh most holy guardians of the four pillars.

Place your astrological chart on the altar and go to the left-hand column of unlit tealights. As you say the name of each of the fates you should light the tealight to her.

Hail to you, the first, CHREPSENTHAES (ΧΡΕΨΕΝΘΑΗΣ) (CHRE-PSEN-THA-'ES) You who are represented by the Moon in the terrestrial world. You are the feminine principle ruling the universe.

Hail to you, the second, MENESCHEES (ΜΕΝΕΣΧΕΗΣ) (ME-NE-SCHE-'ES) You who are represented by the Mercury in the terrestrial world. You are the principle of connection ruling the universe.

Hail to you, the third, MECHRAN (ΜΕΧΡΑΝ) (ME-CHRAN) You who are represented by the Venus in the terrestrial world. You are the principle of Love ruling the universe.

Hail to you, the fourth, ARARMACHES (ΑΡΑΡΜΑΧΗΣ) (A-RAR-MA-CH'ES) You are represented by the Sun in the terrestrial world. You are the male principle ruling the universe.

Hail to you, the fifth, ECHOMMIE (ΕΧΟΜΜΙΗ) (E-CHOM-MEE-'E) You are represented by the Mars in the terrestrial world. You

---

the universe, Sky-Storm, You from the land of silence, You from Khemmis, Red-Hair, Bright Red and Your name flourishes through skill. The Fates of Heaven from PGM IV are the Macrocosmic presences of the seven planets they polarise with the Pole Lords who are invoked next. Sam Block, who has done considerable research on the Pole Lords and the Seven Fates, (see https://digitalambler.com/2018/10/08/pole-lords-and-northern-stars-the-seven-pairs-of-divinities-from-the-mithras-liturgy/)sees the Fates has having a planetary role. If this is the case it is more of a macro-cosmic planetary role rather than the conventional micro-cosmic. They are the planetary forces as experienced everywhere in the universe – the planets behind the planets. The Asps are Uraeus cobra which were symbols of divine authority in Ancient Egypt.

* Possibly a secret name of Hat-hor

are the principle of Chaos ruling the universe.

Hail to you, the sixth, TICHNONDAES (ΤΙΧΝΟΝΔΑΗΣ) (TEECH-NON-DA-'ES) You are represented by the Jupiter in the terrestrial world. You are the principle of Order ruling the universe.

Hail to you, the seventh, EROY ROMBRIES (ΕΡΟΥ ΡΟΜΒΡΙΗΣ) (E-ROO ROM-VREE-E'S) You are represented by the Saturn in the physical world. You are the principle of Time and limitation ruling the universe.

Stand on the northern side of the pole star and talk to these goddesses. When you have finished bow and go to the south.

Shut your eyes and see the arrival of seven other gods, who have the faces of black bulls, in linen loincloths, who possess seven golden diadems.

These are the Pole-Lords of heaven.* You must greet them in the same manner and light a candle to each with his name:

"Hail to you, oh guardians of the pivot. Sacred and brave youths, who turn the revolving axis of the vault of heaven at the command of the One. You send out thunder and lightning and jolts of earthquakes and thunderbolts against the nations of impious people, but to me, who am pious and god-fearing you send health and soundness of body, and acuteness of hearing and seeing and calmness in the present good hours of this day, Oh my Lords you are the ruling Gods!

Light each of the candles as before starting from the bottom.

Hail to you, the first, AIERONTHI (ΑϊΕΡΩΝΘΙ) (A-EE-E-RAWN-THEE) (Violet) you are the star Kochab. Awaken to me.

Hail to you, the second, MERCHEIMEROS (ΜΕΡΧΕΙΜΕΡΟΣ)

---

* The Pole lords are the beings of light that turn the cosmos and decide what is permissible in the world we live in and wield authority (their "golden wands") over the world. They create the structure of everything and bring about order. In my view, they are forms of the rays and appear with coloured auras. These are the seven stars found in Ursa Minor which marks the location of the north celestial pole, as it is home to Polaris, the North Star, which is located at the end of the dipper's handle. In other words, the Pole Lords also show the way for the magician to link with the divine still point in the centre of the universe from which everything revolves. As rays they are partly Macrocosmic planetary force.

(MER-CHEE-ME-ROS) (Orange) you are the star Pherkad. Awaken to me.

Hail to you, the third, ACHRICHIOYR (ΑΧΡΙΧΙΟΥΡ) (ACH-REE-CHEE-OOR) (Green) you are the star Alasco. Awaken to me.

Hail to you, the fourth, MESARGILTO (ΜΕΣΑΡΓΙΛΤΩ) (ME-SAR-GEEL-TAW) (Yellow) you are the star Ahfa al Farkadain Awaken to me.

Hail to you, the fifth, CHICHROALITHO (ΧΙΧΡΩΑΛΙΘΩ) (CHEE-CHRAW-A-LEE-THAW) (Red) you are the star Urodelus Awaken to me.

Hail to you, the sixth, ERMICHTHATHOPS (ΕΡΜΙΧΘΑΘΩΨ) (ER-MEECH-THA-THAWPS) (Blue) you are the star Yildun Awaken to me.

Hail to you, the seventh, EORASICHE (ΕΟΡΑΣΙΧΗ) (E-O-RA-SEE-CH'E) (Indigo) you are the star Polaris. Awaken to me..

Commune with each of the Bull Lords as best as you can. Then sit down and visualise the following

A storm rages around you. There are lightning-bolts and flashing lights. Everything around you is shaking.

Look up, and you will see a god descending, a huge god, having a bright appearance youthful, golden-haired, with a white tunic and golden crown and trousers and holding in his right hand a golden shoulder of a young bull.

He is the Bear which moves and turns heaven around, moving upward and downward by the hour. It is Mithras the Sun behind the Sun who turns the universe. He is also an aspect of your divine self.

You will see lightning-bolts leaping from his eyes and stars from his body — breathe out through your nose hard – pushing the air out with your stomach.

Then take a deep breath of divine air and say
"MOKRIMO PHERIMOPHERERI (ΜΟΚΡΙΜΟ ΦΕΡΙΜΟΦΕΡΕΡΙ) (MO-KREE-MO FE-REE-MO-FE-RE-REE), you are the life of (your name). Stay dwell in my soul. Do not abandon me, for one entreats you, ENTHO PHENEN THROPIOTH (ΕΝΘΟ ΦΕΝΕΝ ΘΡΟΠΙΩΘ) (EN-THO FE-NEN THRO-PEE-AWTH)."

Breathe out through your nose hard – pushing the air out with your stomach while gazing at the god.

Then take a deep breath and say, "Hail, Oh Lord, Oh Master of the water! Hail, Oh Founder of the earth! Hail, Oh Ruler of the wind! O Bright Lightener,

PROPROPHEGGE EMETHIRI (ΠΡΟΠΡΟΦΕΓΓΗ ΕΜΕΘΙΡΙ) **(PRO-PRO-FEG-G'E E-ME-THEE-REE)**

ARTENTEPI THETH MIMEO (ΑΡΤΕΝΤΕΠΙ ΘΗΘ ΜΙΜΕΩ) **(AR-TE-NTE-PEE THEETH MEE-ME-O)**

YENARO PHYRCHECHO PSERI (ΥΕΝΑΡΩ ΦΥΡΧΕΧΩ ΨΗΡΙ) **(Y-E-NA-RAW FYR-CHE-CHAW PS'E-REE)**
DARIO PHRE PHRELBA (ΔΑΡΙΩ ΦΡΗ ΦΡΗΛΒΑ) **(DA-REE-AW FR'E FR'EL-VA)**

Oh Lord, while being born again, I am passing away; while growing and having grown, I am dying; while being born from a life-generating birth, I am passing on, released to death – as you have founded, as you have decreed, and have established the mystery.

I am PHEROYRA MIOYRI (ΦΕΡΟΥΡΑ ΜΙΟΥΡΙ) **(FE-ROO-RA MEE-OO-REE).**

Now is the time that you talk to your *Higher Self.* What happens will be up to you and it. In my experience, he talks in visions and fragments which have a profound effect but do not provide "intellectual" information as such... just transformation. When you have finished thank him and allow yourself to return to Earth.

SUNDAY MORNING

Γνῶθι σεαυτόν
KNOW THYSELF

Today is the last day of the process and is surprisingly less ritually involved as the other days. This is because the pressure has built up due to the last six months' work and the last two days of focused isolation. Today will be intense but it is mostly waiting for the Holy Genius to make contact. The experience (if it happens) will not be what you expect but will open the way for future experiences.

The day's work is based on two small PGM rituals (PGMVII 505-528 and PGM VII 428-539) which were placed alongside each other. The first had the title Meeting with your own *Dæmon* and the second was a *Victory Charm to Helios*. I have slightly expanded both rituals and added important lines from other PGM rituals PGM VIII 40-49 and yesterday's *Mithras liturgy*.

H Betz, in his paper *The Delphic Maxim "Know Yourself" in the Greek Magical Papyri** points out that other than its title, PGM VII 505 does not appear to mention the personal *Dæmon* at all, but it does reveal the procedure for a magician to approach one. Firstly there is a prayer to Tyche, followed by an invocation to Helios-Aion and then some form of purification.

The answer to this problem can be found in Plato's myth of Er† which said after the souls had chosen their life stories, went before Lachesis who "sent with each, as the guardian of his life and the fulfiller of his choice, the genius that he had chosen."

"This divinity led the soul first to Clotho, under her hand and her turning of the spindle to ratify the destiny of his lot and choice; and after contact with her the genius again led the soul to the spinning of Atropos to make the web of its destiny irreversible, and then without a backward look it passed beneath the throne of Necessity."

Iamblichus and Proculus both considered the *Higher Genius* the key to fulfilling destiny and that it acted as a guide to helping to archive it. Given the importance of fate and destiny when approaching your *Higher Genius*, it makes sense then to invoke the goddesses of fate to assist your awakening. Indeed, you saw these goddesses in their Egyptian forms yesterday.

It is important that the person realise that the *Higher Genius* is their divine self and this divine being is no greater or smaller than any other mortal. There was a cautionary tale mentioned in the *Enneads*, the philosopher Porphyry tells how his teacher Plotinus met his *Higher Genius* using the skills of an Egyptian priest.

> *"An Egyptian priest who came to Rome and wanted to give a display of his wisdom asked Plotinus to see a visible manifestation of his holy Dæmon. Plotinus readily agreed, and the evocation took place in the temple of Isis which the Egyptian said it was the only pure spot he could find in Rome. When the spirit was*

---

*   Betz, H. (1981). The Delphic Maxim "Know Yourself" in the Greek Magical Papyri. *History of Religions, 21*(2), 156-171. Retrieved from http://www.jstor.org/stable/1062222

† Plato Resp. 10.616

summoned to appear a god came and not a being of the spirit order, and the Egyptian said "Blessed are you who have a god for a spirit and not a companion of the subordinate order!"

The priest might have been a good magician, but his philosophy was wrong, or at least different from Plotinus. A *Higher Genius* is never a *Dæmon* , but always an example of the unity behind all *Dæmons*. That does not mean that Plotinus was a god, as some who have read this passage claim, or that all humans are gods as the New Age movement insists. It is just that a part of us is divine and we can communicate and co-operate with it.

Take two eggs and write on them:

ΑΒΡΑΣΆΞ ΙΑΩΑΙ ΑΕΩ ΕΩΑ ΩΑΗ ΙΑΩ ΙΗΟ ΕΥ ΑΗ ΕΥ ΙΕ ΙΑΩΑΙ. (A-VRA-SAX EE-A-AW-A-EE A-E-AW E-AW-A AW-A-'E EE-A-AW EE-'E-O E-Y A-'E E-Y EE-A-AW-A-EE)

Place one egg on the left side of the altar next to a small bowl and the other on the right.

In the morning awaken and perform your ritual ablutions.

Perform the lesser invoking pentagram. Perform the entire morning, noon and evening Sun rite together.

1. Perform your confessions
2. Perform the third Sun breath process.
3. Open the quarters, balance the elements and purify and consecrate the space.

Your temple should be set up with your Holy Guardian Genius candle on the altar placed on top of your astrological chart. You should have plenty of incense ready.

Face East and invoke Tyche:

Hail, Tyche, I invite you into this place, oh bringer of rich abundance, Humanity has never conquered you, and endless praise is yours, While others complain that you never give them blessings. I invoke you to ask for your true gifts – the ability to understand my destiny.

You are my Holy Genius' companion I ask you this day to help lead me to it so that I might develop a close relationship to the spindle of Necessity.

I offer you this spice that you may be my helper as I ascend to meet my True Self.

Now invoke the *Dæmon* of the space.

Salva lar familiaris (salute). Salvete De Penates (Salute), Salve Gen Patris familias (salute), Salve Vesta Mater (salute), Salve Larunda (salute).

I offer thee this incense in honour of thee and in recognition of your work as I have strived in your space. I ask that you continue to be a pillar for its growth that I may lean on.

Rather than insisting that life is carried out in the old way, that you must accept that you need to help us establish the new. Give me the ancestral powers, not to recreate your past, which has gone, but to bring my future happiness and well-being.

Quod Bonum Faustum Felix Fortunatum Salutareque Sit Mihi Ita Est.

Now invoke the *Dæmon* of the space who rules the decan of the time that you are doing the ritual (see chapter).
Invoke Helios:

Hail, Helios who has established himself in invisible light over the holy firmament ORKORÈTHARA (ΟΡΚΟΡΘΑΡΑ) (OR-KOR-THA-RA)
You are the father of the reborn Aion ZARACHTHÒ (ΖΑΡΑΧΘΩ) (ZA-RACH-THAW).

You are the father of awful Nature Thortchophano* (ΘΟΡΧΟΦΑΝѠ)
You are the one who has in yourself the mixture of universal nature and who begot the five wandering stars, which are the entrails of heaven, the guts of earth, the fountainhead of the waters, and the violence of fire AZAMACHAR ANAPHANDAO EREYA ANEREYA PHENPHENSO IGRAA

(ΑΖΑΜΑΧΑΡ,ΑΝΑΦΑΔΑΩ, ΕΡΕΝΑ, ΑΝΕΡΕΥΑ, ΦΕΝΕΝΣΩ, ΙΥΡΑΑ)

(A-ZA-MA-CHAR, A-NA-FA-DA-AW, E-RE-NA, A-NE-REV-A, FE-NEN-SAW, EE-Y-RA-A)

You are the youthful one, highborn, scion of the holy temple, kinsman of Abyss. You are the waters of Nun located between the two pedestals of the evening bark SKIATHI and the morning bark MANTO, in the Temple which contains the whole world.†

---

* This name was written in Coptic.

† There are some similarities to this PGM spell and the 25ᵗʰ chapter of the Book of the Dead. Eleni Pachoumi in her Concept of the Divine in the *Greek*

The earth's four basements were shaken by the holy Scarab when you, the master of all were born.

AO SATHREN ABRASAX IAOAI AEO EOA OAE IAOIEO EY AE EY IE IAOAI.

ΑΩ ΣΑΘΡΕΝ ΑΒΡΑΣΆΞ ΙΑΩΑΙ ΑΕΩ ΕΩΑ ΩΑΗ ΙΑΩ ΙΗΟ ΕΥ ΑΗ ΕΥ ΙΕ ΙΑΩΑΙ

(A-AW SATH-REN A-VRA-SAKS EE-A-AW-A-EE A-E-AW E-AW-A AW-A-'E EE-A-AW EE-'E-O E-Y A-'E E-Y EE-E EE-A-AW-A-EE)

Take the left-hand egg and rub it all over your body. As you do think about all the things in yourself which you need to get rid of. All the things that stop you expressing your *Higher Genius.* Take your time.

Take the egg and mentally absorb the divine letters into your *Sphere of Sensation.* Then Say all the following:

"This egg is the universe, which was created by my family, by me, by all I have come into contact. This universe is no longer enough. This universe must end so that my **Higher Genius** and Tyche can build a new universe based on divine principles, where I am the magician."

Crush the egg into a bowl. Lie back and say,

Oh Lord, while being born again, I am passing away; while growing and having grown, I am dying; while being born from a life-generating birth, I am passing on, released to death – as you have founded, as you have decreed, and have established the mystery.

I am PHEROYRA MIOYRI (ΦΕΡΟΥΡΑ ΜΙΟΥΡΙ) (FE-ROO-RA MEE-OO-REE).

Wait a while. The feeling will be similar to death because you are starting from scratch and making a sacrifice of yourself to allow your *Higher Genius* to take over.
You will feel a little blank. Take the other egg in your right hand out into the Sun and hold it up so that it absorbs the Sun's light.

Magical Papyri suggests that has something to do with Kephri theology. The barks's names are taken from Me-Sektet which was the night-bark and Mane-djet which was the day-bark.

Say *AO SATHREN ABRASAX IAOAI AEO EOA OAE IAOIEO EY AE EY IE IAOAI.*

ΑΩ ΣΑΘΡΕΝ ΑΒΡΑΣΆΞ ΙΑΩΑΙ ΑΕΩ ΕΩΑ ΩΑΗ ΙΑΩ ΙΗΟ ΕΥ ΑΗ ΕΥ ΙΕ ΙΑΩΑΙ

(A-AW SA-THREN A-VRA-SAKS EE-A-AW-A-EE A-E-AW AW-A-'E EE-A-AW EE-'E-O E-Y A-'E E-Y EE-E EE-A-AW-A-EE) Seven times.

Take the egg into your temple. Enter the inner temple. And put incense on your burner.

———————

I have made an offering to you Oh *Higher Genius.*
I have surrendered myself and this life to you.
Now I ask that you come to me,
As I emerged alive from my mother's womb.
Come to me *Higher Genius,*
Awaken to me that I might be an effective tool for you
And that might live the destiny that you require.
Teach me *Higher Genius.*

HARPONKNOUPHI, BRINTANTENOPHRI, BRISSKULMA, ARAOUAZARBA, MESENKRIPHI, NIPTOUMI, KHMOUMAOPHI*.

I come then PSOI PNOUTHI NINTHER†

AO SATHREN ABRASAX IAOAI AEO EOA OAE IAOIEO EY AE EY IE IAOAI.

(ΑΩ ΣΑΘΡΕΝ ΑΒΡΑΣΆΞ ΙΑΩΑΙ ΑΕΩ ΕΩΑ ΩΑΗ ΙΑΩ ΙΗΟ ΕΥ ΑΗ ΕΥ ΙΕ ΙΑΩΑΙ)

(A-AW SA-THREN A-VRA-SAKS EE-A-AW-A-EE A-E-AW AW-A-'E EE-A-AW EE-'E-O E-Y A-'E E-Y EE-E EE-A-AW-A-EE)

Repeat below the line seven times. Then wait. You might find the *Higher Genius* appears in your inner temple but not physically. Practically it makes little difference. If nothing happens repeat below the line another seven

———————

*HARPONKNOUPHI is probably an epithet of Horus BRINTANTENOPHRI could be the Egyptian meaning 'good', often used in titles of Osiris, such as Osoronnophris. MESENKRIPHI may be Egyptian for 'Child in his chapel' found explanations for the other names.
† Egyptian for 'Agathodaimon, God of the Gods'

times and pause. Repeat the sequence until you get a result or finally give up. It could take some time which is why I allocated all day to this. If you take a break, then you should perform the *Lesser Ritual of the Pentagram*, confess, open and balance the quarters etc again and then do the complete invocations (without the egg rituals) and continue to repeat the mantra.

You can insert the following prayer to request victory* at any time:

Rejoice with me, You who are set over the East Wind and the World, for whom all the gods serve as Body-Guards at Your Good Hour and on Your Good Day, You who are the Good *Dæmon* (God) of the World, the Crown of the Inhabited World, You who arise from the Abyss, You who Each Day rise a Young Man and set an Old Man. I beg You, Lord, do not allow me to be Over-Thrown, to be Plotted Against, to receive Dangerous Drugs, to go into Exile, to fall upon Hard Times. Rather, I ask to obtain a vision of my Holy Genius and be able to speak to it.
Yes, Lord, awaken to me and give me victory over this divine process by means of Your Power, so that I know"

WHAT SHOULD YOU EXPECT?

This is a complicated question as after all your efforts you should obtain some mystical experience connected to your true spiritual self. How that happens will be unique to you and your perspective on the world.

Some used to using imaginative forms have a clear image of their Genius in the form of an Angel, or spirit or something similar. One person said that the image started with their Genius with his back to him, which slowly turned to face him. Another said that they saw flakes of gold falling on the floor. Images are not that important to the experience as both reported intense feelings of emotion and power.

In my case, I had a vision which seemed initially totally disconnected from the working. Indeed, the only reason I knew that it was not just a random image was that it came with heart-stopping emotion and a flood of certainty. I found myself in tears at the vision and shaken to my core. The state was repeatable and could be found each time I called upon it. Later the relationship between the image and the being behind it deepened.

One person did not see anything but reported that after several hours, she felt like something was watching her. As the hours ticked

---

* [PGM XXXVI.211-30]

on, she felt that there was intense pressure in the room, which then "erupted."

Another thought they had failed. When the chanting stopped, they found themselves in the middle of unnatural calm. It was as if time had stopped. That stillness returned in the coming weeks as they started to integrate the experience within their lives, or when conducting further magical rituals.

What all these experiences have in common was not the "fireworks" but the fact that it was an important starting point for their future life. Invoking the Higher Genius is not the end of the procedure but the beginning. For the last six months to mean anything, you must attempt to merge whatever feeling or experience you have into your life. Knowledge and conversation with your Higher Genius is not a dialogue but surrender to an idea that you have a connection with the Universe. That surrender is giving up what you thought about yourself and building a new existence based around your destiny. A person who has faced their Higher Genius finds happiness in their destiny rather than running from it. It is as if seeing the divine spirit behind our life creates a realisation that we don't have to waste time aspiring to things that we do not need to be. We can be ourselves knowing that we are fulfilling our correct role in the universe. Once we stop wasting time doing things that are not part of the plot (or stressing about those things which cannot be) or acting from fear, we can find happiness. As the stoic Roman Emperor Marcus Aurelius said: "Death smiles at us all; all we can do is smile back."

From a magical point of view, the experience will fix one of the central problems of magic, not working or being blocked. You should reach a point of knowing if a ritual is going to work or not before you do it. This is because the feeling you will have obtained through this experience will not only reveal to you if the universe is behind your actions but also provide you with the knowledge that the ritual will work. Many rituals fail because their success will interfere with another's story and are blocked by the gods or the fates. The Higher Genius will tell you in advance if you are wasting your time. Other rituals, for otherwise hopeless cases, will get the ascent from the Higher Genius to proceed due to magical intervention. I believe that resolving such hopeless cases using magical means often can be a turning point for another person by proving that there is something else in the universe than normal material existence.

It is for this reason that magic systems always require a magician to have this vision of the Higher Genius before they start doing serious work. They might not call it that, or require that person undergo a retreat, but the idea nevertheless empowers all the forms of magic I have seen.

WHAT IF NOTHING HAPPENED?

If you have worked solidly on the system for the last seven months, it is unlikely that you will walk away from your retreat without some form of experience of your Higher Genius. Often those who say they did not experience something from the process found it had; only it was not in the way that they thought. Having undergone six months working on it, they have experienced their Higher Genius working behind the entire operation, and in the weeks and months that followed, they found the voice of the operation speaking to them.

That said, failure is part of this system's story. Usually, this happens long before the retreat. Breaks during the six months cause the magical pressure to defuse, and the *Lower Self* will try everything it can to cause us to relax our discipline. Often the reason you fail at the operation is that the flaws in your personality which have created your life conspire against you, typically using real life to get in the way. Aleister Crowley, for example, failed to perform the Abramelin ritual when he rushed to the assistance of Samuel Mathers in what was to become the comedic farce known as the Battle of Blythe Road. While his diaries are full of real and imagined ghost stories which took place when he was following the operation, Crowley failed, decided it was more important to help Mathers take over the Golden Dawn and take his "rightful role" as a magical leader. It was a classic test which many will experience during the process and one that I do not believe Crowley ever really understood.

However, it is possible that a person may diligently work their way through the six-month process and still not experience anything during the retreat. When it happens, it can be for several different reasons.

YOU DO NOT RESPOND TO THE SYSTEM'S SPIRITUAL IMAGES.

Earlier I explained how the classical Abramelin system did not work for me because I could not react to seeing the divine in the images that the system provided. I effectively shut myself down. It might be that that you do not respond to the spiritual forces described in this system and you must continue seeking your Higher Genius through other methods. It is one thing to call yourself a pagan or Hermetic, but sometimes it is a thin veneer for what you believe.

Since searching for the Higher Genius requires you to be honest, it is unlikely you will get away with it. Abramelin himself mentioned that a person thought he would be better off converting to Judaism to do the operation but failed. His soul was Christian no matter what he intellectually thought.

YOU DO NOT HAVE A BELIEF IN GOD OR GODS

The magical path is developing a relationship with divinity and working with it. The name of that divinity is unimportant, as is how you work with it. What is important is that you see it in a way that you can believe and can follow the concepts which are defined by it. One thing that a magician knows is that their religion is not exclusive, even if that is one of that religion's central premises. Nor can they act like that religion is the only one.

There is a mistaken belief that the magical path can be conducted by atheists or those who do not believe anything. To pull this off they claim that everything is psychological, and spirits and gods are just manifestations of their complexes. Over the years, I have seen such people suffer because it is impossible to work with your Divine Self if you do not believe such an entity exists. What such people usually do is take one of their complexes and make it divine. Religion provides a necessary face for occult teaching to express itself. It tells you that this face is God, and you must see yourself in the light of that being. Without an external face, it is human nature to see themselves as the God of their Universe. While there is some measure of truth behind this, the magician is no more the totality of God than the nail of my big toe is all of me. We are sparks of that central fire, which is God. Religion correctly teaches, however, that there is a separation between that unity which needs to be overcome. Without religion, the central problem behind magic rears its ugly head – narcissism and megalomania. Contacting the Higher Genius puts the ego in its place, and as a result, a belief which makes ego its central platform is going to take a kicking.

YOU DID NOT DO IT LONG ENOUGH

In magical matters, one size does not fit all. Six months of intense working is an arbitrary figure, and it will take some people much longer to get the desired results. The original Abramelin system had six, eight- and 18-month versions. The programme in this book could be easily increased by doing one month's work over two or three months.

AFTERWARDS

WHERE DO YOU GO FROM HERE?

One of my first teachers said that before you could do any magic properly, you needed to make some form of contact with your "*Higher Self.*" He admitted that such an experience was challenging, but after realising it, you could awaken magical abilities which were less limited. Once you had one *Higher Self* experience, it was possible to re-enter that state and effectively take it on as a Godform. Before every ritual, he would remember what his *Higher Self* felt like and open a communication channel with that memory. He would then perform the ceremony. Sometimes the nature of the ceremony caused him to lose the connection with the *Higher Self.* In one case, a disturbance in the ritual caused him to lose that connection, and it noticeably affected his ability to continue because he "lost his *Higher Self.*"

Over the years I have come to see that, with some qualification, he was correct. Before each working, you remember the experience and images of your *Higher Genius* and how it felt. You contact it and explain how you see the rite going and what its goal is. That process starts like a prayer or invocation but rapidly becomes more intimate as it proceeds. Images from the process become increasingly crucial to key into your *Higher Genius* until the barriers between the two states of consciousness dissolve again.

When this happens, you will become aware of the ritual as seen from the view of your divine self. You will instinctively know if it will work or not or if the gods are onside with it. There will be no point continuing with the rite if you have that feeling that it would somehow be a bad idea.

This process as part of the Stage Three *Prima Materia* exercise should not only become an automatic part of your pre-ritual preparation but carried out whenever you get a spare moment. This will enable your *Higher Genius* to have a more significant influence over your life. I have found that when I am considering a problem in my life, attempting to contact that internal divine presence seems to result in solutions coming to mind. However, it does not act as a contact, or as a spirit guide giving advice or use words. It provides perspective, or an idea, which allows the Higher Intellect of the

Lower Self to process its solution. Sometimes that Higher Intellect, due to a lack of study, or faulty philosophy, might get the message wrong, but over time, communications will improve. There have been moments where the intellect has interpreted communications as simple words (No, being the most common) and these I have heard audibly. However, it is essential to realise that the words are not coming from the *Higher Self* but interpreted through the Higher Intellect. It could equally have interpreted the response as a feeling of dread or joy.

Once you have made that connection and feel that it is ok to proceed, it is not necessary or desirable to try and hang onto it throughout the ritual. Making the connection and obtaining that *Higher Genius* certainty will open the way for the ceremony to flow. Since most rites require you to take on different godforms or do other acts which might distract you from maintaining your *Higher Genius*, it seems unreasonable for you to expect to hold it like a godform throughout the rite. What I have found is that such a connection improves my ability to see the ritual from a more spiritual perspective. I tend to pick up more symbols and become aware of forces operating behind the scenes. Once a ritual I was doing for something mundane turned out to be used for something different by the spiritual forces I was invoking. I could see gods and spirits which I had not called taking part. In hindsight, the mundane ritual was simply part of a series of more spiritually orientated work my *Higher Genius* was doing. Linking to my *Higher Genius* enabled me to see the rite in terms of the "bigger picture."

There have been noted moments where I have been unable to make a *Higher Genius* link before a working. Sometimes this has been caused by stress or the fact that I desperately wanted the ritual to work and did not care what my *Higher Genius* thought about it. Other cases have been when the ritual was far removed from what I should have been doing; my *Higher Genius* was making a point. By this, I don't mean that the rite was wrong or immoral, just that it had nothing to do with my destiny.

Working in this way is a habit of a lifetime, and no mortal can do it all the time. However, the door you will have opened with *Helios Unbound* serves as a start to adopting a more spiritually centred life. The discipline you have forged will be the start of your real magical life.

You should be aware of a side effect of your *Higher Genius* experience. While it might initially feel liberating it could cause panic from your *Lower Self*, which shuts you down.

My first experience of my *Higher Genius* took place during my 5=6 initiation into the Hermetic *Order of the Golden Dawn*. For seven years, I hid from direct magical work for some time limiting my practice to carrying out initiations and writing. I was aware of the problem (which was why I forced myself to try the experiments mentioned at the start of this book) to try and re-connect. While my *Higher Genius* was still there, I found that my will to do the sort of magic I wanted was not. It took time for me to integrate the concept, and when I did, I made sudden and dramatic changes in my life that plugged me back into the mainstream current of magic. It might have helped if I had used some of the exercises such as the Stage Three *Prima Materia*, but equally, it could have just my destiny to take a long time to wake up to what I wanted.

This book is based on a pagan eclectic Hermetic system which I have been working on for years. This will be published in a future volume and will cover some of the gaps in the explanations in this book. Space prevented me from going into too many details in some areas which did not necessarily need an explanation as part of the work to connect to your *Higher Genius*. The future book explains the magician system in some detail so that you can build on your seven months of work.

APPENDIX ONE
REQUIREMENTS FOR EACH MONTH

General

An altar (a small table will do)

Box of incense charcoal

A bowl for water

A dagger

Mineral water

A big box of tealights (you will use three a day at least)

Tape recorder for pathworkings

A picture (in a frame which stands up) or statue to represent your *Higher Genius.*

A method of timing your sessions to make sure you carry out your work for the correct amount of time.

Month One

Frankincense or the Abramelin Incense, which is made by Aaron Leitch*.

Month Two

14 black candles marked with the sign of Taurus, Paramah, your name, Hera and an Earth triangle.

14 blue candles marked with the sign of Scorpio, Periton, your name, Persephone and a water triangle.

14 yellow candles marked with the sign of Aquarius, Akramatha, your name, Zeus and an air triangle.

14 red candles marked with the sign of Leo, Zorothion, your name, Hades and a fire triangle

7 white candles marked with a spirit wheel, your name and αἰθήρ

Month three

28 white tea lights

Month four

Four Violet candles marked with the sign of Saturn, your name, and Barimas, Tus, Tamas, Darus, Darjus, Qajus, Harus and Tahitus

Four indigo candles marked with the sign of Moon, your name, and Garnus, Hadis, Maranus, Maltas, Timas, Rabis Minalus and Dagajus.

---

* This can be obtained from Doc Solomon's Occult Curios http://docsolomons.com/wp/

Four Blue candles marked with the sign of Jupiter, your name, and Damahas, Darmas, Matis, Magis, Daris, Tamis, Farus and Dahidas.
Four Green candles marked with the sign of Venus, your name, and Didas, Gilus, Hilus, Dahifas, Ablimas, Basalmus Arhus and Dahtaris.
Four Yellow candles marked with the sign of Sun, your name, and Bandalus, Dahimas, Abadulas, Dahifas, Atiafas, Maganamus, Gadis and Tahimaris.
Four Orange candles marked with the sign of Mercury, your name, and Barhujas, Amiras, Hitis, Sahis, Daris, Hilis, Dahdis and Mahudis.
Four Red candles marked with the sign of Mars, your name, and Dagdijus, Hagidis, Gidijus, Magras, Ardagus, Handagijus, Mahandas and Dahidas.
A set of Tarot cards
Six copies of each of the seven king's seal
Paper crown with one of the six seals on it
Your astrological chart
Frankincense (Sun), Myrrh (Moon), Storax (Saturn), Indian nerd (Venus), Cinnamon (Mercury), Saussurea costus (Mars) and Cinnamomum Tamala (Indian Bay leaf) Jupiter.
A saucer and red wine

Month Five
Set of Tarot cards
Myrrh incense
a picture or statue of Hekate
Your astrological chart
A key.
Red Wine
White Candle marked with Hekate, your name and Geriz
White Candle marked with Hekate, your name and Enedil
White Candle marked with Hekate, your name and Annuncia
White Candle marked with Hekate, your name and Assarez
White Candle marked with Hekate, your name and Cabil
White Candle marked with Hekate, your name and Nedeyrahe
White Candle marked with Hekate, your name and Siely
White Candle marked with Hekate, your name and Annediex
White Candle marked with Hekate, your name and Raubel
White Candle marked with Hekate, your name and Aredafir
White Candle marked with Hekate, your name and Necol

White Candle marked with Hekate, your name and Abdizu
White Candle marked with Hekate, your name and Azerut
White Candle marked with Hekate, your name and Erdegel
White Candle marked with Hekate, your name and Achalich
White Candle marked with Hekate, your name and Azeruch
White Candle marked with Hekate, your name and Egrebel
White Candle marked with Hekate, your name and Annucel
White Candle marked with Hekate, your name and Queyhuc
White Candle marked with Hekate, your name and Bectue
White Candle marked with Hekate, your name and Geliel
White Candle marked with Hekate, your name and Zequebin
White Candle marked with Hekate, your name and Abrine
White Candle marked with Hekate, your name and Aziel
White Candle marked with Hekate, your name and Tagriel
White Candle marked with Hekate, your name and Abliemel
White Candle marked with Hekate, your name and Anuxi

Month Seven
A magical image of Psyche and Eros embracing one another and
beneath Eros's feet these letters: "SSSSSSS (ΣΣΣΣΣΣΣ)," and beneath
Psyche's feet: "EEEEEEEE (ΗΗΗΗΗΗΗΗ).

The Retreat
A candle which can burn day and night for at least three full days.
Prepare it with the sigils and your name on it as described in the
chapter.
Ekklesia seal
A red, black, yellow and blue candle. Write the names of the four holy
creatures Paramara (black) (**Ραράμαρά**) , Zorothion (red) (**Ζοροθιον**),
Periton (blue) (**Περιτον**) and Akramata (yellow) (**Ἀκράμάτά**). Write
your own name on each one
One white candle inscribed with your name, Michael ΜΙΧΑΉΛ,
ΑΕΗΙΟΥΩ, ΝΥΣΕΥ and ΧΥΧ.
One white candle inscribed with your name, RAPHAEL, ΕΗΙΟΥΩΑ
ΝΥΧΙΕU and CHYBACHYCH
One white candle inscribed with your name, GABRIEL, ΗΙΟΥΩΑΕ,
AŌCHE and BACHACHYCH
One white candle inscribed with your name, SOURIEL, ΙΟΥΩΑΕΗ,
MECHEU and BAKAXICHYCH
One white candle inscribed with your name and ZAZIEL, ΟΥΩΑΕΗΙ,
IAO and BAZABACHYCH
One white candle inscribed with your name BADAKIEL, ΥΩΑΕΗΙΟ,

SABVAŌTH and BADETOPTHŌTH
One white candle inscribed with your name SYLIEL, ΩΑΕΗΙΟΥ.
ἈΔΩΝΑΙ and BAINCHŌŌŌCH
Seven coloured cards with the appropriate Greek Vowels

Violet	Ɐ
Indigo	Ω
Blue	꜓
Green	Η
Yellow	ꙇ
Orange	Ǝ
Red	Ο

Inscribe a white candle with your name and ΑΠΑΘΑΝΑΤΙΣΜΟΣ
(Apathanatismos)
14 white tealights
Astrological Chart
Timer
Tape recorder
Two eggs and write on them, your name and ΑΒΡΑΣΆΞ ΙΑΩΑΙ ΑΕΩ
ΕΩΑ ΩΑΗ ΙΑΩ ΙΗΟ ΕΥ ΑΗ ΕΥ ΙΕ ΙΑΩΑΙ.

BIBLIOGRAPHY

Aeschylus., Podlecki, A., Aeschylus. and Aeschylus. (2005). *Prometheus bound*. Oxford: Aris & Phillips.

Agrippa von Nettesheim, H. (1982). *Three Books of Occult Philosophy or magic*. New York: AMS Press.

Assistant, A. (2019). *Acquiring a Supernatural Assistant - Papyri Graecae Magicae - Hermetic Library*. [online] Hermetic.com. Available at: https://Hermetic.com/pgm/assistant [Accessed 16 May 2019].

Bailey, A. (1993). *A treatise on the seven rays*. New York: Lucis Publishing Co.

Betz, H. (n.d.). *Greek Magical Papyri in translation, including the demonic spells*.

Brennan, C. (n.d.). *Hellenistic astrology*.

Cebes Thebanus and Parsons, R. (1892). *Cebes' Tablet*. Boston: Ginn.

Cline, R. (2011). *Ancient angels*. Leiden: Brill.

Daniel, D. (2006). *Paracelsus' "Astronomia Magna" (1537/38)*. Ann Arbor, Mich: UMI.

Diodorus (1985). *Bibliotheca historica*. Lipsiae: Teubner.

Farrell, N. (2011). *Mathers' last secret revised - the rituals and teachings of the alpha et omega*. [Place of publication not identified]: Rosicrucian *Order of the Golden Dawn*.

Farrell, N. (2013). *Magical Imagination: The Keys to Magic*. 2nd ed. London: SKYLIGHT.

Galen. and Johnston, I. (2011). *Galen on diseases and symptoms*. Cambridge: Cambridge University Press.

Greer, J. and Warnock, C. (2010). *The Picatrix*. Place of publication not identified: Adocentyn Press.

Hesiod. and Cooke, T. (1743). *The works of Hesiod*. London: Printed for T. Longman ...

Hesiod. and Lattimore, R. (1991). *Hesiod*. [Michigan]: Ann Arbor Paperbacks.

Jackson, H. and Zoximos (1979). *Zosimos of Panopolis on the letter omega*. Claremont, Calif.: Claremont Graduate School.

Journalpsyche.org. (2019). *The Jungian Model of the Psyche | Journal Psyche*. [online] Available at: http://journalpsyche.org/jungian-model-psyche/ [Accessed 16 May 2019].

Julian and Taylor, T. (1932). *Two orations of the Emperor Julian, one to the Sovereign Sun and the other to the Mother of the gods*. Chicago:

Hermetic Publishing.

Kingsley, P. (1995). *Ancient philosophy, mystery, and magic*. 1st ed. USA: Oxford University Press.

Kingsley, P. (1995). *Ancient philosophy, mystery, and magic*. Oxford: Clarendon Press.

Leitch, A. (2003). *Secrets of the magickal grimoires*. St. Paul, Minn.: Llewellyn.

Mathers, S. (2012). *The Book of the Sacred Magic of Abramelin the Mage*. Newburyport: Dover Publications.

Paracelsus. and Blaser, R. (1960). *Liber de nymphis, sylphis, pygmaeis et salamandris et de caeteris spiritibus.*. Bern: Francke Verlag.

Plato. and Frede, D. (1993). *Philebus*. Indianapolis: Hackett Pub. Co.

Plato., Emlyn-Jones, C. and Preddy, W. (2013). *Republic*. Cambridge, Mass.: Harvard University Press.

Plotinus. (1989). *Enneads*. Cambridge, Mass.: Harvard University.

Plutarch., Dryden, J. and Clough, A. (1952). *The lives of the noble Grecians and Romans*. Chicago: Encyclopdia Britannica.

Pratchett, T. (2013). *Witches abroad*. London: Corgi.

Riley, M. (2019). .

Stratton-Kent, J. (2010). *Geosophia*. [Dover]: Scarlet Imprint/ Bibliothèque Rouge.

Vaughan, R., Cross, T. and Ashmole, E. (1652). *Theatrum chemicum Britannicum* :. London: printed by J. Grismond for Nath: Brooke, at the Angel in Cornhill.

Yunis, H. and Plato. (2011). *Phaedrus*. Cambridge: Cambridge University Press.

Weinfurter, K. (1932). *Man's Higher Purpose*. 1st ed. Paternoster House, Paternoster Row London: RIDER & CO.

By this Author

Non-Fiction

Beyond the Sun: The History, Teachings and Rituals of the Last Golden Dawn Temple.
King Over the Water: Samuel Mathers and the Golden Dawn.
Mathers' Last Secret: The Rituals and Teachings of the Alpha et Omega.
Making Talismans: Creating Living Magical Tools for Change and Transformation.
The Osiris Scroll: Pathworking into the Egyptian underworld
Egyptian Shaman: The Primal Spiritual Path of Ancient Egypt
The Shem Grimoire: Working with the Angels.
The Hidden Path Behind Initiation: The Crata Repoa Decoded
The Magical Machine: The Golden Dawn Vault in Colour
The Druidic Order of Pendragon
The Golden Dawn Temple Tarot (with Harry Wendrich)

Fiction
When a Tree Falls.

You can read articles by Nick Farrell at his blog at www.nickfarrell.it

www.ingramcontent.com/pod-product-compliance
Lightning Source LLC
Chambersburg PA
CBHW020148090426
42734CB00008B/731